International Financial Reporting and Analysis

A Casebook

Kenneth R. Ferris
*The American Graduate School
of International Management*

D1511483

**Irwin
McGraw-Hill**

Boston, Massachusetts   Burr Ridge, Illinois   Dubuque, Iowa
Madison, Wisconsin   New York, New York   San Francisco, California   St. Louis, Missouri

Irwin/McGraw-Hill

A Division of The McGraw·Hill Companies

INTERNATIONAL FINANCIAL REPORTING AND ANALYSIS
A Casebook

Copyright ©1998 by The McGraw-Hill Companies, Inc. All rights reserved.
Printed in the United States of America.

1 2 3 4 5 6 7 8 9 0 EB/EB 9 0 9 8 7

ISBN 0-07-289142-4

http://www.mhhe.com

Tell me, I'll forget;
Show me, I may remember;
Involve me, I'll understand.

The above proverb embodies the fundamental motivation for the emergence of discussion teaching, or what some call the "case method," as a pedagogical style in the classroom, namely the search for an effective teaching paradigm. Case discussion involving both students and a discussion leader has proven to be a highly successful learning format. The use of case studies has been found to facilitate the clinic approach of "learning by doing," and cases have also been found to better reflect the complexities of the business setting and the reality of decision-making with incomplete data.

Discussion teaching is rarely advanced because of its efficiency, but more importantly, it is advocated because of its effectiveness. This is not to suggest that the use of case studies is, in all situations, "the most effective" approach to student learning, but rather that in some situations -- specifically, for graduate management students with prior work experience, for executives, and for advanced undergraduate students -- the case method appears to be more effective than other teaching approaches. Student learning with these groups can be broader in scope, cross functional, multi-disciplinary, and often more realistic in large measure because of the "real world" orientation and student involvement provided by the case studies.

Adding to the complexities of managing in a real world environment is the increasing globalization of business, in particular the financial markets. This casebook reflects this globalization and was developed to serve an emerging need for cases focusing on accounting and financial reporting issues in an international context. While many in North America have been somewhat slow in reaching this point of view, it is now widely recognized by most business corporations that markets are not bounded by a country's borders. Thus, management education and business schools that were once predominately domestically focused are now attempting to meet the needs of its graduates who will be operating in a global business environment by offering increasing numbers of international courses and learning experiences in their programs.

The case studies contained in this book were developed by a number of individuals in a variety of countries. The identification of good case materials is often difficult, particularly in the international arena. Thus, I am particularly indebted to the various contributors to this project. I trust that the materials contained herein will benefit the users, teachers and students, equally.

Kenneth R. Ferris

CONTENTS

CONTENTS

It was August 1996, and the mood at PepsiCo Inc. and its Argentine *super-bottler* Buenos Aires Embotelladora S.A. (hereafter BAESA) was glum. BAESA had just reported a $251 million loss for the third quarter of 1996, and the company disclosed that its fourth quarter loss would, in all likelihood, be even higher[1]. BAESA's U.S.-traded American Depository Receipts (ADRs) had responded to this gloomy prognosis by closing at $ 4 $^7/_8$ [2]. Barely a year ago, the shares had been trading as high as $26. (See Exhibit 1 for a history of BAESA's ADR prices).

Analysts were caught by surprise by the company's poor results as many had predicted a much higher share price -- some as high as $50, but in no case less than $30 per ADR. (See Exhibit 2 for a partial chronology of analysts' estimates.) PepsiCo, with a 24 percent stake in BAESA, was already reeling from the impact of a series of prior and on-going setbacks in Latin America (see Exhibit 3 for details). Almost always a poor second to arch rival Coca Cola, PepsiCo seemed to have allowed itself to fall into a hole, getting out of which seemed extremely difficult in the short-term. Beset with problems in Argentina, Brazil, Mexico, Puerto Rico, and Venezuela, PepsiCo's admiration for its *super-bottler* seemed to be at an all-time low. When asked whether PepsiCo planned an injection of capital into BAESA, Keith Hughes, PepsiCo's public relations manager responded: "the management of BAESA is developing a plan. We will take a look at that plan at the proper time".

Analysts like Shannon O'Neil of Credit Lyonnais must have felt that that "the proper time" was imminent as she implied in her latest review of BAESA: "BAESA has only a few months in which to refinance its enormous debt. If it doesn't, it will go bankrupt. It cannot survive a debt load like this." And Florencia Greco, an analyst for C.S. First Boston, echoed similar fears: "They tried to grow too much. The mistake is Brazil. I don't know whether they were misled in their evaluation of the Brazilian market potential or if they chose the wrong strategy and couldn't reach the market share they expected. Now the company is at the brink of bankruptcy and the situation allows no room for another mistake." In the meantime, a BAESA spokeswoman when contacted to ascertain whether PepsiCo had any plans to bail BAESA out of its present crisis reacted coolly saying "we don't know what PepsiCo's plans are."

While BAESA was facing imminent bankruptcy and PepsiCo was mulling over its Latin American situation, arch rival Coca Cola could not resist the temptation to publicize its achievements in Latin America. Coca Cola, which had seen strong growth in Mexico and South America in recent months, issued a public statement reassuring Wall Street about the health of its own soft-drink business in the region, emphasizing its "focused bottler system" and "excellent results in terms of volume and share of soft-drink sales." Perhaps Coca Cola's announcement was meant to reassure its investors that PepsiCo's problems in Latin America were indicative neither of the region's beverage market nor the general economy of Latin America.

---

[*] This case was prepared by Kenneth R. Ferris and Shankar Venkataraman. Copyright © 1997 by the American Graduate School of International Management. All rights reserved.

[1] BAESA's fiscal year ends on September 30 of each year. Hence, the first quarter for 1996 would be the period ending December 31, 1995; the second quarter would be the period ending March 31, 1996, and so on.

[2] Each ADR represents two Class "B" common shares of BAESA; the sponsored ADRs are listed on the New York Stock Exchange under the symbol "BAE". All amounts are in U.S. dollars unless otherwise noted.

The Global Soft-drink Industry

Soft-drinks are non-alcoholic beverages containing a natural or artificial sweetening agent, natural or artificial flavors, and other ingredients. To an extent unrivaled in any other industry (particularly in consumer non-durables), the global soft-drink industry is dominated by two companies: The Coca-Cola Company and PepsiCo Inc. Within the U.S., which is the world's largest soft-drink market, Coca-Cola products hold 43% of the market, while PepsiCo products account for 31%. In the global market, Coca-Cola holds a 46% market share as compared to PepsiCo's 17%. Exhibit 4 reveals that the Latin American market is second only to North America in terms of the consumption of all brands of soft-drinks. In terms of per-capita consumption of soft-drinks (see Exhibit 5), of the 10 top countries in the world, four are from Latin America[3].

Operations. The soft-drink manufacturing process is quite simple and remarkably similar worldwide. Soft-drink companies manufacture and sell beverage syrups and bases to bottling operations, a growing proportion of which are owned by the soft-drink manufacturers themselves. The bottling operators add sweeteners and carbonated water to produce the final product and distribute it, usually in specific territories assigned by the soft-drink manufacturers through the granting of area franchises.

Global soft-drink manufacturers may license bottlers to sell their products or buy local bottlers outright. While they may import ingredients, bottling is almost always done locally. PepsiCo and Coca-Cola, for example, have company-owned or franchised bottling plants in more than 120 countries. Some soft-drinks, such as mineral waters like Perrier, have distinctive qualities that cannot be reproduced in local markets and consequently are exported in bottled form to foreign markets.

Structure. The key structural components of the soft-drink industry are as follows:

- *Suppliers* (franchisors or brand-owners) wield extraordinary power in their relationship with bottlers. Though this relationship is a symbiotic one, franchises are usually time-bound agreements in which the brand-owner retains the option of terminating a franchise agreement if a bottler fails to perform on a variety of parameters. At the same time, franchisors (like Coca Cola or PepsiCo) realize that it is not possible to be experts in all markets in which they operate, and consequently rely on local bottlers for distribution of their products. The franchisor often tries to ensure a congruence of interests by investing in a franchisee, but a majority interest has both advantages and disadvantages, the principal disadvantage being a host of agency problems and the inflexibility associated with such arrangements that make it difficult for the franchisor to walk away if expectations relating to a market do not materialize. Both Coca-Cola and PepsiCo are in the process of consolidating their bottlers in Latin America. These giant bottlers who, in turn, are expected to consolidate local and regional bottlers, are called *anchor-bottlers* by Coca-Cola and *super-bottlers* by PepsiCo.

- *Buyers* (or consumers) exert a great deal of influence in the soft-drink market and their buying behavior is influenced to a great extent by the marketing of both the franchisor and the franchisee. Buyer behavior is also dictated to a significant extent by the overall state of the local economy. Macro-economic factors play a decisive role in

---

[3] This data suggests that soft-drink consumption bears a weak correlation to per-capita income, a statistic that normally is a reliable indicator of the level of consumption of most other consumer goods.

influencing consumer purchasing behavior, in that consumers can quickly shift their preference to cheaper private label drinks or stop consuming soft-drinks altogether. Thus, the *threat of substitutes* is an ever present one, particularly in an economic downturn. The *threat of new entrants* -- an antecedent to the threat of substitutes -- under normal circumstances does not represent a severe threat; however, in conditions of economic decline, substitutes can and do pose a credible threat. In view of the relative simplicity of the soft-drink production process, the barriers to entry are not significant and a new entrant satisfied with a small geographic segment can do quite well.

In summary:

- The soft-drink industry is a marketing-driven industry whose primary objective is to convince people to drink sweetened water instead of ordinary water or other competing beverages. The crucial determinants of success are promotion and distribution. World-wide, soft-drinks account for approximately 50% of the beverages consumed.

- Most firms view demographics as a critical factor and would like to enter markets where a significant proportion of the population is young -- teenagers are major consumers of soft-drinks and companies believe that these teenagers will continue to consume their products (even if not at the same rate) as they grow in age.

- At the global level, per-capita income apparently has a weak relationship with per-capita soft-drink consumption; however, within a given country, consumption is inextricably linked to the overall well-being of the local economy.

- Latin America represents one of the most important markets to soft-drink manufacturers worldwide.

The Company

BAESA's scope of operations in the beverage industry is quite broad. Apart from being PepsiCo's *super-bottler* in the Southern cone, BAESA

- manufactures and distributes such homegrown brands as Glacier bottled water and La Moderna and Villa del Este fruit drinks;
- distributes such non-Pepsi brands as Lipton Tea in Argentina, Canada Dry & Orange Crush in Chile, and Seagrams in Costa Rica; and,
- has formed a strategic alliance with Compania Cervecerias Unidas S.A. and Anheuseur Busch to distribute Budweiser products in Argentina.

Despite this broad range of activities, the core business of BAESA continues to be the manufacture, bottling, and distribution of soft-drinks, which account for more than 90% of the company's sales revenues.

Exhibit 6 provides a brief chronology of BAESA's history. From sales of just over $25 million in 1990, BAESA's sales for 1995 stood at over $670 million, making it PepsiCo's largest bottler outside the United States. Internationally, BAESA represented approximately 20% of PepsiCo's beverage business.

BAESA's principal business strategy focused on increasing per capita consumption through expanding the market segments in which its products are sold, as well as broadening its product line. The company carved out market share in such growing markets as Argentina in 1990, Costa Rica, Chile, and Uruguay in 1993, and Brazil in 1994. Since Coke was also increasing its share of an expanding Latin American market (except Mexico where the overall market declined following the 1994 peso devaluation), it apparently did not feel threatened by BAESA's market gains. However, when BAESA announced plans to spend $400 million to enter the Brazilian market, even Coca-Cola Co., despite its seemingly unassailable 54% share of the market, took notice.

In recognition of BAESA's quick turnaround of the Argentine market for PepsiCo's products, BAESA was awarded PepsiCo's Chilean, Uruguayan, and Puerto Rican franchises. But the biggest challenge was Brazil, where PepsiCo was saddled with an unmotivated bottler -- Companhia Cervergaria Brahma (BRAHMA). PepsiCo's product sales accounted for only 5% of BRAHMA's profits in 1993. Under such circumstances, it was easy to understand BRAHMA's lack of enthusiasm for pushing PepsiCo's products when it had its own beverage (beer) business to run. Not surprisingly, Pepsi controlled only 5% of the Brazilian soft-drink market in 1994 as compared to Coke's 54%.

BAESA's success in the Southern cone came at an opportune time for PepsiCo as another trend was emerging -- Coca-Cola Co. was consolidating its bottling operations in Latin America and appointing what they called *anchorbottlers*. Anchor-bottlers were expected to consolidate the market, primarily by buying up smaller bottlers. This would save Coca-Cola the administrative headache of dealing with a large number of bottlers in each country. Coke could dictate the broad strategic goals while leaving the anchorbottlers to develop the specific planning and execution of this growth. The decision on whom to appoint as an anchor bottler , however, would become a tricky one as this involved a long-term commitment unlike the much shorter-term franchise contracts with individual bottlers. For PepsiCo Inc., the choice of BAESA as an *anchor bottler* was a natural choice.

In 1995, of BAESA's total sales of $671 million, $388 million came from Argentina, $231 million from Brazil, and the balance from the other regions in which BAESA operated. Sales in Argentina had grown marginally from the corresponding period in 1994 and the entire volume of $231 million from Brazil represented new sales. In 1993, nearly 100% of BAESA's sales occurred in Argentina. Overall, the markets in Argentina seemed to be passing through troubled times in most of 1994 and 1995 with little or no sales growth, due mainly to the troubled Argentine economic situation. The picture in Brazil was a marked contrast. The consumption of soft-drinks in Brazil increased by an incredible 41% between January and September 1995, due in part to the success of the *Real plan* (an economic stabilization package). BAESA took over the Brazilian franchise in December 1994, and its franchise territories included the states of Rio de Janiero, Sao Paulo, and Rio Grande do Sul. In terms of geographic area, the franchise represented less than a third of Brazil, but combined, the territories represented 85% of Brazil's GDP and a population of 70 million. When BAESA assumed control of the Brazilian franchise, Pepsi's share of the Brazilian market was an anemic 5%. By August 1995, BAESA had managed to increase this to 9.1%. In March 1996, BAESA's Brazilian market share rose to 13%, only to slide back to 11.8% in August 1996 when BAESA began to experience the first pains of its scorching growth rate.

Entry into the Brazilian market took BAESA from a company serving a population of under 50 million to a company that served a market of over 120 million people. Brazil seemed to fit perfectly with BAESA's strategy of going into regions with a low per-capita consumption of soft-drinks, just prior to an impending surge in consumption rates. BAESA apparently had again correctly timed its market entry as consumption in Brazil soared by 50% in 1995. Even the rather stiff price tag of $50 million it paid to BRAHMA to accelerate the transfer of PepsiCo's Brazilian franchise seemed justified at the time. Having made the decision to enter Brazil in 1994, two years ahead of schedule, BAESA had barely 4 months in which to hire and train 2000 new employees, build bottling plants, bottling lines, warehouses, and get its distribution system in order. BAESA managed to stick to this punishing schedule and by the end of 1994, had three bottling plants, 9 bottling lines, and 15 warehouses in the southern Brazil franchise. In 1995, strapped for funds, BAESA sold its existing fleet of 700 vehicles (valued at $30 million), and leased them back under operating leases provided by an international financial institution.

Financial Results

Exhibits 7 and 8 contain BAESA's income statement and balance sheet data for the period 1992 to 1995. Most of the company's difficulties seem to have occurred in the post-1995 period; hence, a brief summary of the post-1995 results are presented below:

Abridged Results (Cumulative) Post - 1995

	Net Accounting Loss	Revenues
Q1 (p.e. Dec. 31, 1995)	--$14 million (35.7)	$228.6 million (174.6)
Q2 (p.e. Mar. 31, 1996)	--$49 million (39.2)	$427.5 million (366.6)
Q3 (p.e. June. 30, 1996)	--$310 million (39.4)	$545.6 million (506.2)

(**Note**: The figures in parentheses represent the corresponding figure for the preceding year.)

The sudden slump of the super-bottler to a company in default on both interest and principal payments came as a surprise to many followers, including some analysts who refused to believe the initial flow of bad news. To benchmark BAESA with comparable bottlers, Exhibits 9, 10, and 11 provide statistics for the following soft-drink bottlers, whose operations span Latin America and who are also listed on the NYSE:

- Embotelladora Andina S.A. (ANDINA): a Coca-Cola franchisee in Argentina, Brazil, and Chile

- Grupo Embotelladoras de Mexico (GEMEX): a PepsiCo franchisee in Mexico

- Coca-Cola Femsa S.A. de C.V. (FEMSA): a Coca-Cola franchisee in Argentina and Mexico

- Pan American Beverages (PANAMCO): a Coca-Cola franchisee in Mexico, Brazil, Costa Rica, and Columbia.

Questions

1. Using the data in Exhibits 7 and 8, prepare cash flow statements for BAESA for the period 1993 - 1995.

2. Prepare common-size income statements and balance sheets for BAESA for the period 1993 - 1995 and explain whether those statements provide any indications as to BAESA's current difficulties.

3. Derive some of the key ratios for BAESA for the same period. The major areas of analysis should include Profitability, Liquidity, Solvency (leverage), and Activity (turnover) ratios. Could any of these ratios have helped predict BAESA's predicament in 1996?

4. Using both the generalized model and the Brazilian model, calculate Altman's Z-score for BAESA for the period 1993-1995[4]. Does the score predict the company's financial difficulties?

5. Where did BAESA go wrong strategically? What were the earliest signs? Can any of the mistakes be generalized across industries?

6. What crucial distinctions can you see between BAESA and its competitors?

7. What suggestions do you have for BAESA? Can the situation be salvaged? What options exist? Why did some analysts take so long to react to the bad news?

8. What suggestions do you have for PepsiCo Inc. in Latin America?

---

[4] Altman's Z-score, a predictor of financial difficulty, is defined as follows:

$$Z = 1.2*((CA-CL)/TA) + 1.4*(RE/TA) + 3.3*(EBIT/TA) + 0.6*(MKT.CAP/TL) + 1.0*(SALES/TA)$$

Where:
CA= Current Assets, CL= Current Liabilities, TA= Total Assets, RE= Retained Earnings, EBIT= Earnings Before Interest and Tax, MKT.CAP= Market Capitalization, and TL= Total Liabilities. For Brazil, the Z-score has been refined as follows:

$$Z = -1.44 + 4.03 * (RE/TA) + 2.25 * (EBIT/TA) + 0.14 * (MKT.CAP/TL) + 0.42 * (SALES/TA).$$

Exhibit 1
BAESA:
ADR Price History

	Close	High	Low	Volume[+]
May-93	27.50	28.38	23.00	2224.7
Jun-93	23.38	28.00	23.00	1235.6
Jul-93	26.63	26.75	22.50	736.6
Aug-93	26.88	28.50	25.00	1255.6
Sep-93	32.25	34.75	26.75	2094.7
Oct-93	36.88	40.75	32.50	1730.4
Nov-93	35.00	38.88	31.50	1058.7
Dec-93	45.00	45.50	35.25	1702.3
Jan-94	41.75	46.38	40.25	1020.8
Feb-94	40.50	49.25	37.25	2410.2
Mar-94	34.00	41.13	32.00	4241.7
Apr-94	34.38	35.50	28.25	1857.3
May-94	34.75	36.25	32.88	1233.5
Jun-94	30.88	37.13	30.25	1169.9
Jul-94	34.25	36.00	30.38	1147.1
Aug-94	38.25	39.00	31.00	2402.5
Sep-94	37.38	38.50	36.00	1897.9
Oct-94	38.38	39.50	34.50	1622.0
Nov-94	38.75	41.00	35.00	1379.9
Dec-94	32.25	39.00	30.00	1641.6
Jan-95	31.75	34.88	26.50	2742.3
Feb-95	26.25	34.75	25.75	1949.1
Mar-95	26.00	29.00	19.88	5042.5
Apr-95	27.50	29.25	22.25	1683.2
May-95	30.13	32.75	26.13	1776.7
Jun-95	25.13	32.63	22.00	3081.1
Jul-95	24.88	27.88	24.38	1105.0
Aug-95	23.75	26.75	22.25	1825.7
Sep-95	23.25	26.50	23.00	1076.4
Oct-95	22.88	24.38	22.00	1363.4
Nov-95	25.38	25.88	21.75	1409.6
Dec-95	20.63	26.50	20.25	2613.7
Jan-96	21.25	23.75	20.25	3026.5
Feb-96	16.63	21.50	16.63	3130.6
Mar-96	16.63	17.50	16.38	2597.3
Apr-96	15.88	16.75	13.50	3758.1
May-96	16.00	17.38	15.00	2662.8
Jun-96	13.25	16.25	13.13	1904.9
Jul-96	7.00	13.25	7.00	2895.7

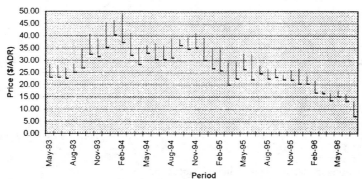

BAESA - ADR - Highs and Lows

*Date of initial N.Y.S.E. listing – May 5, 1993; N.Y.S.E. symbol – BAE
+In thousands

Exhibit 2
BAESA:
Partial Chronology Of Analysts' Estimates

Analyst/Firm	Current Rating	Prior Rating[5]	ADR Price at time of current rating	Expected Target ADR Price	Date of Current Rating	Analyst/Firm Comments
Interacciones Global Inc. Mexico	Buy	Hold	$13	--	July, 1996	*"Anybody selling at today's price must believe that PepsiCo and Anheuser Busch do not have a coherent strategy for Latin America...With the backing of two of the world's biggest companies, we expect BAESA to rebound strongly in fiscal 1997 and have no trouble in securing the necessary financing to service its debt payments due in August."*
Lehman Brothers	Outperform	-- [6]	$24	$33	October, 1995	*"..Brazilian operations will drive BAESA's growth."*
Barings	Buy	Buy	$23 3/4	--	August, 1995	*"We believe that the current share price has discounted all bad news."*
S C Warburg	Buy / Hold	-- [7] / Buy	$31 3/8	$41 / --	January 1995 / July, 1995	The target price of $41 was a 12-month target.
C S First Boston	-- / Hold	-- / Buy	$37 1/4	$45 / --	October, 1994 / June, 1995	The target price of $45 was a 12-month target. Expressed concern about rising debt.
Smith Barney	Outperform	Neutral	$30	--	May, 1995	
Arnold & Bleichroeder	Buy	--	$35 3/8	$50	September, 1994	
Bear Stearns	Avoid	-- [8]	$47	--	February, 1994	The "avoid" rating was based primarily on the view that the consensus opinion(s) on the stock's earnings were "too optimistic". Furthermore, "..(the) next two years will be difficult as they bring in new franchises".
	Neutral	Neutral	$40	--	November, 1994	

---

[5] This column denotes the rating immediately preceding the current rating.

[6] Lehman initiated coverage of BAESA in October 1995; hence, no prior rating is available.

[7] S C Warburg initiated coverage of BAESA in January 1995; hence, no prior rating is available.

[8] Bear Stearns initiated coverage of BAESA in February 1994; hence, no prior rating is available.

Exhibit 3
PepsiCo Inc.
Summary of Latin American Problems

ARGENTINA: In August, 1996, BAESA, PepsiCo's super-bottler in the Southern cone serving the markets of Argentina, Chile, Southern Brazil, and Uruguay, declared that it was unable to pay the interest or principal due on its bank debt. BAESA reported an operating loss of $203 million and negative operating cash flows of $40 million for the third quarter of 1996. Saddled with $647 million in debt, BAESA's solvency remained a question mark.

BRAZIL: In August, 1996, PepsiCo's significant investment in Brazil becomes at risk as BAESA reveals its failing financial condition. In 1994, Coca Cola held a seemingly unassailable 54% share of the Brazilian soft-drink market, compared to Pepsi's 6%. BAESA spent approximately $400 million and, by October 1995, had improved its market share to 9.1%. The future of Pepsi's Brazilian operations were in doubt, however, by the imminent bankruptcy of BAESA which many analysts felt had overextended itself in Brazil.

MEXICO: In September, 1996, Agral Regiomontana, a Monterrey bottling concern in which PepsiCo held a 49% stake, defaulted on $70 million in bank loans. PepsiCo refused to cover the loans, but bankers claim there was a "gentlemen's agreement" that PepsiCo would cover the loans in the event of default.

PUERTO RICO: In August, 1996, Pepsi-Cola Puerto Rico Bottling Co. reported that it had discovered accounting irregularities that would require it to restate first and second quarter earnings, resulting in an operating loss for both quarters. Pepsi-Cola Puerto Rico had previously reported a net profit of $0.01 per share for the first quarter ended December, 31 1995, compared to a profit of $0.23 per share the prior first quarter.

VENEZUELA: In August, 1996, PepsiCo lost its sole bottler in Venezuela when Groupo Cisneros Embotelladoras Hit de Venezuela defected to the company's arch rival, The Coca Cola Co.

Exhibit 4
1994 Global Consumption of All Brands of Soft Drinks

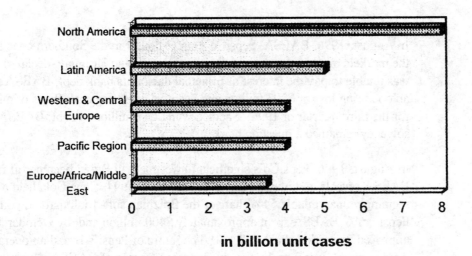

in billion unit cases

Source: Encyclopedia of Global Industries (Gale Research, MI, U.S.A.; 1996)

Exhibit 5

Major Countries Ranked by per capita consumption of soft-drinks (in liters)	
1. United States	180 liters
2. Mexico	135
3. Canada	121
4. Germany	88
5. Australia	79
6. Spain	74
7. Benelux / Denmark	72
8. Argentina	68
9. Chile	68
10. Colombia	67

Source: Encyclopedia of Global Industries (Gale Research, MI, U.S.A.; 1996)

Exhibit 6
BAESA : A Chronology

1988	Charles Beach, a veteran of the soft-drink industry with more than 35 years experience with Coca-Cola, Pepsi, and Royal Crown in the U.S., acquires the PepsiCo operation in Puerto Rico, as well as an interest in the sole Pepsi bottler in Costa Rica.
1989	Beach and his associates buy the existing Argentine PepsiCo franchise out of bankruptcy. Unable to use their dilapidated equipment and machinery, they also buy a 7-Up bottler from PepsiCo and christen the new operation "Buenos Aires Embotelladora S.A." (BAESA). The franchise area covers greater Greater Buenos Aires, the 13th largest city in the world with 40% of Argentina's population. PepsiCo's share of the Argentine cola market is 5.3%.
1990 January	BAESA begins operations.
July	For the 6 month period ended July 31, 1990, BAESA reports sales of 31.14 million pesos.
1991	Soft-drink consumption in Buenos Aires grows by 37%. BAESA's sales volume doubles to 122 million pesos.
1992 September	Argentina soft-drink consumption grows by 15%. BAESA's sales grow to 208.4 million pesos, representing a 34% increase. BAESA's share of the Buenos Aires market exceeds 30%.
April	7.6 million Class B[9] shares are offered to the public at 12 pesos per share. Only 20% of the shares are sold in Argentina, with the remainder sold as ADRs primarily in the United States at $24 per ADR. This equity sale represented the first negotiated stock offering for an Argentine company in the international equity market.
1993 May	A $32.8 million secondary public offering is undertaken in the U.S. at $23.25 per ADR. This was the first SEC-registered NYSE-listed offering for an Argentine company.
September	BAESA's share of the soft-drink market in Argentina grows to approximately 40%. Net sales reach 266.16 million pesos, representing a 28% increase over the previous year.
October	BAESA acquires the Mar de Plata franchise in Argentina.
	BAESA acquires a 100% interest in a company which holds exclusive rights to produce, sell, and distribute certain PepsiCo products in Costa Rica.

---

[9] Class A and B shares are equity shares; however, each Class A share carries the equivalent of 5 voting rights whereas each Class B share carries only one voting right. Class A shares were held exclusively by the company's founders and promoters.

Exhibit 6
BAESA : A Chronology
(continued)

November	BAESA acquires the Chilean and Uruguayan bottling operations of PepsiCo. Impressed by BAESA's stunning growth in Argentina, PepsiCo grants rights to produce, sell, and distribute its products in Southern Brazil as soon as the opportunity arises. (PepsiCo's existing Brazilian franchise agreement did not expire until 1996.)
December	BAESA issues $60 million of seven-year Eurobonds.
	BAESA enters into negotiations with Brahma (PepsiCo's franchisee in Brazil) to accelerate the takeover of Pepsi's Brazilian franchise (originally slated for November 1996). BAESA pays approximately $50 million for the privilege to assume the franchise in December 1994.
1994 March	2.9 million ADRs are sold in a U.S. public offering at $34.50 per ADR, 87,256 of which are issued through a subscription offering to existing shareholders of BAESA, who under Argentine law are entitled to preemptive and accretion rights.
August	BAESA acquires Cordoba franchise in Argentina.
November	Revenues for the fiscal year ending September, 1994, grow to 465 million pesos(from 266 million). Earnings reach $1.47 per ADR.
1995 May	BAESA announces plans to invest an additional $400 million in its Southern Brazil franchise between 1995 and 1997.
October	PepsiCo increases its market share in Brazil to 9.1%. (Just 8 months ago in December 1994, PepsiCo's market share was only 6%.)
November	For the fiscal year ending September 30, 1995, revenues increase to $670 million, from $465 million in 1994. Operating cash flows increase to $127 million from $97 million for the same period.
1996 February	BAESA files a shelf registration with the SEC to offer up to $200 million in debt securities in the U.S.
April	Argentina cuts its excise tax on cola soft-drinks to 4% from 24%. Both Coke & Pepsi expect to benefit, but Coke expects to gain more as colas account for 60% of its sales versus 30% for Pepsi. (Seventy percent of BAESA's sales volume come from fruit-flavored drinks.)

Exhibit 6
BAESA : A Chronology
(continued)

May	BAESA reports a net loss of $26 million for the second quarter versus a profit of $20 million for the corresponding preceding quarter. Added to the first quarter loss of $23 million, the overall picture looks dim -- losses of $49 million for the half year compared to profits of $39 million for the preceding period. Analysts were warned that results would be bad, but the magnitude was underestimated by most.
May	Charles Beach announces retirement. PepsiCo takes operating control effective July 1, 1996. Luis Suarez named CEO. While Beach's retirement was part of PepsiCo's 24% acquisition of BAESA in 1993, he was expected to continue until 1999. His retirement a full three years before schedule raises questions. Several analysts downgrade BAESA.
August	BAESA announces disastrous results for the third quarter -- a $251 million loss, and operating losses of $203 million. For the 9-month period, operating cash flow was a negative $40 million compared to a positive $98 million for the corresponding period in the preceding year. BAESA reports that it will be unable to pay principal or interest on its bank debt (overall indebtedness of $647 million) through October, 1996.
September	PepsiCo cuts its exposure to BAESA by reducing its ownership from 24 to 17 percent.
December	BAESA reports a fourth quarter loss of $151.6 million. Part of the loss involves a charge for $40 million related to "certain accounting irregularities involving inappropriate capitalization of certain expenses as fixed assets."

Note: *All pre-1993 figures are stated in Constant 1993 Pesos*

Exhibit 7
BAESA
Consolidated Balance Sheets
(In thousands of U.S. dollars or Argentine Pesos, except per share data*)

Assets

	September 30, 1995 U.S.$ '000	September 30, 1994 U.S.$ '000	September 30, 1994 Pesos '000	September 30, 1993 Pesos '000	September 30, 1992 Pesos '000
Current Assets					
Cash and cash equivalents	57,617	94,861	94,861	24,790	43,608
Accounts receivable					
Trade, net	74,522	42,274	42,274	19,005	9,678
Due from Pepsi-Cola Argentina	19,923	10,793	10,793	6,440	5,334
Affiliates	2,010	2,071	2,071		
Other	9,023	6,954	6,954	3,133	4,236
Inventories	56,349	26,440	26,440	10,151	7,100
Deferred income Tax	1,264	4,106	4,106	1,537	4,404
Other Current Assets	24,669	7,789	7,789	1,124	519
Total Current Assets	245,377	195,288	195,288	66,180	74,879
Property, Plant and Equipment, Net	655,414	418,845	423,853	136,719	85,855
Intangible Assets, net of accumulated amortization	88,017	90,500	90,500	3,745	4,347
Investment in affiliated company	107,385				
Deferred income tax, net	10,530	3,793			
Other Assets	21,201	36,565	37,694	5,614	73
Total assets	1,127,924	744,991	747,335	212,258	165,154

Liabilities and Shareholders' Equity

	September 30, 1995 U.S.$ '000	September 30, 1994 U.S.$ '000	September 30, 1994 Pesos '000	September 30, 1993 Pesos '000	September 30, 1992 Pesos '000
Current Liabilities					
Current instalments of long-term debt	48,457	15,953	15,953	3,489	372
Current instalments of capital lease obligation					245
Bank loans and overdrafts	182,672	88,662	88,662	3,420	1,902
Accounts Payable:					
Trade	50,550	34,473	34,473	16,455	15,709
Affiliates				811	1,347
Dividends payable					1,849
Income tax payable	903	10,873	10,873	11,295	1,293
Deferred income tax, net	319				
Accrued payroll	10,495	14,569	14,569	6,648	7,765
Accrued other taxes	23,874	10,824	10,824	2,448	3,496
Other accrued expenses	28,809	17,948	18,248	1,066	183
Total current liabilities	346,079	193,302	193,602	45,632	34,161
Long-term debt excluding current installments	323,737	110,761	110,761	8,511	1,023
Deferred income tax, net	7,625	12,273	6,977	12,446	10,365
Capital lease obligation, excluding current installments					65
Other long-term liabilities	10,715	15,622	15,622	1,884	1,648
Total liabilities	688,156	331,958	326,962	68,473	47,262
Shareholders Equity					
Class A common stock of P0.01 par value.	303	303	303	303	336
Class B common stock of P0.01 par value	422	422	422	163	130
Additional paid-in capital	335,547	335,547	344,997	103,485	104,393
Retained earnings					
Appropriated	81,302	75,811	75,124	39,834	13,033
Unappropriated	25,887	3,278			
Cumulative translation adjustment	(3,693)	(2,328)	(473)		
Total shareholders' equity	439,768	413,033	420,373	143,785	117,892
Total liabilities and shareholders' equity	1,127,924	744,991	747,335	212,258	165,154

* In 1993, the Argentine government fixed the official exchange rate between the U.S. dollar and the peso at parity (i.e. $ 1 U.S. = 1 Peso).

Exhibit 8
BAESA
Consolidated Balance Sheets
(In thousands of U.S. dollars or Argentine Pesos, except per share data*)

	September 30, 1995 U.S.$	September 30, 1994 U.S.$	September 30, 1994 Pesos	September 30, 1993 Pesos	September 30, 1992 Pesos
Net Sales	670,449	465,071	465,071	266,160	208,419
Costs and expenses:					
Cost of Sales	345,103	242,790	242,574	137,161	104,138
Selling and marketing expenses	160,644	110,973	110,644	53,689	38,665
Administrative expenses	93,418	41,677	41,827	23,227	22,253
Start-up costs in Brazil	3,162	7,040	7,040		
	602,327	402,480	402,085	214,077	165,056
Income from operations	68,122	62,591	62,986	52,083	43,363
Other income (expenses):					
Price level gain (loss) on monetary items				234	(918)
Interest expense	(39,837)	(8,115)	(8,115)	(541)	(1,874)
Interest income	5,061	4,961	4,961	641	732
Forward contract gain		6,523	6,523		
Foreign exchange gain (loss), net	1,646	1,146	1,146	(227)	(995)
Other, net	2,345	(938)	(1,084)	(768)	(937)
Other income (expenses), net	(30,785)	3,577	3,431	(661)	(3,992)
Income before tax (expense) benefit and equity in net earnings of affiliated company	37,337	66,168	66,417	51,422	39,371
Income tax (expense) benefit	3,079	(17,643)	(17,511)	(15,339)	(9,619)
Income before equity in net earnings of affiliated company	40,416	48,525	48,906	36,083	29,752
Equity in net earnings of affiliated company	4,359				
Net income	44,775	48,525	48,906	36,083	29,752
Earnings per share:					
Income before equity in net earnings of affiliated company	$0.56	$0.73	P0.74	P0.77	P0.72
Equity in net earnings of affiliated company	$0.06				
Net Income	$0.62	$0.73	P0.74	P0.77	P0.72
Weighted average number of shares outstanding (in thousands)	72,500	66,526	66,526	46,600	41,603

Additional Information:					
1. Allowance for doubtful accounts	5486	3258	3258	474	183
2. Accumulated depreciation	127810	79422	95437	51247	36935
3. Accumulated amortization	3258	1530	1530	2242	1640
4. Depreciation and amortization charged to income	61093	35028	33528	14914	9201
5. Reserve for bad and doubtful debts	5486	3258	3258	474	183

Exhibit 9
Latin American Soft-Drink Franchisees
Comparative Annual Ratio Report

	ANDINA Dec-95	GEMEX Dec-95	FEMSA Dec-94	PANAMCO Dec-95
LIQUIDITY				
Current Ratio	1.19	1.28	0.66	0.71
Quick Ratio	0.81	0.62	0.48	0.45
Working Capital Per Share	0.42	0.03	-1.20	-2.74
Cash Flow Per Share	2.27	0.01	1.15	3.57
ACTIVITY				
Inventory Turnover	10.87	4.34	11.03	13.36
Receivables Turnover	7.67	8.31	11.75	15.60
Total Asset Turnover	1.13	0.59	1.06	1.31
Average Collection Per (Days)	47.00	43.00	31.00	23.00
Days to Sell Inventory	33.00	83.00	33.00	27.00
Operating Cycle (Days)	80.00	126.00	63.00	50.00
PERFORMANCE				
Sales/Net PP&E	1.83	0.81	1.32	2.00
Sales/Stockholder Equity	1.59	0.97	1.81	2.64
PROFITABILITY				
Oper.Margin Before Depr (%)	23.72	8.71	13.91	14.61
Oper.Margin After Depr (%)	14.27	1.68	12.05	9.57
Pretax Profit Margin (%)	13.44	-5.11	11.57	8.14
Net Profit Margin (%)	11.77	-5.11	7.78	4.39
Return on Assets (%)	11.20	-3.05	7.05	5.05
Return on Equity (%)	18.74	-4.94	14.08	11.59
Return on Investment (%)	15.82	-3.45	9.96	7.98
Return on Average Assets (%)	13.34	-2.99	8.24	5.74
Return on Average Equity (%)	20.79	-5.44	12.52	12.33
Return on Average Invest.(%)	18.33	-3.71	10.58	8.95
LEVERAGE				
Interest Coverage Before Tax	14.14	0.68	14.55	4.23
Interest Coverage After Tax	12.50	0.68	10.10	2.74
Long-Term Debt/Common Eq.(%)	10.69	43.13	31.83	34.18
Long-Term Debt/Shrhldr Eq.(%)	10.69	43.13	31.83	34.18
Total Debt/Invested Cap.(%)	14.86	35.81	40.94	49.06
Total Debt/Total Assets (%)	10.52	31.64	28.98	31.05
Total Assets/Common Equity	1.67	1.62	2.00	2.29
DIVIDENDS				
Dividend Payout (%)	26.91	0.00	11.47	18.40
Dividend Yield (%)	0.91	0.00	0.61	1.00

Exhibit 10
Latin American Soft-Drink Franchisees
Comparative Common Size
Balance Sheet Data
(Percentage)

	ANDINA Dec-95	GEMEX Dec-95	FEMSA Dec-94	PANAMCO Dec-95
ASSETS				
Cash & Equivalents	1.36	2.17	2.74	3.05
Net Receivables	14.87	4.68	9.94	9.69
Inventories	5.66	6.23	4.20	5.54
Prepaid Expenses	0.45	0.98	0.51	0.84
Other Current Assets	1.56	0.00	0.00	1.10
Total Current Assets	23.91	14.07	17.39	20.22
Gross Plant,Property & Equipment	88.87	97.95	86.15	78.98
Accumulated Depreciation	36.76	23.89	17.71	21.46
Net Plant,Property & Equipment	52.11	74.06	68.45	57.51
Investments at Equity	16.83	0.00	0.00	3.72
Other Investments	2.35	1.81	0.35	0.00
Intangibles	0.00	8.86	11.19	15.98
Deferred Charges	0.00	0.00	2.62	0.00
Other Assets	4.79	1.20	0.00	2.56
TOTAL ASSETS	100.00	100.00	100.00	100.00
LIABILITIES				
Long Term Debt Due In One Year	2.33	4.42	0.00	6.09
Notes Payable	1.80	0.60	13.04	10.06
Accounts Payable	9.25	3.04	2.43	6.91
Taxes Payable	0.00	0.00	2.87	0.07
Accrued Expenses	5.59	0.00	0.00	0.68
Other Current Liabilities	1.18	2.93	8.16	4.74
Total Current Liabilities	20.16	10.98	26.50	28.56
Long Term Debt	6.39	26.62	15.94	14.90
Deferred Taxes	0.15	0.25	0.00	2.13
Minority Interest	4.65	0.00	4.75	4.82
Other Liabilities	8.87	0.41	2.72	6.02
TOTAL LIABILITIES	40.21	38.27	49.91	56.42
EQUITY				
Common Stock	29.70	8.74	18.97	0.05
Capital Surplus	0.00	42.79	16.41	36.07
Retained Earnings	30.09	10.21	14.71	13.32
Less: Treasury Stock	0.00	0.00	0.00	5.86
Common Equity	59.79	61.73	50.09	43.58
TOTAL EQUITY	59.79	61.73	50.09	43.58
TOTAL LIABILITIES & EQUITY	100.00	100.00	100.00	100.00

Exhibit 11
Latin American Soft-Drink Franchisees
Comparative Common Size
Income Statement
(Percentage)

	ANDINA (Dec-95)	GEMEX (Dec-95)	FEMSA (Dec-94)	PANAMCO (Dec-95)
Sales	100.00	100.00	100.00	100.00
Cost of Goods Sold	52.25	51.90	49.23	56.15
Gross Profit	47.75	48.10	50.77	43.85
Selling, General, & Administrative Expense	24.03	39.39	36.86	29.24
Operating Income Before Deprec	23.72	8.71	13.91	14.61
Depreciation, Depletion, & Amortization	9.45	7.04	1.86	5.04
Operating Profit	14.27	1.68	12.05	9.57
Interest Expense	1.02	15.96	0.85	2.52
Non-Operating Income/Expense	0.19	9.17	0.38	0.40
Special Items	0.00	0.00	0.00	0.69
Pretax Income	13.44	-5.11	11.57	8.14
Total Income Taxes	1.77	0.00	3.79	2.80
Minority Interest	-0.10	0.00	0.00	0.96
Income Before Extraordinary Items & Discontinued Operations	11.77	-5.11	7.78	4.39
Available for Common	11.77	-5.11	7.78	4.39
Adjusted Net Income	11.77	-5.11	7.78	4.39

It was May, 1997, and the winter's accumulation of snow was finally beginning to melt outside the Kitchener, Ontario (Canada) offices of the Waterloo Division of CompX International, Inc. (CXI). Inside the CXI facility, Ron Simmons, president of the Waterloo Division, was working on his presentation for CXI's board of directors. Ron had been given the responsibility for developing the financing plan for a proposed expansion into Asia; and, although a final decision on the proposed site (the city of Cebu in the Philippines or Bangkok in Thailand) had not been reached, the CXI directors had unanimously voted to build a new manufacturing facility to more competitively access the growing Asian marketplace for office equipment.

To fully understand his alternatives, Ron had held a series of meetings with CXI's independent auditors, Coopers & Lybrand, and with representatives from CXI's lead lender, the Royal Bank of Canada. On the basis of these discussions, Ron decided to further consider 5 financing alternatives for the proposed $100 million expansion into Asia.[1]

Interest-bearing debentures. Ron felt that a 10-year offering of 9.8 percent coupon rate, interest payable semi-annually, subordinated debentures would be well received by both Canadian and U.S. investors. He had been advised by bank officials that by the date of the expected debt placement (July 1, 1997), CXI should expect a real cost of borrowing of 10 percent; and thus, he should anticipate that the bonds would sell at a slight discount to their face value -- an outcome that Ron considered positive from the standpoint of marketing the securities.

Zero-coupon debentures. Concerned about the adverse effect that the interest-bearing debentures might have on CXI's reported earnings and cash flows, Ron also decided to consider an offering of zero-coupon debentures. Coopers & Lybrand had advised Ron that while the "zeros" would require no periodic cash payments for interest, the unpaid interest charges would still be currently deductible for Canadian tax purposes. Thus, the company's cash flows would remain healthy during the expensive start-up phase of the new manufacturing facility. The auditors' cautioned, however, that because the zeros would be sold at such a large discount from their face value, CXI would need to raise substantially both the number and maturity value of the bonds to be sold. They also alerted Ron that since the bonds would be non-interest bearing, potential investors would expect a higher yield, possibly as much as 200 basis points (2 percent) more.

Payment-in-kind debentures. When Ron expressed concern about the company's cash flows during the critical start-up phase, the Coopers & Lybrand representatives had urged him to also evaluate a hybrid security known as a "payment-in-kind" or PIK bond. These securities were, in effect, a combination zero/interest-bearing debenture, providing all of the advantages and none of the disadvantages of the two types of securities. According to CXI's auditors, most PIK bonds were designed to be non-interest bearing in the early portion of their life and to become interest-bearing securities in the latter part -- just how many periods would be interest-bearing versus non-interest bearing was up to the seller to decide. Ron concluded that since the start-up phase could last as long as 18 months and "debottle-necking" (or fine-tuning the machine tolerances) could last another 6 months, he would consider a PIK debenture which was non-

[*] This case was prepared by Kenneth R. Ferris. Copyright © 1997 by the American Graduate School of International Management. All rights reserved

[1] All amounts are in Canadian dollars unless otherwise noted.

interest bearing for years 1 through 3, and then which became interest-bearing in years 4 thorough 10. On the advice of CXI's auditors, Ron decided to assume that the hybrid debentures would be sold to yield 11 percent and that beginning July 1, 2000, the hybrids would offer a coupon rate of 9.8 percent, payable semi-annually.

Century bonds. Ron also decided to consider the latest fad in debt financing -- century bonds, or 100-year debentures. The <u>Wall Street Journal</u> had recently reported (February 4, 1997) that conditions were ideal for these new, very long-term securities: Interest rates were relatively low, and there was considerable demand for the long-term debt investments by pension funds and insurance companies. Ron had read that such well-known U.S. companies as Dresser Industries, IBM, and the Walt Disney Company had sold century bonds during 1996, and surprisingly, at yields only 20 to 30 basis points above the rates on comparable 30-year bonds. Ron was aware that investors would demand higher yields the longer they were asked to invest their money, but he found the relatively small spread between the 30 and 100-year securities to be enticing.

Offsetting the seemingly low interest cost on the century bonds, was the concern that the Canadian government might adversely rule that the bonds were a form of "permanent capital", and hence disallow the deductibility of the interest charges on the grounds that the payments were more like dividend payments (which were not tax deductible) than interest payments. Coopers & Lybrand had warned Ron that the U.S. Treasury Department had recently proposed to eliminate the corporate tax deduction for interest paid during the last 60 years of century bonds (i.e. permitting deductions for interest payments only for the first 40 years), and that the Canadian government might adopt this same position. Nonetheless, Ron felt that the potential for locking in financing for 100 years at such low rates, or even slightly higher, was worth the potential adverse decision on the deductibility of some interest payments.

Perpetuity debentures. During Ron's investigation of the century bonds, he had come across a <u>Financial Times</u> article describing the sale of $87.3 million (U.S. equivalent) in "gold bonds" by the Imperial Government of Russia in 1894. A unique feature of the gold bonds was that redemption was only by drawing, conducted at the pleasure of the Russian government; thus, the bonds had effectively been sold in perpetuity in that there was no guarantee that they would ever be retired. Given the bond market's current appetite for century bonds, Ron decided that it was only a matter of time before some corporation picked up on the notion and issued perpetuity debentures. He concluded that there was really very little difference between a century bond and a perpetuity bond, and hence for completeness, retained the idea on his list of financing alternatives.

Required:

1.   Calculate the expected proceeds from the sale of the 9.8 percent subordinated debentures on July 1, 1997, assuming that they are sold to yield 10 percent; calculate the interest expense to be reported by CXI for the year-ended 30 June 1998. (Use Exhibits 1 and 2 as needed.) If market interest rates on comparable debt securities rise to 14 percent (in response to changes in investor expectations regarding the rate of inflation), calculate the market value of the CXI subordinated debentures on January 1, 2000.

2.   Calculate the maturity value of the zero-coupon debentures assuming CXI needs to raise $100 million and assuming that the bonds are sold to yield 12 percent; calculate CXI's "interest expense" for the year-ended 30 June 1998. If market interest rates rise to 14 percent, calculate the market value of the zeros on January 1, 2000. What kind of investors would be most interested in this type of security?

3.   Calculate the expected proceeds from the sale of the PIK debentures, assuming they are sold to yield 11 percent. What disadvantages exits with this type of financing?

4.   Calculate the expected proceeds from the sale of the century bonds (assume a coupon rate of 9.8 percent, interest payable semi-annually), assuming they are sold to yield 11 percent. Would you consider the purchase of such a security as an investment? Why or why not?

5.   Calculate the expected proceeds from the sale of the perpetuity bonds (coupon rate of 9.8 percent, interest payable semi-annually), assuming they are sold to yield 11 percent. Do you consider the purchase of a debenture-in-perpetuity a good investment? Why or why not? Under what conditions would a company (or the Russian government) be likely to exercise its right to redeem the perpetuity bonds?

Exhibit 1
Present Value of $1 at the End of N Periods

$$\left(PVIF = \frac{1}{(1+k)^t} \right)$$

Period	4%	5.0%	5.5%	6%	7%	10%	11%	12%
1	.9615	.9524	.9479	.9434	.9346	.9091	.9009	.8929
2	.9246	.9070	.8985	.8900	.8734	.8264	.8116	.7972
3	.8890	.8639	.8516	.8396	.8163	.7513	.7312	.7118
4	.8548	.8227	.8072	.7921	.7629	.6830	.6587	.6355
5	.8219	.7835	.7651	.7473	.7130	.6209	.5935	.5674
6	.7903	.7462	.7253	.7050	.6663	.5645	.5346	.5066
10	.6756	.6139	.5862	.5584	.5083	.3855	.3538	.3220
15	.5553	.4810	.4492	.4173	.3624	.2394	-	.1827
20	.4564	.3769	.3444	.3118	.2584	.1486	-	.1037
30	.3083	.2314	.2028	.1741	.1314	.0573	-	.0334
40	.2082	.1420	.1196	.0972	.0668	.0221	-	.0107
50	.1407	.0872	.0708	.0543	.0339	.0085	-	.0035
60	.0951	.0535	.0403	.0303	.0173	.0033	.0019	.0011
70	.0642	.0329	.0236	.0169	.0088	.0013	.0007	.0004
80	.0434	.0202	.0138	.0095	.0045	.0005	.0003	.0001
90	.0293	.0124	.0081	.0053	.0023	.0002	.0001	-
100	.0198	.0076	.0047	.0030	.0012	.0001	-	-

Exhibit 2
Present Value of an Annuity of $1 per period for N Periods

Period	4%	5.0%	5.5%	6%	7%	10%	11%	12%
1	0.9615	0.9524	0.9479	0.9434	0.9346	0.9091	0.9009	0.8929
2	1.8861	1.8594	1.8464	1.8334	1.8080	1.7355	1.7125	1.6901
3	2.7751	2.7232	2.6980	2.6730	2.6243	2.4869	2.4439	2.4018
4	3.6299	3.5460	3.5052	3.4651	3.3872	3.1699	3.1025	3.0373
5	4.4518	4.3295	4.2703	4.21247	4.1002	3.7908	3.6959	3.6048
6	5.2421	5.0757	4.9956	4.9173	4.7665	4.3553	4.2305	431114
10	8.1109	7.7217	7.5409	7.3601	7.0236	6.1446	-	5.6502
15	11.1181	10.3797	10.0560	9.7122	9.1079	7.6061	-	6.8109
20	13.5903	12.4622	11.9661	11.4699	10.5940	8.5136	-	7.4694
30	17.2920	15.3725	14.5687	13.7648	12.4090	9.4269	-	8.0552
40	19.7928	17.1591	16.1027	15.0463	13.3317	9.7791	-	8.2438
50	21.4822	18.2559	17.0089	15.7619	13.8007	9.9148	-	8.3045
60	22.6235	18.4158	17.4499	16.1614	14.0392	9.9672	9.0736	8.3241
70	23.3945	18.9799	17.7533	16.3845	14.1604	9.9874	9.0848	8.3303
80	23.9154	19.3431	17.9310	16.5091	14.2220	9.9951	9.0888	8.3324
90	24.2673	19.5770	18.0350	16.5787	14.2533	9.9981	9.0902	8.3330
100	24.5050	19.7276	18.0958	16.6176	14.2693	9.9993	9.0906	8.3332

Waterloo Enterprises is a manufacturer of parts used mainly in office equipment (e.g., chairs, desks, file cabinets, etc.). For many years, the company manufactured these parts at several plants in Ontario, Canada. Early in 1994, however, one of the company's principal customers announced its intention to buy equipment completely ready for assembly from Taiwan. The news forced Waterloo to close its Mississauga plant and dispose of its inventories at that location.

The company's 1994 annual report, which appeared early in 1995, disclosed that the closure of the Mississauga facility had precipitated a dramatic deterioration in its business accompanied by a significant liquidation of their inventories. The notes to the financial statements made the following facts about its inventories available to shareholders:

NOTE 1–SUMMARY OF SIGNIFICANT ACCOUNTING POLICIES

Inventories are stated at the lower of cost market value. Cost of inventories is determined by the last-in, first-out method (LIFO) which is less than current cost by $87,609 and $55,952 at December 28, 1993, and December 30, 1994, respectively.

During 1994, inventory quantities were reduced resulting in a liquidation of LIFO inventory quantities carried at lower costs prevailing in prior years as compared with the 1994 cost of production. As a result, income before taxes was increased by $62,310, equivalent to $2.10 per share after applicable income taxes, of which $26,190 before tax, equivalent to $0.88 per share after applicable income taxes, was reflected in cost of product sold and the balance was included as a reduction of the shutdown/disposal provision (see Note 6).

NOTE 6–SHUTDOWN/DISPOSAL PROVISION

In the third quarter of 1994, a provision was recorded for the closing of the Mississauga facilities which are to be sold or otherwise disposed of. The after-tax provision of $55,595 is equivalent to $2.93 per common share and covers estimated losses on the disposition of property, plant, and equipment, and inventories and employee severance and other costs. Net sales of products from these facilities included in consolidated sales totaled $92,465 in 1992, $121,012 in 1993, and $147,554 in 1994.

An examination of Waterloo's financial history revealed that, in 1991, the company had moved from keeping its inventory on a first-in, first-out (FIFO) basis to a LIFO basis.[1] A note to the financial statements at the time described the change:

---

[*] This case was prepared by Kenneth R. Ferris and Michael F. van Breda. Copyright © 1993 by Kenneth R. Ferris. All rights reserved to the authors
[1] Although LIFO is acceptable for financial reporting purposes in Canada, it is not permitted for tax purposes; consequently, LIFO is not widely utilized.

NOTE 2–CHANGE IN INVENTORY VALUATION METHOD

In 1991, the company adopted the last-in, first-out (LIFO) method of determining costs for substantially all of its inventories. In prior years, inventory values were principally computed under the lower of cost or market, first-in, first-out (FIFO) method.

The effect of the change on the operating results for 1991 was to reduce net earnings after tax by $4,714, or 25 cents per share. The inventory balance at December 31, 1991, would have been $7,365 higher if inventory costs had continued to be determined principally under FIFO, rather than LIFO.

It was not practical to determine prior year effects of retroactive LIFO application.

The income statements for the years 1991 through 1994, along with the inventory shown in the balance sheet for each year, appear in Exhibit 1. Details of the units purchased each year appear in Exhibit 2.

QUESTIONS

1. Using the 1991 footnote, explain the change in the inventory valuation from FIFO to LIFO. What are the costs and benefits of such an accounting change?

2. Compute the LIFO reserve for each year and show how the company arrived at the effect of $62,310 for the liquidation of LIFO inventory in 1994. Assume an effective tax rate of 36 percent.

Exhibit 1
Waterloo Enterprises–Selected Financial Data

	1991	1992	1993	1994
Revenue	$1,058,422	$1,236,091	$1,421,526	$1,277,107
Cost of Sales	797,232	958,210	1,085,134	971,550
Gross margin	261,190	277,881	336,392	305,557
Selling and administration	192,775	207,332	209,884	212,567
Loss on write-off (net)	-0-	-0-	-0-	55,595
Income tax	24,629	25,398	45,543	33,476
Net income	43,785	45,151	80,965	3,919
Inventory (per ending balance sheet)	$ 147,304	$ 208,948	$ 232,006	$ 111,904

Exhibit 2
Waterloo Enterprises–Inventory Summary

		Units	Unit Cost
Opening Inventory		60,000	$2.00
Purchases in 1991	- 1st lot	103,652	2.00
	- 2nd lot	293,920	2.10
Sales in 1991		383,920	
Purchases in 1992	- 1st lot	282,220	2.20
	- 2nd lot	153,450	2.60
Sales in 1992		407,650	
Purchases in 1993	- 1st lot	193,210	2.70
	- 2nd lot	202,250	2.90
Sales in 1993		386,920	
Purchases in 1994	1st lot	196,320	2.90
	2nd lot	82,000	3.00
Sales in 1994		332,580	

THE CONSTRUCTIVE CAPITALIZATION OF LEASES[*]

A major problem facing companies operating in capital-intensive industries is the acquisition of revenue-producing assets. These assets are frequently so expensive that they cannot be financed from internal operations, and instead require external financing, often in the form of new debt or equity. Another alternative to the outright purchase of such assets, however, is leasing. Leasing allows a company to hedge against asset obsolescence, often avoiding maintenance, service, and administrative problems, as well as maximizing available tax benefits. There can also be capital structure considerations involved with leasing -- some managers view leasing as a form of "off-balance sheet financing" enabling them to increase the leverage (or borrowing) capacity of their firm.

Lease Accounting

Although the accounting for leases varies from one country to another, there is wide spread agreement that essentially two types of leases exist: capital and operating. Capital leases, which are sometimes referred to as financing leases, are considered to be the equivalent of a purchase contract, consequently requiring the lessee to record a leased asset and a lease liability on its balance sheet. Operating leases, on the other hand, require no balance sheet presentation of the leased asset or liability by the lessee because this type of lease does not transfer any rights, risks, or rewards of ownership from the lessor to the lessee.

Although the specific criteria for distinguishing between the two types of leases varies between countries, a capital lease is generally thought to exist if any of the following tests are satisfied (as assessed at the inception of a lease):[1]

- The lease transfers ownership of the leased asset to the lessee by the end of the lease period (i.e., the ownership test).

- The lease agreement contains a bargain purchase option, under which the lessee is entitled to purchase the leased asset at a substantial discount from its fair market value (i.e., an alternative ownership test).

- The lease term is equal to 75 percent or more of the estimated economic life of the leased asset (i.e., the economic life test).

- The present value of the contractual minimum lease payments is equal to or greater than 90 percent of the leased asset's fair market value at contract inception (i.e., the value test).

Exhibit 1 reveals the specific criteria used to identify capital leases for a selection of 10 countries. If a lease agreement satisfies the necessary tests, it must be accounted for as a capital lease: the minimum lease payments (excluding those payments contingent on future revenue or income levels) are discounted at the lower of the interest rate implicit in a lease or the lessee's incremental borrowing rate, and are then capitalized to the lessee's balance sheet.

---

[*] This case was prepared by Kenneth R. Ferris. Copyright © 1996 by the American Graduate School of International Management. All rights reserved.
[1] The following countries have no criteria for the identification of capital leases, and consequently all leases are accounted for as operating leases: Brazil, China, Finland, France, India, Italy, and Japan. In addition, despite the presence of criteria, the capitalization of capital leases is optional in Denmark, Sweden, and Switzerland.

Once a lease has been capitalized to the lessee's balance sheet, the decision as to how to amortize the leased asset is a management one. Generally, however, if a capital lease transfers ownership of an asset to the lessee, or contains a bargain purchase option, the leased asset should be depreciated over its estimated economic life. Otherwise, the asset should be depreciated in such a way that it is fully written off by the time the lease expires.

If, on the other hand, a lease fails to satisfy any of a country's capital lease criteria, it is classified as an operating lease and no balance sheet disclosure of either a leased asset or a lease liability is required. In most countries, however, certain details regarding any operating leases must be disclosed in the footnotes to the financial statements. Those disclosures usually involve the minimum future lease payments, in total and for each of the succeeding five years.

Analytical Considerations

To cash flow-oriented financial analysts, such as investment and credit analysts, the distinction between a capital lease and an operating lease may exist only in the minds of accounting standard-setters. Both involve, at a minimum, a fixed set of noncancelable future cash outlays. That a distinction exists at all reflects the balance sheet orientation of accounting regulators, in that both types of leases have essentially equivalent effects on the other principal financial statements (i.e., the income statement and the statement of cash flows). The distinction does, however, reinforce the belief held by some corporate managers that the total borrowing capacity of a company can be increased by keeping some (or all) leases off-balance sheet.

The Retail Food Industry

Because of the high cost of constructing and owning large retail facilities, companies in the retail food industry frequently lease many of their assets. Presented in Exhibits 2 and 3 are financial data relating to two such companies: Food Lion, Inc. and Santa Isabel S.A.

Food Lion. Inc. operates a chain of retain food supermarkets in 14 states, principally located in the Southwest United States. As of December 31, 1994, the company operated 1,039 retail food supermarkets, mostly in leased premises. The company's financial statements as of year-end 1994 and selected footnotes are presented in Exhibit 2.

Santa Isabel S.A. is a sociedad anónima abierta (limited liability open stock corporation) organized under the laws of the Republic of Chile. As of March 31, 1995, the company operated 27 supermarkets in Chile and 10 in Lima, Peru; of the 37 stores, 23 are leased. Santa Isabel is the second largest chain of supermarkets in terms of sales in Chile and Peru. The company's financial statements as of year-end 1994 and selected footnotes are presented in Exhibit 3.[2] Santa Isabel prepares its financial statements in pesos and in conformity with accounting principles generally accepted in Chile.

---

[2] This data was obtained from a prospectus, dated July 26, 1995, filed the U.S. Securities and Exchange Commission, associated with the offering of 3.8 million American Depository Shares, representing 57 million shares of Santa Isabel common stock.

Questions

1. Does the use of operating leases increase the borrowing capacity of companies like Food Lion, Inc. and Santa Isabel S.A.?

2. Restate the two companies' financial statements at year-end 1994 to reflect the capitalization of all operating leases. Compare the companies' solvency, both before and after restatement, by calculating the following ratios: total liabilities/total assets, total liabilities/total equity, and long-term debt/equity.

Exhibit 1
Capital Lease Criteria for Lessees by Country

Country	Criteria Utilized by Lessee
•Australia	•A lease is noncancelable and any one of the four tests are satisfied.
•Brazil	•No criteria: all leases are treated as operating leases.
•Canada	•Any one of the 4 tests are satisfied.
•Hong Kong	•Any one of 3 tests: ownership, alternative ownership, and value.
•Israel	•Any one of 2 tests: economic life, value.
•Korea	•Any one of 3 tests: ownership, alternative ownership, and value.
•Norway	•Any one of the 4 tests are satisfied.
•Spain	•The contract contains an option to buy and there is "no reasonable doubt" that the option will be exercised.
•United Kingdom	•Value test only
•United States	•Any one of the 4 tests are satisfied

Exhibit 2
Financial Statement and Selected Footnote
Information: Food Lion, Inc.

A. Income Statements

| | Years Ended | | |
| | December 31, | January 1, | January 2, |
(Dollars in thousands except per share amounts)	1994	1994	1993
Net sales	$7,932,592	$7,609,817	$7,195,923
Cost of goods sold	6,323,693	6,121,274	5,759,534
Gross profit	1,608,899	1,488,543	1,436,389
Selling and administrative expenses	1,129,803	1,096,306	975,111
Interest expense	86,564	72,343	49,057
Depreciation	139,834	143,042	121,616
Store closing charge (Note 13)		170,500	
	1,356,201	1,482,191	1,145,784
Income before income taxes	252,698	6,352	290,605
Provision for income taxes	99,800	2,500	112,600
Net income	$ 152,898	$ 3,852	$ 178,005
Earnings per share	$ .32	$ .01	$ .37

(Results as a percentage of sales)

Net sales	100.00%	100.00%	100.00%
Cost of goods sold	79.72	80.44	80.04
Gross profit	20.28	19.56	19.96
Selling and administrative expenses	14.24	14.41	13.56
Interest expense	1.09	0.95	0.68
Depreciation	1.76	1.88	1.69
Store closing charge (Note 13)		2.24	
	17.09	19.48	15.93
Income before income taxes	3.19	0.08	4.03
Provision for income taxes	1.26	0.03	1.56
Net income	1.93%	0.05%	2.47%

B. Balance Sheets

(Dollars in thousands except per share amounts)	December 31, 1994	January 1, 1994
Assets		
Current assets:		
Cash and cash equivalents	$ 66,869	$ 46,066
Receivables	140,628	109,952
Inventories	855,712	929,138
Prepaid expenses and other	67,905	54,316
Total current assets	1,131,114	1,139,472
Property, at cost, less accumulated depreciation	1,356,673	1,364,211
Total assets	$2,487,787	$2,503,683
Liabilities and Shareholders' Equity		
Current liabilities:		
Notes payable	$ 20,000	$ 10,007
Accounts payable, trade	344,595	346,799
Accrued expenses	298,024	241,187
Long-term debt - current	25	183
Capital lease obligations - current	9,122	7,108
Other liabilities - current	3,293	3,880
Income taxes payable	22,169	10,107
Total current liabilities	697,228	619,271
Long-term debt	355,300	569,350
Capital lease obligations	304,963	301,541
Deferred income taxes	46,190	36,587
Deferred compensation	668	571
Other liabilities	56,085	58,809
Total liabilities	1,460,434	1,586,129
Shareholders' equity:		
Class A non-voting common stock, $.50 par value; authorized 1,500,000,000 shares; issued and outstanding 244,142,000 shares - December 31, 1994 and 244,132,000 shares - January 1, 1994	122,071	122,066
Class B voting common stock, $.50 par value; authorized 1,500,000,000 shares; issued and outstanding 239,571,000 shares	119,786	119,786
Additional capital	337	289
Retained earnings	785,159	675,413
Total shareholders' equity	1,027,353	917,554
Total liabilities and shareholders' equity	$2,487,787	$2,503,683

C. Selected Footnotes

2 PROPERTY

Property consists of the following:

	1994	1993
Land and improvements	$ 185,403	$ 172,980
Buildings	393,012	382,186
Furniture, fixtures and equipment	947,126	907,640
Vehicles	95,198	90,518
Leasehold improvements	107,392	85,698
Construction in progress (estimated costs to complete and equip at December 31, 1994 are $34.5 million)	32,501	26,322
	1,760,632	1,665,344
Less accumulated depreciation	676,930	573,135
	1,083,702	1,092,209
Property under capital leases (less accumulated depreciation of $67,869 and $55,987 for 1994 and 1993, respectively)	272,971	272,002
	$1,356,673	$1,364,211

Property is recorded net of provisions totaling $80.2 million and $87.1 million for 1994 and 1993, respectively, to reflect the realizable value of properties that are held for sale as part of the Company's 1994 store closing program (Note 13).

5 LONG-TERM DEBT

Long-term debt consists of the following:

	1994	1993
Senior note agreement, due from 1998 to 2003. Interest ranges from 6.97% to 8.00%.		$214,000
Medium term notes, due from 1999 to 2006. Interest ranges from 8.32% to 8.73%.	$150,300	150,300
Note purchase agreements, due 1998. Interest is at 10.21%.	50,000	50,000
Note purchase agreements, due 1997. Interest is at 8.25%.	40,000	40,000
Convertible subordinated debentures, due 2003. Interest is at 5%. The debentures are convertible at any time into shares of the Company's Class A non-voting common stock at a conversion price of $7.90 per share, subject to adjustment under certain circumstances.	115,000	115,000
Other	25	233
	355,325	569,533
Less current portion	25	183
	$355,300	$569,350

C. Selected Footnotes (continued)

7 LEASES

The Company's stores operate principally in leased premises. Lease terms generally range from ten to twenty-five years with renewal options ranging from ten to twenty years. The following schedule shows future minimum lease payments under capital leases, together with the present value of net minimum lease payments, and operating leases that have initial or remaining noncancelable lease terms in excess of one year as of December 31, 1994.

	Capital Leases	Operating Leases
1995	$ 52,221	$ 108,736
1996	52,169	108,384
1997	51,866	107,927
1998	51,818	107,987
1999	50,771	107,685
Thereafter	592,147	993,945
Total minimum payments	850,992	$1,534,664
Less estimated executory costs	108,352	
Net minimum lease payments	742,640	
Less amount representing interest	428,555	
Present value of net minimum lease payments	$314,085	

Minimum payments have not been reduced by minimum sublease rentals of $5.4 million due in the future under noncancelable subleases or the remaining rent payments on leased stores that have been closed.

Total rent expense for operating leases, excluding those with terms of one year or less that were not renewed, is as follows:

	1994	1993	1992
Minimum rents	$113,606	$102,390	$93,034
Contingent rents, based on sales	490	608	727
	$114,096	$102,998	$93,761

In addition, the Company has signed lease agreements for additional store facilities, the construction of which was not complete at December 31, 1994. The leases expire on various dates extending to 2019 with renewal options generally ranging from ten to twenty years. Total future minimum rents under these agreements are approximately $216.0 million.

A. Consolidated Statement of Income

Restated for general price-level changes and expressed in thousands of
constant Chilean pesos (ThCh$) of December 31, 1994 and thousands of US dollars (ThUS$)

| | For the years ended December 31, | | | |
| | 1992 | 1993 | 1994 | 1994 |
	ThCh$	ThCh$	ThCh$	ThUS$ Unaudited (Note 2q)
Operating results				
Net sales	62,985,050	88,060,633	128,427,142	317,881
Cost of sales	(53,265,328)	(70,849,001)	(102,698,330)	(254,197)
Gross profit	9,719,722	17,211,632	25,728,812	63,684
Administrative and selling expenses (Note 18)	(7,260,538)	(14,683,162)	(19,937,428)	(49,349)
Operating income	2,459,184	2,528,470	5,791,384	14,335
Non-operating results				
Non-operating income (Note 19)	199,110	1,513,719	989,563	2,450
Non-operating expense (Note 19)	(622,412)	(1,276,016)	(1,608,280)	(3,981)
Price-level restatement gain (loss) (Note 4) .	179,808	430,444	(906,816)	(2,245)
Non-operating (loss) income	(243,494)	668,147	(1,525,533)	(3,776)
Income before income taxes	2,215,690	3,196,617	4,265,851	10,559
Income taxes	(249,122)	(446,741)	(717,519)	(1,776)
Net income	1,966,568	2,749,876	3,548,332	8,783

B. Consolidated Balance Sheets

Restated for general price-level changes and expressed in thousands of
constant Chilean pesos (ThCh$) of December 31, 1994 and thousands of US dollars (ThUS$)

ASSETS

	As at December 31,			
	1992	1993	1994	1994
	ThCh$	ThCh$	ThCh$	ThUS$ Unaudited (Note 2q)
Current Assets				
Cash	930,490	2,973,997	3,089,695	7,648
Time deposits	353,381	2,640,518	67,567	167
Marketable securities (Note 5)	7,871	—	2,539,288	6,285
Accounts receivable (Note 6)	3,222,232	4,312,313	5,654,577	13,996
Notes and accounts receivable from related companies (Note 21)	9,610	790,738	1,965,272	4,864
Inventories (Note 7)	5,241,078	8,042,307	10,668,088	26,405
Prepaid expenses (Note 8)	94,285	247,018	391,294	969
Recoverable taxes (Note 14)	159,021	393,103	162,994	403
Other current assets (Note 9)	499,216	—	—	—
Total current assets	10,517,184	19,399,994	24,538,775	60,737
Property, plant and equipment (net) (Note 10)	18,119,496	24,784,304	29,308,942	72,545
Other assets (Note 11)	72,162	3,705,271	3,541,042	8,765
Total assets	28,708,842	47,889,569	57,388,759	142,047

LIABILITIES AND SHAREHOLDERS' EQUITY

	1992	1993	1994	1994
Current liabilities				
Short-term obligations with banks (Note 13)	964,896	1,615,113	893,801	2,212
Current portion of long-term liabilities (Note 13)	1,037,461	1,240,221	1,540,302	3,813
Accounts payable—trade	7,617,173	11,306,904	14,205,345	35,160
Notes payable (Note 13)	1,174,035	4,695,628	5,252,263	13,000
Other accounts payable	230,036	626,947	869,602	2,152
Notes and accounts payable to related companies (Note 21)	15,064	138	7,494	19
Provisions (Note 12)	93,228	202,874	353,992	876
Withholdings (Note 12)	302,104	444,646	538,389	1,333
Total current liabilities	11,433,997	20,132,471	23,661,188	58,565
Long-term bank obligations (Note 13)	3,442,607	1,431,925	5,238,615	12,967
Capital lease obligations and other long-term liabilities (Note 13)	2,567,407	3,021,504	2,791,183	6,908
Total long-term liabilities	6,010,014	4,453,429	8,029,798	19,875
Minority interest	—	53,804	123,667	306
Commitments and contingencies (Note 20)	—	—	—	—
Shareholders' equity (Note 15)				
Common stock (no par value; authorized: 1,200 shares, 249,600,000 shares, and 249,600,000 shares in 1992, 1993 and 1994, respectively; issued and outstanding: 1,200 shares, 249,392,165 shares and 249,600,000 shares in 1992, 1993 and 1994, respectively)	9,717,285	14,694,848	21,993,962	54,439
Additional paid-in capital	—	5,836,292	31,81279	
Retained earnings	1,547,546	2,718,725	3,548,332	8,783
Total shareholders' equity	11,264,831	23,249,865	25,574,106	63,301
Total liabilities and shareholders' equity	28,708,842	47,889,569	57,388,759	142,047

C. Selected Footnotes

NOTE 10—PROPERTY, PLANT AND EQUIPMENT

Property, plant and equipment (net) is summarized as follows:

	At December 31,		
	1992	1993	1994
	ThCh$	ThCh$	ThCh$
Land	4,173,144	5,425,848	5,743,538
Buildings and installations	2,108,076	3,538,739	5,083,993
Machinery and equipment:			
Machinery	1,488,310	3,505,954	4,007,093
Vehicles	210,860	212,322	265,855
Machinery and equipment	1,699,170	3,718,276	4,272,948
Other fixed assets:			
Furniture and fixtures	1,190,162	1,893,234	2,000,786
Leased assets	3,715,434	5,332,505	6,139,216
Other	1,109,009	2,895,912	4,858,103
Other fixed assets	6,014,605	10,121,651	12,998,105
Revaluation from technical appraisal of property, plant and equipment	5,837,201	5,635,299	5,635,299
Property, plant and equipment at restated cost	19,832,196	28,439,813	33,733,883
Accumulated depreciation	(1,712,700)	(3,655,509)	(4,424,941)
Property, plant and equipment (net)	18,119,496	24,784,304	29,308,942

Depreciation expense for 1994 includes ThCh$8,015 for depreciation of the revaluation from technical appraisal (ThCh$9,249 in 1993 and ThCh$14,211 in 1992).

Leased assets at December 31, 1994 are summarized as follows:

	ThCh$
Land and buildings	
Warehouse	446,878
Household goods store	877,420
Supermarket No. 20	448,728
Administrative Office Building	538,137
	2,311,163
Machinery and equipment	3,828,053
Total	6,139,216

Estimated useful lives of the principal categories of property, plant and equipment are as follows:

	Years
Buildings and installations	60
Machinery and equipment	10 - 20
Furniture and fixtures	10
Leased assets	10 - 20
Revaluation from technical appraisal	27
Other	10

C. Selected Footnotes (continued)

NOTE 13—SHORT-TERM BANK OBLIGATIONS, NOTES PAYABLE AND OTHER LIABILITIES

a) *Short-term bank obligations*

Short-term bank obligations are summarized as follows:

	At December 31,		
	1992	1993	1994
	ThCh$	ThCh$	ThCh$
Payable in:			
United States dollars	169,082	1,469,117	421,594
Peruvian nuevos soles	—	43,398	68,970
Chilean pesos (not indexed)	795,814	102,598	403,237
	964,896	1,615,113	893,801

Weighted average interest rates are as follows:

	At December 31,		
	1992	1993	1994
	%	%	%
Loans in US dollars	5.68	7.99	8.19
Loans in Peruvian nuevos soles	—	76.90	50.60
Loans in Chilean pesos (not indexed)	8.99	15.66	13.08

b) *Notes payable (short-term)*

Interest-free notes payable to suppliers are summarized as follows:

	At December 31,		
	1992	1993	1994
	ThCh$	ThCh$	ThCh$
Payable in:			
United States dollars	—	810,766	1,188,330
Inflation-linked units (UFs)	—	97,595	45,201
Peruvian nuevos soles	—	506,443	1,127,995
Chilean pesos (not indexed)	1,174,035	3,280,824	2,890,737
	1,174,035	4,695,628	5,252,263

C. Selected Footnotes (continued)

NOTE 13—SHORT-TERM BANK OBLIGATIONS, NOTES PAYABLE AND OTHER LIABILITIES (continued)

c) *Long-term bank obligations*

Long-term bank obligations are summarized as follows:

	At December 31,		
	1992	1993	1994
	ThCh$	ThCh$	ThCh$
Payable in:			
Inflation-linked units (UFs)	3,809,087	1,662,004	1,433,227
United States dollars	—	—	4,029,200
	3,809,087	1,662,004	5,462,427
Less: Current portion	(366,480)	(230,079)	(223,812)
Long-term portion	3,442,607	1,431,925	5,238,615

Weighted average interest thereon:

	At December 31,		
	1992	1993	1994
	%	%	%
Inflation-linked units (UFs)	8.46	9.79	9.50
United States dollars	—	—	7.94

d) *Capital lease obligations and other long-term liabilities*

Capital lease obligations and other long-term liabilities are summarized as follows:

	At December 31,		
	1992	1993	1994
	ThCh$	ThCh$	ThCh$
Present value of net minimum lease payments under capital leases payable in inflation-linked units (UFs) . . .	3,739,898	4,993,479	4,795,758
Interest portion	(566,499)	(1,066,876)	(885,927)
Capital lease obligations (net)	3,173,399	3,926,603	3,909,831
Less: Short-term portion	(670,981)	(1,010,142)	(1,316,490)
Long-term portion	2,502,418	2,916,461	2,593,341
Deferred income taxes (Note 14)	—	—	197,842
Other long-term obligations	64,989	105,043	—
Total long-term obligations	2,567,407	3,021,504	2,791,183

Future minimum lease payments on the long-term portion of Capital lease obligations at December 31, 1994 are as follows:

Principal payments during the years ending December 31,	ThCh$
1996	2,823,584
1997	807,365
1998	380,593
1999	371,363
2000	325,213
2001 and thereafter	87,640
Less: deferred interest	(885,927)
	3,909,831

C. **Selected Footnotes** (continued)

NOTE 20—COMMITMENTS AND CONTINGENCIES

Operating leases

The Company leases 22 of its 27 supermarkets in Chile, nine of its ten supermarkets in Peru and other properties in Chile and Peru.

The Company's leases for its supermarket locations in Chile are generally for fixed amounts, while eight leases provide for a payment to the lessor equal to a percentage of gross or net sales. Most of the leases in Chile are renewable, over differing time periods. They expire during the years 1997 to 2010.

Most of the leases for the Company's Peruvian facilities are not automatically renewable and all leases for its Peruvian supermarkets provide for a payment to the lessor equal to a percentage of gross or net sales. The leases expire during the years 1997 to 2003.

The following is a schedule by years of future minimum rental payments required under operating leases and future minimum rentals to be received under subleases that have initial or remaining noncancelable lease terms in excess of one year at December 31, 1994:

Year Ending December 31,	Gross future minimum rental payments	Future minimum rentals to be received under subleases	Net future minimum rental payments
1995	1,906,705	(47,299)	1,859,406
1996	1,906,705	(47,299)	1,859,406
1997	1,906,705	(47,299)	1,859,406
1998	1,906,705	(47,299)	1,859,406
1999	1,906,705	(47,299)	1,859,406
2000 and thereafter	1,906,705	(47,299)	1,859,406
	11,440,230	(283,794)	11,156,436

The future minimum lease payments reflect only scheduled fixed payments as required by the lease contracts. Contingent payments, calculated as a percentage of sales at the applicable location, are required under certain contracts. Rent expense under operating leases was ThCh$569,921, ThCh$726,075 and ThCh$1,141,511 in 1992, 1993 and 1994, respectively. The Company made contingent rental payments of ThCh$57,494, ThCh$15,974 and ThCh$135,301 in 1992, 1993 and 1994, respectively. The Company also realized sublease income of ThCh$8,698, ThCh$10,515 and ThCh$47,299 in 1992, 1993 and 1994, respectively.

Economic woes in Mexico and Argentina are applying the brakes to Coca-Cola Femsa. Since 1988, Coca-Cola Femsa (CCF) has generated excellent sales and operating growth. By investing heavily in capacity and acquisitions, the company consistently increased its profitability, and ROEs charged up to 51% in the early 1990s. Although an international equity issuance in 1993 has since diluted CCF's ROEs, the company raised the capital necessary to move to the next level: expansion abroad. In September 1994, CCF bought Argentina's largest Coke bottler.

CCF had the right idea -- expansion throughout South America has been successful for other regional bottlers -- but its timing proved poor. Soon after the Argentine acquisition, both Mexico and Argentina fell into deep recessions. With high interest rates, unruly inflation, and rising unemployment, Mexico and Argentina suddenly became no-growth markets for bottlers.

Beyond the short term, however, CCF still holds considerable promise. The company plans to continue investing in expansion, and will spend up to $90 million over the next two years.

Thanks to the cola industry's long-term promise, CCF's ADRs have suffered less than most Mexican equities. Still they have shed close to 50% of their value since mid-1994. With a P/E of 18, they are now one of Latin America's cheapest bottling plays.[+]

Juanita Carlos, a senior credit analyst with a large bank headquartered in Houston, Texas, noted the above review of Coca-Cola Femsa, S.A. de C.V. (Coca-Cola Femsa) by Matthew Desmond in International Stocks (January 11, 1996). Because Juanita spoke fluent Spanish and had taken courses in international finance and accounting in her MBA program, she had become the bank's specialist in Latin and South America. The bank she worked for was interested in developing a strong presence in Latin and South America because it believed the region offered lucrative returns. She had been asked to take a close look at Coca-Cola Femsa to evaluate the possibility to making a term loan of at least $US100 million. Juanita searched for recent stories in the financial press on Coca-Cola Femsa. A "Heard on the Street" column in *The Wall Street Journal* described Coca-Cola Femsa in the following terms:

Another company that stood out from the pack in negotiating the difficulties of last year's recession was Mexico-based bottler Coca-Cola Femsa. It not only coped with the sharp devaluation at home but had recently taken over the Coca-Cola concession in Argentina's capital, Buenos Aires, when a harsh recession took hold. One New Jersey-based global fund manager says Coke Femsa did 'a terrific job of not only controlling damage, but building on their franchise (August 15, 1996, p. C1).'

Juanita Carlos also checked the recent stock price performance of Coca-Cola Femsa which is traded on the NYSE as an American Depository Receipt (ADR) (see Exhibit 1). The stock closed on December 31, 1995 at $18.50 per share, down from $24.63 at December 31, 1994. Over the same period, Juanita recalled that the Standard & Poor's 500 index had reported returns of about 35%.

+ Reproduced with permission from Morningstar, Inc.

* This case was prepared by Graeme Rankine for the purpose of class discussion using publicly available data. Erik Solomon and Andrew Springer provided research assistance on this case. Copyright © 1996 by the American Graduate School of International Management. All rights reserved.

The Mexican Economy

Juanita was also aware that the Mexican Government's decision to allow the peso to float freely against the world's currencies had a dramatic impact on the Mexican economy. She found that interest rates were currently in the vicinity of 40% per year and the inflation rate was around 14% annually. Additional data on the Mexican economy and on the soft drink industry is provided in Exhibit 2. By December, 1995, the outlook for the Mexican economy provided in International Stocks (January 11, 1995) suggested that "the dark clouds above the economy parted slightly. President Zedillo's strategy -- short-term pain for long-term gain -- seemed like it was beginning to yield some results."

Company Background

Coca-Cola Femsa is a Mexican joint-venture whose shares are listed on the New York Stock Exchange and on the Bolsa Mexicana de Valores (Mexican Stock Exchange). Prior to 1993, Coca-Cola Femsa was operated as a wholly-owned subsidiary of Femsa. Now, 51% of the company's capital stock is owned by *Fomento Economico Mexicano, S.A. de C.V.* (Femsa), 30% by a wholly-owned subsidiary of *The Coca-Cola Company* and 19% by the public. The company is a bottler and distributor of soft drink products including Coca-Cola, Sprite, Fanta, Diet Coke, Coca-Cola Light, Diet Sprite, Fresca, Lift, Quatro, Powerade, Extra Poma, Etiqueta Azul and Kin. The company distributes soft drink products in three geographic regions: the Valley of Mexico (Mexico City and surrounding areas), Southeast of Mexico City (States of Oaxaca and Tabasco and some areas of the States of Chiapas and Veracruz), as well as Buenos Aires, Argentina. Bottling operations include eight plants in the Valley of Mexico City, five in the southeast of Mexico and two in Buenos Aires, Argentina. In 1995, the company sold 355 million cases in the three areas, which represented a market share of cola sales of 62.2% (Valley of Mexico), 74.6% (Southeast of Mexico City), and 77.1% (Buenos Aires, Argentina).

In 1994, the company acquired an interest in Coca-Cola, S.A., Industrial, Comercial y Financiera which was later renamed Coca-Cola Femsa de Buenos Aires, S.A. At December 31, 1995, Coca-Cola Femsa held a 51% interest in the subsidiary (49% was held by the Coca-Cola Export Corporation), but the company increased its share to 75% on February 20, 1996. Juanita obtained the latest annual report for Coca-Cola Femsa (see Exhibit 3) to prepare a financial analysis of the company.

Mexican Accounting Practices

Juanita recalled from her MBA program that Mexican companies were required to report their financial statements in constant purchasing power and that any gains or losses from inflation were reported in income. Juanita reviewed an accounting textbook for an example of how the procedure is implemented in practice (see Exhibit 4). Haywood Kelly of Morningstar's, International Stocks (February 9, 1996) provided the following assessment of Mexican inflation accounting:

> *When Mexican companies report their 1995 earnings over the next couple of months, some odd-looking numbers will pop up on their income statements. While the peso crisis has resulted in foreign-exchange-related gains and losses for Mexican firms, 1995 results will also include huge gains and losses resulting from inflation - which reemerged with a vengeance in Mexico. In some cases, inflation-induced gains and losses could be the difference between reporting a profit and reporting a loss.*
> *...Whether a company posts a gain or loss because of inflation depends on its mix of monetary assets and monetary liabilities. Basically, the more monetary liabilities a firm has, and the fewer monetary assets, the better. When inflation nibbles away at the*

value of a monetary liability, it's a positive for the company, because the real value of that liability drops. When it nibbles away at items like cash reserves, however, it's a negative.

... Purchasing-power gains or losses are important, but throwing them on the income statement complicates the interpretation of earnings. That's because earnings for a company ... reflect not just the earning power of the company - which is what one expects earnings to reflect - but also management's choice as to the mix of monetary assets and liabilities.

... In general, to understand how a company's core business is doing when the firms uses inflation accounting, operating income is a much better measure than net earnings, as is earnings before interest expense and taxes.

...[M]onetary gains may represent a net increase in purchasing power on the balance sheet, but they're not the same thing as cash flowing in that can be used to invest in working capital or pay suppliers.[++]

Juanita also remembered from her MBA accounting courses that Mexican GAAP was different from U.S. GAAP, particularly with respect to deferred taxes, other post-employment benefits, and foreign currency translation. She obtained information about the principal differences between Mexican GAAP and U.S. GAAP (see Exhibit 5).

Comparable Companies

As part of a complete analysis, Juanita thought it was important to compare Coca-Cola Femsa to other Mexican companies in the same industry. Panamerican Beverages, Inc. (Panamco) is the largest soft drink bottler in Latin America and one of the world's largest bottlers of the soft drink products of the Coca-Cola Company. Panamco produces and distributes soft drink products, beer, bottled water and other beverages in Mexico, Brazil, Columbia and Costa Rica. In Mexico, Panamco serves consumers through its 74% owned Azteca subsidiary in five states including Guanajuato (where it began operations), Puebla, Tlaxcala, Michoacan and most of Veracruz. Panamco reports according to U.S. GAAP and includes financial statements for Azteca (see Exhibit 6).

Grupo Embotellador de Mexico, S.A. de C.V. (Gemex) is a major bottler and distributor of Pepsi products in Mexico. It is also engaged in the production and distribution of mineral water, purified water and soft drinks including Squirt, Mirinda, Garci Crespo, San Lorenzo and Delaware Punch. Juanita obtained the more recent financial statements for Gemex, whose financial statements were computed in accordance with Mexican GAAP, but are reconciled to U.S. GAAP (see Exhibit 7).

Required:

1. Using Coca-Cola Femsa's income statement, prepare a common-size income statement for the company. Compare 1993 to 1995. Why has Coca-Cola Femsa's return on sales decreased from 8.50 percent to 5.80 percent? Look at the comparable data for Azteca (Exhibit 6) and Gemex (Exhibit 7). How does Coca-Cola Femsa's profit performance compare to the other two companies? Why do the companies differ in profit performance?

[++] Reproduced with permission from Morningstar, Inc.

Required (continued)

2. Using Coca-Cola Femsa's income statement and balance sheet, prepare a Dupont analysis (return on equity = net income/revenues * revenues/assets * assets/equity) for Coca-Cola Femsa for 1994-1995. Why has return on equity (ROE) (excluding minority interest) increased from 13.26% to 13.37%? Using comparable data (Exhibits 6 and 7), calculate the same ratios for Azteca and Gemex. How does Coca-Cola Femsa compare to Azteca and Gemex?

3. Using Coca-Cola Femsa's income statement and balance sheet, calculate the debt ratio (total liabilities / total assets, and long-term debt / total assets), and interest coverage ratio (operating income / interest expense). Using comparable data (Exhibits 6 and 7), compute the same ratios for Axteca and Gemex. What is your assessment of Coca-Cola Femsa's default risk? Consider the information on $US denominated debt in Notes 11 and 13. What are the implications for Coca-Cola Femsa's future performance?

4. Using Coca-Cola Femsa's income statement, compute the annual growth rate in revenues from 1993 to 1995. Consider Coca-Cola Femsa's statement of cash flows. How has Coca-Cola Femsa financed its growth? Using comparable data (Exhibits 6 and 7), compute the annual growth rate in revenues for Azteca and Gemex. How have Azteca and Gemex financed their growth? What is your assessment of Coca-Cola Femsa's cash flow situation?

5. Consider the illustration of inflation-adjusted financial statements in Exhibit 4 and the information in Note 4. How would you interpret the change in the item, Cumulative Result of Holding Non-monetary Assets, reported in Coca-Cola Femsa's balance sheet? How would you interpret the item, Gain on Monetary Position, reported in Coca-Cola Femsa's income statement? Do you agree with Morningstar's assessment of Mexican inflation accounting? Would focusing on operating income affect your assessment of the default risk of Coca-Cola Femsa?

6. Consider the information in Exhibit 5 on Mexican and U.S. GAAP. For each issue, would net income and stockholders' equity generally be higher or lower under Mexican GAAP?

7. Consider the information on Coca-Cola Femsa's Argentinean subsidiary in Notes 1 (a), 3, 4 (n) and 19. Explain and evaluate how Coca-Cola Femsa accounts for this subsidiary in its consolidated financial statements? [Hint: How important is the argument that the subsidiary is a "hedge"?]

8. Consider the reconciliation between Mexican and U.S. GAAP provided in Notes 16 and 17 for Coca-Cola Femsa and Exhibit 7 for Gemex. Does this information affect your assessment of Coca-Cola Femsa?

9. Using the data provided in Exhibit 2 (Panel A), what is your assessment of the Mexican economy through 1995? Using the data provided in Exhibit 2 (Panel B), what are the future prospects for the soft drink industry? What are the implications for Coca-Cola Femsa.

10. Should Juanita recommend that the bank make the $US100 million loan to Coca-Cola Femsa?

Exhibit 1
Coca-Cola Femsa, S.A. de C.V. - Monthly Data on Coca-Cola Femsa's Stock Price and Trading Volume During the period August 1992-August 1996

DATE	HIGH PRICE	LOW PRICE	CLOSE PRICE	VOLUME	CUM. ADJ. FACTOR
Aug96	$27.88	$23.88	$26.25	2,388,800	1.000000
Jul96	$28.63	$22.50	$23.88	2,977,100	1.000000
Jun96	$29.38	$27.13	$28.63	2,177,400	1.000000
May96	$32.38	$26.38	$28.88	2,762,800	1.000000
Apr96	$28.63	$22.13	$26.88	3,666,800	1.000000
Mar96	$23.88	$22.00	$22.63	2,562,500	1.000000
Feb96	$25.00	$21.38	$22.13	3,274,000	1.000000
Jan96	$26.13	$18.50	$25.13	6,321,398	1.000000
Dec95	$21.13	$18.00	$18.50	3,130,000	1.000000
Nov95	$22.38	$16.50	$20.50	4,696,597	1.000000
Oct95	$19.88	$16.88	$18.00	3,289,400	1.000000
Sep95	$23.75	$18.38	$19.88	3,242,100	1.000000
Aug95	$24.25	$21.00	$23.13	3,607,800	1.000000
Jul95	$27.38	$21.00	$23.38	5,109,898	1.000000
Jun95	$21.63	$16.63	$21.25	3,524,200	1.000000
May95	$20.88	$16.63	$17.13	2,596,900	1.000000
Apr95	$21.25	$16.88	$19.88	3,829,700	1.000000
Mar95	$19.00	$12.88	$18.50	7,994,796	1.000000
Feb95	$19.25	$13.00	$15.13	5,993,296	1.000000
Jan95	$24.63	$16.00	$19.00	9,163,398	1.000000
Dec94	$32.00	$20.00	$24.63	4,060,200	1.000000
Nov94	$32.63	$28.13	$31.63	1,943,700	1.000000
Oct94	$36.13	$30.63	$30.88	1,836,400	1.000000
Sep94	$38.38	$34.63	$36.13	1,632,900	1.000000
Aug94	$36.50	$30.00	$34.88	3,385,700	1.000000
Jul94	$30.63	$25.13	$30.25	1,446,400	1.000000
Jun94	$31.13	$24.63	$25.13	1,439,600	1.000000
May94	$32.00	$27.50	$31.13	1,701,800	1.000000
Apr94	$31.75	$21.63	$31.75	2,628,400	1.000000
Mar94	$32.25	$26.50	$27.38	3,166,300	1.000000
Feb94	$36.75	$30.13	$32.00	2,153,300	1.000000
Jan94	$35.75	$30.88	$34.75	2,089,600	1.000000
Dec93	$33.75	$28.63	$32.75	1,627,300	1.000000
Nov93	$31.63	$26.13	$28.50	2,601,000	1.000000
Oct93	$31.75	$23.50	$28.00	4,748,699	1.000000
Sep93	$24.00	$21.38	$23.75	8,304,500	1.000000
Aug93	@NA	@NA	@NA	0	1.000000
Jul93	@NA	@NA	@NA	0	1.000000
Jun93	@NA	@NA	@NA	0	1.000000
May93	@NA	@NA	@NA	0	1.000000
Apr93	@NA	@NA	@NA	0	1.000000
Mar93	@NA	@NA	@NA	0	1.000000
Feb93	@NA	@NA	@NA	0	1.000000
Jan93	@NA	@NA	@NA	0	1.000000
Dec92	@NA	@NA	@NA	0	1.000000
Nov92	@NA	@NA	@NA	0	1.000000
Oct92	@NA	@NA	@NA	0	1.000000
Sep92	@NA	@NA	@NA	0	1.000000
Aug92	@NA	@NA	@NA	0	1.000000

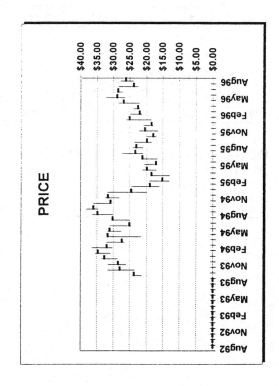

COCA-COLA FEMSA DE C V -ADR
KOF
MONTHLY ADJUSTED PRICES

PRICE

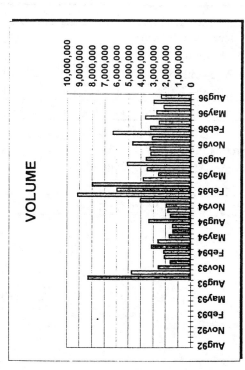

VOLUME

Exhibit 2
Coca-Cola Femsa, S.A. de C.V. - Data on the Mexican Economy and Retail Soft Drink Sales

Panel A:

	1989	1990	1991	1992	1993	1994	1995
Market Price Return (%)	80.7	46.0	120.0	29.8	44.0	-44.0	-23.2
+/- S&P 500 (%)	49.0	49.1	89.5	22.2	33.9	-45.7	-60.7
Consumer-Price Inflation (%)	20.1	26.6	22.7	15.5	9.7	6.9	35.0
Av. Cost of Funds (%)	44.6	37.1	22.6	18.8	18.6	15.5	45.1
Money Supply Growth (%)	na	63.1	123.9	15.1	17.7	1.1	3.5
Trade Balance (US$b)	0.4	-0.9	-7.3	-15.9	-13.5	-18.5	7.1
Current Account Balance (US$b)	-5.8	-7.5	-14.9	-24.8	-23.4	-29.4	-0.7
Real GDP Growth (%)	na	4.5	3.6	2.8	0.7	3.5	-7.0
Exchange Rate (New Pesos per US$)	2.641	2.945	3.071	3.115	3.106	5.325	7.643
Average Price / Earnings	na	9.3	12.0	13.7	20.6	26.5	23.1
Average Price / Book	na	2.2	2.3	2.3	3.0	3.3	2.0
Average Price / Cash Flow	na	8.0	8.5	9.2	15.1	19.4	13.4
Number of ADRs in Average	na	1	5	8	22	35	35

Source: Morningstar, Inc., International Stocks, Mexico Overlook (January 11, 1996), International Monetary Fund, International Financial Statistics (September 1996).

Panel B:

	1990	1991	1992	1993	1994	1995
Retail Sales of Soft Drink:						
Litres Million	11,958	12,691	13,175	14,310	15,461	15,071
New Pesos Million	16,582	20,230	25,582	28,554	33,193	31,074
US$ Million	5,901	6,721	8,279	9,152	10,028	4,972
	1995	**1996**	**1997**	**1998**	**1999**	**2000**
Forecasted Retail Sales of Soft Drink						
...Litres Million	15,071	15,427	15,975	16,620	18,052	19,464
Constant 1995 New Pesos Million	31,074	29,535	31,575	32,316	34,729	37,185
Constant US$ Million	4,972	4,726	5,012	5,171	5,556	5,950

Source: Consumer Mexico (1996).

ARTHUR ANDERSEN & CO

Mexico, D.F.

REPORT OF INDEPENDENT ACCOUNTANTS

To the Stockholders of Coca-Cola FEMSA, S.A. de C.V.:

We have audited the accompanying consolidated balance sheet of COCA-COLA FEMSA, S.A. DE C.V. (incorporated in Mexico) AND SUBSIDIARIES (collectively referred to as the "Company") as of December 31, 1995 and 1994, and the related consolidated statements of income, changes in stockholders' equity and changes in financial position for each of the three years in the period ended December 31, 1995. These financial statements have been prepared in accordance with accounting principles generally accepted in Mexico and, therefore, have been expressed in Mexican pesos with purchasing power as of December 31, 1995. These financial statements are the responsibility of the Company's management. Our responsibility is to express an opinion on these financial statements based on our audits.

We have conducted our audits in accordance with the auditing standards generally accepted in Mexico, which are substantially the same as those followed in the United States. Those standards require that we plan and perform the audit to obtain reasonable assurance about whether the financial statements are free of material misstatement. An audit includes examining, on a test basis, evidence supporting the amounts and disclosures in the financial statements. An audit also includes assessing the accounting principles used and significant estimates made by management, as well as evaluating the overall financial statement presentation. We believe that our audits provide a reasonable basis for our opinion.

Accounting practices used by the Company in preparing the accompanying consolidated financial statements conform with the accounting principles generally accepted in Mexico but do not conform with the accounting principles generally accepted in the United States. A description of these differences and a partial reconciliation as permitted by Form 20-F of consolidated net income and of stockholders' equity to the accounting principles generally accepted in the United States is set forth in Note 17.

In our opinion, the financial statements referred to above present fairly, in all material respects, the consolidated financial position of Coca-Cola FEMSA, S.A. de C.V. and Subsidiaries as of December 31, 1995 and 1994, and the consolidated results of their operations and the changes in their financial position for each of the three years in the period ended December 31, 1995, in accordance with the accounting principles generally accepted in Mexico.

Also, in our opinion, the translated amounts in the accompanying consolidated financial statements translated into U.S. dollars have been computed on the basis set forth in Note 2.

February 23, 1996

Arthur Andersen & Co.

Coca-Cola FEMSA, S.A. de C.V. and Subsidiaries
MEXICO, D.F.

Consolidated Balance Sheet
At December 31, 1995 and 1994
Expressed in Constant Pesos as of December 31,1995 - Thousands of Mexican Pesos (Ps.) and Thousands of U.S. Dollars ($)

ASSETS		1995	1994
Current Assets:			
Cash and cash equivalents	$19,844	Ps.152,483	Ps.136,132
Accounts receivable:			
Trade	37,609	288,987	283,162
Notes	330	2,538	3,819
Other	7,191	55,255	118,016
	45,130	346,780	404,997
Tax recoverable	1,102	8,467	78,461
Inventories	33,402	256,664	215,831
Prepaid expenses	5,761	44,267	45,439
Total Current Assets	105,239	808,661	880,860
Property, Plant and Equipment:			
Land	48,486	372,563	264,311
Buildings,machinery and equipment	486,054	3,734,840	3,228,387
Accumulated depreciation	(122,319)	(939,901)	(863,228)
Construction in progress	21,088	162,037	454,247
Bottles and cases	38,866	298,649	264,838
Total Property, Plant and Equipment	472,175	3,628,188	3,348,555
Investment in Shares	1,439	11,060	16,932
Deferred Charges, Net	8,363	64,258	100,104
Goodwill, Net	124,215	954,468	538,314
TOTAL ASSETS $711,431	Ps.5,466,635	Ps.4,884,765	Ps.4,884,765

LIABILITIES AND STOCKHOLDERS' EQUITY	1995		1994
Current Liabilities:			
Short-term bank loans and interest payable	$11,518	Ps.88,504	Ps.647,619
Short-term maturity of long-term debt	3,219	24,737	5,331
Notes payable	653	5,017	-
Suppliers 42,990	330,335	340,584	
Accounts payable	17,325	133,127	104,643
Taxes payable	10,214	78,487	159,741
Other liabilities	9,355	71,883	57,736
Total Current Liabilities	95,274	732,090	1,315,654
Long-Term Liabilities:			
Private placement notes	100,000	768,400	767,071
Long-term bank loans	152,580	1,172,425	22,405
Notes payable	7,397	56,836	-
Short-term maturity	(3,219)	(24,737)	(5,331)
Pension plan	5,221	40,120	41,255
Seniority premium	1,553	11,929	15,671
Other liabilities	8,034	61,734	61,918
Total Long-Term Liabilities	271,566	2,086,707	902,989
Total Liabilities	366,840	2,818,797	2,218,643
Stockholders' Equity:			
Minority interest in consolidated subsidiary	36,582	281,096	242,086
Majority interest:			
Capital stock	118,799	912,853	912,853
Additional paid-in capital	102,763	789,631	789,631
Retained earnings	93,114	715,487	430,473
Net income for the year	41,187	316,481	321,461
Cumulative result of holding nonmonetary assets	(47,854)	(367,710)	(30,382)
Total Majority Interest	308,009	2,366,742	2,424,036
Total Stockholders' Equity	344,591	2,647,838	2,666,122
TOTAL LIABILITIES AND STOCKHOLDERS' EQUITY	$711,431	Ps.5,466,635	Ps.4,884,765

The accompanying notes are an integral part of this consolidated balance sheet.

Mexico, D.F., February 23, 1996

Alfredo Martí nez Urdal   Hé ctor Treviñ o Gutí errez
Chief Executive Officer   Chief Financial and Administrative Officer

Coca-Cola FEMSA, S.A. de C.V. and Subsidiaries
MEXICO, D.F.

Consolidated Income Statement
For the Years Ended December 31, 1995, 1994, and 1993
Expressed in Constant Pesos as of December 31,1995 - Thousands of Mexican Pesos (Ps.) and Thousands of U.S. Dollars ($)

	1995	1995	1994	1993
Net sales	$795,771	Ps.6,114,707	Ps.4,672,777	Ps.3,090,905
Other operating revenues	3,773	28,991	50,604	26,332
Total revenues	799,544	6,143,698	4,723,381	3,117,237
Cost of sales	464,153	3,566,552	2,432,862	1,430,643
Gross profit	335,391	2,577,146	2,290,519	1,686,594
Operating expenses:				
Administrative	50,764	390,068	348,016	261,534
Selling	228,745	1,757,679	1,343,901	990,038
	279,509	2,147,747	1,691,917	1,251,572
Goodwill amortization	3,645	28,012	6,442	-
Income from operations	52,237	401,387	592,160	435,022
Integral result of financing:				
Interest, net	13,472	103,521	42,261	179,725
Foreign exchange loss (gain), net	14,528	111,636	50,464	(1,806)
Gain on monetary position	(24,556)	(188,690)	(17,630)	(121,008)
	3,444	26,467	75,095	56,911
Other income, net 11,066	85,034	53,049	33,951	
Income before income tax, tax on assets and employee profit sharing	59,859	459,954	570,114	412,062
Income tax, tax on assets and employee profit sharing	13,507	103,788	199,638	147,133
Net income for the year	$46,352	Ps.356,166	Ps.370,476	Ps.264,929
Majority income	$41,187	Ps.316,481	Ps.321,461	Ps.264,929
Minority income	5,165	39,685	49,015	-
Net income for the year	$46,352	Ps.356,166	Ps.370,476	Ps.264,929
Weighted average shares outstanding (thousands)	475,000	475,000	475,000	371,299
Net majority income per weighted average share outstanding (dollars and Mexican pesos)	$0.09	Ps.0.67	Ps.0.68	Ps.0.71

The accompanying notes are an integral part of this consolidated income statement.

Coca-Cola FEMSA, S.A. de C.V. and Subsidiaries
MEXICO, D.F.

Consolidated Statement of Changes in Financial Position
For the Years Ended December 31, 1995, 1994, and 1993
Expressed in Constant Pesos as of December 31,1995 - Thousands of Mexican Pesos (Ps.) and Thousands of U.S.
Dollars ($)

	1995	1995	1994	1993
RESOURCES GENERATED BY (USED IN):				
Operations:				
Net income for the year	$46,352	Ps.356,166	Ps.370,476	Ps.264,929
Depreciation	26,720	205,316	74,691	73,772
Other	13,687	105,174	21,695	12,649
	86,759	666,656	466,862	351,350
Working capital:				
Accounts receivable	7,576	58,217	(48,973)	(19,568)
Inventories	(10,502)	(80,695)	(8,534)	(14,067)
Prepaid expenses	1,072	8,239	8,038	11,542
Suppliers	(1,334)	(10,249)	33,700	32,292
Accounts payable and other	5,548	42,631	19,128	18,336
Taxes payable	(10,574)	(81,254)	(81,334)	63,913
	(8,214)	(63,111)	(77,975)	92,448
RESOURCES GENERATED BY OPERATIONS	78,545	603,545	388,887	443,798
Investments:				
Property, plant and equipment	(97,483)	(749,059)	(484,355)	(364,036)
Shares and deferred charges	(57,445)	(441,399)	(699,400)	(50,711)
RESOURCES USED IN INVESTMENT ACTIVITIES	(154,928)	(1,190,458)	(1,183,755)	(414,747)

Financing Activities:				
Amortization in real terms of financing due to purchase of shares of Coca-Cola FEMSA Buenos Aires	(33,028)	(253,789)	(16,634)	-
Increase (decrease) in notes and interest payable	8,050	61,853	25,517	(638,557)
Increase in bank loans	105,789	812,885	152,146	13,562
Dividends paid	(4,743)	(36,447)	(38,935)	-
Other liabilities	(823)	(6,324)	-	-
Pension plan and seniority premium	233	1,786	2,478	2,022
Payments in real terms of the pension plan and seniority premium	(1,869)	(14,363)	(2,796)	-
Financing for purchase of shares of Coca-Cola FEMSA Buenos Aires	-	-	777,563	-
Additional paid-in capital from The Coca-Cola Co. in Coca-Cola FEMSA Buenos Aires	4,902	37,663	-	-
Increase in capital stock	-	-	-	1,387,757
Financing from FEMSA	-	-	-	(765,829)
RESOURCES GENERATED BY FINANCING ACTIVITIES	78,511	603,264	899,339	(1,045)
Net increase in cash and cash equivalents	2,128	16,351	104,471	28,006
Cash and cash equivalents at beginning of the year	17,716	136,132	31,661	3,655
CASH AND CASH EQUIVALENTS AT END OF THE YEAR	$19,844	Ps.152,483	Ps.136,132	Ps.31,661
Supplementary cash flow information:				
Interest paid	$13,428	Ps.103,177	Ps.11,828	Ps.-
Income tax and tax on assets paid	16,554	127,200	71,182	77,702
Employees profit sharing paid	4,437	34,092	26,999	16,608

The accompanying notes are an integral part of this consolidated statement of changes in financial position.

Coca-Cola FEMSA S.A. de C.V. and Subsidiaries
MEXICO, D.F.

Consolidated Statement of Changes in Stockholders' Equity
For the Years Ended at December 31, 1995, 1994 and 1993
Expressed, in Constant Pesos as of December 31, 1995 - Thousands of Mexican Pesos (Ps.)

Description	Capital Stock	Additional Paid-in Capital	Retained Earnings	Net Income for the Year	Cumulative Result of Holding Nonmonetary Assets	Minority Interest	Total Stockholders' Equity
Consolidated Balances at December 31, 1992	Ps.496,673	Ps.-	Ps.20,910	Ps.183,569	Ps.(340,557)	Ps.-	Ps.360,595
Transfer of income of prior year			183,569	(183,569)			
Subscription by FEMSA and Impulsora de Mercados	173,548				181,946		355,494
Subscription by Inmex Corporation	242,632	789,631					1,032,263
Net income for the year				264,929			264,929
Results from holding nonmonetary assets					(16,200)		(16,200)
Consolidated Balances at December 31, 1993	Ps.912,853	Ps.789,631	Ps.204,479	Ps.264,929	Ps.(174,811)	Ps.-	Ps.1,997,081
Transfer of income of prior year			264,929	(264,929)			
Dividends paid			(38,935)				(38,935)
Acquisition of Coca-Cola FEMSA Buenos Aires						142,665	142,665
Net income for the year				321,461		49,015	370,476
Results from holding nonmonetary assets					144,429	50,406	194,835
Consolidated Balances at December 31, 1994	Ps.912,853	Ps.789,631	Ps.430,473	Ps.321,461	Ps.(30,382)	Ps.242,086	Ps.2,666,122

53

Transfer of income of prior year			321,461	(321,461)			-
Dividends paid			(36,447)				(36,447)
Subscription by minority in Coca-Cola FEMSA Buenos Aires						37,663	37,663
Net income for the year				316,481		39,685	356,166
Results from holding nonmonetary assets					(337,328)	(38,338)	(375,666)
Consolidated Balances at December 31, 1995	Ps.9,912,853	Ps.789,631	Ps.715,487	Ps.316,481	Ps.(367,710)	Ps.281,096	Ps.2,647,838

The accompanying notes are an integral part of this consolidated statement of changes in stockholders' equity.

Coca-Cola FEMSA, S.A. de C.V. and Subsidiaries
MEXICO, D.F.

Notes to the Consolidated Financial Statements
At December 31, 1995, 1994 and 1993
Expressed in Constant Pesos as of December 31, 1995 - Thousands of Mexican Pesos (Ps.) and Thousands of U.S. Dollars ($)

Activities of the Company
Coca-Cola FEMSA, S.A. de C.V. (Coca-Cola FEMSA) is a Mexican corporation controlled by Fomento Economico Mexicano, S.A. de C.V. (FEMSA), whose main activity is the acquisition, holding and transferring of all types of bonds, capital stock, shares and marketable securities.

Coca-Cola FEMSA and its Subsidiaries (the Company), as an economic unit, are engaged in the production and distribution of soft drinks in two Coca-Cola territories located in Mexico and one territory in Argentina. The Valley of Mexico territory includes all of Mexico City and a substantial portion of the State of Mexico. The Southeastern Mexican territory covers the State of Tabasco and contiguous portions of the States of Oaxaca, Chiapas and the southern portion of the State of Veracruz. The Argentine territory includes a substantial portion of the city of Buenos Aires and the greater Buenos Aires area. As mentioned in Note 1, in 1994 Coca-Cola FEMSA acquired control of Coca-Cola FEMSA de Buenos Aires, S.A., formerly Coca-Cola, S.A., Industrial, Comercial y Financiera (Coca-Cola FEMSA Buenos Aires).

Note 1. Important Events
a)   Acquisition of Coca-Cola FEMSA Buenos Aires

On September 1, 1994, Coca-Cola FEMSA acquired 51 % of the capital stock and effective control of Coca-Cola FEMSA Buenos Aires from a subsidiary of The Coca-Cola Company (Coca-Cola Co.). Additionally, Coca-Cola FEMSA also has the option to acquire the remaining 49%, at the same price plus an annual cost of 12%.

The purchase price for this transaction was U.S. $94.7 million and was financed through a private placement of long-term notes outside Mexico in the amount of U.S. $100 million (see Note 13).

The acquisition of the Buenos Aires subsidiary was made at a price above book value; consequently, goodwill of 70.3 million Argentine pesos was generated and is maintained in that currency since the investment will be recovered in such currency. Goodwill is being amortized over a period of 20 years. Since 1991 the Argentine peso (A$) has been equivalent to one U.S. dollar.

The net investment in Coca-Cola FEMSA Buenos Aires is considered a hedge against the U.S. dollar debt used to finance the acquisition. Therefore, the foreign exchange loss, net of the related tax benefit, was recorded directly in stockholders' equity, together with the surplus generated by the restatement of the investment.

The gain on monetary position resulting from this liability which was included in income for the year was computed using the inflation rate of the country in which the subsidiary is located, since in accordance with International Accounting Standards (IAS 21) it was considered to be an integral part of the investment in the foreign subsidiary. Had the Mexican inflation rate been used, the gain on monetary position would have increased by Ps. 271,418.

b)   Acquisition of SIRSA San Isidrio Refrescos, S.A.I. y C. (SIRSA) and Refrescos del Norte, S.A. (RDN)

In July 1995, Coca-Cola FEMSA Buenos Aires signed a letter of intent to acquire the franchises of Coca-Cola which were operated by SIRSA and RDN in territories contiguous to that which is currently operated. The negotiations to carry out this transaction concluded at the end of 1995, establishing February 1, 1996, as the latest closing date of this transaction.
As of December 31, 1995, 37.5 million U.S. dollars had been advanced to formalize this transaction, which with such amount being financed as follows:

In July 1995, Coca-Cola FEMSA and Coca-Cola Co. made advances for future capital increases to Coca-Cola FEMSA Buenos Aires of 5.1 and 4.9 million U.S. dollars, respectively, which were capitalized in February 1996.

In November 1995, Coca-Cola FEMSA Buenos Aires took out a bridge loan in the amount of 27.5 million U.S. dollars, which was repaid in February 1996.

As planned, on February 1, 1996, closing date of the transaction, Coca-Cola FEMSA Buenos Aires paid 22.5 million U.S. dollars as the final balance of the transaction, which were placed in escrow for any possible claims by SIRSA's creditors, which in accordance with the current legislation in Argentina may be filed within a period of 90 days after the closing of the transaction, period during which Coca-Cola FEMSA Buenos Aires is jointly liable for any claims exceeding the above-mentioned escrow.

The total cost of the transaction amounted to 60 million U.S. dollars, resulting in the acquisition of the following:

The SIRSA franchise (territory in which the Company began operating as of February 1, 1996.

The right to operate in the territory of RDN beginning in 1998, year in which the current franchise contract expires.

The land and building where the plant of RDN is located, whose book value amounts to 3.5 million U.S. dollars.

Since this transaction was in process on December 31, 1995, and Coca-Cola FEMSA was already bound by the terms of the agreement, the cost of the franchise and real state were included in the balance sheet as of December 31, 1995.

c)   Financing to Acquire SIRSA and Consolidation of Short-Term Debt

On February 15, 1996, Coca-Cola FEMSA obtained a syndicated loan in the amount of 165 million U.S. dollars (see Note 12), of which 47.5 million U.S. dollars were used to refinance short-term liabilities of Coca-Cola FEMSA and 88.5 million U.S. dollars were advanced to Coca-Cola FEMSA Buenos Aires for future capital stock increases, which were capitalized in February 1996, and were used to pay the remainder of the balance of 22.5 million U.S. dollars due on the SIRSA and RDN acquisitions and to repay short-term liabilities.

Since as of February 23, 1996, the date of issuance of these financial statements, this refinancing had been concluded, the Company decided to classify all debt as of December 31, 1995, based on the new loan agreements.

The remaining 29 million U.S. dollars were primarily used to partially exercise the purchase option of Coca-Cola FEMSA Buenos Aires and to pay commissions.

d) Capitalization of Contributions for Future Capital Increases of Coca-Cola FEMSA Buenos Aires and Partial Exercise of the Purchase Option

In February 1996, the contributions for future capital increases which Coca-Cola FEMSA had contributed to Coca-Cola FEMSA Buenos Aires were capitalized. Coca-Cola Co. did not participate in this capitalization, and consequently, Coca-Cola FEMSA increased its equity in Coca-Cola FEMSA Buenos Aires by 17.5% and resulted in a goodwill of 21.9 million U.S. dollars. Also. on February 20, 1996, an additional 6.5% of Coca-Cola Femsa Buenos Aires was acquired; 27.2 million U.S. dollars were paid and 15.1 million U.S. dollars of goodwill were generated. As a result of this transaction, the equity in this subsidiary increased to 75%. Due to the materiality of this transaction and its impact on the Company's financial statements, the pro forma effects of it are presented below, based on the consolidated financial statements as of December 31, 1995:

	Financial Statements as of December 31, 1995	Pro forma Effects	Financial Pro forma Statements as of December 31, 1995
Current assest	Ps.808,661	Ps.6,174	Ps.814,808
Fixed Assets	3,628,188		3,628,188
Goodwill	954,468	284,891	1,239,359
Other assets	75,318		75,318
Total Assets	Ps.5,446,635	Ps.291,038	Ps.5,757,673
Short-term bank loans	Ps.113,241	Ps.	Ps.113,241
Operating liabilities	618,849		618,849
Total liabilities	732,090		732,090
Long-term bank loans	1,940,825	222,836	2,163,661
Other liabilities	145,882		145,882
Total liabilities	2,818,797	222,836	3,041,633
Stockholders' equity:			
Majority interest	2,366,742	(7,684)	2,359,058
Minority interest	281,096	75,886	356,982
Total stockholders' equity	2,647,838	68,202	2,716,040
Total liabilities and stockholders' equity	Ps.5,446,635	Ps.291,038	Ps.5,757,673

Additionally, The Coca-Cola Co. has granted Coc-Cola Femsa a two year option to purchase the remaining 25% of Coca-Cola Femsa Buenos Aires's capital stock held by it on similar terms and conditions as the stock purchase mentioned above, plus an amount that accrues at an agreed upon rate until such option is exercised. If Coca-Cola Femsa does not exercise this option in whole at expiry, The Coca-Cola Co. will have the right to require Coca-Cola Femsa to purchase the remaining shares of Coca-Cola Femsa Buenos Aires then owned by The Coca-Cola Co. on the same terms and conditions as Coca-Cola Femsa's two year option described above.

e)   Detail of Goodwill and Translation Effect on Stockholders' Equity

Once the pro forma effects have been included, the detail of goodwill as of December 31, 1994 and 1995, is as follows:

Goodwill:	
Acquisition of Coca-Cola FEMSA Buenos Aires (51%)	Ps.544,756
Accumulated amortization as of December 31, 1994	(6,442)
Balance as of December 31, 1994	538,314
Restatement for the year	10,020
Amortization for the year	(28,012)
New acquisitions	434,146
Balance as of December 31, 1995 according to financial statements	954,468
Pro forma effects of partial exercising of the option and capitalization of advances	284,891
Balance as of December 31, 1995 Pro forma	Ps.1,239,359

The total translation effect of the financial statements in stockholders' equity at December 31, 1995 and 1994, amounted Ps. 258,957 and Ps. 151,773, respectively, and is presented in the cumulative result of holding nonmonetary assets.

Note 2. Basis of Presentation

The consolidated financial statements of the Company are prepared in accordance with generally accepted accounting principles in Mexico (Mexican GAAP), which differ in certain significant respects from those applicable in the United States (U.S. GAAP), as further explained in Note 16. A reconciliation from Mexican GAAP to U.S. GAAP is included in Note 17.

U.S. dollar amounts shown in the consolidated financial statements are included solely for the convenience of the reader and are translated from Mexican pesos, as a matter of arithmetic computation only, using the exchange rate as of December 31, 1995, of 7.684 Mexican pesos per U.S. dollar.

Note 3. Basis of Consolidation

The consolidated financial statements as of and for the years ended December 31, 1995, 1994 and 1993, include the financial statements of Coca-Cola FEMSA and its subsidiaries which are majority owned and controlled by Coca-Cola FEMSA. All intercompany balances and transactions have been eliminated

The following companies are the subsidiaries of Coca-Cola FEMSA:

Valley of Mexico:
Industria Embotelladora de Mexico, S.A. de C.V.
Industria Embotelladora del Valle, S.A. de C.V.
Distribuidora de Bebidas del Valle de Mexico, S.A. de C.V.
Propimex, S.A. de C.V.
Distribuidora Comercial Dico, S.A. de C.V.
Refrescos y Aguas Minerales, S.A. de C.V.
Direccion y Servicios, S.A. de C.V.
Refrescos y Aguas Nacionales, S.A. de C.V.
Industria Refresquera del Valle, S.A. de C.V.
Administracion y Asesoria Integral, S.A. de C.V.
Inmobiliaria Cermoc, S.A. de C.V.

Southeastern Mexico:
Refrescos de Oaxaca, S.A. de C.V.
Embotelladora Sin Rival, S.A. de C.V.
Inmuebles del Golfo, S.A. de C.V.

Argentina:
Coca-Cola FEMSA de Buenos Aires, S.A.

Coca-Cola FEMSA Buenos Aires' financial statements were prepared in accordance with the Company's policies and generally accepted accounting principles in Argentina (Argentine GAAP), which are similar to Mexican GAAP. The financial statements of Coca-Cola FEMSA Buenos Aires, previously restated with the Argentine inflation rate, are incorporated into the consolidated financial statements of Coca-Cola FEMSA, translating them from Argentine pesos to Mexican pesos using the exchange rate as of the end of the year.

The 1994 consolidated financial statements of Coca-Cola FEMSA and its Mexican subsidiaries were restated to 1995 Mexican pesos using the National Consumer Price Index (N.C.P.I.), and the Coca-Cola FEMSA Buenos Aires figures were restated using first the Argentine Price Index and then translated into Mexican pesos using the exchange rate as of the end of the year.

The income statement as of December 31, 1994, includes only the results from Coca-Cola FEMSA Buenos Aires beginning in September 1994, acquisition date of this subsidiary; consequently, the information is not comparable.

During the year, some mergers of subsidiaries occurred, in order to optimize resources and reduce administrative costs, reducing the number of subsidiaries from 21 in 1994 to 15 in 1995.

Note 4. Significant Accounting Policies
The consolidated financial statements are prepared in "Mexican pesos" (Ps.), name of the Mexican currency which was readopted effective January 1, 1996. The financial statements as of December 31, 1994, have been reclassified in certain accounts to make them comparable to the December 31, 1995, figures, for which reason they differ from those originally issued.

The principal accounting policies of the Company, which comply with Mexican GAAP, are presented below:

a)   Recognition of the Effects of Inflation in the Consolidated Financial Statements
        The consolidated financial statements have been prepared in accordance with Bulletin B-10 "Recognition of the Effects of Inflation in the Financial Information," as amended, issued by the Mexican Institute of Public Accountants.

        The consolidated financial statements were restated in terms of the purchasing power of the respective currencies as of December 31, 1995, using the inflation rates for each country.

        Bulletin B-10 requires:

        1.   Restating nonmonetary assets, including related costs and expenses such as inventories, cost of goods sold, fixed assets and depreciation using current replacement cost, and restating other nonmonetary assets using the N.C.P.I.

        2.   Restating common stock, additional paid-in capital and retained earnings by the amount necessary to maintain the purchasing power equivalent in Mexican pesos on the dates such capital was contributed or income generated.

        3.   Including in stockholders' equity the cumulative effect of holding nonmonetary assets (net difference between changes in the replacement cost of nonmonetary assets and adjustments based on the N.C.P.I.).

59

4. Including in the cost of financing the purchasing power gain or loss from holding monetary items.

Income statements must be restated using the N.C.P.I. determined from the month in which the transaction occurred to the date of the most recent balance sheet. The statement of changes in financial position, in accordance with Bulletin B-12, "Statement of Changes in Financial Position," identifies the sources and uses of resources representing differences between beginning and ending financial statement balances expressed in constant Mexican pesos, adjusted for the effect of holding nonmonetary assets.

The consolidated financial statements of current and prior periods presented for comparison purposes must be restated in terms of the purchasing power of the Mexican peso as of the most recent balance sheet date.

In Argentina the recognition of the effects of inflation in the financial information is similar to the recognition in Mexico, except for the use of the Argentine inflation rate instead of the N.C.P.I.

b) Cash and Cash Equivalents
Cash consists of non-interest-bearing demand deposits. Cash equivalents consist principally of short-term bank deposits and fixed-rate investments with brokerage houses, valued at quoted market prices.

c) Inventories and Cost of Sales
The value of inventories is adjusted to replacement cost, without exceeding market value. Cost of sales is determined principally based on replacement cost at the time of sale.

d) Promotional Expenses
Promotional costs are charged to expense when they are incurred, except for those promotional costs related to the launching of new products or presentations. These costs are recorded as prepaid expenses and amortized over the period during which they are estimated to increase sales of the related products or presentations to normal operating levels, which is generally one year. At December 31, 1995 and 1994, prepaid expenses include Ps. 8,317 and Ps. 7,380, respectively, of costs related to the launching of new presentations.

For U.S. GAAP purposes, the promotional costs were fully expensed in 1995, 1994 and 1993, as set forth in Note 17.

e) Investment in Shares
The investment in shares of associated companies is recorded at cost of acquisition and adjusted by the equity method.

f) Advances to Suppliers
The balances are adjusted by applying the N.C.P.I. factors, determined from the date from which they were contracted to the date of the most recent balance sheet. These balances are included in inventories.

g) Property, Plant, and Equipment
These assets are initially recorded at cost of acquisition and/or construction and are updated quarterly using specific rates determined by independent appraisers and are adjusted annually to reflect the net replacement cost reported by the same independent appraisers.

Depreciation of fixed assets is computed using a straight-line method, based on the average appraised value of the assets reduced by their residual values and is restated to Mexican pesos at year-end using N.C.P.I. factors. Depreciation rates are determined by independent appraisers, considering the remaining useful lives of the assets. Depreciation of new property, plant, and equipment commences in the year after placement in service.

The estimated useful lives of assets are as follows:

	Years
Building and improvements	41-43
Machinery and equipment	15-26
Distribution equipment	15-17
Other	14-17

The Company has started a process of reviewing the value of assets in anticipation of the expected changes in Mexican GAAP, regarding the restatement of fixed assets based on the N.C.P.I. This process, in combination with Mexico's economic situation, in which inflation is greater than changes in specific cost, has resulted in a decrease in equity during 1995.

h)   Construction in Progress
These assets are adjusted annually to reflect their replacement cost, using specific indices provided by independent appraisers.

i)   Bottles and Cases
Bottles and cases are classified as fixed assets and are recorded at acquisition cost. Their value is subsequently adjusted to replacement cost. Depreciation is computed only for tax purposes using the straight-line method at a rate of 8% per year. For accounting purposes, breakage is charged to expense as incurred. For the years ended December 31, 1995, 1994 and 1993, breakage expense amounted to Ps. 206,986, Ps. 103,746 and Ps. 70,635, respectively, and was included in the consolidated income statement.

Bottles and cases in circulation, which have been placed in the hands of customers, are presented net from deposits received from the customers, and the difference between the cost of these assets and the deposits received is amortized over a period of 50 months.

j)   Deferred Charges
These are restated by applying the N.C.P.I. factors, determined from the date in which they were contracted to the date of the most recent balance sheet, and are amortized on a straight-line basis over the term in which the benefits are expected to be received. Deferred charges principally include leasehold improvements and start-up expenses of a new plant.

k)   Payments from The Coca-Cola Co.
The Coca-Cola Co. has participated in the advertising and promotional programs, and payments received are recorded as a reduction of selling expenses.

In addition, Coca-Cola Co. has made payments in connection with the Company's capital expenditure program. These payments are related to the increase in volume of Coca-Cola products that result from such expenditures and represent a recovery of the cost of concentrate incurred by the Company. Such payments are included in other income, net, and for the years ended December 31, 1995, 1994 and 1993, amounted to Ps. 90,193, Ps. 53,395 and Ps. 33,218, respectively.

l)   Employee Severance Benefits
The Company recognizes in the results of the year the increase in the liability for pension and retirement plans and seniority premiums based on actuarial calculations, recognizing the projected benefit obligation as incurred.

The principal subsidiaries of Coca-Cola FEMSA have established funds for the payment of pension benefits through irrevocable trusts with the employees as beneficiaries.

Severance indemnities are charged to expenses for the year in which they are paid.

m) Income Taxes, Tax on Assets and Employee Profit Sharing
Coca-Cola FEMSA and its subsidiaries recognize, by means of the liability method, the future effect of income taxes, and the Mexican subsidiaries recognize such effect for employee profit sharing related to the cumulative temporary differences between accounting and taxable income, which arise from specific items whose turnaround period can be determined and which are not expected to be replaced by items of a similar nature and amount. Since there are no nonrecurring temporary differences, the Company has not recorded any deferred or prepaid income taxes and employee profit sharing effects.

Each of Coca-Cola FEMSA's individual Mexican subsidiaries determines and records its income taxes and each Mexican subsidiary its tax on assets as if it had filed separately for the income tax incurred during the year based on the applicable tax regulations. Therefore, the tax provisions reflected in the financial statements represent the sum of the provisions for the subsidiaries and the holding company. Valores Industriales, S.A. de C.V. (parent company of FEMSA) is authorized by the Secretaria de Hacienda y Credito Publico (Ministry of Finance) to prepare its income tax and tax on assets returns on a consolidated basis, which includes the proportional taxable income or loss of its Mexican subsidiaries.

n) Integral Result of Financing
The integral result of financing includes:
Interest:
Included in results when earned or incurred.

Foreign Exchange Gains or Losses:
Transactions in foreign currency are recorded in Mexican pesos using the exchange rate applicable on the date they occur. At the end of the year, assets and liabilities in foreign currencies are adjusted to Mexican pesos using the exchange rate applicable at that time, and exchange rate fluctuations are recorded as a foreign exchange gain or loss directly in the results of the year, except for the exchange loss on the U.S. dollar debt used to finance the acquisition of Coca-Cola FEMSA Buenos Aires (see Note 1).

Gain on Monetary Position:
This is the result of the effects of inflation on monetary items. The gain on monetary position is computed on the net monetary position at the beginning of each month, adjusted by changes in the N.C.P.I., in Coca-Cola FEMSA and its subsidiaries in Mexico and the Argentine Price Index in Coca-Cola FEMSA Buenos Aires, and the monthly result is restated in terms of the purchasing power of the Mexican peso at year-end.

o) Restatement of Stockholders' Equity
The objective of this restatement is to present stockholders' equity in terms of purchasing power as of December 31, 1995.

The cumulative effect of holding nonmonetary assets represents the difference between replacement value and restatement value, as determined by applying the N.C.P.I. for nonmonetary assets such as inventory and fixed assets, and their effect in the income statement when the assets are consumed or depreciated.

Note 5. Other Accounts Receivables

	1995	1994
The Coca-Cola Co.	Ps.35,329	Ps.81,363
Travel advances to employees	788	6,239
Advances to employees	3,037	5,579
Escrow	2,957	3,082
Insurance claims	1,457	932
Other	11,687	20,821
	Ps.55,255	Ps.118,016

Note 6. Inventories

	1995	1994
Finished products	Ps.88,200	Ps.52,170
Work in process	5,283	4,082
Raw materials	122,876	122,841
Spare parts	31,317	21,037
Promotional materials	4,977	6,299
Advances to suppliers	4,011	9,402
	Ps.256,664	Ps.215,831

Note 7. Investment in Shares

Investment in shares at December 31, 1995, includes 95,232 shares of Industria Envasadora de Queretaro, S.A. de C.V. (IEQSA), equivalent to 19% of its outstanding capital stock, recorded at its cost of acquisition, Ps. 11,060, which amount is similar to the equity method of valuation. IEQSA produces the most part of Coca-Cola in aluminum cans sold in Mexico and is owned by the Coca-Cola soft drink bottling companies of

Note 8. Intercompany Balances and Transactions

The consolidated balance sheet and income statement include the following balances and transactions with affiliated companies:

FEMSA and Subsidiaries	1995	1994
Balances:		
Assets (trade)	Ps.2,791	Ps.2,208
Liabilities (suppliers)	25,423	18,792

	1995	1994	1993
Transactions:			
Sales and other revenues	Ps.11,285	Ps.23,313	Ps.21,352
Purchases of inventories	198,929	157,441	161,440
Operating expenses	41,280	46,247	29,407
Allocated overhead cost	9,972	9,729	31,709
Interest expense or notes due to FEMSA	-	-	171,541

Coca-Cola Co.	1995	1994
Balances:		
Assets (other accounts receivable)	Ps.35,329	Ps.81,363
Liabilities (long-term notes payable)	56,836	-

	1995	1994	1993
Transactions:			
Purchases of concentrate	Ps.854,749	Ps.689,753	Ps.489,608
Interest expense	3,713	-	-
Income from capital expenditures program	90,193	53,395	33,218

Note 9. Related Party Transactions

At December 31, 1995, 1994, and 1993, the Company received services from companies in which some stockholders of the Company also own stock.

	1995	1994	1993
Service expense	Ps.17,648	Ps.11,131	Ps.5,979
Interest:			
Expense	5,926	4,009	5,431
Income	17,941	2,739	-

Note 10. Pension Plan and Seniority Premiums

The Company has defined benefit pension and disability benefit plans for all administrative personnel and production workers in accordance with established pension plan. Additionally, under Mexican labor law, Mexican companies must pay seniority premiums to all employees who are terminated with 15 or more years of service.

The balances of the liability and the trust assets, as well as the expense, are as follows:

Pension Plan:.	1995	1994
Projected benefit obligation	Ps.78,686	Ps.75,845
Pension plan trust assets	(16,563)	(20,973)
Items to be amortized:		
Modification of pension plan	2,357	4,404
Past service cost	(13,656)	(16,336)
Actuarial loss	(10,988)	(2,107)
Additional liabilities	284	422
Recorded liability	Ps.40,120	Ps.41,255

Seniority Premiums:	1995	1994
Projected benefit obligation	Ps.9,714	Ps.18,976
Actuarial gain (loss)	2,215	(3,305)
Recorded liability	Ps.11,929	Ps.15,671

	1995	1994
Expense for the year:		
Service cost	Ps.5,456	Ps.6,757
Interest cost	5,755	4,261
Amortization of modifications to the pension plan	(127)	(382)
Amortization of past service cost of the pension plan and actuarial loss	2,710	925
Expense before gain on monetary position	13,794	11,561
Gain on monetary position of the liability	(14,363)	(2,796)
Expense (income) after gain on monetary position	Ps.(569)	Ps.8,765

The amortizable items shown above are applied to the results over the estimated period in which the workers will receive plan benefits, which the actuaries estimate to be 14 years.

Note 11. Balances and Transactions in Foreign Currency

Assets and liabilities denominated in U.S. dollars, excluding those of Coca-Cola FEMSA Buenos Aires (see Note 19), are as follows:

December 31, 1995
Amounts in Thousands of U.S. Dollars

	Exchange Rate*	Short-Term	Long-Term	Total
	7.684			
Assets		$123	$-	$123
Liabilities		3,033	248,429	251,462

December 31, 1994
Amounts in Thousands of U.S. Dollars

	Exchange Rate*	Short-Term	Long-Term	Total
	4.995			
Assets		$113	$-	$113
Liabilities		23,764	100,000	123,764

*Mexican pesos.

In December 1994, Banco de Mexico eliminated the limits between which the Mexican peso-U.S. dollar exchange rate traded, thereby allowing the Mexican peso to float freely against the U.S. dollar. This resulted in a significant devaluation with respect to the U.S. dollar.

As of February 23, 1996, the issue date of these consolidated financial statements, the foreign currency position (unaudited) differs significantly from that at December 31, 1995, as a result of the events mentioned in Note 1c, and the exchange rate, which has not stabilized during the year, at this date is 7.50 Mexican pesos per U.S. dollar.

The transactions in foreign currency converted into U.S. dollars, excluding those of Coca-Cola FEMSA Buenos Aires (see Note 19), were as follows:

	Amounts in Thousands of U.S. Dollars	
	1995	1994
Interest income	$716	$81
Interest expense and commissions	14,630	3,694

Note 12. Stockholders' Equity

The outstanding capital stock of Coca-Cola FEMSA is comprised of 475 million shares, with a par value one Mexican peso, of fixed capital stock consisting of the following:

Series	Number of Shares (Thousands)
A	242,250
D	142,500
L	90,250
	475,000

The series "A" shares may only be acquired by Mexican individuals and may not represent less than 51% of total subscribed :capital stock of Coca-Cola FEMSA. The series "A" shares and the series "D" shares have full voting rights but are subject to transfer restrictions. The series "L" shares have limited voting and other corporate rights.

In addition, 90,250 thousand series "B" shares and 68,000 thousand series "L" shares have been authorized and issued but not subscribed.

The restatement of stockholders' equity is distributed to each of its components that gave rise to such restatement, as follows:

	Historical Value	Restatement	Restated Value
Capital stock	Ps.475,000	Ps.437,853	Ps.912,853
Additional paid-in capital	463,755	325,876	789,631
Retained earnings	419,508	295,979	715,487
Net income for the year	281,325	35,156	316,481

The net income for each subsidiary is subject to a legal requirement that 5% thereof be transferred to a legal reserve until the reserve equals 20% of the capital stock. This reserve may not be distributed to stockholders during the existence of the subsidiary, except as stock dividends. As of December 31, 1995, this reserve for Coca-Cola FEMSA amounted to Ps. 18,533 (nominal value).

Retained earnings and other reserves distributed as dividends, as well as reductions of capital, are subject to a 34% income tax charged to the Company when the distribution is not made from net taxable income and is paid to minority shareholders. Since the Company is part of a group that consolidates for tax purposes, these dividends will not be subject to income taxes. The net taxable income at December 31, 1995, was Ps. 183,012 (nominal value).

At an ordinary stockholders' meeting held on April 6, 1995, dividends in the amount of .063 Mexican pesos per share (nominal value) were declared and paid beginning on July 15, 1995.

Note 13. Bank Loans

At December 31, 1995 and 1994, the long-term bank loans of the Company are as follow:

Type of Credit/Bank	Currency	Interest Rate	1995	1994
Bank loans:				
Private Placement to acquire Coca-Cola FEMSA Buenos Aires	Dlls.	9.40%	Ps.768,400	Ps.767,071
Syndicated credit to acquire SIRSA, RDN and Consolidated Liabilities	Dlls.	Libor + 3.25	1,045,024	
Banque Paribas	Dlls.	7.69%	50,046	
Bank Loans to acquire Fixed Assets:				
Various Banks	Dlls.	Variable	61,065	
Capital Leasing:				
Leasing in Coca-Cola FEMSA Buenos Aires	A$		16,290	22,405
			Ps.1,940,825	Ps.789,476

Maturities of the long-term bank loans are as follows:

1996	Ps.24,737
1997	1,085,470
1998	29,950
1999	19,672
2000 and thereafter	780,996
	Ps.1,940,825

As of the date of issue of these financial statements, the Company has complied with all covenants established in the bank loan agreements.

Note 14 Minority Interest

The minority interest related to the incorporation of Coca-Cola FEMSA Buenos Aires is comprised in the consolidated financial statements as follows:

	1995	1994
Capital stock	Ps.244,992	Ps.244,992
Advances for future increases in capital stock	37,663	-
Additional paid-in capital	1,322	1,322
Accumulated deficit	(50,649)	(99,664)
Net income for the year	39,685	49,015
Cumulative result of holding nonmonetary asset	8,083	46,421
	Ps.281,096	Ps.242,086

Note 15. Tax System

Taxes are computed in terms of the currency as of the date on which the transaction occurred. For purposes of presentation in the consolidated financial statements, taxes are restated as of December 31, 1995, by applying factors based on the N.C.P.I.

Mexico:

Income taxes are computed on taxable income, which differs from accounting income principally due to the difference between purchases and cost of sales, the treatment of the integral result of financing, depreciation and the cost of the pension plan. Taxable income is increased or reduced by the effects of inflation on certain monetary assets and liabilities through the tax inflationary component, which is similar in concept to the financial gain from monetary position.

The tax on assets was computed at an annual rate of 1.8% in 1995 and 2.0% in 1994 based on the average of certain assets at tax restated value less certain liabilities. Tax on assets is paid only to the extent that it exceeds income taxes for the year. If in the period there is a tax on asset payment, this amount can be carried back to the income tax paid over the tax on assets in each of the preceding three years. Additionally, this payment can be restated and credited against the excess of income taxes over asset taxes for the following ten years. The balance of creditable asset taxes at December 31, 1995, is Ps. 4,934.

Employee profit sharing is computed at 10% of the individual income of each of the Mexican subsidiaries companies, based on taxable income, with the exception that depreciation of historical, rather than restated, values is used, foreign exchange gains and losses are not included until the asset or liability is due, and the other effects of inflation are also excluded.

Argentina:

Income taxes are computed based on taxable income, which differs from accounting income principally due to differences in depreciation and certain provisions for expenses. For the years ended December 31, 1995 and 1994, Coca-Cola FEMSA Buenos Aires did not generate any income tax expense due to the availability and amortization of tax loss carryforwards, as mentioned below.

	1995	1994	1993
Income tax and tax on assets	Ps.96,601	Ps.169,297	Ps.131,887
Amortization of carryforwards loss	(6,026)	(3,751)	(11,753)
Employee profit-sharing	13,213	34,092	26,999
	Ps.103,788	Ps.199,638	Ps.147,133

As of December 31, 1995, the tax loss carryforwards amounted to Ps. 164,293 and were generated by Coca-Cola FEMSA Buenos Aires. The expiration dates of those tax losses are as follows

Years	
1996	Ps.95,838
1998	42,684
1999	25,771
	Ps.164,293

Note 16. Differences Between Mexican and United States Generally Accepted Accounting Principles
The consolidated financial statements of the Company are prepared in accordance with Mexican GAAP, which differs in certain significant respects from U.S. GAAP.

A reconciliation of the reported net income and stockholders' equity to U.S. GAAP is presented in Note 17. It should be noted that this reconciliation to U.S. GAAP does not include the reversal of the restatement of the financial statements to recognize the effects of inflation, as required under Mexican GAAP Bulletin B-10, as amended (see Note 4a).

The application of Bulletin B-10 represents a comprehensive measure of the effects of price-level changes in the Mexican economy and, as such, is considered a more meaningful presentation than historical cost-based financial reporting for both Mexican and U.S. accounting purposes.

The principal differences between Mexican GAAP and U.S. GAAP that affect the consolidated financial statements of the Company are described below:

a)   Statement of Cash Flows
     Under Mexican GAAP, the Company presents consolidated statements of changes in financial position in accordance with Bulletin B-12. The financial statements have been restated in constant Mexican pesos and prior period amounts have been price-level adjusted accordingly. Bulletin B-12 identifies the generation and application of resources as representing differences between beginning and ending financial statement balances in constant Mexican pesos. It also requires that monetary and unrealized foreign exchange gains and losses be treated as cash items in the determination of resources provided by operations.

     In accordance with Mexican GAAP, the reduction in long-term debt due to restatement in constant Mexican pesos is presented in the consolidated statement of changes in the financial position as a resource used by financial activities, and the gain or loss from monetary position is presented as a component of resources generated by operations. Under U.S. GAAP, Statement of Financial Accounting Standards (SFAS) No. 95, "Statement of Cash Flows," no guidance is provided with respect to inflation-adjusted financial statements.

b)   Deferred Income Taxes and Employee Profit Sharing
     The Company adopted SFAS No. 109, "Accounting for Income Taxes," effective January 1, 1988, for U.S. GAAP reconciliation purposes, the objective of which is to recognize deferred tax liabilities and assets for future tax consequences of temporary differences between the book and tax bases of assets and liabilities.

     The primary temporary differences which generated the deferred tax liability under U.S. GAAP are the deduction of purchases for tax purposes versus cost of sales for financial statement purposes, different depreciation rates and related statements, and the tax loss carryforwards that reduce future taxes payable.

     All of the changes in the required deferred tax liability during the period are charged to the results of the period. A major portion of the temporary differences arising with respect to fixed assets is due to the differences in depreciation rates and restatement effects.

     Employee profit sharing is based on taxable income, adjusted as mentioned in Note 15, and is subject to the future consequences of temporary differences in the same manner as income taxes. The deferred effects not recorded under Mexican GAAP are included in the reconciliation of Mexican to U.S. GAAP.

The tax effect of temporary differences that generated deferred tax liabilities (assets) under SFAS No. 109 are as follows:

Deferred Income Taxes	1995	1994
Fixed assets	Ps.350,454	Ps.331,716
Inventories	43,056	37,285
Seniority premium	(4,056)	(5,264)
Pension plan cost	(12,183)	(11,317)
Tax loss carryforwards	(79,139)	(56,584)
Valuation allowance for tax loss carryforwards*	39,005	11,098
Recoverable asset taxes	(4,934)	(6,668)
Other reserves (Coca-Cola FEMSA Buenos Aires)	(30,418)	(28,848)
	Ps.301,785	Ps.271,418

* The Coca-Cola FEMSA Buenos Aires temporary differences generating a deferred tax asset are recognized to the extent of the deferred tax liability, as the Company considers it is more likely than not that the excess deferred tax asset will not be realizable.

Deferred Employee Profit Sharing	1995	1994
Fixed assets	Ps.101,258	Ps.70,336
Inventories	12,959	10,658
Seniority premium	(1,193)	(1,548)
Pension plan cost	(2,206)	(3,406)
Exchange loss	-	(12,694)
	Ps.110,818	Ps.63,346

c)   Cost of Pension Plan and Other Employee Benefits

Under Mexican GAAP, the requirement to record liabilities for employee benefits using actuarial computations was applicable beginning in 1993, in accordance with Bulletin D-3, "Labor Obligations", which is substantially the same as SFAS No. 87, "Employers' Accounting for Pensions".

The Company has no post-retirement health care insurance or other benefit plans, other than the pension plan referred to in Note 10. Therefore, SFAS No. 106, "Accounting for Post-Retirement Benefits," would have no effect on the Company's financial position.

The Company has prepared a study of pension costs under U.S. GAAP based on actuarial calculations, using the following assumptions:

	1995	1994	1993
% Annual discount rate	10.0	10.0	10.0
% Salary increases	5.9	5.9	5.9
% Return on assets	10.0	10.0	10.0
% Projected inflation rate	3.8	3.8	3.8

The net periodic pension cost and the funded status of the pension plan under SFAS No. 87 are as follows:

	1995	1994	1993
Net periodic pension cost:			
Service cost	Ps.3,685	Ps.4,229	Ps.3,503
Interest cost	5,088	4,896	3,199
Actual return on plan assets	(1,272)	(1,860)	(1,440)
Net amortization and deferral	2,919	1,218	421
Net pension cost (U.S. GAAP)	10,420	8,483	5,683
Net pension cost recorded (Mexican GAAP)	(11,362)	7,529	5,048
Additional expense that must be recognized under U.S. GAAP	Ps.(942)	Ps.954	Ps.635

	1995	1994
Pension liability:		
Vested benefit obligation	Ps.26,665	Ps.21,378
Nonvested benefit obligation	27,945	32,263
Accumulated benefit obligation	54,610	53,641
Impact of projecting salary increases	24,152	29,127
Projected benefit obligation	78,762	82,768
Plan assets at fair value	(15,017)	(20,395)
Unfunded projected benefit obligation	63,745	62,373
Unrecognized net transition obligation	(16,077)	(21,020)
Unrecognized gain	(11,702)	(6,956)
Additional minimum liability	728	355
Total unfunded accrued pension cost under U.S. GAAP	36,694	34,752
Total unfunded accrued pension cost under Mexican GAAP	(40,120)	(40,762)
Excess liability that must be canceled under U.S. GAAP	Ps.(3,426)	Ps.(6,010)

d) SFAS No. 105

With respect to SFAS No. 105, "Disclosure Information about Financial Instrument with Off-Balance-Sheet Risk and Finance Instruments with Concentrations of Credit Risk", the Company's accounts receivable, which represent receivables from numerous retail customers, and the Company's cash balances do not represent any significant concentration of risk to the Company.

e) Accrued Vacation Costs

As of December 31, 1995, the Company has recognized the vacation liability amount for Mexican GAAP purposes; therefore, the corresponding item in the reconciliation of Mexican to U.S. GAAP is no longer applicable at that date.

f) Minority Interest

Under Mexican GAAP, the minority interest in consolidated subsidiaries is presented as a separate component within stockholders' equity in the consolidated balance sheet. According to U.S. GAAP, this item should be excluded from consolidated stockholders' equity and classified as a noncurrent liability in the consolidated balance sheet.

Note 17. Reconciliation of Mexican GAAP to U.S. GAAP

The net income and stockholders' equity adjusted to take into account the material differences between Mexican GAAP and U.S. GAAP, except for the comprehensive effects of price-level changes (see Note 16), are as follows:

	Thousands of Mexican Pesos Except for Shares and per Share Data		
	1995	1994	1993
Majority net income under Mexican GAAP	Ps.316,481	Ps.321,461	Ps.264,929
Approximate U.S. GAAP adjustments:			
Deferred income tax * (Note 16b)	(147,373)	(77,332)	(50,080)
Deferred employee profit sharing (Note 16b)	(81,993)	(7,726)	(7,528)
Pension plan cost (Note 16c)	(942)	(954)	(634)
Accrued vacation costs (Note 16e)		8,396	(322)
Deferred promotional expenses (Note 4d)	(4,138)	4,734	11,111
Gain on monetary position resulting from			
U.S. GAAP adjustments (Note 4n)	152,403	11,725	20,186
Monetary gain on labor liabilities	(14,363)	(2,796)	(2,190)
	(96,406)	(63,953)	(29,457)
Approximate majority net income under U.S. GAAP	Ps.220,075	Ps.257,508	Ps.235,472
Weighted average common shares outstanding (thousands) (Note 12)	475,000	475,000	371,299
Approximate majority net income per share under U.S. GAAP	Ps.0.46	Ps.0.54	Ps.0.63

	1995	1994
Majority stockholders' equity under Mexican GAAP	Ps.2,366,742	Ps.2,424,036
Approximate U.S. GAAP adjustments:		
Deferred income tax * (Note 16b)	(301,785)	(271,417)
Deferred employee profit sharing (Note 16b)	(110,818)	(63,345)
Accumulated pension plan cost (Note 16c)	3,426	6,691
Deferred promotional expenses (Note 4d)	(8,317)	(7,380)
	(417,494)	(335,451)
Approximate majority stockholders' equity under U.S. GAAP	Ps.1,949,248	Ps.2,088,585

* The available tax loss carryforwards in each year were offset against the deferred tax expense.
The gain on monetary position resulting from U.S. GAAP adjustments affects income (retained earnings) and the cumulative effect of holding nonmonetary assets; therefore, the net effect on stockholders' equity is zero.

Under U.S. GAAP, employee severance liabilities are considered a monetary liability and, accordingly, are included in the calculation of the gain on monetary position. However, under U.S. GAAP such liabilities are considered to be nonmonetary and, accordingly, should not be included in the calculation of the gain on monetary position. The elimination of the gain on monetary position for this item has been included in the reconciliation to U.S. GAAP and consequently the previously reported in 1994 and 1993 figures were modified.

Note 18. Summary Financial Data by Geographic Areas

The following sets forth certain financial information of the Company for the two distinct geographical areas in which it operates.

	1995	1994	1993
Total Revenues:			
Mexico	Ps.3,508,882	Ps.3,571,732	Ps.3,117,237
Argentina	2,640,675	1,155,788	-
Adjustments	(5,859)	(4,139)	-
Consolidated	Ps.6,143,698	Ps.4,723,381	Ps.3,117,237
Operating Income:			
Mexico	Ps.437,215	Ps.492,678	Ps.435,022
Argentina	(35,612)	97,280	-
Adjustments	(216)	2,202	-
Consolidated	Ps.401,387	Ps.592,160	Ps.435,022
Capital Expenditures:			
Mexico	Ps.397,419	Ps.1,183,755	Ps.414,747
Argentina	793,039	120,780	-
Consolidated	Ps.1,190,458	Ps.1,304,535	Ps.414,747
Total Assets:			
Mexico	Ps.2,892,633	Ps.2,901,369	
Argentina	2,574,002	1,983,396	
Consolidated	Ps.5,466,635	Ps.4,884,765	

Note 19. Relevant Information Concerning Coca-Cola FEMSA Buenos Aires

The consolidated balance sheet and income statements include the following balances and transactions corresponding to the operations of Coca-Cola FEMSA Buenos Aires:

	1995	1994
Balance Sheet:		
Current assets	Ps.419,331	Ps.413,633
Fixed assets	1,161,875	996,561
Deferred charges, net	38,328	34,888
Goodwill *	954,468	538,314
Short-term liabilities	478,975	859,899
Long-term liabilities	148,116	91,135
Stockholders' equity **, ***	1,946,911	1,032,362

	1995	Sept.-Dec. 1994
Income Statement:		
Total revenues	Ps.2,640,675	Ps.1,155,788
Cost of sales and operating expenses	2,648,275	1,052,066
Goodwill amortization *	28,012	6,442
Income from operations	(35,612)	97,280
Integral result of financing	12,340	16,913
Other income	100,929	13,223
Net income	52,977	93,590

* Includes goodwill effect.
** Includes advances for future increases in capital stock of Ps. 852,924.
*** Includes goodwill from the acquisition from SIRSA of Ps. 434,146.

Note 20. Contingencies

During the last quarter of 1995, the Mexican tax authorities (Secretaria de Hacienda y Credito Publico) levied assessments for additional payments of income taxes on some subsidiaries of the Company related primarily to the procedure followed to restate tax loss carryforwards, and additionally the authorities have challenged the tax loss carryforwards utilized in 1990 and 1991. The subsidiaries disagree with and have challenged the assessments by filing a nullification suit for the amounts determined by the authorities, which amount to Ps. 23,690, including penalties and surcharges. In the opinion of the Company's tax attorneys, there are legal bases to obtain a favorable resolution.

Exhibit 4
Coca-Cola Femsa, S.A. de C.V. - Illustration of Restating Financial Statements for the Effects of Inflation

Assume the following:

- The company began operations on December 31, 1994 with $110 in cash, 100 units of inventory acquired at $1.00 per unit, and property, plant and equipment (PPE) costing $200. Property, plant and equipment (PPE) has an estimated life of ten years and is depreciated for half a year at December 31, 1994 (i.e., half year convention). The company was financed by issuing $100 in notes payable and $300 in common stock. The Consumer Price Index (CPI) was 100 at December 31, 1994.

- The company uses FIFO for inventory valuation. During the year, 100 units of inventory was acquired at $1.20 per unit and 100 units were sold when the replacement cost (RC) was $1.30 per unit. Revenue and expenses, except depreciation, are settled in cash. Taxes are ignored. The replacement cost of the inventory on hand at December 31, 1995 was $1.50 per unit. The replacement cost of the PPE at December 31, 1995 was $300. The CPI was 110 at December 31, 1995 and averaged 106 over the period December 31, 1994-December 31, 1995.

- During the year, the company issued an additional $100 of notes payable. The company paid no dividends.

Historic Cost:

	At Dec. 31, 1994	At Dec. 31, 1995
Cash	110	290
Inventory (FIFO)	100	120
Property, Plant and Equipment	200	200
Accumulated Depreciation	(10)	(30)
Total Assets	400	580
Notes Payable	100	200
Common Stock	300	300
Retained Earnings	0	80
Liabilities & Stockholders' Equity	400	580

	For Year Ending Dec. 31, 1995
Sales	200
Cost of Sales	(100)
Gross Profit	100
Depreciation	(20)
Net Income	80

Restated for the Effect of Inflation:

	At Dec. 31, 1994			At Dec. 31, 1995		
	Historic	Factor	Restated	Historic	Factor	Restated
Cash	110	110/100	121	290	---	290
Inventory (FIFO)	100	110/100	110	120	RC	150
Property, Plant and Equipment	200	110/100	220	200	RC	300
Accumulated Depreciation	(10)	110/100	(11)	(30)	RC	(45)
Total Assets	400		440	580		695.0
Notes Payable	100	110/100	110	200	---	200
Common Stock	300	110/100	330	300	110/100	330
Retained Earnings	0	110/100	0	80		43.5
Cumulative Gain on						
Non-monetary Assets	---		---	---		121.5 *
Liabilities & Stockholders' Equity	400		440	580		695.0

	For Year Ending Dec. 31, 1995		
	Historic	Factor	Restated
Sales	200	110/106	207.6
Cost of Sales	(100)	RC	(130.0)
Gross Profit	100		77.6
Depreciation	(20)	110/100	(30.0)
Net Income	80		47.6
Net Purchasing Power Loss			(4.1)**
Constant Dollar Income			43.5

* See below for computation of Cumulative Gain on Non-monetary Assets

** See below for calculation of Net Purchasing Power Loss

Computation of Purchasing Power Gains and (Losses) on Monetary Assets / Liabilities:

Monetary Assets:

	Historic	Factor	Restated
Cash (Beg. Bal.)	110	110/100	121.0
Sales	200	110/106	207.6
Cost of Sales	(120)	110/106	(124.5)
Cash from borrowing	100	110/106	103.8
			307.9
Cash (Ending Bal.)	290		290.0
Purchasing Power Gain (Loss)			(17.9)

Monetary Liabilities:

	Historic	Factor	Restated
Notes Payable (Beg. Bal.)	100	110/100	110.0
New Loan	100	110/106	103.8
			213.8
Notes Payable (Ending Bal.)	200		200.0
Purchasing Power Gain (Loss)			13.8

Net Purchasing Power Gain (Loss)			(4.1)

Computation of Cumulative Gain on Holding Non-monetary Assets:

Unrealized:

	Historic	Factor	Restated
Inventory		RC	150.0
	120	110/106	(124.5)
			25.5
Property, Plant and Equipment (book value)		RC	255.0
	170	110/100	(187.0)
			68.0
			93.5

Realized:

	Historic	Factor	Restated
Cost of Goods Sold		RC	130.0
	100	110/100	(110.0)
			20.0
Depreciation		RC	30.0
	20	110/100	(22.0)
			8.0
			28.0

Cumulative Gain (Loss) on Holding Non-monetary Assets			121.5

Exhibit 5
Coca-Cola Femsa, S.A. de C.V. - Comparison Between Mexican GAAP and U.S. GAAP for Selected Accounting Issues

Accounting Issue	Mexican GAAP	U.S. GAPP
Changing Prices	Inflation adjustments required	• Primarily historic costs
Business Combinations	• No standard to distinguish when purchase vs. pooling used • Goodwill over not more than 20 years •	Pooling-of-interest only used if specified criteria met; otherwise purchase accounting • Goodwill over not more than 40 years
Consolidation and Equity Accounting	• Control is principal criteria for consolidation; control evidenced by majority ownership (more than 50%); control may be evidenced by less than 50% • Equity method used when investee can exercise significant influence	• Control of a majority of voting interest for concolidation • Equity method used if significant influence; usually 20% or more
Foreign Currency Translation	• Translation gains and losses not specifically addressed • Transaction gains and losses on long-term debt and other long-term monetary items included in income of period in which exchange rate changes	• Gains and losses on translation of foreign functional currency statements are accumulated as component of stockholders' equity • Transaction gains and losses on long-term debt and other long-term monetary items included in income of period in which exchange rate changes
Income Taxes	• Partial liability method - recognized only to the extent that differences between accounting and tax income expected to give rise to a tax benefit or tax payment within definite time period	• Comprehensive liability method - recognized for all future taxes or benefits relating to temporary differences
Earnings per Share	• No accounting standard	• EPS must be presented for all public companies; primary and fully diluted required
Retiree Medical and Life Insurance Benefits	• No accounting standard because these benefits are uncommon	• Expense accrued over working life; liability recognized for unfunded amounts

Source: Financial Reporting in North America (CICA, IMCP, FASB, 1994)

Exhibit 6
Coca-Cola Femsa, S.A. de C.V. - Selected Financial Statement Data Computed in Accordance with U.S. GAAP for AZTECA, Panamco's Mexican subsidiary.

Year Ended December 31,	1995		1994		1993	
Income Statement Data:						
Net sales	$372,296	100.0%	$547,045	100.0%	$455,814	100.0%
Cost of sales	176,863	47.50	253,304	46.30	201,568	44.22
Operating expenses	136,970	36.79	205,158	37.50	176,033	38.62
Operating income	58,463	15.70	88,583	16.19	78,213	17.16
Interest income (expense) - net	(10,186)	(2.74)	(5,940)	(1.09)	(2,673)	(0.59)
Other income (expense) - net	(16,443)	(4.42)	7,944	1.45	11,503	2.52
Nonrecurring income (expense)	-	-	(4,332)	(0.79)	(1,405	(0.31)
Income before income taxes	31,834	8.55	86,255	15.77	85,638	18.79
Income taxes	11,099	2.98	29,598	5.41	26,415	5.80
Income before minority interest	20,735	5.57	56,657	10.36	59,223	12.99
Minority interest in AZTECA subsidiaries	2,006	0.54	7,043	1.29	17,868	3.92
Net income attributable to AZTECA's holding company	18,729	5.03	49,614	9.07	41,355	9.07
Minority interest in AZTECA holding company	5,077	1.36	14,746	2.70	19,141	4.20
Net income attributable to Panamco	13,652	3.67	34,868	6.37	22,214	4.87

Year Ended December 31,	1995	1994	1993
Other Data:			
Soft drink cases (in millions)	195.2	216.0	198.0
Water unit cases (in millions)	39.3	16.7	3.0
Depreciation and amortization	$23,096	$28,177	$23,924
Capital expenditures	$32,366	$106,287	$47,861

At December 31,	1995	1994
Balance Sheet Data:		
Cash and equivalents	$3,331	$4,971
Property, plant and equipment, net	134,406	183,368
Total assets	242,577	325,931
Long-term debt	51,121	54,241
Total liabilities	112,296	105,901
Minority interest	- *	3,072
Stockholders' equity	130,281	216,958

* The minority interest was reduced to zero in 1995 due to the allocation of the cumulative translation adjustment.

Exhibit 7
Coca-Cola Femsa, S.A. de C.V. - Selected Financial Statement Data for Gemex

MEXICAN GAAP

Year Ended December 31,	1995		1994	
Income Statement Data:				
Net sales	Ps.2,780,329	100.0%	Ps.3,146,870	100.0%
Costs and expenses:				
Cost of sales	1,425,032	51.25	1,417,350	45.04
Selling, general and administrative expenses	1,075,968	38.70	1,206,372	38.34
Depreciation and amortization	193,200	6.95	133,129	4.23
	2,694,200	96.90	2,756,851	87.61
Operating income	86,129	3.10	390,019	12.39
Integral cost of financing:				
Interest expense	310,589	11.17	130,974	4.16
Interest income	(25,959)	(0.93)	(24,010)	(0.76)
Exchange loss	671,484	24.15	508,381	16.16
Monetary position gain	(735,348)	26.45	(68,026	(2.16)
	220,766	7.94	547,319	17.39
(Loss) Income before provisions and extraordinary item	(134,637)	(4.84)	(157,300)	(5.00)
Provision for:				
Income tax and asset tax	17,608	0.63	34,407	1.09
Employee statutory profit sharing	5,608	0.20	3,309	0.11
	23,216	0.84	37,716	1.20
Income before extraordinary item	(157,853)	(5.68)	(195,016)	(6.20)
Extraordinary item:				
Tax reduction from utilization of tax loss carryforwards	17,508	0.63	31,766	1.00
Net income (loss)	(140,285)	(5.05)	(163,250)	(5.19)

At December 31,	1995	1994
Balance Sheet Data:		
Cash and equivalents	Ps.99,976	Ps.63,904
Property, plant and equipment, net	3,409,807	3,095,278
Total assets	4,604,205	4,608,858
Long-term debt	1,225,861	1,135,546
Total liabilities	1,762,009	2,371,162
Stockholders' equity	2,842,196	2,237,696

RECONCILIATION BETWEEN MEXICAN AND U.S. GAAP

	Thousands of Mexican Pesos Except for Shares and per Share Data	
	1995	1994
Net income under Mexican GAAP	Ps.(140,285)	Ps.(163,250)
U.S. GAAP adjustment for:		
Deferred income tax	(188,413)	179,054
Deferred profit-sharing	120	702
Amortization of goodwill	12,074	10,913
Accrued vacation costs	3,308	(3,721)
Reversal of capitalized exchange losses, interest income and monetary position gains	(2,827)	(113,135)
Net income (loss) under U.S. GAAP	(316,023)	(89,437)
Earnings (loss) per share	Ps.(0.37)	Ps. (0.12)
Weighted average shares outstanding (thousands)	1,144,846	1,056,656

	1995	1994
Total stockholders' equity reported under Mexican GAAP	Ps.2,842,196	Ps.2,237,697
Approximate U.S. GAAP adjustments:		
Deferred income tax	(324,621)	(308,492)
Deferred profit-sharing	(79,447)	(115,961)
Goodwill	(168,913	(180,988)
Accrued vacation costs	(7,779)	(11,087)
Reversal of capitalized exchange losses, interest income and monetary position gains	(115,962)	(113,134)
Stockholders' equity under U.S. GAAP	Ps.2,145,474	Ps.1,508,034

NO DEPOSIT, NO RETURN
Citi and Pepsi Squabble Over a Loan Gone South of the Border

Welcome to the Latin American debt crisis redux -- or at least a nasty little after effect of it. With the 1980s and mid-1990s crises still being felt, Citicorp, which led the world's banking community into Third World lending in the mid-1970s, is fighting to recover a bum $20 million loan to a Mexican soft-drink bottler. Normally, such a loan by the nation's second-largest bank wouldn't make much of a ripple inside or outside Citibank.

This was no ordinary bottler, however. It is a joint venture partly owned by PepsiCo Inc., which is trying to make a big push into emerging markets, especially Latin America. Pepsi is refusing to cover not only the $20 million Citi loan, which was made for bottle purchases, but another $50 million in credits and leasing agreements extended by other banks and suppliers.

Business Week, September 23, 1996, p. 134.

The Latin Cola Wars between Pepsi and Coca-Cola began in earnest in September 1993. Working with its bottlers in Argentina, Mexico, Puerto Rico, and Venezuela, PepsiCo was determined to win the early battles. PepsiCo's leadership had concluded that success would only come if the company took more control of its bottlers' operations in-country, while simultaneously injecting substantial capital into their operations. Pepsi could gain a larger share of some of the world's most promising soft drink markets, but only by accepting *lower margins* at the cost of substantial *new investments*. The company's return on capital employed, however, was not going to be pretty.

However, all had not gone according to plan. In only three years -- by September 1996 -- it appeared that PepsiCo's entire Latin American initiative was on the brink of failure. Instead of gaining market share, Pepsi was facing a net loss of market share south of the equator. Roger Enrico, PepsiCo's Chief Executive Officer since April of 1996, surveyed the company's competitive position and performance and found little to brag about. Traditional arch-rival Coca-Cola and its charismatic leader, Mr. Robert Guizeta, was retaking much of the marketshare lost previously to Pepsi in the opening days of the war. Margins were down across Latin America, and economic conditions had only served to emphasize the weaknesses in PepsiCo's strategy which senior management was only now beginning to admit. Pepsi also now had a second enemy -- the Mexican Peso -- in addition to its old nemesis Coca-Cola.

Mexico, the second largest soft drink market in the world, had been a major front in the Latin Cola wars. By the fall of 1996, however, it appeared the war was lost. Pepsi's market share had dropped to little more than 21%, down from 26% in 1995. Pepsi still trailed Coca-Cola in all but one of the top ten cola markets in the world (see Exhibit 1). Roger Enrico now pondered where the war had been lost, and what was to be done.

The Latin Cola Wars

In 1993, PepsiCo was the second largest soft drink company in the world, with a 21% world market share to Coca-Cola's 46%. PepsiCo, however, was determined to change that. Many of the world's industrial-country markets for soft drink products were already mature, but the host of emerging-country markets represented immense potential. Countries such as China and India were only in the first stages of consumer product growth -- the war would be waged in their markets for decades to come.

But the markets of Latin America, already some of the world's largest soft drink consumers, were thought to still contain substantial potential for growth. With rising per capita incomes and a proven proclivity for soft drink consumption, Latin America was ripe for a cola war. In addition to cola drinks, an added feature of the Latin American market was the growing popularity of flavored drinks. The flavored drink segment was thought to be still in its infancy in Latin America, and both Coke and Pepsi had recently been expanding their soft drink product lines. Thankfully, sales of flavored drinks did not cannibalize cola drink markets, only the markets of other flavored drinks.

Exhibit 1 Global Market Share Comparison of Coke & Pepsi		
Top 10 Countries	Coke	Pepsi
United States	42%	31%
Mexico	61%	21%
Japan	34%	5%
Brazil	51%	10%
East-Central Europe	40%	21%
Germany	56%	5%
Canada	37%	34%
Middle East	23%	38
China	20%	10%
Britain	32%	12%

Source: *Fortune*, October 28, 1996, p. 78 (Andrew Conway, Morgan Stanley).

PepsiCo's Latin American initiative was spearheaded by PepsiCo's Chief of International Operations, Chris Sinclair. Sinclair had taken over Pepsi-Cola International (PCI), the international side of PepsiCo, Inc., in March of 1990 with the express purpose of doubling PepsiCo's overseas business during the 1990's. Sinclair pursued a go-for-broke expansionist strategy, attacking Coca-Cola head-on in every major market. Sinclair would be PepsiCo's standard-bearer in the Latin cola wars.

Pepsi saw Latin America as prime territory for a major initiative. With the exception of Venezuela, however, Pepsi was trailing Coke in every major country market in

Exhibit 2 Soft Drink Market Shares in South America, 1993-94			
Country	Coke	Pepsi	Other
Argentina	57.4%	36.0%	6.6%
Bolivia	54.4%	18.3%	27.3%
Brazil	54.9%	8.0%	37.1%
Chile	64.1%	18.0%	17.9%
Colombia	43.6%	11.2%	45.2%
Ecuador	55.5%	17.4%	27.1%
Mexico	61.0%	21.0%	18.0%
Peru	42.1%	23.5%	34.4%
Venezuela	11.6%	42.0%	46.4%
Uruguay	67.0%	30.3%	2.7%

Source: "A Huge Defection Leaves Pepsi Flat in Venezuela," *Houston Chronicle*, August 25, 1996; *Fortune*, October 28, 1996.

Latin America. Pepsi's market share ranged from as low as 8% in Brazil, to a high of 42% in Venezuela (see Exhibit 2). With the exceptions of Argentina and Uruguay, Pepsi's market share was not only trailing Coke across the southern hemisphere, it was often third to other soft drinks. Late in 1993, the reality was that Pepsi -- at best -- was a distant second to Coke.

But a cola war is not easily won. The first problem was the structure of the market. Soft drink companies like Coca-Cola and PepsiCo had traditionally serviced country markets via a two-stage presence. First, the soft drink syrup concentrate was sold in-country via a local affiliate. This local affiliate was frequently wholly-owned or majority-controlled by the soft drink parent. Access to the consumer, however, was through a second level of local bottlers and distributors. These companies had traditionally been local franchisees in which the soft drink originator (eg., Coca-Cola or Pepsi) had no real equity interest. They were *cooperative joint ventures*, not *equity joint ventures*. These bottlers and distributors were granted exclusive regional rights, and operated independently in their own markets.

This lack of control was frustrating for the strategists back in the home offices of the major soft drink powers (Atlanta, Georgia for Coca-Cola; Purchase, New York for PepsiCo). In 1993 both Coca-Cola and PepsiCo had moved to gain additional management control over their Latin American markets via a chosen *anchor bottler* (Coca-Cola) or *super-bottler* (PepsiCo). Both Pepsi and Coke had decided that if they were to effectively take marketshare from the other, they would need a single voice in the regional market. It was hoped that through a single representative, the product would be able to gain market preferences from local retail distributors, as well as present a singular image to the consuming public.

The anchor bottler strategy was dependent on two critical components. First, the chosen bottler needed the resources to implement the strategy, a strategy which was often a combination of technology, packaging, distribution, and marketing. Secondly, the bottler must have the product focus to see the strategy through in a highly competitive marketplace. PepsiCo was now moving quickly to put both components in place.

By taking an equity interest in these local bottlers, the soft drink makers intended to have direct managerial and financial control in the implementation of their strategic goals. The equity injections associated with these joint ventures were to provide much of the badly needed capital to up-grade the production and distribution facilities needed to compete in an emerging Latin market. So *venture* they did. What PepsiCo -- and specifically Chris Sinclair -- did not anticipate, however, was the role that personalities and families would play in the development of their Latin American strategy.

Argentina. Pepsi-Cola International (PCI) moved in October 1993 to gain a 26% equity interest in a number of its key bottlers across Latin America. In the late 1980s, a group of investors led by Charles Beach had gained control of bottlers and distributors, first in Puerto Rico (1986) , then in Argentina (1989). Buenos Aires Embotelladora S.A. (Baesa), the firm for which Beach served as CEO, had been Pepsi's greatest success story in the early 1990s, as the local Argentine bottler had expanded market share and influence to Brazil, Chile, and eventually Uruguay. Beach had increased Pepsi's market share in Buenos Aires from about 1% to 39% by 1992. In exchange for several existing Chilean and Uruguayan 19bottling operations, PCI pumped $35 million in cash into Baesa. Baesa was also guaranteed control over several expiring Brazilian bottlers, most notably franchises in Rio de Janeiro and Porto Alegre (1994) and Sao Paulo (1996). Baesa undertook a massive expansion and recapitalization of its production facilities throughout South America, raising over half a billion U.S. dollars between 1992 and 1994.

Venezuela. Hit de Venezuela, PCI's primary bottling operation in Venezuela, was owned and operated by the Cisneros Group. Headed by Guastavo Cisneros and his brother Oswaldo, the Cisneros Group was a highly diversified financial empire involved in businesses ranging from sporting goods to telecommunications products and services.[1]

The Cisneros family, friends of PepsiCo's President Roger Enrico and the holders of a franchise for over 50 years, were actively negotiating with PCI to sell the parent company a sizeable equity share in the Venezuelan bottler. Although Venezuela was the only country in South America in which Pepsi held a larger share of the market than Coca-Cola, the Cisneros Group believed that in order to continue to hold, and possibly expand, their market dominance a sizeable capital injection would be necessary. Negotiations with Pepsi had proceeded slowly, however, as PepsiCo was not comfortable with some of the Group's ambitions to expand outside the Venezuelan borders into other markets.

Mexico. In March 1993, concurrent with the adoption process of NAFTA, Chris Sinclair announced that PepsiCo was undertaking a $750 million investment initiative in Mexico. The $750 million would be used over the next five years to bolster bottling and marketing efforts, recapitalize operations, and update bottlers with the latest technology.[2] The purpose was clear: to cut into Coca-Cola's dominant Mexican market share. Coca-Cola had also been busy of late, taking a 30% interest in Fomento Economico de Mexico (Femsa), and naming it Coke's anchor bottler in Mexico.

> It takes at least three Diet Pepsis -- Pepsi Lights, actually -- to down your plate of tacos al pastor, the delectable house specialty at El Tizoncito. Pepsi has pouring rights at this popular chain, which brings seasoned proficiency to fast food throughout Mexico City -- and typifies the renewed battle for cola one-upmanship on the mean streets of the Mexican capital. Try getting near the place during "lunch hour," customarily between 3:00 and 5:00 PM.
>
> Source: "The Mexican Insurrection," *Beverage World*, August 1993.

Approximately 80% of all soft drink sales in Mexico were through mom-and-pop stores called *tienditas*. Market analysts believed that as long as the tienditas controlled the market, price wars between bottlers would be nearly impossible. According to the President of Pepsi-Cola Latin America, "The only way to win against a giant like Coke is to put them on the ropes. We've got to constantly innovate and act very quickly."[3]

---

[1] The Cisneros Group held controlling interest in a number of U.S. and South American businesses including Spalding (sport equipment), Evenflo (baby products), Galaxy Latin America (satellite TV services), and Pueblo (supermarkets).

[2] The first phase of the initiative was a US$115 million equity interest in three Mexican bottlers: a 29% interest in Grupo Embotelladoras Unidas, a 49% interest in Grupo Protexa's bottling subsidiary, Agral, and a 20% interest in Grupo Rello

[3] Luis Suarez,"The Mexican Insurrection," *Beverage World*, August, 1993.

Exhibit 3 Major States and Cities of Mexico

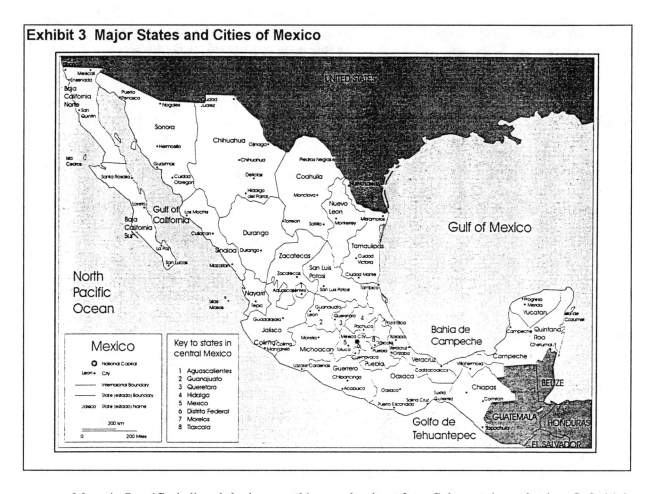

Many in PepsiCo believed the key to taking marketshare from Coke was in packaging. Soft drink makers had long considered the Mexican market an emerging market, and emerging markets consistently showed a preference for the refillable and returnable packages -- the returnable glass bottle.[4] The logic was simple, the returnable package was the cheaper delivery vehicle for the product. But if Mexico was industrializing rapidly, and more of its high soft drink consuming populace grew increasingly affluent, the desire of the affluent for convenience would grow. The convenient package was the slightly higher cost, non-returnable package, the non-returnable plastic bottle. Pepsi was thinking plastics.

Grupo Embotellador de Mexico (Gemex) was PepsiCo's largest bottler outside of the United States, serving Pepsi's largest market outside the United States. Gemex had grown from a small bottling operation in the city of Acapulco in 1964 to a major player in one of the world's largest metropolitan areas, Mexico City. Gemex was owned and operated by Enrique C. Molina Sobrino and the Molina family. Gemex was considered the most successful of PCI's Mexican operations, with a 1992 soft drink market share in the Mexico City area estimated at 50.8% as compared to Coke's 49.2%. This made Gemex exceptionally successful compared to other major PepsiCo bottlers, inside and outside of Mexico.

Agral was a joint venture of Grupo Protexa (51%), the sixth largest construction company in Mexico, and Pepsi-Cola International (49%). This was PCI's largest equity interest in any of the regional bottlers, and reflected Pepsi's grand ambitions for its market. Agral currently held a 20% market share in

---

[4] Coca-Cola, in fact, believed that there was no consumer goods package more critical to a product, more recognizable to its consumers, than Coke's contour bottle. Coke was determined to stay with the returnable glass bottle.

the Monterey market of northern Mexico, the third largest city in Mexico. Monterey's prospects centered on its ranking as one of the highest per capita consumption regions for soft drinks in the country. Unfortunately, it was also one of Pepsi's weakest markets. Although Agral's prospects were considered good, Grupo Protexa itself was a US$1.2 billion conglomerate with a multitude of interests, including telecommunications, rail transportation, petrochemicals, and heavy construction. Its commitment to expanding PepsiCo's interests in the region had been hotly debated both in northern Mexico and northern New York.

The other regional bottlers were enjoying only modest degrees of success against the historical dominance of Coca-Cola. Grupo Rello was the bottler and distributor in Toluca and Tlanepantla, rapidly expanding suburbs of Mexico City. Although successful, many suspected that it would be eventually absorbed into Gemex. Grupo Embotelladoras Unidas, located in Guadalajara, Mexico's second largest metropolitan area, was also a joint venture partner with PCI, but was suffering flat growth in sales.

With PCI's Chris Sinclair at the helm, PepsiCo was determined to launch a revitalized attack on Coca-Cola throughout Mexico. Sinclair moved swiftly in 1993, acquiring a 20% equity interest in Grupo Rello. With the lone exception of Agral in northern Mexico, it appeared from the start that Sinclair intended to lead his attack thru Gemex. But the Molina family, the owners of Gemex, had rebuffed suggestions by PCI that it take an equity interest in the other bottler.

Grupo Embotellador de Mexico (Gemex)

Gemex is a holding company which produces, distributes, and sells bottled soft drinks, mineral water, returnable plastic bottles, and a variety of other packaging materials through its various subsidiaries. The Company's flavored soft drink products include Pepsi Cola®, 7-Up®, Clearly Canadian®, Seagram's Mixers®, Squirt®, Mirinda®, in addition to two mineral waters, Garci Crespo® and Electropura®. With its head office in Mexico City, Gemex owns and operates 97 soft drink warehouses and 23 bottling plants in four regions around and including Mexico City and the cities of Iguala, Tehuacan (a city famous for its natural waters), Acapulco, and Cuernavaca. The Company employs more than 15,000 people throughout Mexico, and holds the exclusive rights to the bottling and distribution of Pepsi products in these four regions.[5]

Grupo Embotellador de Mexico, was established on December 21, 1981, under the name Grupo Troika, by Enrique Molina and family.[6] In 1984, Mr. Molina acquired the exclusive right to produce and distribute PepsiCo soft drink products in the Mexico City area. In late 1991, the name of the Company was officially changed from Grupo Troika to Grupo Embotellador de Mexico (Gemex). Over the following decade the company acquired a number of soft drink and beverage bottlers and distributors throughout Mexico. Gemex was listed on the Mexico City stock exchange on December 17, 1991. One

---

[5] Gemex has exclusive rights to the following four regions:
    1. Mexico City Area, which consists of Mexico City and portions of the states of Hidalgo and Mexico;
    2. Southwest Area which consists of the states of Guerrero and Morelos;
    3. Southeast Area which consists of the states of Campeche, Quintana Roo and Yucatan;
    4. North Central Area which consists of the states of Aguascalientes, Durango, and Zacatecas.

[6] Certain operating subsidiaries of the Company had previously been formed or acquired by Mr. Molina between 1964 and 1981.

year later, it was listed on the London Stock Exchange via Global Depositary Shares (GDSs) and the New York Stock Exchange (symbol GEM) through American Depositary Receipts (ADRs).[7]

Gemex's growth was rapid in the 1990s. In 1993, the company signed two new exclusive agreements which expanded product lines and market areas. The first was with Seagrams & Company, giving Gemex the exclusive right to produce, distribute, and sell Seagrams' products throughout Mexico. The second was with Natural Beverage Company, in which Gemex obtained the rights to exclusively distribute the Clearly Canadian beverage line. Gemex's competitive position against other soft drink producers, such as Coca-Cola, strengthened, as it now possessed a wider product line -- flavored drink and bottled water segments -- beyond the traditional cola segment.

Sales and income continued to grow at healthy rates in 1993 and 1994. Although the Mexican economy grew only 0.4% in 1993, the beverage and bottled water market grew 2.7%; Gemex's sales volume itself grew 5.6%, and net revenues increased by 8%.[8] Gemex's Annual Report in 1993 highlighted how financially healthy the firm was:

> Financial ratios show that Gemex is a sound profitable company. In terms of net income to net revenues, the ratio improved 7.5%, reaching 14.4% in 1993, from 13.4% in 1992. Noteworthy is the growth in return on capital. The ratio of net income to stockholders' equity increased 15.3%. Finally, it is a pleasure to inform you that the annual increase in the market value of Gemex's stock during 1993 was 109.6%, a percentage that is five times above the average investment instruments denominated in new pesos in the Mexican market and 22% over the food, beverage and tobacco industry stock market increase.

In 1994 the Company expanded once again. On January 14, 1994, Gemex purchased all of the shares of Grupo Seser, S.A. de C.V. and Electropura for a total of US$80 million.[9] Electropura was the leading bottled water company in the Mexico City market, and the most widely recognized name across Mexico. With the addition of Electropura, net revenues rose 28.5% over 1993 (although not directly comparable due to the acquisition), reaching NP$2.07 billion.

Growth required capital. The Company raised US$29.76 million in needed equity through an ADR offering on March 29, 1994. The issue, representing 5,900,000 *CPOs* -- Ordinary Participating Certificates (equivalent to 2,950,000 *GDSs*, Global Depositary Shares) -- was offered through Goldman Sachs, Merrill Lynch, and Oppenheimer, with Citibank, New York, acting as the depositary bank. At the same time as the ADR issue in New York, 900,000 GDSs representing 1.8 million CPOs were offered outside the United

---

[7] An American Depositary Receipt, or *ADR*, is a certificate of ownership issued by a U.S. bank representing a claim on underlying foreign securities (such as shares of Gemex). Firms which are incorporated and traded on foreign stock exchanges wishing to have their shares listed on U.S. stock exchanges are typically traded via ADRs. In the case of Gemex, each ADR (simultaneously termed a Global Depositary Receipt or GDR) was equal to three *Ordinary Participating Certificates* (CPOs), which in turn was a combination of one B share, one D share, and one L share in Gemex (described in Exhibit 6).

[8] Gemex's financing costs also decreased substantially in 1993, falling 14.6% from the previous year, mostly as a result of a successful Eurobond issuance at the end of 1992.

[9] The Company also acquired the following bottling subsidiaries: Purificadora de Aqua Perula, S.A. de C.V.; Purificadora de Aqua Ecatepec, S.A. de C.V.; Purificador de Aqua Los Reyes, S.A. de C.V.; Purificadora de Agua Andalucia, S.A. de C.V.; Purificadora de Aqua Cancun, S.A. de C.V. The Company also acquired real estate subsidiaries (Inmobiliaria Operativa, S.A. de C.V., and Inmobiliaria Imalbi, S.A. de C.V.), plastic bottle subsidiary (Plasticos EP, S.A. de C.V.), and a distribution subsidiary (Serviagua, S.A. de C.V).

States and Mexico, and 1.3 million GDSs were offered in Mexico itself. Proceeds of the offerings were used to repay much of the debt associated with the Electropura acquisition two months prior, and for general corporate financing.

Towards the end of 1994, Gemex -- and particularly Enrique Molina -- felt that Gemex was making major market share in-roads against arch rival Coca-Cola. It continued to invest heavily in the latest production and distribution plant and equipment, positioning itself to thwart any new-found competitors with a cost structure which would be the lowest in the region. Unfortunately, Gemex did not foresee the fall of the New Peso and its repercussions on Gemex's competitiveness.

The Fall of the Peso

The value of the Mexican peso had fallen throughout the 1980s as Mexico continually fought high domestic inflation. Beginning in 1982, the value of the peso was allowed to float by the government within a narrow band, the "controlled rate," which allowed the currency's value to depreciate slowly rather than fall freely. This exchange rate control system allowed Mexican residents and companies to purchase foreign currency, and required them to sell foreign currency earned, at the official exchange rate established daily by the Banco de México. But the peso's value still fell continuously throughout the 1980s, approaching 3,000 pesos to the dollar in the early 1990s. Finally, on November 11, 1991, after years of hardship and costly austerity measures, the Mexican economy and inflation rate stabilized sufficiently to allow the removal of the controlled rate. On January 1, 1993, the Mexican government replaced the peso (Ps) with the New Peso (NP) and revalued it, with one New Peso equaling 1,000 Pesos.

The New Peso was allowed to fluctutate over a relatively narrow range during the following two years. Although the Mexican government allowed it to depreciate, the New Peso's value was not allowed to change proportionately in value to the domestic rate of inflation in Mexico.[10] Any fluctuation in the New Peso's value outside the established limits resulted in direct open market intervention by Banco de México -- typically a buying of New Pesos on the open market with hard currency reserves such as the U.S. dollar. The New Peso became increasingly overvalued, and contributed to a rapid growth in Mexico's current account deficit.

In 1994 a number of events led to a crisis in the New Peso's value. The Mexican current account deficit rose to 8% of Mexico's Gross Domestic Product (GDP). At the same time, U.S. dollar-denominated interest rates began rising due to the implementation of a relatively tight monetary policy by the U.S. Federal Reserve, making it more attractive to move out of New Pesos into U.S. dollars. Finally, political events within Mexico, such as the armed insurgency in the southern Mexican state of Chiapas, led international investors to fear for the stability of the government. On December 22, 1994, the New Peso was allowed to float (it sank) from NP$3.45/US$ to NP$4.65/US$.

---

[10] Mexican consumer prices rose 11.9% in 1992, 8.0% in 1993, 7.1% in 1994, and 52.0% in 1995. According to Purchasing Power Parity, a country's currency value relative to other currencies should change in proportion to relative inflation rates. If Mexico's inflation rate was higher than the U.S.'s inflation rate in 1993 and 1994 as it was, the peso should have fallen in value relative to the dollar; it would probably have fallen *gradually* if allowed to trade freely.

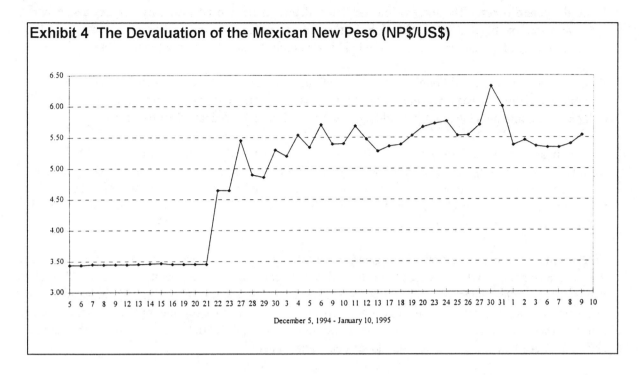

Exhibit 4 The Devaluation of the Mexican New Peso (NP$/US$)

December 5, 1994 - January 10, 1995

The Mexican government's policy, which allowed the New Peso to fall only a prescribed daily amount, had not kept the peso in line with economic fundamentals such as the consistently higher Mexican inflation rate and the continually escalating merchandise trade deficit.[11] The fall of the New Peso -- in the eyes of many currency analysts -- was inevitable.

The devaluation of the peso was devastating for Gemex, as it was for most multinational firms in Mexico. Gemex shares on the NYSE plummeted from a high of nearly $30 per share in mid-1994 to under $8 in January, 1995. The fall in Gemex share values reflected not only the lower U.S. dollar-value of Gemex's Mexican peso-based earnings, but also the fallen expectations for the Mexican economy and the purchasing power of the Mexican consumer, both factors leading to a downward revision in Gemex's earnings expectations.

On January 20, 1995, Gemex released a statement attempting to respond to numerous investor inquiries regarding how it had been impacted by the fall of the New Peso:[12]

♦ **The company's debt.** Noting that the firm had switched the currency of denomination of the majority of its debt in 1992, Gemex now had U.S. dollar-denominated debt totaling $264 million or 78% of total liabilities. Although offering no current strategies to manage the exposure, the company noted that it possessed significant additional debt capacity (bank lines and an open Euro-Commercial Paper program) to assure liquidity.

---

[11] Eventually, on January 1, 1996, the New Peso was renamed the Peso, without any change in its value.

[12] "Grupo Embotellador de Mexico, S.A. de C.V. Addresses Financial Condition," January 20, 1995, Mexico City.

♦ **Capital expenditures.** The increase in the firm's debt had been used primarily for expansion and modernization of fixed assets. Although further future capital expenditures would obviously be reduced, the firm felt that these assets would aid in its ability to maintain its competitiveness.

♦ **Profit & loss impact.** Although as "a result of the devaluation, the dollar denominated debt will generate an estimated negative impact on the Company's profit and loss of approximately NP$260 million," the company noted that it would enjoy a NP$100 million tax loss carry-forward.

♦ **Financial statement and ratios.** Even with the exposure of U.S. dollar-denominated debt, Gemex would still be in compliance with its Eurobond covenants requiring: a) a consolidated debt/total capitalization ratio of no more than 0.55; it was 0.47; b) a fixed charge coverage ratio of at least 2.25 to 1, currently 3.79; and c) consolidated net worth of at least NP$526.3 million, currently NP$1.5 billion (as of December 31, 1994).

♦ **Operations.** The cost structure of the Company was only slightly exposed to currency pressures, as 9% of cost of goods sold was sourced in U.S. dollars.[13] According to management, Gemex would offset the exchange rate-related cost increases by reducing sales discounts and enjoying newly-derived efficiencies from the intensive fixed capital investment undertaken over the previous three years. Further, the firm's *integral cost of financing* would increase substantially as a result of the higher effective interest expenses arising from dollar-denominated debt.[14]

With the release of 1994 earnings and revenues on March 6, 1995, the full impact of the peso's devaluation on Gemex's performance was revealed. Net income for 1994 was a sizeable loss of NP$163.3 million, despite a positive operating income of NP$390.0 million. The difference was, predictably, the massive losses associated with the devaluation (listed under *integral cost of financing*), foreign exchange losses of NP$508.4 million and interest expenses of NP$131.0 million.[15] Operating profits indicated that the basic business of Gemex was still competitive, but its financing/financial structure appeared to be a major liability. Gemex's ADR prices on the New York Stock Exchange were down, and staying down (see Exhibit 5).

---

[13] Import costs included aluminum, pet resins, crowns and twist-off bottle caps.

[14] Under Mexican accounting practices, the *integral cost of financing* is composed of four separate financially-based cash flow components: 1) foreign exchange gains and losses on debt; 2) interest expense; 3) interest earnings; and 4) gains and losses on monetary assets and liabilities. See Appendix A for additional details.

[15] All values are in constant New Pesos as of December 31, 1995. As described in Appendix A, Mexican Generally Accepted Accounting Practices (GAAP) require that all financials be adjusted for the effects of inflation, and as a result, all historical financial statistics are revised annually for reporting and comparison purposes.

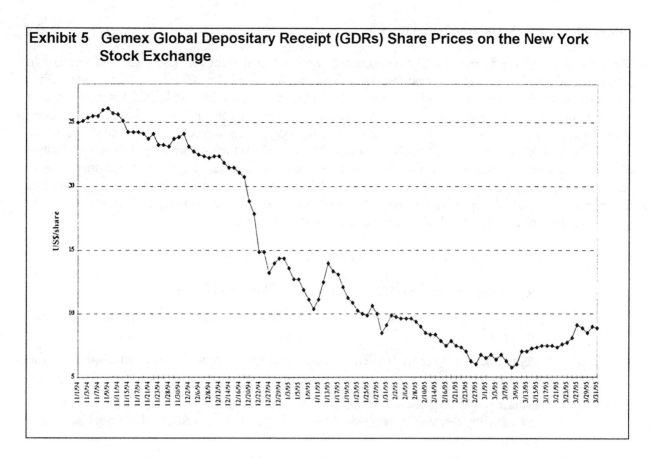

Exhibit 5 Gemex Global Depositary Receipt (GDRs) Share Prices on the New York Stock Exchange

The peso's slide continued into the new year, falling from NP$5.5/US$ to just over NP$6.0/US$. Accompanying the first quarter results for 1995, Enrique C. Molina, Chairman and President of Gemex, made the following statement:

> This was a difficult quarter for Gemex. The peso's devaluation increased our foreign exchange loss and cost of goods sold increased faster than our price in the first two months of this year. In fact, margins in March reached 1994 levels due to the implementation of a price increase in mid-March but, given the timing of such increase, the net sales figure for this quarter does not reflect the favorable effect we expect such increase to have on the net sales figure in the next quarter.[16]

To date, the pass-through of exchange rate-related costs and losses to customers had not sustained the firm's profitability. In the following months, Gemex's actual sales volume fell as a result of price increases. Second quarter results indicated a decrease in the sales volume of soft drink products of 5%, however, a 21% increase in the sales volume of purified jug water sales buoyed firm earnings. But PepsiCo's and Gemex's relationship was about to change, and the result would hopefully allow Gemex to recover something of its former glory.

---

[16] Gemex, April 28, 1995.

The Joint Venture Agreement With PepsiCo

The next major step in Gemex's evolution occurred before the dust from the peso's fall had settled. In January 1995, Pepsi-Cola International (PCI) purchased a 10% interest in Gemex's bottling subsidiaries operating in the Southeast area of Mexico for NP$4.6 million. On July 27, 1995, PCI announced that it would be moving in principle to acquire a 25% interest in Gemex for cash and ownership of several other Pepsi-Cola bottling enterprises in Mexico. The purpose of PepsiCo's movement was to establish Gemex as -- officially and financially -- Pepsi's anchor bottler in Mexico. Market analysts now estimated that Gemex could soon account for over half of Pepsi's sales in the entire country, and PepsiCo's senior management felt that it was critical to inject new life, and new capital, into its major Mexican bottler.[17] Enrique Molina had previously rebuffed PepsiCo's advances, but now conceded that his company's dependence on U.S. dollar-denominated debt left it little choice in the wake of the peso's fall.

The investment by PepsiCo in Gemex contained five basic features:

1) Pepsi would contribute US$217 million in cash directly to Gemex;

2) Pepsi would transfer its company-owned bottling operations in several north central cities to Gemex;

3) Pepsi would transfer its 10% equity stake in Gemex's southeastern bottling operations to Gemex;

4) Gemex would be granted bottling rights to *white territories* (i.e., areas where Pepsi was not currently distributed) and would have the option to acquire all other franchises which became available;

5) Pepsi would participate in key Gemex management decisions.

There was one other notable feature of the transaction. The founding Molina family of Gemex was to maintain operational control for seven years. At the end of the seven years, the Molina family would sell all of its voting shares to PepsiCo.[18] PepsiCo agreed to pay a premium of US$50 million to the family for controlling interest.

The restructuring of corporate control was complex (see Exhibit 6). According to the joint venture agreement, Mr. Molina, PepsiCo, and PepsiCo's Mexican subsidiaries formed the "Molina/PepsiCo Gemex Shares Trust," a Delaware statutory business trust. After all participants contributed their specific shares to the trust, the management of the shares in the trust was divided into two separate phases. In Phase I, from October 1995 to December 2002, Mr. Molina would continue as Chairman and CEO of Gemex, and

---

[17] PepsiCo's motivations are clear in light of several public statements since that time. For example, Roger Enrico, CEO of PepsiCo recently stated "The financial crisis in Mexico brought things to a head. If there was ever a time to invest and show confidence in Mexico and Gemex, it was then" (*Financial Times*, November 27, 1996, p.14).

[18] According to PepsiCo's 1996 10-K filed with the U.S. SEC (p.44), "In 1995, PepsiCo issued a seven-year put option in connection with the formation of a joint venture with the principal shareholder of GEMEX, an unconsolidated franchised bottling affiliate in Mexico. The put option allows the principal shareholder to sell up to 150 million GEMEX shares to PepsiCo at 66 2/3 cents per share. PepsiCo accounts for this put option by marking it to market with gains or losses recognized currently as an adjustment to equity in net income of unconsolidated affiliates, which is included in selling, general and administrative expenses in the Consolidated Statement of Income. The put option liability, which was valued at $26 million at the date of the original transaction, increased to $30 million by year-end, resulting in a $4 million charge to earnings."

would have the right to vote all of the B shares and ordinary participation certificates (CPOs) in the Trust (over 50% of the voting control of Gemex). During Phase II, commencing in January 2003, PepsiCo would acquire the sole power to direct the vote of all B shares and CPOs in the Trust. PepsiCo would thereafter control the company as long as the Trust held the majority of the outstanding B shares. Although PepsiCo now held only 26.74% of the total shares in Gemex, it held 51.5% of the voting shares (B shares). According to the agreement, however, PepsiCo would not exercise its voting rights until the end of 2002.

In August 1995, Gemex continued its recapitalization efforts, successfully refinancing US$85 million in short-term debt in two tranches. One tranche was financed through a private placement arranged by Chemical Bank (US), while the second was a commercial paper issue sponsored by the Weston Group (US). Both were denominated in U.S. dollars.

On October 12, 1995, Gemex and PepsiCo confirmed the consummation of the joint venture agreement. In a press release, Gemex's President Enrique Molina noted the joint venture's primary advantage to Gemex: "It strengthens our balance sheet, reduces our leverage and opens greater access for Gemex in capital markets." On October 18, 1995, Gemex announced a 3 for 1 stock split of its CPOs listed on the Mexican bolsa.[19] As part of the new venture structure, Steve Lawrence was named President and Chief Operating Officer, and would report to Gemex's CEO and Chairman, Enrique Molina.[20] Lawrence was considered a turn-around artist, and was another indication of PepsiCo's commitment to not only make the new venture work, but to revitalize Gemex's anchor bottler position. The question for Lawrence was what to do?

---

[19] Although these same CPOs are the underlying security for the ADRs (or GDRs) traded on the New York Stock Exchange, it did not affect the valuation of the ADRs due to a ratio change of the underlying shares from 2:1 to 6:1.

[20] Mr. Lawrence had most recently served as Senior V.P. of Pepsi-Cola, Europe, and President and CEO of PepsiCo International, Spain.

Exhibit 6 Ownership of the Share Capital of Gemex, April 26, 1996

Owner	B Shares Number	%	D Shares Number	%	L Shares Number	%	Total Outstanding Shares
Enrique C. Molina Sobrino	344,351,117	47.2%	328,926,889	97.3%	328,926,889	97.3%	71.29%
PepsiCo	375,900,831	51.5%	---	0.0%	---	0.00%	26.74%
All other officers & directors	9,234,152	1.3%	9,234,152	2.7%	9,234,152	1.97%	1.97%
	729,486,100	100.0%	338,161,041	100.0%	338,161,041	100.0%	100.00%
Molina/PepsiCo Shares Trust							
Molina Family	57,468,714	13.3%	57,468,714	100.0%	57,468,714	100.0%	12.26%
PepsiCo	375,900,831	86.7%	---	0.0%	---	0.0%	26.74%
	433,369,545	100.0%	57468,714	100.0%	57,468,714	100.0%	39.00%

B Shares: Listed on the Mexican Stock Exchange (symbol GGEMEX). Effected a 3 for 1 stock split on October 6, 1995. According to the Company's amended and restated bylaws, non-Mexicans are prohibited from owning 50% or more of Series B shares. On March 9, 1994, shareholders approved a capital stock restructuring whereby 63.5% of the Series B outstanding shares, including those represented by Depositary Shares that represented 93.4% of the outstanding Series B shares that were not held by the majority shareholder, and 49.4% of the Series B shares held by the majority shareholder, were converted into Ordinary Participation Certificates (CPOs) on March 28, 1994.

D Shares: Entitled to vote only in limited circumstances and to receive an annual cumulative dividend of 5% of the capital attributed to Series D shares. Effected a 3 for 1 stock split on October 6, 1995. Series D shares cannot be traded individually but will be represented by CPOs for ten years from the date of issue with Banco Nacional de Mexico S.A. as CPO Trustee. The CPOs are listed on the Mexican Stock Exchange for ten years, after which they may continue to be represented as CPOs or may be removed from the CPO Trust and traded separately. Series D shares may not be withdrawn from the CPO Trust until the tenth anniversary of the issue.

L Shares: Entitled to vote only in limited circumstances and to liquidation preference only after Series D shares are paid in full. Effected a 3 for 1 stock split on October 6, 1995. Series L shares cannot be traded individually but will be represented by CPOs for ten years from the date of issue, with the Banco Nacional de Mexico S.A. as CPO Trustee. The CPOs will be listed on the Mexican Stock Exchange for ten years, after which they may continue to be represented as CPOs or may be removed from the CPO Trust and traded separately. Series L shares may not be withdrawn from the CPO Trust until the tenth anniversary of the issue

Global Depositary Shares: Each Global Depositary Share (GDS) represents six Ordinary Participation Certificates (CPOs). Each CPO represents one Series B share, one Series D share, and one Series L share. Each GDS is entitled to the voting rights and dividend rights of the shares represented by the underlying CPOs. GDS custodian depositary bank: Citibank, N.A., Mexico City.

Source: *Moody's International Company Data Report on Grupo Embotellador de Mexico*, S.A. de C.V., p. 3.

Status 1996: The Cola War in Mexico

By late summer 1996, PepsiCo's strategy in Mexico had begun to unravel. A review by Pepsi-Cola International of Gemex's operations and performance to date was unsettling. The full impact of the damage of the peso's devaluation could now be accurately assessed.

Operating Income & Integral Cost of Financing. Exhibit 7 provides an overview in constant pesos of the Company's profitability for the years 1991-1995. The rapid expansion in market share and business lines in the early 1990s had more than tripled operating income from NP$117.0 million in 1991 to NP$390.0 million in 1994. In 1995, following the fall of the peso and the resurgence of competition from Coca-Cola, operating income fell to NP$86.1 million. Operating income was in many ways a measure of the business's basic competitiveness independent of financing expenses.

**Exhibit 7 Grupo Embotellador de Mexico's Income Statement, December 31
(thousands of constant New Pesos)**

	1995	1994	1993	1992	1991
Net sales	2,745,891	3,114,965	1,581,681	1,370,985	941,725
Other revenues	34,438	31,905	30,005	23,498	15,270
Total revenues	2,780,329	3,146,870	1,611,686	1,394,483	956,995
Less cost of sales	(1,425,032)	(1,417,350)	(676,686)	(601,192)	(430,071)
Less selling, G&A expenses	(864,234)	(940,026)	(572,817)	(485,377)	(378,637)
Less administrative expenses	(211,734)	(266,346)	---	---	---
Less depreciation & amortization	(193,200)	(133,129)	(59,291)	(50,895)	(31,255)
Total costs and operating expenses	(2,694,200)	(2,756,851)	(1,308,794)	(1,137,464)	(839,963)
Operating income	86,129	390,019	302,892	257,019	117,032
Interest/financial income	25,959	24,010	---	---	---
Less interest expenses	(310,589)	(130,974)	---	---	---
Foreign exchange loss	(671,484)	(508,381)	---	---	---
Monetary position gain	735,348	68,026	---	---	---
Integral income (cost) of financing, net	(220,766)	(547,319)	(24,368)	(26,642)	(11,094)
Income before provisions & extraord. items	(134,637)	(157,300)	278,524	230,377	105,938
Provision for income and asset taxes	(40)	(2,641)	(45,299)	(43,193)	(11,937)
Employee statutory profit sharing	(5,608)	(3,309)	(6,829)	(7,721)	(8,941)
Provision for income tax & employee profits	(5,648)	(5,950)	(52,128)	(50,914)	(20,878)
Income before equity losses in associated companies	(140,285)	(163,250)	226,396	179,463	85,060
Equity in income (losses) of assoc companies	---	---	---	(10,743)	---
Income after equity inclusions	(140,285)	(163,250)	226,396	179,463	85,060
Tax reduction from operating loss carryforward	---	---	5,576	12,235	5,638
Recovery of lease charge in prior years	---	---	---	5,789	---
Gain on acquisition of shares	---	---	---	---	7,758
Total extraordinary items	---	---	5,576	18,024	13,396
Net consolidated income (loss)	(140,285)	(163,250)	231,972	186,744	98,456

Source: Gemex, Form 10-K, December 31, 1995.

The integral cost of financing indicates the impact of the peso's devaluation on the firm's capital structure: total integral cost of financing had risen from NP$24.4 million in 1993 to NP$547.3 million in 1994 -- immediately following the peso's initial plunge -- remaining high in 1995 at NP$220.8 million. Foreign exchange losses were devastating: NP$508 million in 1993 and NP$671 million in 1995. Interest expenses continued to rise, nearly tripling from 1994 to 1995. Because the peso's fall was late in 1994 (December), most of the actual dollar-denominated interest payment impact was not fully felt until 1995.

Net income for Gemex had now been negative for two full years. With profits having peaked in 1993 at about NP$232 million; 1994 and 1995 witnessed losses of NP$163 million and NP$140 million, respectively. Given the significant drop in operating income and the rising costs of financing, it appeared that structural changes in Gemex might be in order.

Operating Costs. Soft drinks are produced by mixing water, concentrate, and sweetener, and then injecting carbon dioxide gas to create carbonation. Cost of sales is therefore dominated by two components, sweetener and the cost of concentrate. As part of its franchise agreement with PepsiCo, Gemex is obligated to purchase all concentrate and syrup for the production of soft drink products from the franchisor (PepsiCo). Gemex purchases are made from Pepsi-Cola Mexicana S.A. de C.V., at a unit price of 16.5% of the wholesale price (net of value-added taxes) of the finished product.

Gemex buys all of its sugar from Consorcio Industrial Escorpión S.A. de C.V. (Escorpión), a company owned and controlled by Mr. Enrique Molina. Escorpión accounted for 45% of Mexico's total refined sugar production in 1995.[21] Escorpión's agreement with Gemex states that it "has agreed to supply the Company with sugar, at a price no less favorable than that charged by Escorpión to third parties, for as long as Escorpión and the Company remain under the common control of Mr. Molina and his immediate family."[22]

An overview of Gemex's cost of sales for the 1993-1995 period is provided in Exhibit 8. As a percentage of sales, cost of sales were 42.0%, 45.0%, and 51.3% in 1993, 1994, and 1995, respectively. Cost of sales increased substantially from 1993 to 1994 as a result of the acquisition of Electropura (bottled water). From 1993 to 1994, Gemex participated in a marketing arrangement with PepsiCo, in which PepsiCo reimbursed Gemex for all marketing costs above 16.5% of the wholesale price paid by the company for concentrate for the year following a price increase for soft drinks in Mexico, if Gemex reinvested the proceeds of the reimbursement in fixed assets. The marketing arrangement expired in October 1994.

Gemex, like PepsiCo, markets its products predominantly in nonreturnable plastic bottles. Although plastic bottle production and sale constitutes nearly half of Gemex's current revenues, the bottles are more expensive than the returnable glass bottles used by Coca-Cola for over 50 years.[23] In 1995, approximately 42% of Gemex's Pepsi Products were sold in returnable glass bottles, 16% in plastic returnable bottles (PRBs), and 42% in non-returnable bottles and cans.[24] The actual proportion of sales volume in non-returnable bottles increased in 1994 and 1995, however, as a result of consumer preferences.

---

[21] Sugar prices have long been controlled on world markets and within national boundaries. The government of Mexico regulated the price of sugar with price controls and import duties until August 1995. Prior to April 1993 sugar prices in Mexico were adjusted monthly according to the rate of inflation in the United States and the official devaluation of the peso by the government. In April 1993 this price control was eliminated, and an allowed 9.0% increase was set for the remainder of the year (1993). Following price adjustments allowed were 6.0% in January 1994, 15% in February 1995, 9.8% in May 1995, and 10.8% in August 1995. Price controls were then eliminated following the August 1995 adjustment. The total increase in sugar prices for 1995, for all price adjustments and exchange rate changes, was 60.7%. Although price controls kept sugar costs for Gemex under control in 1994 and 1995, it was expected that subsequent costs might rise significantly.

[22] Gemex, Form 20-F, December 31, 1995, p. 19.

[23] Morningstar research report, June 13, 1996, p. 1105.

[24] Gemex first used plastic returnable bottles (PRBs) in 1991 in the 1.5 liter size. The company estimates that PRBs can be reused approximately twenty times before being recycled. Market studies conducted by Gemex indicate that PRBs are increasingly popular with consumers because of their lighter weight, larger size, higher durability, and lower cost per ounce of soft drink.

Exhibit 8 Gemex' Cost of Sales, December 31, 1995 (thousands of constant New Pesos)			
	1993	**1994**	**1995**
Raw materials			
Sugar	320,817	352,909	334,397
Concentrate	333,303	406,226	315,530
Packaging	41,941	231,721	349,909
Other	115,272	143,800	150,459
Total raw materials	811,333	1,134,656	1,150,295
Labor	35,983	43,981	36,410
Overhead	181,246	238,713	238,327
Total cost of sales	1,028,563	1,417,350	1,425,032

Concentrate amounts for 1993 and 1994 are shown net of reimbursements from PepsiCo under the "Plan 16.5" marketing arrangement. In 1993 and 1994 these PepsiCo reimbursements totaled NP11.6 million and NP7.4 million, respectively. Plan 16.5 expired on October 1, 1994. Source: Gemex, Form 20-F, December 31, 1995, p. 52.

Financial Structure & Costs. Gemex's debt structure changed drastically in the early 1990s in order to support the bottler's rapidly expanding operational goals. The long-term debt structure on December 31, 1995, was composed of the following four elements (see Exhibit 9 for a detailed description):

- **Financial leases.** The firm was a party to financial lease obligations totaling NP$201,677,000, payable in U.S. dollars, with interest payments of LIBOR plus 2.25%.[25]

- **Credit lines.** The Company possessed two major credit lines totaling NP$296,530,000, payable in U.S. dollars, with interest rates of LIBOR plus 0.85% and LIBOR plus 1.25%.

- **Long-term debt.** A long-term debt obligation to an individual lender of NP$84,205,000 payable in U.S. dollars.

- **Euronotes.** On November 10, 1992, Gemex issued a guaranteed U.S. dollar five-year euronote. The note, due November 19, 1997, paid 10.75% semi-annually (May 19th and November 19th). On December 31, 1995, the Ba3 rated issue had US$110,000,000 outstanding (NP$847,000,000).[26] The issue's covenants required the firm to maintain certain financial ratios and limit dividend payments, in addition to the primary restriction that it could not increase long-term debt.

---

[25] LIBOR, the London Interbank Offer Rate, the interest rate at which high creditworth banks lend amongst themselves in the London market, serves as the base rate for many loan agreements worldwide.

[26] The December 31, 1995 financials were valued (marked-to-market) at an exchange rate of NP$7.70/US$.

Exhibit 9 Grupo Embotellador de Mexico, S.A. de C.V. Liabilities & Net Worth, December 31 (thousands of constant New Pesos)

	1995	1994	1993	1992	1991
Notes payable to banks	27,499	735,791	35,898	9,946	309,646
Current portion of long-term debt	203,551	191,009	44,086	36,576	24,003
Trade accounts payable	139,852	145,057	45,698	30,377	32,335
Accrued income tax & expenses	128,749	116,924	70,559	83,109	46,157
Income tax payable	---	---	2,614	1,673	---
Employee statutory profit-sharing	---	4,445	10,267	11,502	11,606
Affiliated companies	6,093	---	9,257	15,402	10,662
Total current liabilities	505,744	1,193,226	218,379	188,585	434,409
Long-term debt	1,225,861	1,135,546	485,985	488,737	93,438
Seniority benefits	18,720	23,417	12,182	8,744	7,244
Deferred taxes payable	11,684	18,973	---	---	---
Total liabilities	1,762,009	2,371,162	716,546	686,066	535,091
Common stock	402,359	302,764	189,177	177,376	152,506
Additional paid-in capital	1,969,951	792,865	277,573	241,632	41,132
Retained earnings	241,226	381,511	462,932	336,432	184,720
Reserves	106,119	131,296	35,461	35,535	---
Excess in restatement of stock's equity	122,541	629,260	97,951	195,466	45,945
Total stockholders' equity	2,842,196	2,237,696	1,063,094	986,441	424,303
Total liabilities & stockholders' equity	4,604,205	4,608,858	1,779,640	1,672,507	959,394

Source: Gemex, Form 20-F, December 31, 1995.

As of December 31, 1995, Gemex possessed US$188.5 million in dollar-denominated debt, constituting 99.8% of its outstanding indebtedness. Gemex did not currently engage in any hedging of its foreign currency denominated exposures, and did not enter into any transactions related to the management of the foreign currency or interest rate risks of the company. According to statements filed in conjunction with the company's SEC filings, however, Gemex sought to "optimize its mix of U.S. dollar- and Peso-denominated debt and it may in the future consider entering into hedging and other arrangements considering the then relevant risks, costs and other factors."[27]

Market Share. Although profits *run* businesses, market share *drives* consumer product firms like PepsiCo. The bottom line in the Cola Wars had always been market share. According to the latest data, however, Coca-Cola was kicking PepsiCo's can.[28] As Exhibit 10 illustrates, Coca-Cola seemed to be enjoying a very strong offensive. Whereas Gemex's total soft drink market share was at a three-year low, Coke was setting new records. PepsiCo's turn-around artist, Steve Lawrence, had already been reassigned from Gemex to Pepsi-Cola Mexico.

The Latin Cola Wars had, in the eyes of many, been either *won* by Coca-Cola or *lost* by PepsiCo. It appeared that Chris Sinclair's go-for-broke expansionist strategy had failed -- PepsiCo's major bottlers across Latin America were going broke and Sinclair was sacked in the summer of 1996.

---

[27] Gemex, Form 20-F, December 31, 1995, p. 30.

[28] Referring to the article in *Fortune* magazine October 28, 1996, entitled "How Coke is Kicking Pepsi's Can."

Exhibit 10 Pepsi's and Coca-Cola's Respective Market Shares in the Mexico City Area
(percent)

Year	Cola Segment		Flavored Soft Drink		Total Market	
	Gemex	Femsa	Gemex	Femsa	Gemex	Femsa
1991	48.9	51.1	17.3	6.4	35.2	32.1
1992	50.0	50.0	19.6	6.8	37.7	32.8
1993	47.7	52.3	28.1	6.1	40.1	32.9
1994	48.0	52.0	29.9	8.7	40.7	31.2
1995	44.0	56.0	33.4	17.4	39.8	45.2

Coca-Cola FEMSA, S.A. de C.V., is the Company's primary competitor in the Mexico City Area. The Coca-Cola Company, U.S., owned approximately 30% of Coca-Cola FEMSA. Source: Gemex Form 20-F, December 31, 1995, p. 24.

In August of 1996, PepsiCo's anchor bottler in Caracas, Venezuela, owned by the Cisneros family, was lost to Coca-Cola. In an overnight coup, the Cisneros Group sold out 50% of the bottler's ownership to Coca-Cola for approximately $500 million, turning Venezuela's largest Pepsi-Cola bottler and distributor into Coca-Cola's largest bottler and distributor in a matter of hours.[29] The turnabout was reportedly achieved out of Cisneros' frustration in negotiating an equity injection from PepsiCo. Despite extended negotiations, PepsiCo was unwilling to take a substantial equity position in the Venezuelan bottler. The problems with Pepsi, according to Cisneros, began twenty years before when Pepsi began diversifying out of soft drinks into snacks and restaurants. "Pepsi-Cola was a religion for them," he said. "Then it was no longer that important."[30] Whereas Pepsi was unwilling to take more than a 10% to 20% stake in the Venezuelan bottler, Coca-Cola offered US$500 million for a 50% stake and would invest millions in refrigeration equipment and trucks that the bottler believed it needed. Change was swift, with the former PepsiCo delivery trucks repainted in a matter of days from Pepsi blue to Coke red. Pepsi's market share in the fall of 1996 in Venezuela was estimated at less than 1%.[31]

Baesa, PepsiCo's success story in southern South America, was on the edge of bankruptcy. In September 1996, PepsiCo announced that it would be taking special charges of $525 million, mostly against the losses associated with its 24% interest in Baesa. Baesa lost an estimated $300 million in the first six months of 1996. Most of Baesa's losses resulted from an ugly combination of rapid asset expansion -- which was debt-financed -- and low asset utilization. Baesa's plant and equipment had reportedly been running at under 40% capacity as a result of Coca-Cola's aggressive counter-offensives throughout Brazil and Argentina.

---

[29] *Fortune* magazine reported that Coca-Cola referred to the negotiation process in Venezuela as "Project Swan," a label derived from the Cisneros family name, *cisne* meaning *swan* in Spanish. Many within Pepsi refer to it as Roger Enrico's potential *swan song*.

[30] "PepsiCo Fumble in Venezuela Traced To Its Losing Its 'Religion'," *The Dallas Morning News*, September 1, 1996, p. 3H.

[31] On November 14, 1996, PepsiCo announced the establishment of a new joint venture bottling agreement in Venezuela with Empresas Polar. Polar is Venezuela's largest beer brewer with an estimated 80% to 90% market share. Polar will hold 70% interest to PepsiCo's 30%. Polar had 1995 sales of US$1.6 billion, 60% derived from the sale of beer. Polar also has its own softdrink brand, Golden, which holds a 5% market share in Venezuela. PepsiCo intends to spend more than US$400 million in Venezuela in an attempt to re-take its market share.

Even Agral, PepsiCo's joint venture with Grupo Protexa in northern Mexico was in trouble. The aggressive marketing campaign launched originally by Chris Sinclair in 1993 had intended to increase Pepsi's market share from the then 8% to 40%.[32] Successful in its early stages (as was the case with Gemex farther south), Agral had quickly expanded its market share to 20%. Coca-Cola, however, responded in kind with an aggressive marketing campaign which destroyed both firms' operating margins. Agral defaulted on $70 million in bank loans in July 1996, including a $20 million loan from Citibank for the financing of new bottles (working capital).[33] Agral announced in September that it would remain a PepsiCo bottler only if PCI would sell its 49% share back to Grupo Protexa.

As illustrated in Exhibit 11, PepsiCo's combined segments operating profits and identifiable assets by world region showed a frightening trend -- a larger investment in assets producing a declining level of earnings. Whereas Mexico had been a major source of earnings in 1993 and 1994, 1995 saw an operating profit which was less than one-third the previous year's level, and was accompanied by a deterioration in asset value.

The 1990s had been eventful for PepsiCo, and Gemex in particular. With all of the changes in ownership, product lines, capitalization, currencies, and earnings, questions still remained as to whether PepsiCo was winning any of the country-battles in the Cola Wars.

Exhibit 11 PepsiCo, Inc's Operating Profits and Identifiable Assets for Combined Segments (millions US$)

	Operating Profit			*Identifiable Assets*		
Region	1995	1994	1993	1995	1994	1993
United States	$2,758	$2,706	$2,523	$14,505	$14,218	$13,590
Europe	(65)	17	47	3,127	3,062	2,666
Mexico	80	261	223	637	995	1,217
Canada	86	82	102	1,344	1,342	1,364
Other	342	258	182	2,629	2,196	1,675
Total	$3,171	$3,324	$3,077	22,242	21,813	20,512
Unconsolidated Affiliates				1,635	1,295	1,091
Corporate				1,555	1,684	2,103
Total				$25,432	$24,792	$23,706

Notes: a) The results of centralized concentrate manufacturing operations in Puerto Rico and Ireland have been allocated based upon sales to the respective geographic areas; b) The initial charges upon adoption of SFAS 121 reduced combined segment operation profit by $503 (United States - $302, Europe - $119, Mexico - $21, Canada - $30, Other - $31).
Source: PepsiCo, Inc. 10-K, pp 59-60.

---

[32] The marketing war undertaken by Agral in the northern Mexico market against Coca-Cola's dominant market share in 1993 was called "Desert Storm."

[33] Agral, like Gemex, had expanded and recapitalized predominantly with U.S. dollar-denominated debt. What made the problem with Agral even more difficult was that Citibank's chairman is a board member of PepsiCo, Inc.

Case Questions

1. What went wrong with PepsiCo's Mexican strategy?

2. What role did capital play, and what role did business relationships play, in the process of building and expanding PepsiCo's presence in Latin America?

3. How did the peso interact with the structure of Gemex's operations to impact Gemex's competitiveness in the Mexican marketplace?

4. What would you have done differently than Pepsi in the Mexican market?

Appendix A: Inflation Accounting [34]

During an inflationary period, historic cost financial statements show illusory profits and capital erosion is masked. The adjustments required by Mexican GAAP are intended to correct these misleading results. The U.S. SEC, recognizing this, does not require that inflation adjustments be removed from Mexican financial statements when reconciling them to U.S. GAAP. Thus, inflation adjusted Mexican results may be directly compared to those of U.S. companies without subjective adjustments for inflation.

Mexican inflation accounting practices fall into three basic areas:

1. Fixed assets and inventories are revalued to current cost. Fixed assets and inventory are restated using either replacement value or by application of the National Consumer Price Index (NCPI) published by the Bank of Mexico.

The difference between historic cost and updated value is an *unrealized holding gain* that is included in the equity section of the balance sheet (often listed as "excess (deficiency) in restated equity", "accumulated gain (loss) on nonmonetary assets" or simply "holding gain (loss) on nonmonetary items"). Depreciation and cost of sales are computed from the adjusted values.

2. All financial statements are stated in pesos with purchasing power as of the latest year end.

3. Gain or loss on net monetary position is included in the income statement as part of financing cost (the section entitled *integral cost of financing, net*). Monetary assets and liabilities are those that are automatically expressed in pesos with end-of-period purchasing power; their value is fixed in money terms. Examples include cash, accounts receivable, and accounts payable.

Integral cost of financing. During periods of inflation, a company with monetary liabilities in excess of monetary assets will have a gain because liabilities will be repaid with pesos having lower purchasing power. Because lenders increase interest rates to compensate, a firm will ordinarily have higher interest expenses in an inflationary economy. The combined net interest expense, foreign currency and monetary gain or loss, approximates the company's real (as opposed to nominal) financing cost. [35]

Note that even in a period of high inflation, incurring additional debt will not necessarily be beneficial. For example, holding the proceeds of a loan in cash produces an offsetting monetary loss as purchasing power erodes. To be effective, the proceeds must be invested in assets that produce a return greater than inflation.

Note: Mexican accounting also requires that prior years' financial statements be updated to pesos with purchasing power as of the most current balance sheet date. That means that last year's financial statements will look different in this year's annual report. This is done so that year-to-year comparisons are not distorted by inflation.

Source: Adapted by authors from "Accounting Issues," Bear, Stearns & Company, Inc., dated October 11, 1991, May 13, 1994, and February 10, 1995.

---

[34] This section draws upon information presented in a series entitled "Accounting Issues" published by Bear, Stearns & Company, Inc., dated October 11, 1991, May 13, 1994, and February 10, 1995.

[35] Even in a period of high inflation, incurring additional debt will not necessarily be beneficial. For example, holding the proceeds of a loan in cash produces an offsetting monetary loss as its purchasing power erodes. To be effective, the proceeds must be invested in assets that produce a return greater than inflation.

Appendix B: Grupo Embotellador de Mexico, S.A. de C.V. (Gemex) Assets, December 31 (thousands of constant New Pesos)

	1995	1994	1993	1992	1991
Cash & equivalents	99,976	63,904	68,347	359,534	20,614
Trade accounts receivable	167,686	185,464	228,026	129,909	246,939
Less allowance for doubtful accounts	(39,113)	(27,482)	---	---	---
Trade accounts receivable, net	128,573	157,982	228,026	129,909	246,939
Other receivables from related companies	4,283	---	---	---	---
Affiliated companies	23,333	47,704	13,290	11,174	122,048
Recoverable taxes	36,786	128,851	---	---	---
Other receivables	22,608	96,446	---	---	---
Raw materials	188,365	222,738	138,583	74,228	19,133
Work in process	---	---	2,200	1,173	1,244
Finished products	61,494	70,403	20,943	11,987	8,004
Advances to suppliers	---	---	2,170	4,266	759
Materials & spare parts	31,193	56,290	26,726	23,568	16,815
Merchandise in transit	---	---	---	---	23,554
Other inventories	5,742	8,181	---	---	---
Total inventories	286,794	357,612	190,622	115,222	69,509
Prepaid expenses	45,339	108,900	6,234	5,968	6,163
Total Current Assets	647,692	961,399	507,149	621,807	465,273
Other investments	33,437	23,995	16,612	---	---
Investment in associated companies	50,020	76,030	53,546	54,021	5,346
Land	382,935	328,481	138,842	98,197	64,968
Buildings	578,227	536,821	166,949	131,577	65,222
Improvements & additions	86,806	72,363	40,676	21,030	7,218
Machinery & equipment	1,392,661	1,181,189	403,977	432,565	304,967
Furniture & fixtures	272,041	80,352	30,905	28,580	11,964
Vehicles	1,210,983	946,378	361,289	295,642	236,254
Construction in progress	242,998	445,950	83,525	57,039	21,184
Cases & bottles	342,994	441,540	283,021	195,792	93,748
Property, plant & equipment, gross	4,509,645	4,033,074	1,509,184	1,260,422	805,525
Less accumulated depreciation	(1,099,838)	(937,796)	(478,748)	(412,356)	(322,193)
Property, plant & equipment, net	3,409,807	3,095,278	1,030,436	848,066	483,332
Other assets	55,455	51,781	30,242	23,972	5,443
Goodwill, net	407,794	400,375	131,104	124,642	---
Deferred taxes	---	---	10,551	---	---
Total Assets	4,604,205	4,608,858	1,779,640	1,672,507	959,394

Source: Gemex, Form 20-F, December 31, 1995.

Appendix C: Grupo Embotellador de Mexico's (Gemex) Sales, 1995 (thousands of New Pesos)

Brand	Sales volume (000s cases)	Percent of soft drink sales volume (percent)	Net sales (000s cases)	Percent of net sales (percent)	Percent of soft drink net sales (percent)
PEPSI PRODUCTS					
Pepsi	109,864	56.7	1,338,093	48.7	54.8
Pepsi Light	1,202	0.6	19,173	0.7	0.8
Pepsi Max	2,254	1.2	37,815	1.4	1.5
Mirinda	23,872	12.3	315,251	11.5	12.9
Seven-Up	8,232	4.2	121,149	4.4	5.0
Kas	3,974	2.1	60,347	2.2	2.5
Total	149,398	77.1	1,891,828	68.9	77.4
MINERAL WATER PRODUCTS					
Garci Crespo	16,793	8.7	182,735	6.7	7.5
San Lorenzo	2,385	1.2	19,031	0.7	0.8
Total	19,178	9.9	201,766	7.3	8.3
OTHER SOFT DRINK PRODUCTS					
Manzanita Sol	9,515	4.9	118,023	4.3	4.8
Squirt	12,188	6.3	166,183	6.1	6.8
Titan	335	0.2	14,268	0.5	0.6
Delaware Punch	2,500	1.3	38,646	1.4	1.6
Other	717	0.4	13,177	0.5	0.5
Total	25,255	13.0	350,297	12.8	14.3
TOTAL SOFT DRINK PRODUCTS	193,831	100.0	2,443,891	89.0	100.0
PURIFIED WATER & OTHER PRODUCTS					
Electropura	32,433		230,930	8.4	
Bottled water	3,060		34,152	1.2	
Total	35,493		265,082	9.7	
Other			36,916	1.3	
TOTAL			2,745,889	100.0	

Source: Gemex, Form 20-F, December 31, 1995.

Appendix D: Consolidated Statement of Income, PepsiCo (US) and Subsidiaries Fiscal years ended December 30, 1995, December 31, 1994 and December 25, 1993 (millions of US dollars except per share amounts)

	1995 (52 weeks)	1994 (53 weeks)	1993 (52 weeks)
Net sales	$ 30,421	$ 28,472	$ 25,021
Costs and expenses, net:			
Cost of sales	(14,886)	(13,715)	(11,946)
Selling, general & administrative expenses	(11,712)	(11,244)	(9,864)
Amortization of intangible assets	(316)	(312)	(304)
Impairment of long-lived assets	(520)	---	---
Operating profit	$ 2,987	$ 3,201	$ 2,907
Gain on stock offering by an unconsolidated affiliate	---	18	---
Interest expense	(682)	(645)	(573)
Interest income	127	90	89
Income before taxes & cumulative effect of accounting changes	$ 2,432	$ 2,664	$ 2,423
Provision for income taxes	(826)	(880)	(835)
Income before cumulative effect of accounting changes	$ 1,606	$ 1,784	$ 1,588
Cumulative effect of accounting changes:			
Post-employment benefits	---	(55)	---
Pension assets	---	23	---
Net income	$ 1,606	$ 1,752	$ 1,588
Income per share:			
Before cumulative effect of accounting changes	$2.00	$2.22	$1.96
Cumulative effect of accounting changes			
Post-employment benefits	---	(0.07)	---
Pension assets	---	0.03	---
Net income per share	$2.00	$2.18	$1.96
Average shares outstanding	804	804	810

Source: Gemex, Form 20-F, December 31, 1995.

109

Appendix E: PepsiCo & Coca-Cola Share Prices, NYSE, June 1994 - October 1996

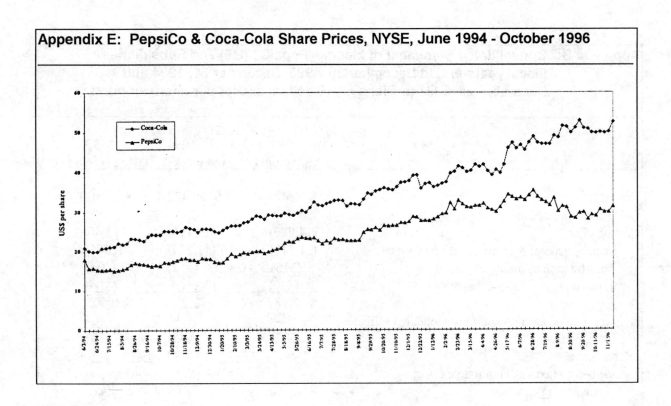

Katherine Miller, director of mergers and acquisitions for International Acquisitions, Inc. (IAI), was sitting in her office evaluating what appeared to be a significant stumbling block for a deal that had been brought to her for approval by the company's U.S. subsidiary. IAI was an international holding company for a group of independent hotel chains and resorts located around the world. Headquartered in Phoenix, Arizona, IAI had significant operations in Germany, Japan, the United Kingdom, the United States, Mexico, and five Caribbean countries.

Organizationally, the company was structured into 10 largely autonomous operating companies based on geographical location and country boundaries. Holding company-level executives encouraged executives of the various operating companies to operate independently, even to the point of competing for convention business. This philosophy was felt to be the best way to keep the various units at peak operating efficiency -- a characteristic considered essential in the highly competitive hotel and resort industry. The only area in which operating company-level executives were required to seek holding company-level approval involved the acquisition (or divestiture) of hotels and resorts.

THE DEAL

The proposal that Miller was currently reviewing involved the acquisition of a chain of six resort hotels, located in Florida, California, and Hawaii. The properties were very desirable, and holding company-level executives were highly enthusiastic about the prospects of acquiring the resorts. The resort hotels were being sold as a package, and Miller expected that they would also be of considerable interest to such well-known companies as Hilton, ITT-Sheraton, and Marriott. In fact, Miller's current concern over the deal evolved from her expectation that a number of foreign hotel companies would, in all likelihood, also be bidding on the six-hotel package.

Since the properties were all located within U.S. boundaries, the acquisition proposal had originated within IAI's U.S. operating company (IAI-U.S.). As Miller reviewed the proposed acquisition price data (see Exhibit 1), she realized that U.S. accounting and tax regulations might cause them to lose this acquisition opportunity. Miller was concerned that if a foreign bidder for the properties emerged, the more lenient treatment of goodwill for accounting or tax purposes in other countries might permit such a company to outbid IAI-U.S. for the resort package.

In anticipation of this possibility, Miller decided to evaluate the bid price that IAI might be able to pay if the acquisition were handled through its German, Japanese, and U.K. operating companies. As a first step in this process, she developed a table comparing the prevalent accounting and tax treatments for goodwill in each of the four countries (see Exhibit 2).

---

[*] This case was prepared by Kenneth R. Ferris. Copyright © 1993 by Kenneth R. Ferris. All rights reserved to the author.

QUESTIONS

1. Using the assumptions and valuation approach described in Exhibit 1, calculate the maximum bid price that IAI could offer for the six-hotel package through its German, Japanese, and U.K. subsidiaries.
2. Is Miller's concen about losing the properties to a foreign bidder justified? Why, or why not?
3. How will harmonization affect this type of problem for IAI in the future?

Exhibit 1
Comparative Acquisition Bid Price Data Source: IAI-U.S.

I. Maximum bid price based on projected accounting earnings (before goodwill amortization and taxes) of $4 million per year for a 20-year horizon, discounted at various hurdle rates:

Hurdle (Discount) rate	10%	15%	20%
Maximum bid price (000s)	$21,154	$16,318	$13,088
Goodwill (000s)	6,154	1,318	(1,912)

Assumptions:

1. Constant tax rate of 34 percent.
2. Fair market value of the resort properties is $15 million.
3. Acquisition price is that price (P) which would render the purchase a zero net present value (NPV) project; that is, if the hurdle rate = 10%, then

$$NPV = PV - P = 0$$
$$= PV - [15,000 + GW]$$

where GW = Goodwill
PV = [PV factor for n = 20, i = 10%
× Projected annual accounting earnings]

4. Projected annual accounting earnings are calculated as follows:

	(000's)
Accounting earnings before goodwill amortization and Income taxes	4,000
Less. Amortization of goodwill (GW)	- GW/40
Accounting earnings before income taxes	[4,000 - GW/40]
Less: Income taxes (.34 x 4,000)	(1,360)
Projected annual accounting earnings	[2,640 - GW/40]

II. Maximum bid price based on after-tax cash flow, discounted at 10%:

Hurdle (Discount) rate	10%
Maximum bid price (000s)	$22,466
Goodwill (000s)	7,466

Exhibit 1
Comparative Acquisition Bid Price Data Source: IAI-U.S. (continued)

Assumptions:

1. Constant tax rate of 34 percent.
2. Fair market value of the resort properties is $15 million.
3. Acquisition price is that price (P) which would render the purchase a zero net present value (NPV) project; that is,

$$
\begin{aligned}
NPV \;=\; & PV - P = 0 \\
=\; & PV - [15{,}000 + GW] \\
\text{where} \quad GW \quad & \text{Goodwill} \\
PV \;=\; & [PV \text{ factor for } n = 20,\ i = 10\% \\
& \times \text{After-tax cash flow}] \\
=\; &
\end{aligned}
$$

4. After-tax cash flow Is calculated as follows:

	(000s)
Earnings before goodwill amortization and income taxes	
Less: Amortization of goodwill (GW)	$4,000
Taxable earnings	-0-
Less: Income taxes (@ .34)	$4,000
Taxable earnings after tax	(1,360)
Add: Noncash amortization of goodwill	$2,640
After-tax Cash Flow	-0-
	$2,640

Exhibit 2
Alternative Accounting and Tax Treatment of Goodwill

Country	Accounting Treatment	Tax Treatment
Germany	Goodwill capitalized to the balance sheet and amortized against earnings over 5 years	Goodwill capitalized and amortized over 15 years
Japan	Goodwill capitalized to the balance sheet and amortized against earnings over 5 years	Goodwill capitalized and amortized over 5 years
United Kingdom	Goodwill charged off (in total) against equity reserve at the time of acquisition	Goodwill not tax deductible
United States	Goodwill capitalized to the balance sheet and amortized against earnings over 40 years	Goodwill not tax deductible.[*]

---

[*] Effective 1994, Goodwill became tax-deductible In the United States over a 15-year-period.

[DuPont's pollution prevention performance is] *"defined more by adroit lobbying efforts to kill legislation than by innovative approaches to pollution prevention. For example, DuPont successfully delayed the phase-out of CFC's for 15 years because it was the world's largest producer of the ozone destroyers. As the inevitable deadline approached, the company stepped up its promotion of substitute HCFC's, which are less potent but still ozone depleting, instead of developing alternatives that do not harm the environment"* (Fortune, July 26, 1993, p. 118).

In July, 1996, Christine Miller, a financial analyst at Ranking and Sellene Inc., a small investment firm, was considering adding a position in DuPont common stock to the firm's large company mutual fund. As part of her analysis, Christine obtained summary financial data for DuPont. (Exhibit 1 contains condensed balance sheets and income statements for the years 1992-1995). In addition, she reviewed recent publications in which DuPont was mentioned. One of the articles that she reviewed had appeared in Fortune in 1993 in which DuPont had been labeled an environmental "laggard."

While Christine had always considered herself "pro-environment," her primary concern was with the possibility that DuPont's environmental excesses might lead to a decline in DuPont's stock price in the future. She also obtained information about the financial effects of DuPont's environmental record (see Exhibits 2-6) from previous DuPont annual reports.

Company Background

E.I. DuPont de Nemours and Company (DuPont) was founded in 1802 in Delaware. The company has five business segments -- Chemicals, Fibers, Polymers and Diversified Businesses, operating under the DuPont name, and Petroleum, operating as Conoco, Inc. The company is the largest U.S. chemical producer, and one of the world's largest, with consolidated 1992 sales of $37.8 billion. DuPont currently operates approximately 90 businesses in numerous industries, and has operations in about 70 nations. Approximately 46% of consolidated 1992 revenues were derived from sales outside the U.S. As of 1992, the company employed approximately 125,000.

DuPont's reputation as an environmental laggard hit bottom in 1993. Since the Toxic Release Inventory was first compiled by the U.S. government in 1987, DuPont had consistently been identified as the company with the largest quantities of toxic releases in the United States (see Exhibit 2).

The company's consistently poor environmental showing required a strategic response. DuPont had two alternatives. One alternative was to continue to attempt to resist the rising tide of environmentalism. Many felt that DuPont had the political clout to influence the outcome of the legislative process regarding environmental laws. A second alternative was to embrace the environmental movement. (See Appendix I for a brief summary of significant United States environmental regulation.)

DuPont opted for the latter strategy, deciding to become an environmental leader. There were two necessary aspects of this transformation. First, DuPont would have to develop internal tactics for improving its

---

* This case was prepared by David Shields. Copyright ©1997 by the American Graduate School of International Management. All rights reserved.

environmental performance. The company responded with a Corporate Environmental Plan (CEP), which consisted of a method for identifying cost-effective projects for waste elimination (see Appendix II). Second, DuPont would need to decide how to disclose their environmental performance to the public. The remainder of this case focuses on DuPont's external reporting of its environmental activities.

External Disclosure Of Environmental Issues

In the U.S., companies are required to file numerous environmental reports with federal, state and local governmental agencies. In addition, publicly-held companies are required to follow Generally Accepted Accounting Principles in the preparation of their annual reports and reports to the Securities and Exchange Commission, and as part of this process, provide certain environmental disclosures. A summary of this GAAP is given in Exhibit 7.

As of 1995, DuPont reported significant progress. In the 1995 DuPont annual report, E. S. Woolard Jr., Chairman of DuPont, claimed that:

> *Environmental progress has clearly established DuPont as a worldwide environmental leader. DuPont was recognized as an "Early Achiever" by the U.S. Environmental Protection Agency for our progress in the voluntary 33/50 Program. We exceeded 50 percent reductions in emissions of 17 large-volume toxic chemicals before the target year of 1995. The U.S. EPA also recognized DuPont as one of the top 20 partners in the agency's Waste Wi$e program for waste reduction. Other recognitions during the year included the United Nations University Unique Business Leadership Award for DuPont's commitment to a "zero" waste and emissions goal and the Banksia Award, one of Australia's most prestigious honors for environmental leadership.*

QUESTIONS:

1. Do a t-account analysis of DuPont's Environmental Liability, and summarize its Environmental Expenses and Environmental Capital Expenditures for the years 1992-1995. What are the relative magnitudes?

2. How have environmental accounting and disclosure rules changed over the period 1992-1996?

3. How might Christine estimate DuPont's "true" environmental liability? Could she use the environmental expenditure and liability data to improve her estimate?

4. What incentives does DuPont have to increase its level of environmental disclosures? What incentives does DuPont have to not increase its environmental disclosures? Why did DuPont provide environmental disclosures that exceed those required by GAAP?

5. Does DuPont's stock price reflect the company's unrecognized environmental liability? What risks does Christine's large company fund face if she acquires the DuPont stock? Is the market biased towards highly publicized environmental events such as the spillage by the Exxon Valdez or Union Carbide's Bhopal incident?

Exhibit 1
E.I. DuPont de Nemours
Consolidated Financial Statements

A. Consolidated Balance Sheets (Condensed):1992-1995

(Dollars in Millions)

| | December 31 | | | |
	1992	1993	1994	1995
ASSETS				
Current Assets	$12,228	$10,899	$11,108	$10,955
Property, Plant and Equipment (net)	21,882	21,423	21,120	21,341
Investments and Other Assets	4,760	4,731	4,664	5,016
TOTAL ASSETS	$38,870	$37,053	$36,892	$37,312
LIABILITIES AND STOCK-HOLDERS' EQUITY				
Current Liabilities	$10,226	$ 9,439	$ 7,565	$12,731
Long-Term Liabilities and Deferred Taxes	16,879	16,384	16,505	16,145
Stockholders' Equity	11,765	11,230	12,822	8,436
TOTAL LIABILITIES AND STOCKHOLDERS' EQUITY	$38,870	$37,053	$36,892	$37,312

B. Consolidated Income Statements (Condensed):1992-1995

(Dollars in Millions)

| | For the Year | | | |
	1992	1993	1994	1995
Sales (net)	$ 38,352	$ 37,841	$ 40,221	$ 43,222
Cost of Goods Sold	(21,856)	(21,396)	(21,810)	(23,363)
General Selling & Administrative Expenses	(8,091)	(7,635)	(7,255)	(7,115)
Other Gains and Loses	(6,594)	(7,852)	(6,774)	(7,354)
Earnings Before Income Taxes	$ 1,811	$ 958	$ 4,382	$ 5,390
Income Taxes	(836)	(392)	(1,655)	(2,097)
Extraordinary Items[*]	(4,902)	(11)	--	--
Net Income	($3,927)	$ 555	$ 2,727	$ 3,293

---

[*] None of the extraordinary items relate to environmental issues.

Exhibit 2
DuPont Toxic Release Inventory
(In Millions Of Pounds)[**]

Toxic Release Inventory (millions of pounds)

DU PONT U.S. CHEMICALS & SPECIALTIES (C & S)

	1987	1988	1989	1990	1991
RELEASES[1]					
Air[2]	60.9	55.6	52.7	46.4	44.7
Water	1.7	1.5	1.9	1.4	1.4
Land	1.4	4.4	0.6	0.7	0.3
RELEASES TO ENVIRONMENT	64.0	61.5	55.2	8.5	46.4
Injection Wells[3]	175.0	181.5	196.5	166.5	186.9
TOTAL RELEASES	239.0	243.0	251.7	215.0	233.3
TRANSFERS[4]					
Off Site	22.9	25.6	25.2	22.1	19.0
POTW[5]	5.5	2.6	2.1	2.4	1.8
TOTAL TRANSFERS	28.4	28.2	27.3	24.5	20.8
TOTAL C& S	267.4	271.2	279.0	239.5	254.1

CONOCO NORTH AMERICAN REFINING

	1987	1988	1989	1990	1991
Air	1.9	1.7	1.3	.9	1.1
Water	.01	.03	.03	.02	.17
Land	.15	.07	.04	.03	.05
TOTAL REFINING	2.1	1.8	1.4	1.0	1.3

[**] (Source: DuPont Environmental Report, 1992)

118

Exhibit 3
E.I. DuPont de Nemours
1992 Annual Report Environmental Disclosure

Management's Discussion and Analysis

Environmental Matters

The company complies worldwide with current government regulations and internal standards relating to the protection of the environment. Compliance with these increasingly stringent environmental regulations usually results in higher expenditures, both capital and expense.

An estimated $300 million was spent for environmental capital projects in 1992, with 1993 authorizations for environmental-related capital projects currently forecast at $400 million. Such amounts may increase in future years. Estimated pre-tax environmental expenses, including accruals for certain remediation activities (described below), totaled about $900 million in 1992, 1991, and 1990. Environmental operating expenses may increase over the next several years as new pollution control equipment is installed.

The company accrues for certain environmental remediation activities related to past operations, including Superfund cleanup and Resource Conservation and Recovery Act compliance activities, for which commitments have been made and reasonable cost estimates are possible. During 1992, the company accrued 180 million for such activities, compared with $130 million in 1991 and $135 million in 1990. Actual expenditures related to the accrual were $121 million in 1992, $91 million in 1991 and $52 million in 1990. The company's balance sheet at December 31, 1992 reflects an accrual for remediation costs of $465 million, compared to $426 million and $387 million at year-end 1991 and 1990, respectively.

Although future remediation expenditures could be significant, the effect on future financial results in not subject to reasonable estimation because considerable uncertainty exits, principally from evolving requirements and their effects on individual sites, selection of technology to meet compliance standards and the cost and timing of expenditures. These expenditures in the aggregate, however, are not expected to have a material impact on the company's competitive or financial position.

27. Commitments and Contingent Liabilities

The company is also subject to contingencies pursuant to environmental laws and regulations that in the future may require the company to take action to correct the effects on the environment of prior disposal or release of chemical or petroleum substances by the company or other parties. The company has accrued for certain environmental remediation activities for which commitments have been made and reasonable estimates are possible. Although future remediation expenditures could be significant, the effect on future financial results is not subject to reasonable estimation. Management does not anticipate, however, that they will have a material adverse effect on the consolidated financial position of the company.

Management's Discussion and Analysis

Environmental Matters

Recognizing that some risk to the environment is associated with the company's operations, as it is with other companies engaged in similar businesses, the company is committed to protecting the environment and has a program to reduce emissions and generation of hazardous waste. The company complies worldwide with government regulations relating to the protection of the environment. Expenditures to comply with these increasingly stringent environmental laws and regulations could be significant over the next ten to twenty years but are not expected to have a material impact on the company's competitive or financial position. If new laws and regulations containing more stringent requirements are enacted, expenditures may be higher than the assessments of potential environmental costs provided below.

New waste treatment facilities and pollution control and other equipment are being installed to satisfy legal requirements and to make progress in achieving the company's waste elimination and prevention goals. About $600 million was spent for capital projects related to environmental requirements and company goals in 1993. The company currently forecasts expenditures for environmental-related capital projects totaling about $600 million in 1994. These amounts may increase in future years. The company anticipates significant capital expenditures may be required over the next decade for treatment, storage, and disposal facilities for solid and hazardous waste. In addition, compliance costs under the 1990 Clean Air Act Amendments are expected to be significant. Environmental capital expenditures in 1992 and 1993 included expenditures in the Petroleum segment to meet federal requirements related to reformulated gasoline/clean fuels. Additional environmental capital expenditures are anticipated for plant air emission controls, primarily in the Chemicals and Petroleum segments; however, considerable uncertainty will remain with regard to estimates of capital expenditures until regulatory requirements are known.

Estimated pretax environmental expenses charged to current operations, including the remediation accruals discussed below, totaled about $1 billion in 1993, as compared to $900 million in 1992 and 1991. These expenses include operating, maintenance, and depreciation costs for solid waste treatment, storage and disposal facilities and for air and water pollution control facilities; costs incurred in conducting environmental research activities; and other matters. The largest of these expenses results from the operation of water pollution control facilities (related to compliance with the Clean Water Act and the operation of solid waste management facilities, each of which accounts for about one quarter of the total. More than 30 percent of total annual expenses relate to the company's Chemicals, Fibers, Polymers, and Diversified Businesses segments in the United States, primarily the Chemicals and Polymers segments. Expenses may increase over the next several years as a result of additional operating expenses associated with expected new pollution prevention and control equipment.

The company accrues for certain environmental remediation activities relating to past operations, including those under the Comprehensive Environmental Response, Compensation and Liability Act (CERCLA, often referred to as Superfund) and the Resource Conservation and Recovery Act (RCRA) described below, when it is probable that a liability has been incurred and reasonable estimates can be made. Accrued liabilities are exclusive of claims against third parties and are not discounted. During 1993, the company accrued $183 million for environmental remediation activities, compared to $160 million and $130 million in 1992 and 1991, respectively. At December 31, 1993, the company's balance sheet included an accrued liability of $522 million as compared to $465 million and $426 million at year-end 1992 and 1991, respectively. Expenditures for such previously accrued remediation activities were $126 million in 1993, $121 million in 1992 and $91 million in 1991.

Notes to Financial Statements (dollars in millions, except per share)

1. Summary of Significant Account Policies

DuPont observes the generally accepted accounting principles described below. These, together with the other notes that follow, are an integral part of the consolidated financial statements.

Environmental Liabilities and Expenditures

Accruals for environmental matters are recorded in operating expenses when it is probable that a liability has been incurred and the amount of the liability can be reasonably estimated. Accrued liabilities are exclusive of claims against third parties and are not discounted.

In general, costs related to environmental remediation are charged to expense. Environmental costs are capitalized if the costs increase the value of the property and/or mitigate or prevent contamination from future operations.

27. Commitments and Contingent Liabilities

The company is also subject to contingencies pursuant to environmental laws and regulations that in the future may require the company to take action to correct the effects on the environment of prior disposal or release of chemical or petroleum substances by the company or other parties. The company has accrued for certain environmental remediation activities consistent with the policy set forth in Note 1. Although future remediation accruals and expenditures could be significant, the effect on future financial results is not subject to reasonable estimation. Management does not anticipate, however, that they will have a material adverse effect on the consolidated financial position of the company.

1994 Management's Discussion and Analysis (excerpt)

Environmental Matters

The company operates about 150 manufacturing facilities, five petroleum refineries, 20 natural gas processing plants and numerous product-handling and distribution facilities around the world, all of which are significantly affected by a broad array of laws and regulations relating to the protection of the environment. It is the company's policy to comply fully with or to exceed all legal requirements worldwide. In addition, since some risk to the environment is associated with the company's operations, as it is with other companies engaged in similar businesses, voluntary programs are in place to minimize that risk. These programs are designed to reduce air emissions, curtail the generation of hazardous waste, decrease the volume of wastewater discharges and improve the energy efficiency of operations. The cost of complying with increasingly complex environmental laws and regulations, as well as the company's own internal programs, is significant, and will continue to be so for the foreseeable future, but is not expected to have a material impact on the company's competitive or financial position. The enactment of broader or more stringent environmental laws or regulations in the future, however, could lead to an upward reassessment of the potential environmental costs provided below.

New waste treatment facilities and pollution control and other equipment are routinely installed to satisfy both legal requirements and the company's waste elimination and pollution prevention goals. About $400 million was spent for capital projects related to environmental requirements and company goals in 1994. The company currently estimates expenditures for environmental-related capital projects will total about the same in 1995. The company anticipates significant capital expenditures may be required over the next decade for treatment, storage and disposal facilities for solid and hazardous waste and for compliance with the 1990 Amendments to the Clean Air Act (CAA). For example, environmental capital costs in 1993 and 1994 related to the CAA Amendments included expenditures in the Petroleum segment to meet federal requirements for reformulated gasoline/clean fuels, and additional environmental capital expenditures are anticipated for plant air emission controls, primarily in the Chemicals and Petroleum segments. Although considerable uncertainty will remain with regard to future estimates of capital expenditures until all new CAA regulatory requirements are known, related capital costs over the next two years are currently estimated to total approximately $20 million.

Estimated pretax environmental expenses charged to current operations totaled about $950 million in 1994, as compared to $1 billion in 1993 and $900 million in 1992. These expenses included the remediation accruals discussed below, operating, maintenance and depreciation costs for solid waste, air and water pollution control facilities and costs incurred in conducting environmental research activities. The largest of these expenses resulted from the operation of water pollution control facilities and solid waste management facilities, each of which accounted for about $200 million. About 75 percent of total annual expenses resulted from the operations of the company's Chemicals, Fibers, Polymers and Diversified Businesses segments in the United States, primarily the Chemicals and Polymers segments. Expenses are expected to increase over the next several years as a result of additional operating costs associated with new pollution prevention and control equipment.

Remediation Accruals

The Comprehensive Environmental Response, Compensation and Liability Act (CERCLA, often referred to as Superfund) and the Resource Conservation and Recovery Act (RCRA) both require that the company undertake certain remediation activities at sites where the company conducts or once conducted operations or at sites where company-generated waste was disposed. DuPont accrues for those remediation activities when it is probable that a liability has been incurred and reasonable estimates can be made. Accrued liabilities are exclusive of claims against third parties and are not discounted. During 1994 the company accrued $185 million for environmental remediation activities, compared to $183 million and $160 million in 1993 and 1992, respectively. At December 31, 1994, the company's balance sheet included an accrued liability of $616 million as compared to $522 million and $465 million at year-end 1993 and 1992, respectively. Approximately 75 percent of the company's environmental accrual is attributable to RCRA and similar remediation liabilities and 25 percent to CERCLA liabilities. Expenditures for such previously accrued remediation activities were $91 million in 1994, $126 million in 1993 and $121 million in 1992.

The company's assessment of the potential impact of these two principal remediation statutes is subject to considerable uncertainty due to the complex, ongoing and evolving process of generating estimates of remediation costs. The various stages of remediation include initial broad-based analysis of a site, on-site investigation, feasibility studies to select from among various remediation methods, approval by applicable authorities and, finally, the actual implementation of the remediation plan. Remediation activities occur over a relatively long period of time and vary in cost substantially from site to site depending on the mix of unique site characteristics, the development of new remediation technologies and the evolving regulatory framework. The company's assessment of those costs is a continuous process which takes into account the factors affecting each specific site. DuPont Environmental Remediation Services, a wholly owned subsidiary, provides technical capability to address the company's remediation needs in a cost-effective manner, while protecting human health and the environment.

RCRA, as amended in 1984, provides for extensive regulation of the treatment, storage and disposal of hazardous waste. The regulations currently provide that companies seeking to periodically renew RCRA permits, or close facilities with permits, must, as a condition of renewal or closure, undertake certain corrective measures to remediate contamination caused by prior operations. The RCRA corrective action program affects the company differently than the CERCLA program in that the cost of RCRA corrective action activities is typically borne solely by the company. The company anticipates that significant ongoing expenditures for RCRA corrective actions may be required over the next two decades. Annual expenditures for the near term are not expected to vary significantly from the range of such expenditures over the past few years. Longer term, expenditures are subject to considerable uncertainty and may fluctuate significantly, perhaps between $50 million and $300 million in any one year. The company's expenditures associated with RCRA and similar remediation activities were approximately $70 million in 1994, $90 million in 1993 and $103 million in 1992.

The company from time to time receives requests for information or notices of potential liability from the Environmental Protection Agency (EPA) and state environmental agencies, alleging that the company is a "potentially responsible party" (PRP) under CERCLA or equivalent state legislation. In addition, the company has on occasion been made a party to cost recovery litigation by those agencies. These requests, notices and lawsuits assert potential liability for remediation costs of various waste treatment or disposal sites that are not company owned but allegedly contain wastes attributable to the company from past operations. As of December 31, 1994, the company was aware of potential liability under CERCLA or state laws at about 310 sites around the United States. The CERCLA or state remediation process is actively under way at one stage or another at about 145 of those sites. In addition, the company has resolved its liability at 48 sites, either by completing necessary remedial actions with other PRPs or by participating in "de minimis buyouts" with other PRPs whose waste, like the company's, only represented a small fraction of the total waste present at a site.

The company's expenditures associated with CERCLA or state remediation activities were approximately $21 million in 1994, $36 million in 1993 and $18 million in 1992. Over the next decade the company may incur significant costs under CERCLA. Considerable uncertainty exists with respect to these costs, and under the most adverse circumstances potential liability may exceed amounts accrued as of December 31, 1994. The company's share of the remediation cost at these sites in many instances cannot be precisely estimated due to the large number of PRPs involved, the scarcity of reliable data pertaining to many of these sites, uncertainty as to how the laws and regulations may be applied to these sites and the multiple choices and costs associated with diverse technologies that may be used in remediation. For most sites, the company's potential liability will be significantly less than the total site remediation costs because the percentage of material attributable to the company versus that attributable to other PRPs is relatively low. There are a few sites where the company is a major participant, but neither the cost to the company of remediation at those sites, nor at all CERCLA sites in the aggregate, is expected to have a material impact on the competitive or financial position of the company. The process of estimating CERCLA remediation costs, the financial viability of other PRPs and the PRPs' respective shares of liability is ongoing. Often these estimates are performed by third parties and, thus far, have not been subject to material uncertainty or dispute. Moreover, other PRPs at sites where the company is a party typically have the financial strength to meet their obligations and, where they do not, or where certain PRPs cannot be located, the company's own share of liability has not materially increased. The company's general experience has been that, in most cases, its share of estimated costs at any given site has trended downward as this process has matured.

Although future remediation expenditures in excess of current reserves could be significant, the effect on future financial results is not subject to reasonable estimation because considerable uncertainty exists as to the cost and timing of expenditures. The company is actively pursuing claims against insurers with respect to RCRA and CERCLA liabilities. Potential recoveries in this litigation have not been offset against the accruals discussed above.

1994 Summary of Significant Accounting Policies Footnote:
Environmental Liabilities and Expenditures

Accruals for environmental matters are recorded in operating expenses when it is probable that a liability has been incurred and the amount of the liability can be reasonably estimated. Accrued liabilities are exclusive of claims against third parties and are not discounted.

In general, costs related to environmental remediation are charged to expense. Environmental costs are capitalized if the costs increase the value of the property and/or mitigate or prevent contamination from future operations.

1994 Footnote on Commitments and Contingencies (excerpt):

The company is also subject to contingencies pursuant to environmental laws and regulations that in the future may require the company to take action to correct the effects on the environment of prior disposal practices or releases of chemical or petroleum substances by the company or other parties. The company has accrued for certain environmental remediation activities consistent with the policy set forth in Note 1. At December 31, 1994, such accrual amounted to $616 and, in management's opinion, was appropriate based on existing facts and circumstances. Under the most adverse circumstances, however, this potential liability could be significantly higher. In the event that future remediation expenditures are in excess of amounts accrued, management does not anticipate that they will have a material adverse effect on the consolidated financial position of the company.

1995 Management's Discussion and Analysis (excerpt)

Environmental Matters

DuPont operates manufacturing facilities, petroleum refineries, natural gas processing plants and product-handling and distribution facilities around the world. Each facility is significantly affected by a broad array of laws and regulations relating to the protection of the environment, and it is the company's policy to fully meet or exceed legal and regulatory requirements wherever it operates. Although some risk to the environment is associated with the company's operations, as it is with other companies engaged in similar operations, facilities are run in accordance with the highest standards of safe operation regardless of where they are located even though those standards may exceed the requirements of local law. DuPont has also implemented voluntary programs to reduce air emissions, curtail the generation of hazardous waste, decrease the volume of wastewater discharges and improve the efficiency of energy use. The cost of complying with increasingly complex environmental laws and regulations, as well as the company's own internal programs, is significant and will continue to be so for the foreseeable future. It is not, however, expected to have a material impact on the company's competitive or financial position. The enactment of broader or more stringent environmental laws or regulations in the future, however, could lead to an upward reassessment of the potential environmental costs discussed below.

In 1995 DuPont spent about $300 million for environmental capital projects either required by the law or necessary to meet the company's internal waste elimination and pollution prevention goals. The company currently estimates expenditures for environmental-related capital projects will total $400 million in 1996. Significant capital expenditures may be required over the next decade for treatment, storage and disposal facilities for solid and hazardous waste and for compliance with the 1990 Amendments to the Clean Air Act (CAA), although thus far expenditures related to the CAA Amendments have been relatively modest, amounting to about $2 million in 1995. Considerable uncertainty will remain, however, with regard to future estimates of capital expenditures until all new CAA regulatory requirements are known. Related capital costs over the next two years are currently estimated to total approximately $6 million.

Estimated pretax environmental expenses charged to current operations totaled about $800 million, before insurance recoveries, in 1995 as compared to $950 million in 1994 and $1 billion in 1993. These expenses include the remediation accruals discussed below, operating, maintenance and depreciation costs for solid waste, air and water pollution control facilities and the costs of environmental research activities. The largest of these expenses resulted from the operation of wastewater treatment facilities and solid waste management facilities, each of which accounted for about $200 million. About 80 percent of total annual expenses resulted from the operations of the company's Chemicals, Fibers, Polymers and Diversified Businesses segments in the United States.

Remediation Accruals

DuPont accrues for remediation activities when it is probable that a liability has been incurred and reasonable estimates of the liability can be made. These accrued liabilities exclude claims against third parties and are not discounted. Much of this liability results from the Comprehensive Environmental Response, Compensation and Liability Act (CERCLA, often referred to as Superfund), the Resource Conservation and Recovery Act (RCRA) and similar state laws that require the company to undertake certain investigative and remedial activities at sites where the company conducts or once conducted operations or at sites where company-generated waste was disposed. The accrual includes a number of sites identified by the company that may require environmental remediation but which are not currently the subject of CERCLA, RCRA or state enforcement activities. Over the next one to two decades the company may incur significant costs under both CERCLA and RCRA. Considerable uncertainty exists with respect to these costs and under adverse changes in circumstances, potential liability may exceed amounts accrued as of December 31, 1995.

It is difficult to develop reasonable estimates of future CERCLA and RCRA site remediation costs because of the inherent uncertainty associated with the remediation process. Remediation activities tend to occur over a relatively long period of time and vary in cost substantially from site to site depending on the mix of unique site characteristics, evolving remediation technologies, diverse regulatory agencies and enforcement policies and the presence or absence of potentially liable third parties. Nevertheless, the company's assessment of such costs is a continuous process that takes into account the relevant factors affecting each specific site. At December 31, 1995, the company's balance sheet included an accrued liability of $602 million as compared to $616 million and $522 million at year-end 1994 and 1993, respectively. Approximately 77 percent of the company's environmental reserve at December 31, 1995 was attributable to RCRA and similar remediation liabilities and 23 percent to CERCLA liabilities. During 1995, remediation accruals of $82 million, offset by $161 million in insurance proceeds, resulted in a credit to income of $79 million, compared to accruals of $185 million and $183 million in 1994 and 1993, respectively.

Remediation Expenditures

RCRA extensively regulates the treatment, storage and disposal of hazardous waste. The law requires that companies operating hazardous waste treatment, storage or disposal facilities be permitted and must, as part of such permit, undertake an assessment of environmental conditions at the facility. If conditions warrant, the companies may be required to remediate contamination caused by prior operations. The RCRA corrective action program has a substantially different effect on the company than does CERCLA in that the cost of RCRA corrective action activities is typically borne solely by the company.

The company anticipates that significant ongoing expenditures for RCRA corrective actions may be required over the next two decades, although annual expenditures for the near term are not expected to vary significantly from the range of such expenditures over the past few years. Longer term, expenditures are subject to considerable uncertainty and may fluctuate significantly. The company's expenditures associated with RCRA and similar remediation activities were approximately $94 million in 1995, $70 million in 1994 and $90 million in 1993.

The company from time to time receives requests for information or notices of potential liability from the Environmental Protection Agency (EPA) and state environmental agencies alleging that the company is a "potentially responsible party" (PRP) under CERCLA or an equivalent state statute. In addition, the company has on occasion been made a party to cost recovery litigation by those agencies or by private parties. These requests, notices and lawsuits assert potential liability for remediation costs at various waste treatment or disposal sites that typically are not company owned but allegedly contain wastes attributable to the company's past operations. As of December 31, 1995, the company had been notified of potential liability under CERCLA or state law at about 327 sites around the United States. The remediation process is actively under way at one stage or another at about 158 of those sites. In addition, the company has resolved its liability at 73 sites, either by completing remedial actions with other PRPs or by participating in "de minimis buyouts" with other PRPs whose waste, like the company's, represented only a small fraction of the total waste present at a site. The company received notice of potential liability at 16 new sites during 1995 compared with 17 similar notices in 1994 and 24 in 1993. The company's expenditures associated with CERCLA and similar state remediation activities were approximately $25 million in 1995, $21 million in 1994 and $36 million in 1993.

For most Superfund sites, the company's potential liability will be significantly less than the total site remediation costs because the percentage of waste attributable to the company versus that attributable to all other PRPs is relatively low. The process of estimating CERCLA remediation costs, the financial viability of other PRPs and the PRPs' respective shares of liability is ongoing, and, thus far, the estimates have not been subject to material uncertainty or dispute. Moreover, other PRPs at sites where the company is a party typically have the financial strength to meet their obligations and, where they do not, or where certain PRPs cannot be located, the company's own share of liability has not materially increased. The company's general experience has been that, in most cases, its share of estimated costs at any given site has trended downward over time. There are relatively few sites where the company is a major participant, and neither the cost to the company of remediation at those sites, nor at all CERCLA sites in the aggregate, is expected to have a material impact on the competitive or financial position of the company.

Total expenditures for previously accrued remediation activities under CERCLA, RCRA and similar state laws were $119 million in 1995, $91 million in 1994 and $126 million in 1993. Although future remediation expenditures in excess of current reserves is possible, the effect on future financial results is not subject to reasonable estimation because of the considerable uncertainty that exists as to the cost and timing of expenditures. The company is actively pursuing claims against insurers with respect to CERCLA and RCRA liabilities.

1995 Summary of Significant Accounting Policies Footnote:
Environmental Liabilities and Expenditures

Accruals for environmental matters are recorded in operating expenses when it is probable that a liability has been incurred and the amount of the liability can be reasonably estimated. Accrued liabilities are exclusive of claims against third parties and are not discounted.

Costs related to environmental remediation are charged to expense. Environmental costs are capitalized if the costs increase the value of the property and/or mitigate or prevent contamination from future operations.

1995 Footnote on Commitments and Contingencies (excerpt):

...The company is also subject to contingencies pursuant to environmental laws and regulations that in the future may require the company to take further action to correct the effects on the environment of prior disposal practices or releases of chemical or petroleum substances by the company or other parties. The company has accrued for certain environmental remediation activities consistent with the policy set forth in Note 1. At December 31, 1995, such accrual amounted to $602 and, in management's opinion, was appropriate based on existing facts and circumstances. Under adverse changes in circumstances, potential liability may exceed amounts accrued. In the event that future remediation expenditures are in excess of amounts accrued, management does not anticipate that they will have a material adverse effect on the consolidated financial position of the company.

Exhibit 7
U.S. Generally Accepted Accounting Principles for Environmental Liability Disclosure

As of 1992, environmental uncertainties were covered by Statement of Financial Accounting Standards No. 5, *Accounting for Contingencies*. Companies were required to accrue a liability if (a) information available prior to issue of the financial statement indicates that it is probable that an asset has been impaired or a liability has been incurred at the date of the financial statements, and (b) the amount of the loss can be reasonably estimated. FASB Interpretation No. 14, *Reasonable Estimation of the Amount of a Loss* (1976) indicates that a reasonable estimate might be a range of loss, rather than a single dollar estimate. In most cases, the liability may not be offset against planned recoveries from third parties, such as insurance companies or other Potentially Responsible Parties (According to FASB Interpretation No. 39, *Offsetting of Amounts Related to Certain Contracts*, which was issued in 1992.) For year-ends beginning on December 15, 1996, Statement of Position 96-1, *Environmental Remediation Liabilities* requires that environmental liabilities should be accrued in accordance with FASB Statement No. 5, and that the accrual should include (a) incremental direct costs of the remediation effort, as well as (b) costs of compensation and benefits for remediation workers. The amount to be accrued should include the entity's share of liability for a specific site, plus the entity's allocated share of the cost to remediate at the site that is the responsibility other PRP's or governmental units, but that will not be paid by them. The estimate should be based on the entity's current estimate of costs to remediate, discounted by an appropriate interest rate if the timing and amounts are reliably determinable.

Appendix I
U.S. Federal Environmental Remediation and Pollution Control Laws

The Comprehensive Environmental Response, Compensation, and Liability Act (CERCLA) of 1980. This "Superfund" law established a program of identifying sites throughout the United States where hazardous substances present a danger to the environment; it was also designed to ensure that (a) such sites be remediated by those responsible, or by the government; (b) to compensate governmental entities for damages to natural resources caused by hazardous substances; (c) to develop a procedure for claims against Potentially Responsible Parties (PRP's) by parties who have spent money to remediate such sites; and (d) to create a trust fund to cover the costs associated with orphan sites and the costs incurred while awaiting reimbursement by PRP's. The original Superfund was $1.6 billion.

Under CERCLA, liability for remediation of Superfund sites is both strict, and joint and several. Strict liability means that PRP's of a hazardous waste site are liable for remediation costs regardless of fault. Liability is also joint and several. This means that if multiple parties contributed to a hazardous waste site, each individual party may be responsible for cleaning up the entire site; if the other PRP's are unable to contribute, even if that party was responsible for only a small part of the waste at the site and did nothing improper.

The Superfund Amendments and Reauthorization Act (SARA) of 1986. This second "Superfund" law provides more detailed standards for remediation and settlement of costs, broadened criminal sanctions against PRP's, and increased the Superfund to $8.5 billion. This increased trust fund is supported by taxes on the petroleum industry and a tax on corporate alternative minimum tax income.

The Resource Conservation and Recovery Act of 1976 (RCRA). This legislation provides comprehensive U.S. government regulation of hazardous wastes from the point of generation to final disposal. All generators and transporters of hazardous waste and owners and operators of hazardous waste treatment, storage or disposal facilities must comply with this Act. Generators of hazardous waste must track the types and amounts of hazardous waste generated and must meet requirements regarding packaging and labeling, annual reporting of amounts, and extensive technological standards for managing this waste. RCRA also contains provisions for closing hazardous waste facilities, at the owners' expense.

Appendix II
Corporate Environmental Plan (CEP)

To balance environmental commitments with business imperatives, DuPont defined a methodology for rank-ordering environmental projects by considering cost/benefit, regulatory and competitive factors. This approach, called the Corporate Environmental Plan (CEP), utilizes a general Pareto approach to cost-effectiveness, which attempts to achieve an 80% reduction in total waste for 20% of the total implementation cost. This approach forms the basis for an Environmental Index (EI) for the cost-effectiveness of any given initiative. The EI measures the cost per pound of reduction in TRI releases, and is normalized around a value of 1.0. Any initiative with an EI of 1.0 or lower is considered efficient, while EI values greater than 1.0 constitute marginally efficient projects. The timing of implementation of these initiatives is linked to both business viability (from a competitive standpoint) and risk-based prioritization.

One of the benefits of project prioritization is that it offers a consistent and formal way to evaluate trade-offs between two currently proposed initiatives that require capital investment. For instance, the desirability of reducing the last drop of waste A can be weighed against the costs and benefits of reducing the first drop of waste B. Likewise, prioritization can extend to evaluating trade-offs over time (e.g., between current environmental initiatives and those addressing future environmental regulations). Additionally, since prioritization is in terms of waste generated, cross-media effects are taken into account.

An inevitable shortcoming of the prioritization procedure is its inability to identify synergistic projects. Each initiative is evaluated separately. This weakness can be offset, however, by identifying potentially synergistic projects as the projects and initiatives are formulated.

Overview

This case focuses on analyzing financial statement data from four non-U.S. companies in the energy industry.[1] The companies -- The British Petroleum Company PLC, Royal Dutch Petroleum Company, The Shell Transport and Trading Company PLC, and Total S.A. -- have some common characteristics. The four firms are all classified as principally operating in petroleum refining (Standard Industrial Classification (SIC) 2911) on Standard and Poor's Compustat database. The common stock of each of the four firms are listed on the New York Stock Exchange and traded as American Depository Receipts (ADR) under the symbols BP, RD, SC and TOT, respectively. Thus, U.S. investors are provided with a low-cost method of owning shares in these international companies. Information about each of the company's recent stock price can be found on the Internet using the company's ticker symbol at StockMasters' web site (www.stockmaster.com). In addition, British Petroleum and Total have web pages on the Internet (www.bp.com and www.total.com) that provide additional information about their business activities. With regard to their business organization, the firms are all vertically integrated since they are involved in both upstream (i.e., exploration and production) as well as downstream activities (i.e., refining and marketing).

Yet, there are also differences between the four firms. For example, they are headquartered in different cities throughout Europe. They also differ in size. Royal Dutch reported $65.923 billion in sales revenues in 1995, more than double Total's sales revenues of $27.736 billion.

Company Descriptions

The British Petroleum Company PLC was registered in the United Kingdom in 1909 as Anglo-Persian Oil Co., Ltd. to develop oil resources in what is now known as Iran. The company's name was changed to Anglo-Iranian Oil Co., Ltd. in 1935, and to The British Petroleum Company Limited in 1954, before finally adopting the present name in 1982. The company's business is conducted by several operating units. BP Exploration is responsible for the Group's upstream activities as well as its midstream activities (i.e., processing and marketing natural gas and the management of the crude oil and gas pipeline assets). The downstream activities (i.e., the supply and trading, refining, marketing and transportation of crude oil and petroleum to wholesale and retail customers) are undertaken by BP Oil. BP Oil transports crude oil to its refineries by ship and through pipelines linking its refineries with import terminals and oil fields. Another unit, BP Shipping, owns or operates an international fleet of crude oil and oil products tankers and a LPG vessel, carrying cargoes for the company and for third parties; it also operates support vessels for offshore exploration and production. BP Chemicals is a major producer of chemicals in the USA, Europe and other parts of the world and also supplies, markets and distributes chemical products to bulk, wholesale and retail customers.

---

* This case was prepared by Graeme Rankine for the purpose of class discussion. Copyright © 1997 by the American Graduate School of International Management. All rights reserved.

[1] The data used in the case was obtained from, and used with permission of, Compustat PC Plus, an analytic software system integrating financial statement and market information produced by Standard & Poor's Compustat, Englewood, CO.

Royal Dutch Petroleum Company was incorporated in the Netherlands in 1890 as Royal Dutch Co. to work petroleum wells in the Netherlands Indies, now known as Indonesia. In 1907, the company and Shell Transport and Trading Co., PLC of the United Kingdom merged to form the Royal Dutch/Shell Group of Companies. The Royal Dutch/Shell Group is the holding company for the group's two operating companies, Royal Dutch Petroleum, which controls 60% of the groups' overall assets and Shell Transport and Trading Company PLC, which controls the other 40%. The company operates through five different operational divisions: oil and gas, natural gas, chemicals, coal, and research.

The Shell Transport and Trading Company PLC was incorporated in Great Britain in 1897 to consolidate various oil companies, owning tank steamers and plants and engaged in the wholesale business of transportation, distribution, and trade in petroleum products. The company is a holding company which owns, directly or indirectly, investments in the numerous companies constituting the Royal Dutch/Shell Group of companies ("The Group"). Shell Transport and Trading holds interests in service companies which provide advice and services to other Group and associated companies and operating companies which operate in oil and natural gas, chemicals, coal, metals and other businesses in many countries.

Total S.A., headquartered in Paris, France is one of the largest firms in the international energy and specialty chemicals business and operates in over 80 countries around the world. The company was founded by a syndicate of industrialists and financiers as Compagnie Francaise des Petroles (CFP), an oil exploration and production company. The name was changed to TOTAL Compagnie Francaise des Petroles (Total CFP) in 1985 and to the present name in 1991. The company's shares were listed on the New York Stock Exchange (NYSE) in the form of ADRs in 1991. Total manufactures and trades in all solid, liquid or gas fuels, petroleum and its derivatives, motor fuels, lubricants, fuel oils and miscellaneous by-products. The company organized into three profit centers: upstream, downstream and chemicals. Upstream includes exploration and production, and the coal, gas and electricity activities. Downstream activities include refining, marketing, trading and shipping, while chemicals includes rubber processing and the four coatings businesses (resins, inks, adhesives and paints).

Questions:

Part A:

1. Consider Tables 1 and 2. Evaluate each company in terms of growth in sales, operating profit, net income (adjusted net income plus preferred dividends), total assets, and stockholders' equity over the period 1993-1995. Which company experienced the fastest growth? Can a company grow too fast? What are the consequences of fast growth?

2. Consider Table 3 which presents the common size balance sheets [i.e., all items shown as a percentage of total assets]. Why are the values reported in the common size balance sheet for Royal Dutch and Shell the same? [Hint: Review the descriptions of the two companies' ownership structure above.] Compare 1993 to 1995. Why did Total's current assets increase from 45.52 percent to 49.72 percent? Did the other three firms also experience an increase in current assets? Can a company have too much invested in current assets? Why did British Petroleum's total liabilities decrease from 68.57 percent to 63.48 percent? Did the other three firms experience an increase or a decrease in total liabilities? Is this situation good or bad? Why?

3.   Consider Table 4 which presents the common size income statements [i.e., all items shown as a percentage of sales]. Compare 1993 with 1995. Why is Total's gross profit around 8 percent, yet the gross profit for each of the other firms is greater than than 20 percent? Why did Total's adjusted net income (after deducting preferred dividends) decrease from 2.19 percent to 1.66 percent? Did the other three firms experience an increase or a decrease in adjusted net income? What were the main causes of the change in adjusted net income for the other firms?

4.   Consider Table 5 showing the statement of cash flows. Compare 1993 with 1995. Why did Shell's operating cash flow increase from $4,975.0 million to $5,951.0 million? Did the other three firms experience an increase in operating cash flows? If so, why? In 1993, Total's operating cash flow of $2,170.4 million was less than the $2,316.1 million spent on investing activities. Where did Total get the additional cash to finance the investment? Can this situation continue indefinitely? What have the other firms done with the excess of operating cash flow over cash flow from investing?

Part B:

Consider the definitions of some common performance indicators as shown in Exhibit 1. For Table 7, compute the values of the missing ratios for 1995 using the data in Tables 1-6 before answering the following questions:

1.   Which firm has the most (least) liquidity at December 31, 1995? Can a firm have too much liquidity? Too little liquidity?

2.   Which firm is best (worst) at managing its assets at December 31, 1995? Can a firm have receivables that are too low?

3.   Which firm is the most (least) financially leveraged at December 31, 1995? Can a firm have too much debt? Too little debt?

4.   Which firm experienced the best (worst) profitability during 1995? Consider the Dupont analysis. What were the factors that caused the change in return on equity for each company during 1993-1995?

5.   Which investors should be the happiest (unhappiest) at 1995 year-end? Why?

6.   Are any of the firms likely takeover candidates? Which firm is the most (least) likely to be taken over? Why?

7.   Why is the "book" value of stockholders' equity so different from the "market" value of stockholders' equity for these firms?

8.   Which firm would you predict to be the best (worst) performer for investors in 1996? In 1997? Test your predictions by looking up the recent stock price performance of the companies on Stockmaster's web site on the Internet (www.stockmaster.com).

Questions (continued)

<u>Part C</u>:

The financial data reported for these energy companies are converted to U.S. dollar amounts using a country-specific currency exchange rate. However, GAAP (Generally Accepted Accounting Principles) used in the U.S., U.K., the Netherlands and France are different from each other in many respects. For example, U.S. GAAP does not permit companies to revalue their assets upwards, but it is permitted in the other three countries.

1. Does the issue of differences in GAAP affect the answers you provided to questions 1, 2, 3, 4, 6 and 7 in Part B? Why or why not?

2. If you learn that the financial statement data in Tables 1-7 have been converted to U.S. GAAP, does this affect the answers you provided to questions 1, 2, 3, 4, 6 and 7 in Part B? Why or why not?

Exhibit 1
Definitions of Some Key Ratios

LIQUIDITY RATIOS:

Cash & Market Sec. to Total Assets	=	(Cash + Marketable Securities) / Total Assets
Acid Test Ratio	=	(Cash + Marketable Securities + Receivables) / Current Liabilities (CL)
Current Ratio	=	Current Assets / CL

ASSET MANAGEMENT:

Day's Receivable	=	365 / (Sales / Receivables)
Day's Inventory	=	365 / (Cost of Goods Sold / Inventories)
Asset Turnover	=	Sales / Total Assets

FINANCIAL LEVERAGE:

Debt to Total Assets	=	(CL + L-T Debt + Other L-T Debt) / Total Assets
Stockholders' Equity to Total assets	=	Stockholders' Equity / Total Assets
Long-term Debt to Stockholder's Equity	=	(L-T Debt + Other L-T Debt) / Stockholders' Equity
Coverage Ratio	=	Operating Profit / Interest Expense

PROFITABILITY:

Gross Margin Ratio	=	Gross Profit / Sales
Return on Sales	=	Net Income / Sales
		(Adj. Net Income + Preferred Dividends) / Sales)
Return on Assets (1)	=	Net Income / Total Assets
		(Adj. Net Income + Preferred Dividends) / Total Assets
Return on Assets (2)	=	Pretax Income / Total Assets
Return on Equity	=	Net Income / Stockholders' Equity
		(Adj. Net Income + Preferred Dividends) /Stockholders' Equity
Return on Common Equity	=	(Net Income - Preferred Dividends) / Common Stockholders' Equity
		Adj. Net Income / Common Stockholders' Equity

STOCK MARKET PERFORMANCE:

Dividend Yield	=	Cash Dividends / Market Price per Share (12/31)
Annual Common Stock Return	=	$(\text{Price}_t + \text{Divs}_t - \text{Price}_{t-1}) / \text{Price}_{t-1}$
Book-to-Market Ratio	=	Common Stockholders' Equity / (Market Price per Share * # Common Shares Outstanding)

DUPONT ANALYSIS:

Return on Equity	=	Return on Sales * Asset Turnover * Leverage
=	=	(Net Income / Sales) * (Sales / Assets) * (Assets / Stockholders' Equity)

137

Financial Analysis of International Energy Firms
Table 1

Financial Analysis of International Energy Firms

Table 1

ANNUAL BALANCE SHEET ($ MILLIONS)

	BRITISH PETROLEUM			ROYAL DUTCH			SHELL			TOTAL		
	Dec95	Dec94	Dec93	Dec95	Dec94	Dec93	Dec95	Dec94	Dec93	Dec95	Dec94	Dec93
ASSETS												
Cash & Equivalents	616.2	293.3	310.3	6,814.0	6,961.0	5,754.0	4,542.0	4,641.0	3,836.0	5,968.6	4,586.4	4,195.6
Net Receivables	7,141.7	6,639.4	5,245.1	9,656.0	8,190.0	7,300.0	6,437.0	5,459.0	4,866.0	4,749.3	4,024.3	3,316.4
Inventories	4,389.8	4,302.5	3,942.0	4,536.0	4,219.0	3,976.0	3,024.0	2,813.0	2,651.0	2,390.0	2,220.3	1,981.5
Prepaid Expenses	2,031.1	1,703.5	1,613.4	@CF	@CF	@CF	@CF	@CF	@CF	@CF	@CF	@CF
Other Current Assets	1,020.2	940.7	1,168.7	2,363.0	2,164.0	1,824.0	1,576.0	1,443.0	1,216.0	1,000.2	996.5	787.4
Total Current Assets	15,199.0	13,879.3	12,279.5	23,369.0	21,534.0	18,854.0	15,579.0	14,356.0	12,569.0	14,107.9	11,827.5	10,280.9
Gross Plant,Property & Equipment	66,856.8	63,034.9	59,622.9	82,492.0	75,747.0	70,226.0	54,995.0	50,499.0	46,817.0	20,600.5	18,145.7	15,680.2
Accumulated Depreciation	35,160.8	31,749.1	29,149.5	40,951.0	37,871.0	34,197.0	27,301.0	25,248.0	22,798.0	10,823.2	9,051.0	7,667.4
Net Plant,Property & Equipment	31,696.0	31,285.8	30,473.4	41,541.0	37,876.0	36,029.0	27,694.0	25,251.0	24,019.0	9,777.3	9,094.7	8,012.8
Investments at Equity	3,263.5	2,669.2	2,433.4	4,986.0	4,724.0	4,659.0	3,324.0	3,149.0	3,107.0	980.6	850.2	720.7
Other Investments	157.6	525.7	484.6	665.0	577.0	356.0	444.0	385.0	237.0	1,612.8	1,564.5	1,504.4
Intangibles	152.9	137.3	156.6	0.0	0.0	0.0	0.0	0.0	0.0	1,648.5	1,607.4	1,541.0
Deferred Charges	0.0	0.0	0.0	0.0	0.0	0.0	0.0	0.0	0.0	0.0	0.0	0.0
Other Assets	0.0	0.0	0.0	0.0	0.0	0.0	0.0	0.0	0.0	248.7	279.5	526.1
Total Assets	50,469.1	48,497.2	45,827.6	70,561.0	64,711.0	59,898.0	47,041.0	43,141.0	39,932.0	28,375.8	25,223.8	22,585.9
LIABILITIES												
Long Term Debt Due In One Year	@CF	837.7	817.1	989.0	912.0	980.0	660.0	608.0	654.0	449.9	487.4	424.6
Notes Payable	1,151.3	787.8	1,009.1	2,270.0	2,483.0	2,269.0	1,514.0	1,656.0	1,512.0	2,505.7	2,066.0	1,727.8
Accounts Payable	6,809.4	5,959.2	4,476.8	5,115.0	4,078.0	3,722.0	3,410.0	2,719.0	2,482.0	3,187.4	3,054.4	2,519.8
Taxes Payable	1,725.4	1,054.6	1,155.4	2,056.0	1,924.0	1,112.0	1,370.0	1,282.0	741.0	@CF	@CF	@CF
Accrued Expenses	2,717.5	2,375.9	2,309.3	2,533.0	2,235.0	2,191.0	1,689.0	1,490.0	1,460.0	403.9	346.5	319.2
Other Current Liabilities	2,730.0	2,383.7	2,579.7	5,972.0	5,230.0	4,528.0	3,981.0	3,487.0	3,019.0	2,343.2	1,783.8	1,589.5
Total Current Liabilities	15,133.5	13,398.8	12,347.4	18,935.0	16,862.0	14,802.0	12,624.0	11,242.0	9,868.0	8,890.0	7,738.1	6,581.0
Long Term Debt	7,425.6	8,899.8	10,555.2	4,409.0	3,571.0	3,675.0	2,940.0	2,381.0	2,451.0	5,063.5	4,267.2	4,066.8
Deferred Taxes	586.6	444.6	366.4	4,797.0	4,583.0	5,451.0	3,198.0	3,055.0	3,634.0	829.7	897.5	1,029.1
Investment Tax Credit	0.0	0.0	0.0	0.0	0.0	0.0	0.0	0.0	0.0	0.0	0.0	0.0
Minority Interest	168.5	170.0	147.8	1,864.0	1,128.0	938.0	1,242.0	752.0	625.0	736.8	703.1	623.6
Other Liabilities	8,725.1	8,335.1	8,008.0	5,287.0	4,882.0	4,077.0	3,525.0	3,254.0	2,718.0	2,117.4	1,889.5	1,605.1
Total Liabilities	32,039.2	31,248.3	31,424.8	35,292.0	31,026.0	28,943.0	23,529.0	20,684.0	19,296.0	17,637.4	15,495.4	13,905.5
EQUITY												
Preferred Stock - Redeemable	0.0	0.0	0.0	0.0	0.0	0.0	0.0	0.0	0.0	0.0	0.0	0.0
Preferred Stock - Nonredeemable	18.7	18.7	17.7	1.0	1.0	1.0	19.0	19.0	18.0	0.0	0.0	0.0
Total Preferred Stock	18.7	18.7	17.7	1.0	1.0	1.0	19.0	19.0	18.0	0.0	0.0	0.0
Common Stock	2,174.6	2,146.6	2,013.8	1,667.0	1,543.0	1,382.0	1,283.0	1,293.0	1,226.0	2,400.0	2,126.4	1,854.4
Capital Surplus	3,347.8	3,244.8	2,968.3	995.0	1.0	1.0	0.0	0.0	0.0	2,179.2	1,713.5	1,355.4
Retained Earnings	12,888.7	11,838.8	9,402.8	32,606.0	32,140.0	29,571.0	22,210.0	21,145.0	19,392.0	6,159.3	5,888.6	5,470.7
Less: Treasury Stock	0.0	0.0	0.0	0.0	0.0	0.0	0.0	0.0	0.0	0.0	0.0	0.0
Common Equity	18,411.1	17,230.2	14,384.9	35,268.0	33,684.0	30,954.0	23,493.0	22,438.0	20,618.0	10,738.4	9,728.4	8,680.4
Total Equity	18,429.8	17,248.9	14,402.7	35,269.0	33,685.0	30,955.0	23,512.0	22,457.0	20,636.0	10,738.5	9,728.4	8,680.4
Total Liabilities & Equity	50,469.0	48,497.2	45,827.5	70,561.0	64,711.0	59,898.0	47,041.0	43,141.0	39,932.0	28,375.8	25,223.9	22,586.0
Common Shares Outstanding	464.613	458.552	454.255	536.074	536.074	536.074	552.417	552.417	552.417	470.099	454.588	439.155

Financial Analysis of International Energy Firms
Table 2

	BRITISH PETROLEUM			ROYAL DUTCH			SHELL			ANNUAL INCOME STATEMENT ($ MILLIONS, EXCEPT PER SHARE) TOTAL		
	Dec95	Dec94	Dec93	Dec95	Dec94	Dec93	Dec95	Dec94	Dec93	Dec95	Dec94	Dec93
Sales	57,047.4	50,667.4	51,638.6	65,923.0	56,898.0	57,104.0	43,949.0	37,932.0	38,069.0	27,736.2	25,584.6	22,882.2
Cost of Goods Sold	43,950.8	39,076.2	39,116.8	47,334.0	41,299.0	42,236.0	31,557.0	27,533.0	28,157.0	25,189.2	23,545.4	21,004.9
Gross Profit	13,096.6	11,591.2	12,521.8	18,589.0	15,599.0	14,868.0	12,392.0	10,399.0	9,912.0	2,547.0	2,039.2	1,877.3
Selling, General, & Administrative Expense	5,389.4	4,680.3	5,664.7	7,364.0	6,662.0	6,745.0	4,909.0	4,441.0	4,496.0	@CF	@CF	@CF
Operating Income Before Depreciation	7,707.2	6,910.9	6,857.1	11,225.0	8,937.0	8,123.0	7,483.0	5,958.0	5,416.0	2,547.0	2,039.2	1,877.3
Depreciation, Depletion, & Amortization	3,220.0	3,333.9	3,856.3	4,870.0	4,138.0	3,710.0	3,246.0	2,759.0	2,474.0	1,308.7	1,115.7	974.6
Operating Profit	4,487.2	3,577.1	3,000.8	6,355.0	4,799.0	4,413.0	4,237.0	3,199.0	2,942.0	1,238.3	923.5	902.7
Interest Expense	837.4	872.1	1,086.0	831.0	716.0	811.0	554.0	478.0	541.0	602.0	525.0	496.6
Non-Operating Income/Expense	954.3	729.8	363.5	2,031.0	2,006.0	1,610.0	1,354.0	1,338.0	1,074.0	578.5	631.7	387.8
Special Items	(1,529.4)	55.1	(354.6)	@CF	@CF	@CF	@CF	@CF	@CF	(340.2)	0.0	29.9
Pretax Income	3,074.7	3,489.9	1,923.7	7,555.0	6,089.0	5,212.0	5,037.0	4,059.0	3,475.0	874.6	1,030.2	823.9
Total Income Taxes	1,309.8	1,058.8	1,012.1	3,040.0	2,070.0	2,345.0	2,462.0	1,731.0	1,830.0	413.1	323.7	277.8
Minority Interest	(7.9)	18.4	3.0	110.0	69.0	9.0	73.0	46.0	6.0	2.5	73.2	45.3
Income Before Extraordinary Items & Discontinued Operations	1,772.8	2,412.8	908.7	4,405.0	3,950.0	2,858.0	2,502.0	2,282.0	1,639.0	459.0	633.3	500.8
Preferred Dividends	1.6	1.5	1.5	0.0	0.0	0.0	1.0	1.0	1.0	0.0	0.0	0.0
Available for Common	1,771.2	2,411.3	907.2	4,405.0	3,950.0	2,858.0	2,501.0	2,281.0	1,638.0	459.0	633.3	500.8
Savings Due to Common Stock Equivalents	0.0	0.0	0.0	0.0	0.0	0.0	0.0	0.0	0.0	0.0	0.0	0.0
Adjusted Available for Common	1,771.2	2,411.3	907.2	4,405.0	3,950.0	2,858.0	2,501.0	2,281.0	1,638.0	459.0	633.3	500.8
Extraordinary Items	0.0	0.0	0.0	0.0	0.0	0.0	0.0	0.0	0.0	0.0	0.0	0.0
Discontinued Operations	0.0	0.0	0.0	0.0	0.0	0.0	0.0	0.0	0.0	0.0	0.0	0.0
Adjusted Net Income	1,771.2	2,411.3	907.2	4,405.0	3,950.0	2,858.0	2,501.0	2,281.0	1,638.0	459.0	633.3	500.8
Earnings Per Share (Primary) - Excluding Extra Items & Disc Ops	$3.83	$5.29	$2.00	$8.16	$7.37	$5.38	$4.54	$4.14	$2.98	$0.98	$1.37	$1.14
Earnings Per Share (Primary) - Including Extra Items & Disc Ops	$3.83	$5.29	$2.00	$8.16	$7.37	$5.38	$4.54	$4.14	$2.98	$0.98	$1.37	$1.14
Earnings Per Share (Fully Diluted) Excluding Extra Items & Disc Ops	$3.83	$5.29	$2.00	$8.16	$7.37	$5.38	$4.54	$4.14	$2.98	$0.98	$1.37	$1.14
Earnings Per Share (Fully Diluted) Including Extra Items & Disc Ops	$3.83	$5.29	$2.00	$8.16	$7.37	$5.38	$4.54	$4.14	$2.98	$0.98	$1.37	$1.14
EPS from Operations	$6.88	$5.18	$2.75	$8.52	$6.70	$5.75	$4.77	$3.71	$3.22	$1.61	$1.37	$1.10
Dividends Per Share	$3.33	$2.21	$1.88	$5.47	$4.84	$4.73	$3.40	$2.92	$2.59	$0.82	$0.69	$0.90

Financial Analysis of International Energy Firms

Table 3

	BRITISH PETROLEUM			ROYAL DUTCH			SHELL			COMMON SIZE BALANCE SHEET (TOTAL) (PERCENTAGE)		
	Dec95	Dec94	Dec93	Dec95	Dec94	Dec93	Dec95	Dec94	Dec93	Dec95	Dec94	Dec93
ASSETS												
Cash & Equivalents	1.22	0.60	0.68	9.66	10.76	9.61	9.66	10.76	9.61	21.03	18.18	18.58
Net Receivables	14.15	13.69	11.45	13.68	12.66	12.19	13.68	12.65	12.19	16.74	15.95	14.68
Inventories	8.70	8.87	8.60	6.43	6.52	6.64	6.43	6.52	6.64	8.42	8.80	8.77
Prepaid Expenses	4.02	3.51	3.52	@CF	@CF	@CF	@CF	@CF	@CF	@CF	@CF	@CF
Other Current Assets	2.02	1.94	2.55	3.35	3.34	3.05	3.35	3.34	3.05	3.52	3.25	3.49
Total Current Assets	30.12	28.62	26.79	33.12	33.28	31.48	33.12	33.28	31.48	49.72	46.89	45.52
Gross Plant,Property & Equipment	132.47	129.98	130.10	116.91	117.05	117.24	116.91	117.06	117.24	72.60	71.94	69.42
Accumulated Depreciation	69.67	65.47	63.61	58.04	58.52	57.09	58.04	58.52	57.09	38.14	35.88	33.95
Net Plant,Property & Equipment	62.80	64.51	66.50	58.87	58.53	60.15	58.87	58.53	60.15	34.46	36.06	35.48
Investments at Equity	6.47	5.50	5.31	7.07	7.30	7.78	7.07	7.30	7.78	3.46	3.37	3.19
Other Investments	0.31	1.08	1.06	0.94	0.89	0.59	0.94	0.89	0.59	5.68	6.20	6.66
Intangibles	0.30	0.28	0.34	0.00	0.00	0.00	0.00	0.00	0.00	5.81	6.37	6.82
Deferred Charges	0.00	0.00	0.00	0.00	0.00	0.00	0.00	0.00	0.00	0.00	0.00	0.00
Other Assets	0.00	0.00	0.00	0.00	0.00	0.00	0.00	0.00	0.00	0.88	1.11	2.33
TOTAL ASSETS	100.00	100.00	100.00	100.00	100.00	100.00	100.00	100.00	100.00	100.00	100.00	100.00
LIABILITIES												
Long Term Debt Due In One Year	@CF	1.73	1.78	1.40	1.41	1.64	1.40	1.41	1.64	1.59	1.93	1.88
Notes Payable	2.28	1.62	2.20	3.22	3.84	3.79	3.22	3.84	3.79	8.83	8.19	7.65
Accounts Payable	13.49	12.29	9.77	7.25	6.30	6.21	7.25	6.30	6.22	11.23	12.11	11.16
Taxes Payable	3.42	2.17	2.52	2.91	2.97	1.86	2.91	2.97	1.86	@CF	@CF	@CF
Accrued Expenses	5.38	4.90	5.04	3.59	3.45	3.66	3.59	3.45	3.66	1.42	1.37	1.41
Other Current Liabilities	5.41	4.92	5.63	8.46	8.08	7.56	8.46	8.08	7.56	8.26	7.07	7.04
Total Current Liabilities	29.99	27.63	26.94	26.83	26.06	24.71	26.84	26.06	24.71	31.33	30.68	29.14
Long Term Debt	14.71	18.35	23.03	6.25	5.52	6.14	6.25	5.52	6.14	17.84	16.92	18.01
Deferred Taxes	1.16	0.92	0.80	6.80	7.08	9.10	6.80	7.08	9.10	2.92	3.56	4.56
Investment Tax Credit	0.00	0.00	0.00	0.00	0.00	0.00	0.00	0.00	0.00	0.00	0.00	0.00
Minority Interest	0.33	0.35	0.32	2.64	1.74	1.57	2.64	1.74	1.57	2.60	2.79	2.76
Other Liabilities	17.29	17.19	17.47	7.49	7.54	6.81	7.49	7.54	6.81	7.46	7.49	7.11
TOTAL LIABILITIES	63.48	64.43	68.57	50.02	47.95	48.32	50.02	47.95	48.32	62.16	61.43	61.57
EQUITY												
Preferred Stock - Redeemable	0.00	0.00	0.00	0.00	0.00	0.00	0.00	0.00	0.00	0.00	0.00	0.00
Preferred Stock - Nonredeemable	0.04	0.04	0.04	0.00	0.00	0.00	0.04	0.04	0.05	0.00	0.00	0.00
Total Preferred Stock	0.04	0.04	0.04	0.00	0.00	0.00	0.04	0.04	0.05	0.00	0.00	0.00
Common Stock	4.31	4.43	4.39	2.36	2.38	2.31	2.73	3.00	3.07	8.46	8.43	8.21
Capital Surplus	6.63	6.69	6.48	1.41	0.00	0.00	0.00	0.00	0.00	7.68	6.79	6.00
Retained Earnings	25.54	24.41	20.52	46.21	49.67	49.37	47.21	49.01	48.56	21.71	23.35	24.22
Less: Treasury Stock	0.00	0.00	0.00	0.00	0.00	0.00	0.00	0.00	0.00	0.00	0.00	0.00
Common Equity	36.48	35.53	31.39	49.98	52.05	51.68	49.94	52.01	51.63	37.84	38.57	38.43
TOTAL EQUITY	36.52	35.57	31.43	49.98	52.05	51.68	49.98	52.05	51.68	37.84	38.57	38.43
TOTAL LIABILITIES & EQUITY	100.00	100.00	100.00	100.00	100.00	100.00	100.00	100.00	100.00	100.00	100.00	100.00

Financial Analysis of International Energy Firms
Table 4

Financial Analysis of International Energy Firms

Table 4

COMMON SIZE INCOME STATEMENT (PERCENTAGE)

	BRITISH PETROLEUM			ROYAL DUTCH			SHELL			TOTAL		
	Dec95	Dec94	Dec93	Dec95	Dec94	Dec93	Dec95	Dec94	Dec93	Dec95	Dec94	Dec93
Sales	100.00	100.00	100.00	100.00	100.00	100.00	100.00	100.00	100.00	100.00	100.00	100.00
Cost of Goods Sold	77.04	77.12	75.75	71.80	72.58	73.96	71.80	72.59	73.96	90.82	92.03	91.80
Gross Profit	22.96	22.88	24.25	28.20	27.42	26.04	28.20	27.41	26.04	9.18	7.97	8.20
Selling, General, & Administrative Expense	9.45	9.24	10.97	11.17	11.71	11.81	11.17	11.71	11.81	@CF	@CF	@CF
Operating Income Before Deprec	13.51	13.64	13.28	17.03	15.71	14.22	17.03	15.71	14.23	9.18	7.97	8.20
Depreciation, Depletion, & Amortization	5.64	6.58	7.47	7.39	7.27	6.50	7.39	7.27	6.50	4.72	4.36	4.26
Operating Profit	7.87	7.06	5.81	9.64	8.43	7.73	9.64	8.43	7.73	4.46	3.61	3.95
Interest Expense	1.47	1.72	2.10	1.26	1.26	1.42	1.26	1.26	1.42	2.17	2.05	2.17
Non-Operating Income/Expense	1.67	1.44	0.70	3.08	3.53	2.82	3.08	3.53	2.82	2.09	2.47	1.69
Special Items	-2.68	0.11	-0.62	@CF	@CF	@CF	@CF	@CF	@CF	-1.23	0.00	0.13
Pretax Income	5.39	6.89	3.73	11.46	10.70	9.13	11.46	10.70	9.13	3.15	4.03	3.60
Total Income Taxes	2.30	2.09	1.96	4.61	3.64	4.11	5.60	4.56	4.81	1.49	1.27	1.21
Minority Interest	-0.01	0.04	0.01	0.17	0.12	0.02	0.17	0.12	0.02	0.01	0.29	0.20
Income Before Extraordinary Items & Discontinued Operations	3.11	4.76	1.76	6.68	6.94	5.00	5.69	6.02	4.31	1.66	2.48	2.19
Preferred Dividends	0.00	0.00	0.00	0.00	0.00	0.00	0.00	0.00	0.00	0.00	0.00	0.00
Available for Common	3.10	4.76	1.76	6.68	6.94	5.00	5.69	6.01	4.30	1.66	2.48	2.19
Savings Due to Common Stock Equivalents	0.00	0.00	0.00	0.00	0.00	0.00	0.00	0.00	0.00	0.00	0.00	0.00
Adjusted Available for Common	3.10	4.76	1.76	6.68	6.94	5.00	5.69	6.01	4.30	1.66	2.48	2.19
Extraordinary Items	0.00	0.00	0.00	0.00	0.00	0.00	0.00	0.00	0.00	0.00	0.00	0.00
Discontinued Operations	0.00	0.00	0.00	0.00	0.00	0.00	0.00	0.00	0.00	0.00	0.00	0.00
Adjusted Net Income	3.10	4.76	1.76	6.68	6.94	5.00	5.69	6.01	4.30	1.66	2.48	2.19

Financial Analysis of International Energy Firms
Table 5

Financial Analysis of International Energy Firms

Table 5

ANNUAL STATEMENT OF CASH FLOWS ($ MILLIONS)

	BRITISH PETROLEUM			ROYAL DUTCH			SHELL			TOTAL		
	Dec95	Dec94	Dec93	Dec95	Dec94	Dec93	Dec95	Dec94	Dec93	Dec95	Dec94	Dec93
INDIRECT OPERATING ACTIVITIES												
Income Before Extraordinary Items	1,772.8	2,412.8	908.7	4,405.0	3,950.0	2,858.0	2,502.0	2,282.0	1,639.0	459.0	633.3	500.8
Depreciation and Amortization	3,739.9	3,076.8	3,367.2	4,870.0	4,138.0	3,710.0	3,246.0	2,759.0	2,474.0	1,683.4	1,242.2	980.1
Extraordinary Items and Disc. Operations	0.0	0.0	0.0	0.0	0.0	0.0	0.0	0.0	0.0	0.0	0.0	(64.4)
Deferred Taxes	0.0	0.0	0.0	@CF	@CF	@CF	@CF	@CF	@CF	@CF	@CF	@CF
Equity in Net Loss (Earnings)	@CF	@CF	@CF	20.0	3.0	(47.0)	13.0	2.0	(31.0)	6.9	(5.2)	35.8
Sale of Property, Plant, and Equipment and Sale of Investments - Loss (Gain)	4.7	(55.1)	59.1	0.0	0.0	0.0	0.0	0.0	0.0	(37.2)	(208.1)	(148.5)
Funds from Operations - Other	1,331.9	229.5	663.4	(281.0)	(1,133.0)	559.0	248.0	(404.0)	640.0	224.2	544.6	439.0
Receivables - Decrease (Increase)	@CF	@CF	@CF	(1,044.0)	(875.0)	(19.0)	(696.0)	(583.0)	(13.0)	(365.5)	(461.6)	45.4
Inventory - Decrease (Increase)	(110.6)	(344.3)	595.4	9.0	(26.0)	483.0	6.0	(17.0)	322.0	8.2	(81.4)	183.6
Accounts Payable and Accrued Liabs - Inc (Dec)	@CF	@CF	@CF	947.0	362.0	187.0	631.0	241.0	124.0	396.6	@CF	@CF
Income Taxes - Accrued - Increase (Decrease)	@CF	@CF	@CF	21.0	716.0	(269.0)	14.0	477.0	(180.0)	@CF	@CF	@CF
Other Assets and Liabilities - Net Change	207.0	(335.1)	(901.3)	(20.0)	(117.0)	0.0	(13.0)	(78.0)	0.0	89.8	401.7	198.5
Operating Activities - Net Cash Flow	6,945.7	4,984.7	4,692.5	8,927.0	7,018.0	7,462.0	5,951.0	4,679.0	4,975.0	2,465.5	2,065.6	2,170.4
INVESTING ACTIVITIES												
Investments - Increase	0.0	0.0	0.0	332.0	265.0	19.0	221.0	176.0	12.0	291.8	544.5	1,225.5
Sale of Investments	0.0	0.0	0.0	172.0	599.0	@CF	114.0	399.0	@CF	308.3	@CF	@CF
Short-Term Investments - Change	0.0	0.0	0.0	@CF	@CF	0.0	@CF	@CF	0.0	(11.6)	43.0	(57.9)
Capital Expenditures	4,450.9	3,679.6	4,137.0	6,584.0	5,669.0	5,013.0	4,390.0	3,780.0	3,342.0	@CF	@CF	@CF
Sale of Property, Plant, and Equipment	@CF	@CF	@CF	@CF	@CF	@CF	@CF	@CF	@CF	112.3	71.1	23.5
Acquisitions	0.0	0.0	56.1	533.0	1,024.0	607.0	356.0	683.0	405.0	(1,988.5)	(1,200.8)	(1,009.1)
Investing Activities - Other	658.9	1,202.6	3,031.8									
Investing Activities - Net Cash Flow	(3,792.0)	(2,477.0)	(1,161.3)	(6,211.0)	(4,311.0)	(4,425.0)	(4,141.0)	(2,874.0)	(2,949.0)	(2,095.9)	(1,773.3)	(2,316.1)
FINANCING ACTIVITIES												
Sale of Common and Preferred Stock	66.4	71.9	41.4	0.0	0.0	0.0	0.0	0.0	0.0	@CF	92.6	687.6
Purchase of Common and Preferred Stock	0.0	0.0	0.0	0.0	0.0	0.0	0.0	0.0	0.0	0.0	0.0	0.0
Cash Dividends	829.5	648.7	648.6	2,737.0	2,293.0	2,134.0	1,825.0	1,529.0	1,423.0	140.7	140.7	88.3
Long-Term Debt - Issuance	42.7	348.8	428.5	697.0	1,365.0	@CF	465.0	911.0	@CF	1,360.8	630.7	1,084.0
Long-Term Debt - Reduction	1,431.5	2,024.2	1,981.3	992.0	1,558.0	137.0	661.0	1,039.0	91.0	203.2	263.4	233.1
Current Debt - Changes	(559.3)	47.4	(1,263.2)	(342.0)	249.0	(106.0)	(228.0)	166.0	(71.0)	(267.3)	(278.6)	164.0
Financing Activities - Other	0.0	0.0	0.0	259.0	126.0	164.0	172.0	84.0	109.0	(49.6)	(276.7)	(33.9)
Financing Activities - Net Cash Flow	(2,711.2)	(2,204.7)	(3,423.3)	(3,115.0)	(2,111.0)	(2,213.0)	(2,077.0)	(1,407.0)	(1,476.0)	700.0	(236.1)	(1,580.2)
Exchange Rate Effect	(6.3)	(23.0)	(20.7)	152.0	59.0	(216.0)	102.0	39.0	(144.0)	(116.0)	(69.8)	35.8
Cash and Equivalents - Change	436.1	280.0	87.2	(247.0)	655.0	608.0	(165.0)	437.0	406.0	953.6	(13.7)	1,470.3
DIRECT OPERATING ACTIVITIES												
Interest Paid - Net	@NA	@NA	@NA	@NA	@NA	@NA	@NA	@NA	@NA	506.0	462.9	436.6
Income Taxes Paid	@NA	@NA	@NA	@NA	@NA	@NA	@NA	@NA	@NA	191.3	188.4	232.1

142

Financial Analysis of International Energy Firms

Table 6

	BRITISH PETROLEUM			ROYAL DUTCH			SHELL			TOTAL		
	Dec95	Dec94	Dec93	Dec95	Dec94	Dec93	Dec95	Dec94	Dec93	Dec95	Dec94	Dec93
Common Shares Outstanding (M)	464.613	458.552	454.255	536.074	536.074	536.074	552.417	552.417	552.417	470.099	454.588	439.155
Price per share (12/31)	$102.13	$79.88	$64.00	$141.13	$107.75	$104.38	$81.50	$65.38	$64.75	$34.00	$29.50	$27.13
Market Value of Equity ($M)	$47,451	$36,629	$29,072	$75,656	$57,762	$55,955	$45,022	$36,117	$35,769	$15,983	$13,410	$11,914

Miscellaneous Information

	%	%	%
U.S. Return - Large Common Stocks	37.43	1.31	9.99
U.S. Return - Small Common Stocks	34.46	3.11	20.98
U.S. Return - Long-term Corporate Bonds	27.20	-5.76	13.19
U.S. Return - US Treasury Bills	5.60	3.90	2.90
U.S. Inflation Rate	2.74	2.67	2.75

Financial Analysis of International Energy Firms
Table 7

	BRITISH PETROLEUM			ROYAL DUTCH			SHELL TRAN & TRADE			TOTAL S.A.		
	Dec95	Dec94	Dec93	Dec95	Dec94	Dec93	Dec95	Dec94	Dec93	Dec95	Dec94	Dec93
LIQUIDITY RATIOS:												
Cash & Market Sec to Total Assets		0.006	0.007		0.108	0.096		0.108	0.096		0.182	0.186
Acid Test Ratio		0.517	0.450		0.899	0.882		0.898	0.882		1.113	1.141
Current Ratio		1.036	0.995		1.277	1.274		1.277	1.274		1.528	1.562
ASSET MANAGEMENT:												
Day's Receivable		47.829	37.074		52.539	46.660		52.529	46.654		57.413	52.900
Day's Inventory		40.188	36.783		37.287	34.360		37.291	34.365		34.419	34.433
Asset Turnover		1.045	1.127		0.879	0.953		0.879	0.953		1.014	1.013
FINANCIAL LEVERAGE:												
Debt to Total Assets		0.632	0.674		0.391	0.377		0.391	0.377		0.551	0.542
Stockholders' Equity to Total assets		0.356	0.314		0.521	0.517		0.521	0.517		0.386	0.384
Long-term Debt to Stockholder's Equity		0.999	1.289		0.251	0.250		0.251	0.250		0.633	0.653
Coverage Ratio		4.102	2.763		6.703	5.441		6.692	5.438		1.759	1.818
PROFITABILITY:												
Gross Margin Ratio		0.229	0.242		0.274	0.260		0.274	0.260		0.080	0.082
Return on Sales		0.048	0.018		0.069	0.050		0.060	0.043		0.025	0.022
Return on Assets (1)		0.050	0.020		0.061	0.048		0.053	0.041		0.025	0.022
Return on Assets (2)		0.072	0.042		0.094	0.087		0.094	0.087		0.041	0.036
Return on Equity		0.140	0.063		0.117	0.092		0.102	0.079		0.065	0.058
Return on Common Equity		0.140	0.063		0.117	0.092		0.102	0.079		0.065	0.058
STOCK MARKET PERFORMANCE:												
Dividend Yield		0.028	0.029		0.045	0.045		0.045	0.040		0.023	0.033
Annual Common Stock Return		0.283	0.440		0.079	0.347		0.055	0.317		0.113	0.351
Book-to-Market Ratio		0.470	0.495		0.583	0.553		0.621	0.576		0.725	0.729
DUPONT ANALYSIS:												
Return on Equity =		0.140	0.063		0.117	0.092		0.102	0.079		0.065	0.058
Return on Sales		0.048	0.018		0.069	0.050		0.060	0.043		0.025	0.022
* Asset Turnover		1.045	1.127		0.879	0.953		0.879	0.953		1.014	1.013
* Leverage		2.812	3.182		1.921	1.935		1.921	1.935		2.593	2.602

SELECTED FINANCIAL RATIOS

JILIN CHEMICAL INDUSTRIAL COMPANY LTD.*

In recent years, there has been a growing trend for companies to seek equity and debt capital from foreign sources. In some cases, this trend has resulted from a lack of available capital in home markets, and in others from the desire to find the least expensive financing on a worldwide basis. The U.S. capital market has particularly benefited from this trend, with a growing number of non-U.S. companies choosing to list securities on U.S. exchanges. A foreign company desiring to list its equity investments on a U.S. exchange can do so via a *sponsored* American Depository Receipt, or ADR.[1] These equity-share equivalents are designated as being equal to a predetermined number of foreign-company common shares which have been placed on deposit in a U.S. escrow account with a trust company or other fiduciary agent.[2]

Chinese companies first began listing their equity securities on U.S. exchanges in the early 1990s. Most were state-run enterprises that used this mechanism as a means to raise much needed capital. Although many of these companies have since become "public" companies, in most cases a majority stake is still held by a state-run holding company or government ministry. As of year-end 1996, thirteen Chinese companies had sponsored or unsponsored ADRs listed in the U.S. (see Exhibit 3).

Chinese Equity Markets

The Chinese equity market first began operations in the late 1980s with trading on two primary exchanges -- one in the bustling metropolis of Shanghai and the other in the Special Economic Zone of Shenzhen. Stocks listed on these exchanges included "A" shares, which can only be purchased by Chinese citizens, and "B" shares, which can only be traded by foreigners. Although the shares carry equivalent voting rights, there is often large disparities in price between the A and B shares, in part because of the limited supply faced by A shareholders (e.g. A shares frequently trade at a premium over B shares).

As of year-end 1996, 83 "B" class shares were listed for trading on the Shanghai and Shenzhen exchanges. Begining in 1991, Chinese companies also began issuing "H" shares, or shares of Chinese companies that could be traded on the Hong Kong Stock Exchange, and which could be purchased by foreigners. As of year-end 1996, the number of H shares listed on the Hong Kong exchange numbered 21. Finally, in the early 1990s, Chinese companies also began issuing "N" shares to represent the sponsored ADRs that were being sold over U.S. exchanges. At year-end 1996, the total market capitalization of B, H, and N shares -- those shares in Chinese companies that can be purchased by foreigners -- totaled $6.9 billion (U.S.) Because of the liquidity of these shares, the B, H and N shares trade at equivalent market values (i.e. there is no arbitrage opportunity).

---

[1] American depository receipts are often referred to as American depository shares, or ADSs.

[2] Foreign securities may also be traded in the U.S. via *unsponsored* ADRs. An unsponsored ADR is one in which the foreign-issuer has <u>not</u> requested listing on a U.S. exchange. Instead, the ADR listing is initiated by a brokerage house or investment bank which has purchased the foreign securities on a foreign market and then places the securities in escrow in the U.S. Sponsored ADRs are usually listed on one of three principal U.S. stock exchanges (i.e. the AMEX, the NASDAQ, or the NYSE), whereas unsponsored ADRs remained unlisted but trading occurs over the NASDAQ "bulletin Board" or via "pink sheets". Companies with sponsored ADRs are required to submit an annual report (Form 20-F) to the U.S. Securities and Exchange Commission, whereas no filing requirement exists for unsponsored ADRs.

Company background

Jilin Chemical Industrial Company Ltd. was established on December 13, 1994 following the reorganization of Jilin Chemical Industrial Corporation, a state-run company of the People's Republic of China (P.R.C.). Jilin Chemical is one of China's largest diversified chemical enterprises. The company's principal business consists of the production of petroleum products, petrochemical and organic chemical products, dyestuff and dye intermediates, synthetic rubber products, chemical fertilizer and other chemical products.

Jilin Chemical undertook an initial public offering in May 1995. Merrill Lynch & Company and China Development Finance Company (H.K.) Ltd. underwrote 889.3 million shares on the Hong Kong Stock Exchange at HK$1.589 per H Share and 875.5 million American Depository Shares (ADS) on the New York Stock Exchange (NYSE Symbol: JCC) for US$20.75 per ADS.[3] The company, which in 1995 had RMB ¥2,552 billion in sales, issued a special dividend of RMB ¥0.052 (approximately HK$0.049) per share, which was equivalent to RMB ¥5.20 or US$0.625per ADS.[4] In addition, for the year ending December 31, 1995, the company declared a special interim dividend of approximately RMB ¥110 million (approximately HK$103 million) to its ultimate holding company.

P.R.C. vs. IAS Accounting Standards

Presented in Exhibit 1 are the 1995 financial statements of Jilin Chemical, prepared in accordance with International Accounting Standards (IAS). The notes to the financial statements (see Exhibit 2) distinguish between the accounting standards of the P.R.C. and those of the IASC (International Accounting Standards Commission). Generally, the classification of certain financial statement items differ between PRC accounting standards and those of the IAS; however, certain other specific differences are noted (see note 28):

- **Noncurrent Monetary Assets.** P.R.C. accounting standards call for long-term monetary assets (e.g. VAT receivables) to be stated at face value. Under IASC standards, however, monetary assets (and liabilities) such as deferred VAT receivables should be stated at their net present value (i.e. discounted) using the average long-term borrowing cost for the company.

- **Asset Revaluation**. Under P.R.C. accounting standards, noncurrent assets are not revalued (i.e. the historical cost concept is strictly adhered to), and consequently depreciation expense cannot be taken on any revalued asset values. Under IASC standards, however, noncurrent assets may be periodically revalued, and consequently depreciation expense is calculated to include the effect of any revaluation of noncurrent depreciable assets.

---

[3] Each ADS is equivalent to 100 H Shares.

[4] RMB ¥ refers to the Chinese currency Renminbi. In company publications, the Renminbi has been translated into Hong Kong and United States dollars at HK$1.00 = RMB ¥1.0702 and US$1.00 = RMB ¥8.3175, respectively. The rates are representative of rates quoted by the Bank of China.

- **Timing Issues**. P.R.C. accounting standards dictate that assets may be written off on the income statement only after an asset has been physically disposed of. IASC standards, however, require assets to be written off once they are identified as being obsolete or their value impaired.

- **Currency Translation Capitalization**. Translation differences resulting from foreign currency translation of construction debt are capitalized to the balance sheet during the construction period under P.R.C. Accounting Standards. Under IASC standards, as long as they are not interest adjustments, the currency translation loss cannot be deferred or amortized.

Questions:

1. Considering just the above noted accounting differences, assess the expected impact on Jilin Chemicals' reported net income and total assets if P.R.C. accounting practices, rather than IASC standards, had been used in presenting the 1995 financial results.

2. What accounting entries are necessary in order to restate the company's financial statements from IASC standards to P.R.C. accounting standards?

3. Calculate the following ratios under both IASC standards and PRC accounting standards:

   • Return on sales
   • Return on assets
   • Return on equity
   • Total debt-to-assets
   • L.T. debt-to-equity

   Are the differences material? Is it important to restate Jilin Chemical's financial results using P.R.C. accounting standards to a benchmark like IASC standards?

4. Compare and contrast U.S. GAAP and P.R.C. GAAP. What similarities and differences do you observe?

Exhibit 1
Jilin Chemical Industrial Co., Ltd.
Financial Disclosures

REPORT OF THE INTERNATIONAL AUDITORS

安 永 會 計 師 事 務 所

To the members
Jilin Chemical Industrial Company Limited
(Established in the People's Republic of China with limited liability)

We have audited the financial statements on pages 35 to 63 which have been prepared in accordance with International Accounting Standards.

Respective responsibilities of directors and auditors

The Company's directors are responsible for the preparation of financial statements which give a true and fair view. In preparing financial statements which give a true and fair view it is fundamental that appropriate accounting policies are selected and applied consistently. It is our responsibility to form an independent opinion, based on our audit, on those statements and to report our opinion to you.

Basis of opinion

We conducted our audit in accordance with Statements of Auditing Standards issued by the Hong Kong Society of Accountants. An audit includes an examination, on a test basis, of evidence relevant to the amounts and disclosures in the financial statements. It also includes an assessment of the significant estimates and judgements made by the directors in the preparation of the financial statements, and of whether the accounting policies are appropriate to the Company and the Group's circumstances, consistently applied and adequately disclosed.

We planned and performed our audit so as to obtain all the information and explanations which we considered necessary in order to provide us with sufficient evidence to give reasonable assurance as to whether the financial statements are free from material misstatement. In forming our opinion we also evaluated the overall adequacy of the presentation of information in the financial statements. We believe that our audit provides a reasonable basis for our opinion.

Opinion

In our opinion, the financial statements give a true and fair view, in all material respects, of the state of affairs of the Company and of the Group as at 31st December, 1995 and of the profit and cash flows of the Group for the year then ended and have been properly prepared in accordance with International Accounting Standards and the disclosure requirements of the Hong Kong Companies Ordinance.

Ernst & Young
Certified Public Accountants

Hong Kong
25th March, 1996

CONSOLIDATED PROFIT AND LOSS ACCOUNT

Year ended 31st December, 1995

	Notes	1995 RMB'000	1994 RMB'000
Turnover	3	7,078,551	5,848,916
Operating profit before exceptional item and taxation	4	1,088,069	811,110
Exceptional item	5	–	65,320
Operating profit before taxation and share of profit/(loss) of a joint venture		1,088,069	876,430
Share of profit/(loss) of a joint venture	14	12,212	(16,509)
Taxation	6	(356,715)	(257,724)
Profit after taxation		743,566	602,197
Minority interests		(23)	–
Net profit attributable to shareholders		743,543	602,197
Dividends	7, 24	284,936	194,593
Earnings per share	8	RMB0.25	RMB0.25

CONSOLIDATED BALANCE SHEET

31st December, 1995	*Notes*	**1995** *RMB'000*	**1994** *RMB'000*
Assets			
Current assets			
Cash and bank balances		755,527	180,455
Inventories	16	1,027,319	805,413
Accounts receivable and other receivables		755,606	1,016,910
VAT receivable	17	19,744	22,685
Total current assets		2,558,196	2,025,463
Fixed assets	11	4,691,989	4,269,015
Construction in progress	12	4,541,735	1,983,824
Long term investments	14	319,096	412,747
Deferred VAT receivable	15	66,314	80,171
Total assets		12,177,330	8,771,220
Liabilities and shareholders' equity			
Current liabilities			
Bank and other loans	18	747,770	494,425
Current portion of loans from a fellow subsidiary	18	232,871	68,550
Accounts payable		606,778	1,552,873
Advances from customers		379,593	300,214
Accrued expenses and other payables		708,879	361,332
Dividends payable	7	284,936	–
Total current liabilities		2,960,827	2,777,394
Bank loans	18	68,490	18,660
Loans from a fellow subsidiary	18	605,000	652,500
Amount due to ultimate holding company	19	2,818,985	1,595,285
Other loan	20	1,668	6,417
Deferred taxation	21	5,760	–
Total liabilities		6,460,730	5,050,256
Minority interests		14,965	–
Shareholders' equity			
Share capital	22	3,361,078	2,396,300
Share premium	23	1,828,157	1,290,324
Reserves	24	512,400	34,340
Total shareholders' equity		5,701,635	3,720,964
Total liabilities and shareholders' equity		12,177,330	8,771,220

Liu Shulin	**Jiao Haikun**
Director	*Director*

CONSOLIDATED CASH FLOW STATEMENT

Year ended 31st December, 1995

	1995	**1994**
	RMB'000	*RMB'000*
Operating activities		
Operating profit before taxation and share of profit/(loss) of a joint venture	1,088,069	876,430
Depreciation	347,154	213,829
Interest expense	223,252	135,247
Fixed assets written off	11,595	–
Loss on disposal of fixed assets	4,511	–
Other non-cash income and expenses	(1,742)	(21,376)
Movement in inventories	(221,906)	(61,474)
Movement in trade balance with ultimate holding company	(218,291)	(395,563)
Movement in accounts receivable and other receivables	389,719	(208,837)
Movement in accounts payable	(946,095)	651,046
Movement in advances from customers, accrued expenses and other payables	176,665	290,085
Taxes paid	(360,535)	(257,724)
Net cash inflow from operating activities	492,396	1,221,663
Investing activities		
Capital expenditures for construction in progress	(1,539,699)	(703,733)
Capital expenditures for fixed assets	(17,148)	(3,220)
Purchase of investments	–	(1,784)
Cash not assumed by the Company due to reorganisation on 1st October, 1994	–	(8,193)
Net cash outflow from investing activities	(1,556,847)	(716,930)
Net cash inflow/(outflow) before financing activities	(1,064,451)	504,733
Financing activities		
Share proceeds net of listing expenses	1,502,611	–
Capital contribution from minority shareholder of a subsidiary	14,942	–
Interest paid	(230,507)	(181,348)
Proceeds from borrowings	610,973	411,040
Repayment of borrowings	(258,496)	(356,944)
Distribution to ultimate holding company	–	(328,051)
Net cash inflow/(outflow) from financing activities	1,639,523	(455,303)
Net increase in cash and cash equivalents	575,072	49,430
Cash and cash equivalents at beginning of year	180,455	131,025
Cash and cash equivalents at end of year	755,527	180,455
Non-cash transactions:		
Capital expenditures financed by ultimate holding company	1,505,302	1,196,880
Net asset, net of cash, retained by ultimate holding company in connection with restructuring on 1st October, 1994	–	537,582
Net transfer of assets to ultimate holding company	–	(339,120)
Investment in a joint venture	–	418,082
Investment in a subsidiary	12,726	–

1. BASIS OF PRESENTATION

Jilin Chemical Industrial Company Limited (the "Company") was established in the People's Republic of China (the "PRC") on 13th December, 1994 as a joint stock limited company to hold the assets and liabilities of the principal production units, certain ancillary functions and a subsidiary (hereinafter collectively referred to as the "Contributed Net Assets") of Jilin Chemical Industrial Corporation (the "Predecessor"), a State-owned enterprise controlled by and under the administration of the Jilin Provincial Government and is subject to the industrial oversight of the Ministry of Chemical Industry of the PRC. The Company expects to receive the continued support of the Jilin Provincial Government for its working capital requirements and its capital expenditure in the foreseeable future.

In connection with the restructuring, the Contributed Net Assets of the Predecessor as at 30th September, 1994 were revalued to reflect their then current fair values and the Contributed Net Assets were taken over by the Company from the Predecessor effective 1st October, 1994 in consideration of which 2,396,300,000 domestic invested shares in the form of State-owned shares ("Domestic Shares"), with a par value of RMB1.00 each, were issued by the Company to the Predecessor. The Predecessor was then renamed Jilin Chemical Group Corporation and became the Company's ultimate holding company.

The consolidated financial statements of the Company and its subsidiaries (hereinafter collectively referred to as the "Group") for the year ended 31st December, 1994 presented for comparative purposes have been prepared on the basis that the Group with all its present components had been so constituted during the year ended 31st December, 1994. In the opinion of the directors, the consolidated financial statements of the Group prepared on this basis present more fairly the results, cash flows and state of affairs of the Group as a whole.

Further details of the Company's subsidiaries and the Group's activities are set out in notes 13 and 27 respectively.

2. SUMMARY OF SIGNIFICANT ACCOUNTING POLICIES

Basis of accounting

The financial statements have been prepared in accordance with International Accounting Standards ("IAS") and the disclosure requirements of the Hong Kong Companies Ordinance. This basis of accounting differs from that used in the preparation of the statutory and management accounts of the Company and of the Group, which were prepared in accordance with the accounting principles and the relevant financial regulations applicable to joint stock limited companies established in the PRC. A reconciliation of the Group's results under IAS and PRC accounting standards is presented in note 28. The principal accounting policies adopted are as follows:

Basis of consolidation

The consolidated financial statements incorporate the financial statements of the Company and its subsidiaries. The results of subsidiaries acquired or disposed of during the year are consolidated from or to their effective dates of acquisition or disposal, respectively. All significant intercompany transactions and balances within the Group are eliminated on consolidation.

2. SUMMARY OF SIGNIFICANT ACCOUNTING POLICIES *(Continued)*

Interest in subsidiaries

A subsidiary company is a company over which the Company has the power to govern its financial and operating policies so as to obtain benefits from its activities, notwithstanding its equity interest in that company.

Fixed assets and depreciation

Fixed assets are stated at cost or at revalued amounts, as determined for the purposes of the Group restructuring and in connection with the floatation of the Company, less accumulated depreciation.

Depreciation of fixed assets is calculated on a straight-line basis to write off the cost or revalued amount of each asset over its estimated useful life, after taking into account its estimated residual value. The estimated useful lives of fixed assets are as follows:

Buildings and other constructions	10 to 45 years
Plant, machinery and equipment	8 to 28 years
Land use rights	50 years

No depreciation is provided on construction in progress until the asset is completed and put into productive use.

Construction in progress

Construction in progress represents factory buildings, plant and machinery and other fixed assets under construction and is stated at cost. Cost comprises direct costs of construction as well as interest charges during the period of construction, installation and testing, and certain exchange differences on any related borrowed funds. Capitalisation of interest charges ceases when an asset is ready for its intended use. Construction in progress is transferred to fixed assets when it is capable of producing saleable output on a commercial basis, notwithstanding any delays in the issue of the relevant commissioning certificates by the appropriate PRC authorities.

Joint venture

A joint venture is an interest in a venture between two or more venturers whose rights and obligations with respect to the venture are specified in a contractual joint venture agreement which gives the venturers joint control over the venture and in which no single venturer is in a position to control, unilaterally, the activity of the venture.

Investments in joint ventures are accounted for using the equity method of accounting.

Investments

Investments held on a long term basis, other than investments in joint ventures, are stated at cost less any provisions for permanent diminution in values deemed necessary by the directors.

153

2.   **SUMMARY OF SIGNIFICANT ACCOUNTING POLICIES** *(Continued)*

Deferred VAT receivable

The deferred VAT receivable represents the deemed input value added tax ("VAT") calculated as at 1st January, 1994 in accordance with the relevant PRC regulations as more fully explained in note 15. It is stated at its present value calculated over the estimated period of recovery using the average long term borrowing cost of the Group.

Cash and cash equivalents

Cash and cash equivalent equals cash and bank balances.

Deferred taxation

Deferred taxation is provided, using the liability method, on all significant timing differences to the extent it is probable that the liability will crystallise in the foreseeable future. A deferred tax asset is not recognised until its realisation is assured beyond reasonable doubt.

Inventories

Inventories, other than spare parts and consumables, are stated at the lower of cost and net realisable value. Cost is determined on the weighted average basis and, in the case of work in progress and finished goods, comprises direct materials, direct labour and an appropriate proportion of production overheads. Net realisable value is based on estimated selling prices less further costs expected to be incurred to completion and disposal.

Spare parts and consumables are stated at the lower of cost determined on the weighted average basis and replacement cost.

Foreign currency translation

The Group's financial records are maintained and the financial statements are stated in Renminbi ("RMB").

Transactions in foreign currencies are translated into RMB at exchange rates prevailing on the transaction dates. Monetary assets and liabilities denominated in foreign currencies at the balance sheet date are translated into RMB at rates of exchange quoted by the People's Bank of China.

Foreign currency translation differences relating to borrowed funds to the extent that they are adjustments to the interest costs of funds used to finance the construction of fixed assets are capitalised during the period of construction. The capitalised amount is calculated by applying the interest rate differential between the foreign currency denominated loans and RMB loans to the average foreign currency denominated loans outstanding. The remaining foreign currency differences arising from long term monetary liabilities denominated in foreign currencies are dealt with in the profit and loss account.

Effective 1st January, 1995, IAS 21 has been amended such that the aforesaid exchange losses on long term monetary liabilities denominated in a foreign currency to the extent that they are not adjustments to the interest costs of funds can no longer be deferred and amortised. For details of the prior year's effects of the aforesaid change in the accounting policy, please refer to note 5.

2. SUMMARY OF SIGNIFICANT ACCOUNTING POLICIES *(Continued)*

Sales

Sales are recognised upon delivery of goods to customers.

Repairs and maintenance expenses

Repairs and maintenance expenses are charged to the profit and loss account as incurred.

Research and development expenses

Research and development expenses are written off in the year in which they are incurred.

Government revenue grants

Government revenue grants are recognised as income upon approval by the relevant Government authority, at which stage the eventual collectibility is also ascertainable.

Retirement benefits

Retirement benefits are charged to the profit and loss account based on the contributions to a government retirement benefit scheme.

Prior to 31st December, 1994, retirement benefits were paid to retired employees based on their final salary before retirement.

Effective 1st January, 1995, the Company contributed to a defined contribution plan to the extent of 26% of the actual incurred employees' wages and bonuses.

The result of the above arrangement is that the Group is no longer responsible for the retirement benefits of its current and former employees since 1st January, 1995.

Prior to this change, the financial statements reflect the actual payments made to retired employees and not an estimate of the future pension expense accruing to its current employees. The effect of restating the cost of retirement benefits on the basis of the estimated future pension expenses accruing to the Group's current employees would not have a significant effect on the results of the Group for the year ended 31st December, 1994.

11. FIXED ASSETS

	Buildings and other constructions RMB'000	Plant, machinery and equipment RMB'000	Land use rights RMB'000	Total RMB'000
Group				
Cost or valuation:				
At beginning of year	862,609	2,392,440	1,088,843	4,343,892
Reclassification	(79,757)	79,757	–	–
Revaluation adjustment	14,124	14,909	–	29,033
Additions	700	16,448	–	17,148
Transferred from construction in progress (note 12)	174,326	565,727	–	740,053
Disposals	(1,403)	(18,098)	–	(19,501)
At 31st December, 1995	970,599	3,051,183	1,088,843	5,110,625
Accumulated depreciation:				
At beginning of year	6,281	63,150	5,446	74,877
Provided during the year	28,504	297,236	21,414	347,154
Disposals	(32)	(3,363)	–	(3,395)
At 31st December, 1995	34,753	357,023	26,860	418,636
Net book value:				
At 31st December, 1995	935,846	2,694,160	1,061,983	4,691,989
At 31st December, 1994	856,328	2,329,290	1,083,397	4,269,015
Company				
Cost or valuation:				
At beginning of year	855,497	2,339,395	1,088,843	4,283,735
Reclassification	(79,757)	79,757	–	–
Revaluation adjustment	14,124	14,909	–	29,033
Additions	700	16,410	–	17,110
Transferred from construction in progress (note 12)	174,326	565,494	–	739,820
Disposals	(1,403)	(31,213)	–	(32,616)
At 31st December, 1995	963,487	2,984,752	1,088,843	5,037,082
Accumulated depreciation:				
At beginning of year	6,218	62,287	5,446	73,951
Provided during the year	28,504	294,923	21,414	344,841
Disposals	(32)	(3,363)	–	(3,395)
At 31st December, 1995	34,690	353,847	26,860	415,397
Net book value:				
At 31st December, 1995	928,797	2,630,905	1,061,983	4,621,685
At 31st December, 1994	849,279	2,277,108	1,083,397	4,209,784

11. FIXED ASSETS *(Continued)*

The fixed assets of the Company were revalued as at 30th September, 1994 by independent equipment and property valuers. Plant, machinery and equipment were valued using either the cost approach or the market approach. The former valuation approach was used in respect of those assets which did not have sufficient market information and the valuation was determined by reference to depreciated replacement cost. The latter valuation approach was determined by reference to the most recent prices paid for similar assets. Buildings were valued using depreciated replacement cost. The valuation of land use rights was commonly based on standard land prices determined by the Jilin Province Land Bureau.

Pursuant to the restructuring exercise of the Company and by virtue of a document dated 21st November, 1994 issued by the State-owned Assets Administration Bureau, the total value at which the fixed assets were assumed by the Group as of 1st October, 1994 was RMB3,922,877,000 as at 30th September, 1994 resulting in a revaluation surplus of RMB1,540,039,000 (after the prior year adjustment referred to in note 5 above) to the Company and the Group.

In preparation for the listing of the Company's shares on the Stock Exchange of Hong Kong Limited (the "Hong Kong Stock Exchange"), a separate revaluation was carried out for the Group's fixed assets as at 28th February, 1995. The revaluation was done by American Appraisal Hong Kong Limited, using the same basis as that of the previous 30th September, 1994 revaluation. This resulted in a further revaluation surplus of RMB29,033,000 to the Company and the Group.

The effect of these revaluation surpluses of RMB1,540,039,000 and RMB29,033,000 was to increase the depreciation charge for fixed assets by approximately RMB124 million and RMB1,209,000, respectively, for the current year. Had the fixed assets of the Group been stated at cost, that is, the effect of the two revaluations were excluded, the net book value of buildings and other constructions, plant, machinery and equipment, and land use rights as at 31st December, 1995 would be RMB882,947,000 RMB2,390,571,000 and RMB Nil, respectively.

All of the Company and the Group's buildings are located in the PRC and the land where the Group's buildings are situated is State-owned. Pursuant to an approval document dated 23rd November, 1994 issued by the State Land Administration Bureau, the Group was granted the right to use the land on which the Group's buildings are erected for a period of 50 years commencing 1st October, 1994.

The Group has no plans to revalue its assets on a regular basis.

15. DEFERRED VAT RECEIVABLE

Group and Company

	1995 RMB'000	1994 RMB'000
VAT receivable as at 1st January	98,553	98,553
Amount utilised during the year	(19,711)	–
	78,842	98,553
Less: Present value discount	(12,528)	(18,382)
VAT receivable at end of year	66,314	80,171

This represents the deemed VAT receivable arising from the introduction of the new PRC VAT system on 1st January, 1994. This asset was accounted for by the Group and the Company on 1st January, 1994 by applying a 14% VAT rate to certain inventory values as at 31st December, 1993 with the effect of reducing certain opening inventories of the Group and the Company as at 1st January, 1994 by the same amount. A detailed directive regarding the utilisation of the deferred VAT receivable was issued in May 1995 by the Ministry of Finance and the State General Tax Bureau pursuant to which the Group and the Company will be able to offset the balance of RMB98,553,000 against its VAT payable within a period of five years starting from 1st January, 1995. Accordingly, a discount has been applied using the Group's average rate of borrowing over the estimated period of recovery.

17. VAT RECEIVABLE

This represents principally VAT paid by the Group and the Company in respect of their purchases offset against the VAT payable on their sales during the two years ended 31st December, 1995. The net amount is available to offset against future VAT payable on the sales of the Group and the Company.

28. DIFFERENCES BETWEEN IAS AND PRC ACCOUNTING STANDARDS

Other than the differences in classification of certain financial statement items and the accounting treatment of the items described below, there are no material differences between the Group's financial statements prepared in accordance with IAS and PRC accounting standards. The main differences are:

(i)   Under IAS, the deferred VAT receivable is stated at its net present value calculated over the estimated period of recovery using the average long term borrowing cost of the Group. Such accounting treatment is not permissible under PRC accounting standards.

(ii) Depreciation expenses calculated under IAS include the effect of the revaluation of fixed assets as at 28th February, 1995. Under PRC accounting standards, this revaluation, which was not in connection with the 1994 restructuring, was not recognised. Accordingly, depreciation charges calculated under PRC accounting standards are lower than under IAS.

(iii) Under PRC accounting standards, fixed assets that are written off cannot be charged to the profit and loss account until the assets are physically disposed of. Under IAS, these assets are written off to the profit and loss account once they are identified as obsolete.

(iv) As mentioned in note 2, foreign currency translation differences relating to borrowed funds to the extent that they are adjustments to the interest costs of funds used to finance the construction of fixed assets are capitalised. Under PRC accounting standards, all foreign currency translation differences relating to funds borrowed to finance the construction of fixed assets are capitalised during the construction period.

(v)   Under IAS tax adjustments are made in respect of the deferred tax effects for items (ii) to (iv) above. The deferred tax effect on item (i) had not been recognised in 1994 due to its immateriality and accordingly was not reversed in 1995.

The effects of the above differences on net profit attributable to shareholders are summarised as below:

	Notes	1995 RMB'000	1994 RMB'000
Net profit attributable to shareholders under IAS		743,543	602,197
Adjustments:			
Discount/(write back) on deferred VAT receivable	*(i)*	(5,854)	18,382
Depreciation charges due to revaluation on 28th February, 1995	*(ii)*	1,209	–
Fixed assets written off	*(iii)*	11,595	–
Exchange gains in respect of funds borrowed for fixed assets	*(iv)*	(5,451)	–
Tax adjustments	*(v)*	(2,426)	–
Net profit attributable to shareholders under PRC accounting standards		742,616	620,579

28. DIFFERENCES BETWEEN IAS AND PRC ACCOUNTING STANDARDS *(Continued)*

The effect on shareholders' equity of the significant difference between IAS and PRC accounting standards is shown below.

	1995	**1994**
	RMB'000	*RMB'000*
Shareholders' equity under IAS	5,701,635	3,720,964
Adjustments:		
Discount on deferred VAT receivable	12,528	18,382
Reduction in depreciation charges due to revaluation on 28th February, 1995	1,209	–
Revaluation surplus of fixed assets	(29,033)	–
Deferred tax effect on the revaluation surplus	9,580	–
Fixed assets written off	11,595	–
Exchange gains in respect of funds borrowed for fixed assets	(5,451)	–
Tax adjustments	(2,426)	–
Shareholders' equity under PRC accounting standards	5,699,637	3,739,346

Exhibit 3
Chinese Companies Traded on U.S. Exchanges*

Company	Symbol	Exchange
Brilliance China Automotive Holdings	CBA	NYSE
China Eastern Airlines	CEA	NYSE
China Tire Holdings	TIR	NYSE
China Yuchai International	CYD	NYSE
Ek Chor China Motorcycle	EKC	NYSE
Guagshen Railway	GSH	NYSE
Huaneng Power International	HNP	NYSE
Jilin Chemical Industrial Co.	JCC	NYSE
Shandong Huaneng Power Development	SH	NYSE
Shanghai Chlor-Alkai Chemical	SLLBY	OTC
Shanghai Erfangji	SHFGY	OTC
Shanghai Petrochemical	SHI	NYSE
Shanghai Tyre & Rubber	STRCY	OTC

* Includes sponsored and unsponsored ADRs and ADSs.

HONG KONG LAND DEVELOPMENT COMPANY LTD.[*]

In 1994, the Hong Kong Land Development Company (HKLDC) reported record earnings. In his letter to the shareholders, Ivan Chow, chairman of the board of HKLDC, commented:

> For Hong Kong Land Development Company, 1994 was a year of merger and expansion. The company established itself as one of the most successful real estate developers in Hong Kong. And, our merger with Tianrong Holdings Ltd. provided a solid foundation for growth into China and increased profits in the years ahead.

Background

HKLDC was a real estate development company headquartered in Kowloon, Hong Kong. The company had received considerable media coverage over its proposed development of a series of "complete living" apartment complexes. The complexes contained not only living quarters, but also shopping facilities for food and clothing, restaurants, movie theaters, game arcades, and health clubs. By 1993, HKLDC had two such developments in operation -- one located in Kowloon and the other located in Shatin (in the New Territories). In 1994, the company changed its corporate policy regarding these developments from one of "constructing and operating" to one of "constructing, operating, and selling."

In June of 1993, prior to the adoption of the new policy, HKLDC arranged the sale of its Shatin development to a group of investors. The selling price was approximately $184 million, and the sale resulted in a gain of over $38.4 million.[1] In its 1993 annual report, HKLDC reported the gain as an "extraordinary item".[2]

The sale of the development was financed by a $16 million down-payment and a 30 year, nonrecourse, 7 percent note for $168 million. The note was payable in annual principal installments of $5.6 million beginning in September 2000. Shortly after the transaction, the group of investors contributed the development to a new limited partnership in which the Shatin Land Management Company Ltd. (SLMC) was the general partner. SLMC, a wholly-owned subsidiary of HKLDC, became the exclusive operator and manager of the Shatin complex.

Kowloon Complex

In December of 1994, HKLDC arranged the sale of its second "complete living" complex. The Kowloon property, which had been carried on the books of HKLDC at a net book value of $74.4 million, was sold for $320 million to a group of investors. The sale was financed with a $13.6 million down-payment and a 35 year, 6.5 percent note for $306.4 million. The note was secured by the complex itself and called for a prepayment of $31.44 million, representing interest for the first three years. Beginning in 1997, payments of approximately $18.4 million (principal and interest) per year were to be made for the

---

[*] This case was prepared by Kenneth R. Ferris. Copyright © 1996 by The American Graduate School of International Management. All rights reserved.

[1] Unless otherwise noted, all values are in Hong Kong dollars.

[2] Under generally accepted accounting principles in Hong Kong, an extraordinary item is an event or transaction **outside** the ordinary activities of a business that is both material and not expected to recur frequently or regularly.

next 32 years. At the time of the sale, the preferred client lending rate of the Hang Seng Bank in Hong Kong was approximately 8 percent.

Shortly after the sale was completed, the group of investors transferred title of the development to a limited partnership in which the Kowloon Land Management Company Ltd.,(KLMC) a wholly-owned subsidiary of HKLDC, was the general partner. KLMC thus became the sole and exclusive manager of the Kowloon complex. Under the terms of the new limited partnership, any operating losses, depreciation and amortization charges, and tax credits would accrue to the original group of investors who were now limited partners.

Because of the 1994 change in corporate policy regarding the development complexes, HKLDC treated the gain on the sale of the Kowloon property as an ordinary item.[3] In addition, to establish consistency in the application of this accounting treatment, the gain from the prior year's sale of the Shatin property was reclassified as an ordinary sale. This change in accounting practice was noted in the independent auditor's opinion.

Required

1. Do you agree with the accounting treatment utilized by HKLDC to account for the sale of the Kowloon complex? Substantiate your position.

2. Evaluate the quality of reported earnings and assets. Prepare a list of those items that concern you.

---

[3] Under Hong Kong GAAP, events or transactions **within** the ordinary activities of a business but which are both material and exceptional in terms of size and incidence should be separately identified in the footnotes as "exceptional items".

Exhibit 1
Hong Kong Land Development Company

Consolidated Balance Sheets

	(HK $ M) Year ended 30 June	
Assets	**1995**	**1994**
Cash	$ 66.2	$ 37.8
Receivables (substantially pledged)	1,519.1	956.4
Prepaid Expenses	12.7	3.5
Inventories	20.0	5.5
Property held for resale (substantially collateralized)	833.2	655.6
Investment in joint venture	107.4	117.5
Property, plant, and equipment (net)	288.9	293.1
Deferred charges and other assets (partially pledged)	292.0	158.3
Total Assets	$3,139.5	$2,227.7

Liabilities and Shareholders' Equity		
Accounts payable	$ 37.6	$ 45.7
Accrued liabilities	38.3	33.3
Income taxes payable	244.4	127.1
Bonds, mortgages, and similar debt	1,418.9	969.8
Deferred credits	138.6	242.9
Stockholders' equity		
Shares of HK $0.50 each:		
Authorized: 2,000.0 million		
Outstanding: 1,040.4 million	520.2	436.9
Reserves	179.7	54.4
Retained earnings	561.8	317.6
Total Shareholders' equity	1,261.7	808.9
Total Liabilities and Shareholders' Equity	$3,139.5	$2,227.7

Exhibit 2
Hong Kong Land Development Company

Consolidated Statements of Income

	(HK $ M) Year ended 30 June	
	1995	**1994**
Sales revenue	$ 965.3	$ 838.6
Operating revenue	103.6	187.3
Earnings from joint ventures	15.2	19.1
Interest and other income	69.8	21.9
	1,153.9	1,066.9
Operating expenses		
Cost of sales and selling expenses	529.3	576.1
General and administrative expenses	152.3	167.2
Depreciation	14.6	28.2
Interest and debt expense	45.4	31.0
	741.6	803.1
Earnings before income taxes	412.3	263.8
Income taxes	137.4	44.4
Net earnings	274.9	219.4

Exhibit 3
Hong Kong Land Development Company

Selected Footnotes

4. Receivables

Receivables comprise the following:

	1995	1994
Bulk land sales	$ 572.1	$ 561.2
Mortgages and notes receivable	623.6	244.3
Real estate sales	128.7	87.2
Joint ventures and other accounts	194.7	63.7
	$ 1,519.1	$ 956.4

Receivables from real estate sales are secured by second trust deeds and conditional sales contracts, and are stated net of the reserve for losses of $ .556 and $ .350 in 1995 and 1994, respectively.

7. Bonds, mortgages, and similar debt

	Total	Currently Due
9½% General mortgage bonds	$ 56.8	$ 4.8
Mortgage loans, with interest from $4^7/_8$% to 12%	852.9	302.0
Bank notes, with interest from 7% to $12^1/_4$%	693.3	349.6

16. Exceptional items

On June 30, 1993, the Company sold the Shatin "complete living" complex at a net gain of $38.4 million. On December 31, 1994, the Company sold the Kowloon "complete living" complex at a net gain of $245.6 million. Subsequent to the sale of the Shatin property, the Company changed its policy toward these investments from one of constructing and operating such properties to one of constructing, operating, and selling. Accordingly, the sale of Shatin property has been reclassified from amounts previously reported to reflect the transaction as an ordinary/exceptional sale rather than as an extraordinary item.

1996 would mark a significant milestone for Japan Airlines (JAL), Japan's largest air carrier -- the company would report its first operating profit since 1991. According to company disclosures, JAL's operating profit for the fiscal year ended March 31, 1996, exceeded ¥17.3 billion, as compared to an operating loss of ¥12.6 billion in 1995 (see Exhibit 1). Analysts familiar with the company and the airline industry attributed JAL's improved performance to three factors: a strong yen, an extensive corporate restructuring effort, and strong demand in the growing Asian marketplace. According to a company spokesperson, international passenger traffic for the airline rose more than 13 percent in 1996, an outcome largely attributed to a stronger yen and the resulting increase in Japanese demand for inexpensive overseas travel. During fiscal year 1996, JAL filled over 73 percent of the seats on its international flights -- an impressive performance by airline industry standards. Despite continuing weakness in the Japanese economy, new routes and a more competitive fare structure also produced a nearly 6 percent increase in passenger volume in JAL's domestic market. Analysts expected a partial deregulation of Japan's domestic airline industry to provide further increases to JAL's profits. Previously, highly regulated domestic fares prevented airline revenue growth from keeping pace with increasing passenger loads. Beginning in 1996, however, JAL would have more freedom to set its own domestic fares, which was anticipated to result in increased revenues and profits from its domestic operations.

Industry analysts also cited JAL's on-going restructuring program as a key contributor to the airline's turn-around. According to a company spokesperson, the restructuring program was composed of four components. First, operating expenses would be reduced by ¥100 billion. Second, planned capital investments would be reduced by ¥400 billion over the four year period 1995-1998. Third, personnel costs would be reduced as a result of an increased use of outsourcing, and hence by reducing the number of employees from 22,000 to 17,000 by March of 1998. And fourth, an increased use of leased, rather than purchased aircraft.

Although most airline analysts were impressed by the improvements attained by the company to date, some skeptics remained. The share price of JAL's ADRs, which traded on the NASDAQ exchange in the U.S., had increased over 16 percent by the time the company disclosed its 1996 fiscal year results. Some analysts wondered, however, if the capital markets had over reacted to the company's favorable financial disclosures.

Analysts Concern

Much of the concern centered around a series of accounting policy changes undertaken by the airline during the past three years. According to the company's 1995 footnotes:

> **CHANGES IN ACCOUNTING POLICY**
>
> a. Effective April 1, 1993, the Company changed its basis of accounting for bond issuance expenses, which had previously been charged to income when incurred, to capitalizing and amortizing these over a period of three years. As a result of this change, bond issuance expenses of ¥2,128

---

[*] This case was prepared by Kenneth R. Ferris. Copyright © 1996 by The American Graduate School of International Management. All rights reserved.

million were capitalized for the year ended March 31, 1994. The effect of this change was to decrease the loss before income taxes and the equity in earnings of unconsolidated subsidiaries and affiliates for the year ended March 31, 1994 by ¥1,419 million.

b. Effective April 1, 1994, the Company discontinued the policy of providing for deferred income taxes on special depreciation in accordance with the Special Taxation Measures Law and the Commercial Code of Japan. The effect of this change was to decrease the net loss for the year ended March 31, 1995 by ¥4,108 million.

c. Effective April 1, 1993, the Company changed the estimated useful lives of certain aircraft, with the exception of the Boeing 747-400 (international type), and their spare parts from 10 years, which is prescribed by the Corporation Tax Law of Japan, to 15 years (international type) or 13 years (domestic type), based on a revised estimate by the Company.

This change reflects the fact that the structure of the aircraft has become more durable and the maintenance required is sufficient to warrant such a change.

The effect of this change was to decrease the loss before income taxes and equity in earnings of unconsolidated subsidiaries and affiliates for the year ended March 31, 1994 by ¥17,842 million.

The latest accounting policy change was revealed in the company's 1996 annual report (see footnote 3): JAL had decided to change its method of depreciation accounting for its ground property and equipment. In the past, the airline had used the double-declining balance method; however, effective April 1, 1995, the company adopted the straight-line method of depreciation, and as a consequence, reduced its net loss before income taxes by ¥10.9 billion.[1]

Airline industry analysts had, in the past, applauded JAL's conservative depreciation practices. Few international carriers utilized the more conservative declining-balance method, and most depreciated their fleets over estimated lives in excess of 10 years:

International Carrier	Depreciation Method	Estimated Useful Life
American Airlines	straight-line	8-20 years
British Airways	straight-line	14-25 years
Deutsche Lufthansa	straight-line	10.5 years
Varig	straight-line	5-15 years

Those same analysts now wondered about the reasons behind JAL's decision to switch depreciation methods.

---

[1] Under Japanese tax regulations, depreciation is tax-deductible only if recorded in the company's financial records. For a corporation with paid-in capital in excess of ¥100 million, income tax rates are as follows:

National tax rate	37.5%
Local enterprise tax rate	6.74% (approximately)
Corporate inhabitant tax rate	7.76% (effective rate)

Questions:

1. Why did JAL make the accounting policy decisions listed above? Do you agree with the company's decision to change these accounting policies? Why or why not?

2. Considering only JAL's depreciation policy changes, estimate the company's operating earnings for 1994-1996 assuming that the policy changes had <u>not</u> been implemented.

3. Review Exhibits 1 and 2. Make a list of any differences you observe between Japanese and U.S. GAAP.

4. Evaluate JAL's debt position.

Exhibit 1
Japan Airlines Company Ltd.
Consolidated Financial Statements

A.   **Consolidated Balance Sheets**

CONSOLIDATED BALANCE SHEETS
JAPAN AIRLINES COMPANY, LTD. AND CONSOLIDATED SUBSIDIARIES
MARCH 31, 1996 AND 1995

	Millions of yen		Thousands of U.S. dollars (Note 2)
ASSETS	1996	1995	1996
Current assets:			
Cash and cash equivalents	¥ 112,545	¥ 104,672	$ 1,061,745
Time deposits	8,742	118,031	82,471
Marketable securities, at cost	82,742	78,388	780,584
Accounts receivable:			
Trade	174,856	136,228	1,649,584
Unconsolidated subsidiaries and affiliates	28,794	27,290	271,641
Allowance for doubtful accounts	(2,043)	(1,585)	(19,273)
Flight equipment spare parts, at cost	48,207	50,506	454,783
Prepaid expenses and other	91,720	86,857	865,283
Total current assets	545,565	600,390	5,146,839
Investments and advances:			
Unconsolidated subsidiaries and affiliates	69,580	66,864	656,415
Others, at cost	252,664	213,013	2,383,622
Total investments and advances	322,244	279,877	3,040,037
Property and equipment (Note 4):			
Flight equipment	1,324,529	1,297,981	12,495,556
Ground property and equipment (Note 3)	906,003	872,120	8,547,198
	2,230,532	2,170,101	21,042,754
Accumulated depreciation	(1,115,085)	(1,096,190)	(10,519,669)
	1,115,447	1,073,911	10,523,084
Advances on aircraft purchases and other	75,364	116,416	710,981
Property and equipment, net	1,190,812	1,190,328	11,234,075
Housing loans to employees	4,938	21,362	46,584
Other assets	15,962	29,095	150,584
Translation adjustments	31,529	34,706	297,443
	¥2,111,053	¥2,155,761	$19,915,594

A. Consolidated Balance Sheets (continued)

LIABILITIES AND STOCKHOLDERS' EQUITY	Millions of yen		Thousands of U.S. dollars (Note 2)
	1996	1995	1996
Current liabilities:			
Short-term bank loans (Note 4)	¥ 71,076	¥ 102,479	$ 670,528
Current portion of long-term debt (Note 4)	169,081	134,622	1,595,103
Accounts payable:			
Trade	163,701	134,787	1,544,349
Construction	15,464	13,781	145,886
Unconsolidated subsidiaries and affiliates	8,321	6,815	78,500
Accrued expenses	77,668	79,479	732,716
Accrued income taxes (Note 5)	2,848	3,079	26,867
Other	137,531	125,466	1,297,462
Total current liabilities	645,693	600,512	6,091,443
Long-term debt (Note 4)	1,091,993	1,171,365	10,301,820
Accrued severance indemnities (Note 6)	99,987	96,839	943,273
Minority interests	5,062	7,198	47,754
Commitments and contingent liabilities (Note 8)			
Stockholders' equity:			
Common stock, ¥50 par value;			
Authorized: 6,000,000,000 shares			
Issued: 1,778,943,439 shares	188,323	188,323	1,776,632
Additional paid-in capital	161,776	161,776	1,526,188
Legal reserve (Note 7)	7,330	7,330	69,150
Deficit	(89,095)	(77,577)	(840,518)
	268,334	279,853	2,531,452
Common stock in treasury, at cost:			
26,183 shares in 1996 and 11,502 shares in 1995	(19)	(7)	(179)
Total stockholders' equity	268,315	279,846	2,531,273
	¥2,111,053	¥2,155,761	$19,915,594

The accompanying notes are an integral part of these statements.

B. Consolidated Statements of Operations

	1996	1995	Millions of yen 1994	Thousands of U.S. dollars (Note 2) 1996
Operating revenues:				
Passenger:				
Domestic	¥ 303,160	¥ 296,628	¥ 284,599	$ 2,860,000
International	620,481	560,236	518,246	5,853,594
Cargo:				
Domestic	29,401	28,980	28,463	277,367
International	132.603	126,677	119,559	1,250,971
Incidental and other	363,394	335,893	305,743	3,428,245
	1,449,041	1,348.417	1,256,612	13,670,198
Operating expenses:				
Flying operations	275,577	252,432	270,095	2,599,783
Maintenance	79,090	79,977	73,638	746,132
Passenger services	124.071	122,737	118,665	1,170,481
Aircraft and traffic servicing	196,572	190,738	176,389	1,854,452
Sales and advertising	197,779	189,472	168,971	1,865,839
General and administrative (Note 5)	102,265	110,299	79,945	964,764
Depreciation and amortization (Note 3)	94,779	104,705	88,454	894,141
Cost of incidental and other revenues	361,589	310,685	310,078	3,411,216
	1,431,726	1,361,048	1,286,240	13,506,849
Operating income (loss)	17,315	(12,631)	(29,627)	163,349
Non-operating income (expenses):				
Interest and dividend income	5,726	10,485	13,885	54,018
Interest expenses	(50,759)	(55,809)	(53,915)	(478,858)
Exchange gains (losses), net	4,463	(3,972)	(5,718)	42,103
Aircraft purchase incentives	3,336	27,853	7,100	31,471
Gain on sales of aircraft	18,980	22,027	23,622	179,056
Special termination benefits	(1,010)	(10,038)	(3,845)	(9,528)
Loss on termination of operations of a subsidiary	(1,311)	–	–	(12,367)
Other, net	(5,282)	2,836	5,148	(49,830)
	(25,856)	(6,618)	(13,722)	(243,924)
Loss before minority interests, income taxes, and equity in earnings of unconsolidated subsidiaries and affiliates	(8,540)	(19,249)	(43,349)	(80,566)
Income taxes (Note 5):				
Current	3,675	3,440	3,973	34,669
Deferred	1,167	(4,760)	(4,991)	11,009
	4,842	(1,319)	(1,018)	45,679
Loss before minority interests and equity in earnings of unconsolidated subsidiaries and affiliates	(13,383)	(17,930)	(42,331)	(126,254)
Minority interests	2,252	3,107	3,751	21,245
Equity in earnings of unconsolidated subsidiaries and affiliates	2,032	202	1,115	19,169
Net loss	¥ (9,098)	¥ (14,620)	¥ (37,463)	$ (85,830)

The accompanying notes are an integral part of these statements.

C.   **Consolidated Statements of Stockholders' Equity**

CONSOLIDATED STATEMENTS OF STOCKHOLDERS' EQUITY

JAPAN AIRLINES COMPANY, LTD. AND CONSOLIDATED SUBSIDIARIES
FOR THE YEARS ENDED MARCH 31, 1996, 1995 AND 1994

| | | | | Millions of yen |
	Number of shares of common stock	Common stock	Additional paid-in capital	Legal reserve (Note 7)	Retained earnings (deficit)
Balance at March 31, 1993	1,778,943,439	¥188,323	¥161,776	¥7,330	¥(17,785)
Net loss for the year ended March 31, 1994					(37,463)
Bonuses to directors and statutory auditors					(54)
Decrease resulting from changes in equity interest in subsidiaries and affiliates					(983)
Translation adjustments					1,720
Balance at March 31, 1994	1,778,943,439	188,323	161,776	7,330	(54,566)
Net loss for the year ended March 31, 1995					(14,620)
Bonuses to directors and statutory auditors					(25)
Decrease resulting from changes in equity interest in subsidiaries and affiliates					(11,040)
Translation adjustments					2,676
Balance at March 31, 1995	1,778,943,439	188,323	161,776	7,330	(77,577)
Net loss for the year ended March 31, 1996					(9,098)
Bonuses to directors and statutory auditors					(22)
Decrease resulting from changes in equity interest in subsidiaries and affiliates					(674)
Translation adjustments					(1,722)
Balance at March 31, 1996	1,778,943,439	¥188,323	¥161,776	¥7,330	¥(89,095)

| | | | Thousands of U.S. dollars (Note 2) |
	Common stock	Additional paid-in capital	Legal reserve (Note 7)	Retained earnings (deficit)
Balance at March 31, 1995	$1,776,632	$1,526,188	$69,150	$(731,858)
Net loss for the year ended March 31, 1996				(85,830)
Bonuses to directors and statutory auditors				(207)
Decrease resulting from changes in equity interest in subsidiaries and affiliates				(6,358)
Translation adjustments				(16,245)
Balance at March 31, 1996	$1,776,632	$1,526,188	$69,150	$(840,518)

The accompanying notes are an integral part of these statements.

Exhibit 1
Japan Airlines Company Ltd.
Consolidated Financial Statements
(continued)

D.   Consolidated Statements of Cash Flows

JAPAN AIRLINES COMPANY, LTD. AND CONSOLIDATED SUBSIDIARIES
FOR THE YEARS ENDED MARCH 31, 1996, 1995 AND 1994

		Millions of yen		Thousands of U.S. dollars (Note 2)
	1996	1995	1994	1996
Operating activities				
Net loss	¥ (9,098)	¥ (14,620)	¥ (37,463)	$ (85,830)
Adjustments to reconcile net loss to net cash provided by operating activities:				
Depreciation and amortization	94,779	104,705	88,454	894,141
Net provision for (reversal of) severance indemnities	3,148	1,215	(10,154)	29,698
Provision for (reversal of) deferred income taxes	1,157	(5,694)	(5,239)	10,915
Equity in earnings of unconsolidated subsidiaries and affiliates	(2,032)	(202)	(1,115)	(19,169)
Loss on termination of operations of a subsidiary	1,311	–	–	12,367
Gain on sale, disposal and revaluation of flight equipment spare parts, property and equipment	(17,103)	(19,410)	(22,151)	(161,349)
Minority interests	(2,252)	(3,107)	(3,751)	(21,245)
Foreign currency translation loss (gain)	1,455	(21,973)	(3,243)	13,726
Changes in operating assets and liabilities:				
Accounts receivable	(39,674)	(2,627)	(17,293)	(374,283)
Flight equipment spare parts and prepaid expenses	(2,386)	30,159	(8,950)	(22,509)
Accounts payable and accrued expenses	40,473	21,075	27,994	381,820
Net cash provided by operating activities	69,778	89,521	7,089	658,283
Investing activities				
Decrease (increase) in time deposits and marketable securities	104,923	(33,367)	85,687	989,839
Additions to property and equipment	(95,821)	(252,260)	(225,272)	(903,971)
Proceeds from sales of property and equipment	28,028	51,738	45,556	264,415
Decrease (increase) in investments and advances	(41,646)	66,614	55,731	(392,886)
Decrease (increase) in housing loans to employees	16,424	35,918	(2,380)	154,943
Decrease (increase) in other assets	3,170	(8,031)	(5,643)	29,905
Other	(712)	(7,451)	4,735	(6,716)
Net cash provided by (used in) investing activities	14,366	(146,839)	(41,586)	135,528
Financing activities				
Proceeds from long-term debt	293,799	284,685	360,300	2,771,688
Payments of long-term debt	(338,614)	(284,670)	(301,016)	(3,194,471)
Increase (decrease) in short-term bank loans	(31,403)	16,698	(5,197)	(296,254)
Dividends paid and bonuses to directors and statutory auditors	(53)	(55)	(89)	(500)
Net cash provided by (used in) financing activities	(76,271)	16,658	53,998	(719,537)
Net increase (decrease) in cash and cash equivalents	7,873	(40,660)	19,501	74,273
Cash and cash equivalents at beginning of the year	104,672	145,332	125,831	987,471
Cash and cash equivalents at end of the year	¥112,545	¥104,672	¥145,332	$1,061,745
Supplemental disclosures of cash flow information				
Cash paid during the year for:				
Interest	¥ 69,850	¥ 73,705	¥ 63,361	$ 658,962
Income taxes	6,076	4,466	3,653	57,320

The accompanying notes are an integral part of these statements.

1. SUMMARY OF SIGNIFICANT ACCOUNTING POLICIES

a. Basis of presentation

Japan Airlines Company, Ltd. (the "Company") and its consolidated domestic subsidiaries maintain their accounting records and prepare their financial statements in accordance with accounting principles and practices generally accepted in Japan, and its consolidated foreign subsidiaries in conformity with those of the countries of their domicile. The accompanying consolidated financial statements have been compiled from the consolidated financial statements filed with the Minister of Finance as required by the Securities and Exchange Law of Japan and include certain additional financial information for the convenience of readers outside Japan.

As permitted by the Securities and Exchange Law of Japan, amounts of less than one million yen have been omitted. As a result, the totals shown in the accompanying consolidated financial statements (both in yen and in dollars) do not necessarily agree with the sum of the individual amounts.

Certain amounts previously reported have been reclassified to conform to current year classifications.

b. Principles of consolidation and accounting for investments in unconsolidated subsidiaries and affiliates

The consolidated financial statements include the accounts of the Company and all its significant subsidiaries. All significant intercompany accounts and transactions have been eliminated.

Investments in certain unconsolidated subsidiaries and in significant affiliates (companies owned 20% to 50%) are accounted for by the equity method of accounting.

The difference between the cost and the underlying net equity in the net assets at the dates of acquisition of the consolidated subsidiaries and companies accounted for by the equity method is amortized by the straight-line method over a period of five years.

c. Foreign currency accounts

Foreign currency receivables and payables are translated into yen as follows:
(1) Current receivables and payables are translated at the applicable year-end rates;
(2) Non-current receivables and payables not hedged by forward exchange contracts are translated at historical rates, which approximate the prevailing rates at the time of the transactions; and
(3) Long-term debt hedged by forward exchange contracts is translated at the forward rates, and the resulting translation differences are allocated to income or expenses on the basis of the number of months in the contract period.

The accounts of consolidated foreign subsidiaries are translated into yen as follows:
(1) Capital stock is translated at historical rates; and
(2) Retained earnings (deficit) at the beginning of the year is translated at the preceding year-end rate.
(3) All other accounts are translated at the applicable year-end rates;

The accounts of unconsolidated foreign subsidiaries accounted for by the equity method are translated into yen as follows:
(1) Retained earnings (deficit) at the end of the year and net income (loss) for the year are translated at the applicable year-end rates; and
(2) Retained earnings (deficit) at the beginning of the year is translated at the preceding year-end rates.

d. Property and equipment

Property and equipment are stated at cost except as indicated in the following paragraph.

In Japan, companies are permitted by tax legislation to defer certain capital gains principally arising from insurance claims by crediting them to the cost of certain properties. Such deferred gains at March 31, 1996 and 1995 amounted to ¥11,010 million ($103,867 thousand) and ¥14,814 million, respectively.

Depreciation of property and equipment is as follows:

Flight equipment:
Aircraft and spare engines:

Boeing 747 (with the exception of Boeing 747-400)	– principally the declining-balance method based on their estimated useful lives
Boeing 747-400	– the straight-line method based on their estimated useful lives
Boeing 767	– the straight-line method based on their estimated useful lives
Boeing 777	– the straight-line method based on their estimated useful lives
Boing 737-400	– the straight-line method based on their estimated useful lives
Douglas DC-10	– principally the declining-balance method based on their estimated useful lives
Douglas MD-11	– the straight-line method based on their estimated useful lives

Spare parts contained in flight equipment:
– principally the declining-balance method based on each aircraft's or engine's estimated useful life

Ground property and equipment:
– principally the straight-line method

Effective April 1, 1993, the Company changed the estimated useful lives of the aircraft, with the exception of the Boeing 747-400 (international type), and their spare parts from 10 years, which is prescribed by the Corporation Tax Law of Japan, to 15 years (international type) or 13 years (domestic type), based on a revised estimate by the Company.

This change reflects the fact that the structure of the aircraft has become more durable and the level of maintenance required is sufficient to warrant such change.

The effect of this change was to decrease loss before minority interest, income taxes and equity in earnings of unconsolidated subsidiaries and affiliates for the year ended March 31, 1994 by ¥17.842 million.

Costs for maintenance, repairs and minor renewals and improvements are charged to income in the year incurred: major renewals and improvements are capitalized.

In general, when assets are sold or otherwise disposed of, the profit or loss, computed on the basis of the difference between the net book value of the assets and the sales proceeds, is credited or charged to income in the year of the sale or disposal, and the cost and accumulated depreciation are removed from the accounts.

e. Bond issuance expenses
Bond issuance expenses are principally capitalized and amortized over a period of three years.

f. Accrued severance indemnities
An employee whose employment is terminated is entitled, in most cases, to a lump-sum severance payment, the amount of which is determined by reference to the basic rate of pay, length of service and the conditions under which the termination occurs. The Company has followed the accounting policy of providing for the liability for employees' severance indemnities to the extent to which they are deductible for income tax purposes. The rate of deduction permitted for income tax purposes is 40% of such liability.

In addition to the lump-sum payment plan. the Company and certain significant domestic subsidiaries have established contributory funded defined benefit pension plans pursuant to the Welfare Pension Insurance Law of Japan to substitute for their non-contributory funded pension plans, while most other domestic subsidiaries have maintained non-contributory funded pension plans. The costs of the pension plans are determined actuarially and the amortization of prior service cost is charged to income. Prior service cost is being amortized over a period of between 10 and 20 years.

g. Passenger revenue
Passenger revenue is recognized when the transportation services are rendered.

h. Appropriation of retained earnings (deficit)
Under the Commercial Code of Japan, the appropriation of retained earnings (deficit) with respect to a financial period is made by resolution of the stockholders at a general meeting held subsequent to the close of the financial period and the accounts for that period do not, therefore. reflect such appropriation.

i. Cash equivalents
The Company defines cash equivalents as highly liquid, short-term investments with an original maturity of three months or less.

2. U.S. DOLLAR AMOUNTS
Amounts in U.S. dollars are included solely for the convenience of the reader. The rate of ¥106= S1, the approximate exchange rate prevailing on March 31, 1996, has been used. The inclusion of such amounts is not intended to imply that yen have been or could be readily converted, realized or settled in U.S. dollars at that or any other rate.

3. CHANGES IN ACCOUNTING POLICY
a. Effective April 1, 1993, the Company changed its method of accounting for bond issuance expenses, which had previously been charged to income when incurred, to capitalizing and amortizing these over a period of three years. As a result of this change, bond issuance expenses of ¥2.128 million were capitalized for the year ended March 31, 1994. The effect of this change was to decrease the loss before minority interests, income taxes and equity in earnings of unconsolidated subsidiaries and affiliates for the year ended March 31, 1994 by ¥1,419 million.
b. Effective April 1, 1994, the Company discontinued the policy of providing for deferred income taxes on special depreciation in accordance with the Special Taxation Measures Law and the Commercial Code of Japan. The effect of this change was to decrease the net loss for the year ended March 31, 1995 by ¥4,108 million.
c. Effective April 1, 1995, the Company changed its method of accounting for depreciation expenses related to ground property and equipment to the straight-line method from the declining-balance method. The effect of this change was to decrease operating expenses and the operating loss for the year ended March 31, 1996 by ¥10,974 million (S103,528 thousand) and to decrease the loss before minority interests, income taxes and equity in earnings of unconsolidated subsidiaries and affiliates for the year ended March 31, 1996 by ¥10,915 million ($102,971 thousand).

4. SHORT-TERM BANK LOANS AND LONG-TERM DEBT

The weighted average interest rates for short-term bank loans outstanding at March 31, 1996 and 1995 were 3.46% and 5.42%, respectively, and the approximate weighted average interest rates for such obligations outstanding during the years ended March 31, 1996 and 1995 were 3.56% and 4.91%, respectively.

Long-term debt at March 31, 1996 and 1995 comprised the following:

	Millions of yen		U.S. dollars
	1996	1995	1996
Bonds:			
Bonds in foreign currencies, guaranteed by the Japanese government, due 1996 to 1998 with interest at 6.625% to 11.0%	¥ 62,144	¥ 65,575	$ 586,264
Bonds in U.S. dollars, due 2003 with interest at 6.625%	26,845	26,845	253,254
Bonds in foreign currencies, due 1996 to 2000 with interest at 4.3% to 6.375% and a rate which varies according to LIBOR	16,954	22,022	159,943
Private placements in foreign currencies, due 1996 with interest at 8.4%	1,515	1,344	14,292
Japanese yen bonds, due 2001 to 2002 with interest at 2.3% to 2.6%	70,000	–	660,377
Euro-yen bonds, due 1998 to 2003 with interest at 4.0% to 6.9% and a rate which varies according to LIBOR	193,245	340,327	1,823,066
Convertible bonds, due 1997 to 2005 with interest at 1.4% to 1.6%	56,302	56,302	531,150
Loans with collateral, due 1996 to 2024 with interest at 1.47% to 7.0%	343,888	319,700	3,244,226
Loans without collateral	454,948	441,836	4,291,962
Other	35,232	32,034	332,377
	1,261,074	1,305,987	11,896,924
Less current portion	(169,081)	(134,622)	(1,595,103)
	¥1,091,993	¥1,171,365	$10,301,820

Convertible bonds, unless previously redeemed, are convertible into shares of common stock of the Company at the following current conversion prices:

	Conversion price per share	Conversion Period
1.6% convertible bonds in yen due 2005	¥1,751.10	February 1, 1990– March 30, 2005
1.5% convertible bonds in yen due 1999	¥1,751.10	February 1, 1990– March 30, 1999
1.4% convertible bonds in yen due 1997	¥1,751.10	February 1, 1990– March 28, 1997

Under the provisions of these issues, the conversion prices are subject to adjustment in certain cases which include stock splits.

The aggregate annual maturities of long-term debt subsequent to March 31, 1996 are as follows:

Year ending March 31,	Millions of yen	Thousands of U.S. dollars
1997	¥ 169,081	$ 1,595,103
1998	176,447	1,664,594
1999	151,270	1,427,075
2000	134,345	1,267,405
2001 and thereafter	629,927	5,942,707
	¥1,261,074	$11,896,924

A summary of assets pledged as collateral for long-term debt at March 31, 1996 is as follows:

	Millions of yen	Thousands of U.S. dollars
Flight equipment, net of accumulated depreciation	¥437,493	$4,127,292
Ground property and equipment, net of accumulated depreciation, and other	103,936	980,528
	¥541,429	$5,107,820

In November 1987, the Japan Airlines Company, Ltd. Law was abrogated. However, the section pertaining to the bondholders' entitlement to payments from the Company's assets in priority to other unsecured creditors was reinstated under a new law. Holders of bonds which amounted to ¥62,144 million ($586,264 thousand) at March 31, 1996 are covered by the new law.

The effective interest rates on certain foreign currency bonds, which resulted from hedging such bonds with cross-currency interest rate swaps, were lower than the long-term prime rate in Japan at each issuance date.

5. INCOME TAXES

The Company is subject to a number of taxes based on taxable income, i.e. corporation, inhabitants' and enterprise taxes, which, in the aggregate, resulted in a statutory rate of approximately 52% in 1996, 1995 and 1994.

Corporation tax and inhabitants' taxes are based on taxable income and are included under the caption "Income Taxes – Current," while enterprise tax, which is deductible for corporation and inhabitants' tax purposes when paid, is included under the caption "Operating expenses – General and administrative" in the accompanying consolidated statements of operations. Enterprise tax for the years ended March 31, 1996, 1995 and 1994 was ¥1,306 million ($12,320 thousand), ¥770 million and ¥929 million, respectively.

Deferred income taxes are recognized only insofar as they relate to the elimination of intercompany items on consolidation.

6. ACCRUED SEVERANCE INDEMNITIES

Charges to income for severance indemnities for the years ended March 31, 1996, 1995 and 1994 were as follows:

	Millions of yen			Thousands of U.S. dollars
1996	1995	1994		1996
¥17,723	¥25,395	¥7,737		$167,198

The decrease in accrued severance indemnities for the year ended March 31, 1996 resulted principally from a decrease in the effect of special termination benefits.

The unamortized balance of prior service cost of the pension plans at March 31, 1995, the most recent valuation date, was ¥43,900 million ($414,150 thousand).

7. LEGAL RESERVE

In accordance with the provisions of the Commercial Code of Japan, the Company has provided a legal reserve by appropriating retained earnings. The legal reserve may be used to reduce or eliminate a deficit or may be transferred to stated capital through suitable stockholders' or directors' action, but is not available for the payment of dividends.

8. COMMITMENTS AND CONTINGENT LIABILITIES

Commitments outstanding at March 31, 1996 for purchases of property and equipment amounted to ¥545,346 million ($5,144,773 thousand).

The Company leases aircraft, office space, warehouses and office equipment. These leases are customarily renewed upon expiration.

At March 31, 1996, contingent liabilities for guarantees, principally for unconsolidated subsidiaries, affiliates and employees, amounted to ¥43,430 million ($409,716 thousand).

In addition, at March 31, 1996, the Company was liable under debt assumption agreements for in-substance defeasance of the bonds which amounted to ¥120,000 million ($1,132,075 thousand).

9. AMOUNTS PER SHARE

Net loss per share has been computed based on the weighted average number of shares of common stock outstanding during each year.

The primary and fully diluted net loss per share were the same for the year ended March 31, 1996.

Net assets per share have been computed based on the number of shares of common stock outstanding at each balance sheet date.

		Yen		U.S.dollars
Year ended March 31	1996	1995	1994	1996
Net loss	¥(5.11)	¥(8.22)	¥(21.06)	$(0.048)

		Yen	U.S.dollars
March 31	1996	1995	1996
Net assets	¥150.83	¥157.31	$1.422

10. SEGMENT INFORMATION

The Company and its consolidated subsidiaries conduct worldwide operations in air transportation, hotel and resort operations, card and lease operations, travel services, trading and other airline-related business. The respective businesses other than the air transportation business, hotel and resort operations and card and lease operations, are insignificant to the consolidated results of operations of the Company and its consolidated subsidiaries and, accordingly, are included in "Other."

Business segment information of the Company and its consolidated subsidiaries for the years ended March 31, 1996, 1995 and 1994 is summarized as follows:

Millions of yen

Year ended March 31, 1996	Air transportation (Note 3)	Hotel and resort operations	Card and lease operations	Other	Total	General corporate assets and intercompany eliminations	Consolidated
Operating revenues	¥1,067,351	¥ 52,503	¥ 11,586	¥317,599	¥1,449,041	¥ –	¥1,449,041
Intra-group sales and transfers	97,502	4,529	29,094	158,666	289,793	(289,793)	–
Total	1,164,854	57,033	40,681	476,266	1,738,835	(289,793)	1,449,041
Operating expenses	1,148,191	57,667	39,586	472,373	1,717,819	(286,092)	1,431,726
Operating income (loss)	¥ 16,663	¥ (634)	¥ 1,094	¥ 3,892	¥ 21,015	¥ (3,700)	¥ 17,315
Depreciation and amortization	¥ 75,811	¥ 7,519	¥ 7,697	¥ 4,819	¥ 95,847	¥ (1,068)	¥ 94,779
Capital expenditures	¥ 74,925	¥ 1,480	¥ 8,591	¥ 10,824	¥ 95,821	¥ –	¥ 95,821
Identifiable assets	¥1,428,721	¥183,488	¥329,383	¥287,484	¥2,229,078	¥(118,024)	¥2,111,053

Thousands of U.S. dollars

Year ended March 31, 1996	Air transportation (Note 3)	Hotel and resort operations	Card and lease operations	Other	Total	General corporate assets and intercompany eliminations	Consolidated
Operating revenues	$10,069,349	$ 495,311	$ 109.301	$2,996,216	$13,670,198	$ –	$13,670.198
Intra-group sales and transfers	919,830	42,726	274.471	1,496,849	2,733,896	(2,733.896)	–
Total	10,989,188	538,047	383.783	4,493,075	16,404,103	(2,733.896)	13,670.198
Operating expenses	10,831,990	544,028	373.452	4,456.349	16.205,839	(2,698.981)	13,506.849
Operating income (loss)	$ 157.198	$ (5,981)	$ 10.320	$ 36.716	S 198,254	$ (34.905)	$ 163.349
Depreciation and amortization	$ 715.198	$ 70,933	$ 72.613	$ 45,462	S 904.216	$ (10.075)	$ 894.141
Capital expenditures	$ 706.839	$ 13,962	$ 81.047	$ 102.113	S 903,971	$ –	$ 903.971
Identifiable assets	$13,478,500	$1,731,018	$3,107.386	$2,712,113	S21.029,037	$(1,113.433)	$19,915.594

Millions of yen

Year ended March 31, 1995	Air transportation	Hotel and resort operations	Card and lease operations	Other	Total	Intercompany eliminations	Consolidated
Operating revenues	¥1.007.521	¥50,156	¥12.276	¥278.464	¥1,348,417	¥ –	¥1,348.417
Intra-group sales and transfers	82.128	5,723	25.323	150.291	263,465	(263.465)	–
Total	1,089,650	55,879	37.600	428,755	1,611,882	(263.465)	1,348.417
Operating expenses	1,101.416	57,926	36.518	427.333	1,623,193	(262.145)	1,361.048
Operating income (loss)	¥ (11,766)	¥ (2,047)	¥ 1.082	¥ 1.422	¥ (11,311)	¥ (1,319)	¥ (12.631)

Millions of yen

Year ended March 31, 1994	Air transportation	Hotel and resort operations	Card and lease operations	Other	Total	Intercompany eliminations	Consolidated
Operating revenues	¥ 967,429	¥27,432	¥13.288	¥248.461	¥1,256,612	¥ –	¥1,256.612
Intra-group sales and transfers	69,165	4,964	18.648	126.270	219,047	(219,047)	–
Total	1,036,595	32,396	31.936	374,731	1,475,660	(219,047)	1,256.612
Operating expenses	1,071,239	31,491	31.281	371.353	1,505,364	(219.124)	1,286.240
Operating income (loss)	¥ (34,643)	¥ 904	¥ 654	¥ 3.378	¥ (29,703)	¥ (76)	¥ (29.627)

Operating revenues of foreign operations which include international passenger and cargo services sold in Japan accounted for 55.6%, 54.6% and 52.6% of the total operations revenues for the years ended March 31, 1996, 1995 and 1994 respectively.

REPORT OF CERTIFIED PUBLIC ACCOUNTANTS

JAPAN AIRLINES COMPANY, LTD. AND CONSOLIDATED SUBSIDIARIES

To the Board of Directors of

JAPAN AIRLINES COMPANY, LTD.

We have examined the consolidated balance sheets of Japan Airlines Company, Ltd. and its consolidated subsidiaries as of March 31, 1996 and 1995, and the related consolidated statements of operations, stockholders' equity and cash flows for each of the three years in the period ended March 31, 1996, all expressed in yen. Our examinations were made in accordance with auditing standards generally accepted in Japan and, accordingly, included such tests of the accounting records and such other auditing procedures as we considered necessary in the circumstances.

In our opinion, the accompanying consolidated financial statements, expressed in yen, present fairly the financial position of Japan Airlines Company, Ltd. and its consolidated subsidiaries at March 31, 1996 and 1995, and the results of their operations and their cash flows for each of the three years in the period ended March 31, 1996, in conformity with accounting principles generally accepted in Japan consistently applied during the period except for the changes, with which we concur, in the method of accounting for bond issuance expenses in 1994, for deferred income taxes in 1995, and for depreciation expenses related to ground property and equipment in 1996 as described in Note 3 to the consolidated financial statements.

The U.S. dollar amounts in the accompanying consolidated financial statements with respect to the year ended March 31, 1996 are presented solely for convenience. Our examination also included the translation of yen amounts into U.S. dollar amounts and, in our opinion, such translation has been made on the basis described in Note 2 to the consolidated financial statements.

Showa Ota & Co.

June 27, 1996

Showa Ota & Co.

Mitsui Oil Exploration Company (hereafter MOECO) was founded in the early 1960s by Mitsui & Company Ltd., one of Japan's leading industrial conglomerates. MOECO's emergence resulted from a consolidation of a number of smaller oil and gas companies owned by Mitsui, and reflected the concern of Mitsui executives regarding Japan's dependence on other oil-producing countries (e.g. Australia, the OPEC nations, and the U.S.) for its supply of oil and oil-related by-products.

Over the next 30 years, the company experienced a relatively high rate of growth and by the mid-1990s was regarded as one of Asia's leading companies in the development and operation of oil and gas wells. (The company also maintained a small refining operation.) The end of the Cold War and the normalization of diplomatic relations between Vietnam and the U.S. presented MOECO with new opportunities to replenish, and even increase, its diminishing reserves. This case concerns the financing of one such opportunity.

Malay Basin Project

In late May, 1996, Unocal, the U.S.-based energy company, signed a three-year contract with the state oil agency of Vietnam, PetroVietnam, to explore for natural gas off the southern coast of that country. Exploration was expected to begin in 1997, following nine months of seismic surveying. The site, to be known as Block B, was located in the Malay Basin, adjacent to an area already under exploration by Fina of Belgium.

According to a Unocal spokesperson, the Malay Basin project was a joint venture among three companies: Unocal, with a 45 percent ownership, would be the operator; Repsol, the state-owned oil company of Spain, had a 30 percent interest; and MOECO had a 25 percent interest. (PetroVietnam retained an option to buy a 15 percent interest from the joint venture partners.)

MOECO's share of the project's exploration budget was expected to total approximately ¥200 billion. When reviewing the feasibility of the joint venture, Mitsui executives had been led to believe that 40 percent of the necessary funds could be internally generated from MOECO's existing operations. The remaining 60 percent would need to be obtained from outside sources, probably from one or more of the banks that were members of the Mitsui keiretsu.[1]

---

[*] This case was prepared by Kenneth R. Ferris. Copyright © 1996 by The American Graduate School of International Management. All rights reserved.

[1] A keiretsu (literally, headless combine) is an alliance of technically unaffiliated companies, usually linked by inter-locking directorates and ownership of shares, that provide economic support to one another.

Questions:

1. Using MOECO's financial data in Exhibits 1 - 3, prepare a statement of cash flows for 1996.[2] Using this statement, forecast MOECO's "discretionary cash flows" for 1997.[3].

2. How valid is the assumption that 40 percent of the necessary funds for the Malay Basin Project can be internally-generated from operations? Be prepared to substantiate your answer.

---

[2] In Japan, a statement of cash flows is not a required financial statement, although it is frequently disclosed by large companies as supplemental information (and hence not subject to audit).

[3] Discretionary cash flows (DCF) may be defined in a variety of ways; for purposes of this case, we define DCF as follows:

DCF = Cash flows from operations - dividends - currently maturing debt - asset replacement

Exhibit 1
Mitsui Oil Exploration Company
Consolidated Balance Sheets

	Yen (millions)	
	December 31, 1996	December 31, 1995
Assets		
Current assets:		
Cash (including time deposits of ¥8,000)	¥ 200,133	¥ 220,500
Trade receivables (net)	138,200	106,400
Inventories (Note 2)	117,900	93,600
Prepaid expenses	22,217	27,700
Total current assets	478,450	448,200
Investments:		
In associated companies (note 1)	318,000	302,000
Sinking fund (Note 3)	5,000	--
Long-term assets:		
Undeveloped properties (note 4)	32,700	18,800
Oil and Gas properties, and equipment (Note 5)	670,000	675,000
Less: Accumulated depreciation and depletion	(227,000)	(200,000)
Unamortized goodwill	6,000	7,500
Total assets	¥1,283,150	¥1,251,500
Liabilities and Shareholders' Equity		
Current Liabilities:		
Trade Payables	¥ 3,300	¥ 16,000
Accrued income taxes payable	5,500	6,500
Dividends payable	4,000	--
Total current liabilities	12,800	22,500
Long-term liabilities:		
10% convertible debentures	100,000	--
Premium on debentures	7,014	--
Deferred income taxes (note 1)	92,000	80,000
Accrued retirement benefits	125,000	120,000
Total liabilities	336,814	222,500
Shareholders' equity:		
Common stock, ¥50 par; authorized shares, 50,000,000,000 (Note 6)	206,000	150,000
Preferred stock, ¥250 par; authorized shares, 1,000,000,000 (Note 6)	--	25,000
Capital in excess of par value:		
Common	315,000	300,000
Preferred	--	175,000
Retained earnings	425,336	379,000
Total liabilities and shareholders' equity	¥1,283,150	¥1,251,500

Exhibit 2
Mitsui Oil Exploration Company
Consolidated Balance Sheets For the Year Ended December 31, 1996
(Yen, millions)

Revenues:		
Oil sales	¥ 630,970	
Gas sales	335,300	
		¥ 966,270
Cost and expense:		
Cost of operations and products sold	741,440	
Selling, general and administrative	108,430	
Interest	9,514	
Amortization of goodwill	1,500	
		860,884
		105,386
Other sources of income:		
Income from unconsolidated subsidiaries		73,300
Gain on sales of undeveloped properties		2,000
Earnings before income taxes		180,686
Income taxes (Note 1)		88,350
Net earnings		¥ 92,336

Exhibit 3
Mitsui Oil Exploration Company
Notes to Consolidated Financial Statements

1. Summary of Significant Accounting Policies

Principles of Consolidation

The consolidated financial statements include the accounts of Mitsui Oil Exploration Company and all significant subsidiaries, after elimination of intercompany transactions and balances. Income from subsidiaries in which ownership is 20 to 50 percent is recognized on an equity basis. All associated companies are engaged in the extraction industry.

Depreciation and Amortization

Depreciation has been provided using the declining-balance method, except for depreciation of oil and gas production equipment, which is determined using the unit-of-production method. Goodwill, obtained in conjunction with the acquisition of South China Sea Drilling, Inc., in late 1995, is being amortized on a straight-line basis over a 5-year period.

Exploration and Development Costs

All intangible drilling and development costs are accounted for under the "successful efforts" method of accounting. Geological and geophysical expenses are charged against income as incurred.

Income Taxes

The company and its subsidiaries file consolidated income tax returns. Deferred income taxes arise principally from differences between the financial statement carrying amounts of existing assets and liabilities and their respective tax bases, and relate primarily to inventories, property and equipment, the allowance for doubtful items, and net operating loss carryforwards.

2. Inventories

Inventories of crude oil and products are valued at lower of cost or market, using the first-in, first-out method. The inventory amounts used in the computation of cost of sales were ¥120,220 million and ¥95,300 million for the years ended December 31, 1996 and 1995, respectively.

3. Sinking Fund

The 10 percent convertible debentures issued on January 1, 1996, are payable December 31, 2006. Under the terms of the bond indenture, a sinking fund was established during 1996.

4. Undeveloped Properties

The company follows a policy of both purchasing and leasing undeveloped oil and gas properties. Leasehold costs are initially capitalized. Subsequent accounting treatment of these costs depends upon the size and cost of extraction of discovered reserves. All undeveloped properties acquired during 1996 were found to be economically productive.

During 1996, undeveloped oil and gas properties were acquired from a major shareholder in exchange for 200 million shares of the company's common stock. These properties were recorded at the par value of the issued shares.

During 1996, certain undeveloped properties located in the China Sea were sold to the Mobil Oil Company. The properties were sold for ¥9 billion and had a book value of ¥7 billion.

5. Oil and Gas Properties, and Equipment

Depreciation and depletion taken during 1996 totaled ¥49,600 million. During 1995, the company began a program of replacing certain outdated extraction equipment. New acquisitions in 1996 amounted to ¥24,650 million. The company plans to invest approximately ¥200 billion in new oil and gas properties during 1997-98.

6. Shareholders' Equity

The authorized and issued shares of capital stock at December 31, 1995 and 1996, are summarized as follows:

	Authorized Shares	Issued Shares 1995	1996
Preferred stock, ¥250 par	1,000,000,000	100,000,000	- -
Common stock, ¥50 par	50,000,000,000	3,000,000,000	4,120,000,000

During the month of January, 1996, 200 million shares of common stock were issued in exchange for undeveloped oil and gas properties (see Note 4). In June 1996, a 25 percent common stock dividend was declared and distributed. A public offering of 120 million common shares was held in December 1996; the offering was fully subscribed.

As of December 3, 1995, 100 million shares of ¥250 par value preferred stock were outstanding. The entire amount was redeemed during 1996 for ¥202 billion.

I. Identifying Differences between U.S. and Japanese GAAP

Dave Ando and Yoshi Yashima, recent business school graduates, work as research security analysts for a mutual fund specializing in international equity investments. Based on several meetings, senior managers of the fund decided to invest in the machine tool industry. One international company under consideration is Tanaguchi Corporation, a Japanese manufacturer of machine tools. As staff analysts assigned to perform fundamental analysis on all new investment options, Ando and Yashima obtain a copy of Tanaguchi Corporation's unconsolidated financial statements (Appendix A) and set out to calculate their usual spreadsheet of financial statement ratios. Exhibit 1 presents the results of their efforts. As a basis for comparison, Exhibit 1 also presents the median ratios for U.S. machine tool companies for a comparable year. The following conversation ensues.

Dave: Tanaguchi Corporation does not appear to be as profitable as comparable U.S. firms. Its operating margin and rate of return on assets are significantly less than the median ratios for U.S. machine tool operators. Its rate of return on common equity is only slightly less than its U.S. counterparts, but this is at the expense of assuming much more financial leverage and therefore risk. Most of this leverage is in the form of short-term borrowing. You can see this in its higher total liabilities to total assets ratio combined with its lower long-term debt ratio. This short-term borrowing and higher risk are also evidenced by the lower current and quick ratios. Finally, Tanaguchi Corporation's shares are selling at a higher multiple of net income and stockholders' equity than those of U.S. machine tool companies. I can't see how we can justify paying more for a company that is less profitable and more risky than comparable U.S. companies. It doesn't seem to me that it is worth exploring this investment possibility any further.

Yoshi: You may be right, Dave. However, I wonder if we are not comparing apples and oranges. As a Japanese company, Tanaguchi Corporation operates in an entirely different institutional and cultural environment than U.S. machine tool companies. Furthermore, it prepares its financial statements in accordance with Japanese generally accepted accounting principles (GAAP), which differ from those in the U.S.

Dave: Well, I think we need to explore this further. I recall seeing a report on an associate's desk comparing U.S. and Japanese accounting principles. I will get a copy for us (Appendix B).

Required:

Using the report comparing U.S. and Japanese accounting principles (Appendix B) and Tanaguchi Corporation's financial statements and notes (Appendix A), identify the most important differences between U.S. and Japanese GAAP. Consider both the differences in acceptable methods and in the methods commonly used. For each major difference, indicate the likely effect (increase, decrease, or no effect) (1) on net income, (2) on total assets, and (3) on the ratio of liabilities divided by stockholders' equity of converting Tanaguchi's financial statements to U.S. GAAP.

---

*This case was prepared by Paul R. Brown and Clyde P. Stickney. Copyright (c) 1992 by the American Accounting Association. Reprinted with permission from the American Accounting Association.

Exhibit 1

Comparative Financial Ratio Analysis for Tanaguchi Corporation and U.S. Machine Tool Companies

	Tanaguchi Corporation	Median Ratio for U.S. Machine Tool Companies[a]
Profitability Ratios		
Operating Margin after Taxes (before interest expense and related tax effects)	2.8%	3.3%
x Total Assets Turnover	1.5	1.8
= Return on Assets	4.2	5.9
x Common's Share of Operating Earnings [b]	.83	.91
x Capital Structure Leverage [c]	3.8	2.6
= Return on Common Equity	13.3%[d]	13.9%[d]
Operating Margin Analysis		
Sales	100.0%	100.0%
Other Revenue/Sales	.4	-
Cost of Goods Sold/Sales	(73.2)	(69.3)
Selling and Administrative/Sales	(21.0)	(25.8)
Income Taxes/Sales	(3.4)	(1.6)
Operating Margin (excluding interest and related tax effects)	2.8%	3.3%
Asset Turnover Analysis		
Receivable Turnover	5.1	6.9
Inventory Turnover	6.3	5.2
Fixed Asset Turnover	7.5	7.0
Risk Analysis		
Current Ratio	1.1	6.9
Quick Ratio	.7	.9
Total Liabilities/Total Assets	73.8%	61.1%
Long-Term Debt/Total Assets	4.7%	16.1%
Long-Term Debt/Stockholders' Equity	17.9%	43.2%
Times Interest Covered	5.8	3.1
Market Price Ratios (per common share)		
Market Price/Net Income	45.0	9.0
Market Price/Stockholders' Equity	5.7	1.2

[a] Source: Robert Morris Associates, Annual Statement Studies (except price-earnings ratio).

[b] Common's Share of Operating Earnings = Net Income to Common/Operating Income after Taxes (before interest expense and related tax effects).

[c] Capital Structure Leverage = Average Total Assets/Average Common Stockholders' Equity

[d] The amounts for return on common equity may not be precisely equal to the product of return on assets, common's share of operating earnings and capital structure leverage due to rounding.

II. Comparing Profitability and Risk Ratios for U.S. and Japanese Firms

Dave Ando and Yoshi Yashima spent the next several days converting the financial statements of Tanaguchi Corporation from Japanese to U.S. GAAP. Although their conversions required them to make several estimates, Dave and Yoshi felt comfortable that they had largely filtered out the effects of different accounting principles. Exhibit 2 presents the profitability and risk ratios for Tanaguchi Corporation based on Japanese GAAP (column 1) and as restated to U.S. GAAP (column 2). Column 3 shows the median ratios for U.S. machine tool companies (the same as those reported in Exhibit 1). After studying the financial statement ratios in Exhibit 2, the following conversation ensues.

Dave: The operating profitability of Tanaguchi Corporation, as evidenced by the rate of return on assets, is still lower than comparable U.S. firms, even after adjusting for differences in accounting principles. Although Tanaguchi's rate of return on common equity is now higher than its U.S. counterparts, the higher return occurs at the expense of taking on substantially more debt and therefore more risk. A significant portion of the differences in price-earnings ratios between Tanaguchi Corporation and U.S. companies results from differences in accounting principles. However, large differences still remain. I'm still not convinced that investing in Tanaguchi Corporation makes sense. Yoshi, am I on track with my interpretations or am I missing something?

Yoshi: I'm not sure we are yet to the point where we can recommend that our equity fund purchase shares of Tanaguchi Corporation. We need to develop a better understanding of why the restated financial ratios for Tanaguchi Corporation still differ so much from those for U.S. machine tool companies.

One possible explanation might relate to the practice of many Japanese companies to operate in corporate groups, which the Japanese call *keiretsus*. Tanaguchi Corporation is a member of the Menji *keiretsu*. Each *keiretsu* typically comprises firms in eight or ten different industries (for example, one *keiretsu* might include firms in the steel, chemicals, forest products, retailing, insurance, and banking industries). The companies usually hold stock in each other; investments in the 25 percent to 30 percent range are common. These investments are not made for the purpose of controlling or even significantly influencing other members of the corporate group. Rather, they serve as a mechanism for providing operating links between the entities. It is common for one corporation in the *keiretsu* to source many of its raw materials from another group member and to sell a substantial portion of its products to entities within the group. Each *keiretsu* includes a bank that provides needed funds to group members. It is rare that the bank would allow a member of the group to experience significant operating problems or to go bankrupt due to lack of funds.

A second, but related, institutional difference between the U.S. and Japan concerns stock ownership patterns. Roughly one-third of Japanese companies' shares is held by members of its *keiretsu* and another one-third is held by financial institutions, typically banks and insurance companies not affiliated with the *keiretsu*. This leaves only one-third of the shares held by individuals. The large percentage of intercorporate stock holdings has historically lessened the concern about keeping investors happy by paying large dividends or reporting ever-increasing earnings per share, as seems to be the case in the U.S.

Instead, the emphasis of Japanese companies has been on serving new or growing markets, increasing market share, and strengthening the members of the *keiretsu*. The Japanese economy has grown more rapidly than that of the U.S. during the last several decades. In addition, Japanese companies have built their export markets and added operations abroad. The strategic emphasis has been on gaining market dominance in this growth environment and not on attaining particular levels of profit margin, rates of return, or earnings per share.

Finally, stock price changes in Japan appear related more to changes in real estate values than to the operating performance of individual companies. Real estate values and stock prices moved dramatically upward during the eighties, although significant decreases have occurred recently. The increasing stock prices appeared to keep investors happy, leading them to de-emphasize the kinds of profitability performance evaluation common in the U.S. (Note: Your instructor may assign additional references in conjunction with this case that elaborate on strategic, institutional, and cultural differences between the U.S. and Japan).

Required:
After studying the financial statements and notes for Tanaguchi Corporation, develop explanations for the differences in the profitability and risk ratios for Tanaguchi Corporation reported in column 2 of Exhibit 2 as compared to those reported in column 3 for U. S. machine tool companies.

Exhibit 2

Comparative Financial Ratio Analysis for Tanaguchi Corporation and U.S. Machine Tool Companies

	Tanaguchi Corp (Japanese GAAP) (1)	Tanaguchi Corp (U.S. GAAP) (2)	Median Ratio for U.S. Machine Tool Companies[a] (3)
Profitability Ratios			
Operating Margin after Taxes (before interest expense and related tax effects)	2.8%	2.9%	3.3%
x Total Assets Turnover	1.5	1.5	1.8
= Return on Assets	4.2	4.5%	5.9
x Common's Share of Operating Earnings[b]	.83	.83	.91
x Capital Structure Leverage[c]	3.8	4.0	2.6
= Return on Common Equity	13.3%[d]	14.8%	13.9%[d]
Operating Margin Analysis			
Sales	100.0%	100.0%	100.0%
Other Revenue/Sales	.4	.4	-
Cost of Goods Sold/Sales	(73.2)	(73.4)	(69.3)
Selling and Administrative/Sales	(21.0)	(20.6)	(25.8)
Income Taxes/Sales	(3.4)	(3.5)	(1.6)
Operating Margin (excluding interest and related tax effects)	2.8%	2.9%	3.3%
Asset Turnover Analysis			
Receivable Turnover	5.1	5.0	6.9
Inventory Turnover	6.3	6.5	5.2
Fixed Asset Turnover	7.5	7.2	7.0
Risk Analysis			
Current Ratio	1.1	1.0	1.6
Quick Ratio	.7	.7	.9
Total Liabilities/Total Assets	73.8%	74.5%	61.1%
Long-Term Debt/Total Assets	4.7%	5.1%	16.1%
Long-Term Debt/Stockholders' Equity	17.9%	18.3%	43.2%
Times Interest Covered	5.8	5.7	3.1
Market Price Ratios (per common share)			
Market Price/Net Income	45.0	30.9	9.0
Market Price/Stockholders' Equity	5.7	4.6	1.2

[a] Source: Robert Morris Associates, Annual Statement Studies (except price-earnings ratio).

[b] Common's Share of Operating Earnings = Net Income to Common/Operating Income after Taxes (before interest expense and related tax effects).

[c] Capital Structure Leverage = Average Total Assets/Average Common Stockholders' Equity

[d] The amounts for return on common equity may not be precisely equal to the product of return on assets, common's share of operating earnings and capital structure leverage due to rounding.

UNCONSOLIDATED FINANCIAL STATEMENTS FOR TANAGUCHI CORPORATION

TANAGUCHI CORPORATION
Balance Sheet
(in billions of yen)

	March 31	
Assets	*Year 4*	*Year 5*
Current Assets		
Cash	¥ 30	¥ 27
Marketable Securities (Note 1)	20	25
Notes and Accounts Receivable (Note 2)		
Trade Notes and Accounts	200	210
Affiliated Company	30	45
Less: Allowance for Doubtful Accounts	(5)	(7)
Inventories (Note 3)	130	150
Other Current Assets	25	30
Total Current Assets	¥ 430	¥ 480
Investments		
Investments in and Loans to Affiliated Companies (Note 4)	¥ 110	¥ 140
Investments in Other Companies	60	60
Total Investments	¥ 170	¥ 200
Property, Plant and Equipment (Note 6)		
Land	¥ 25	¥ 25
Buildings	110	130
Machinery and Equipment	155	180
Less: Depreciation to Date	(140)	(165)
Total Property, Plant and Equipment	¥ 150	¥ 170
Total Assets	¥ 750	¥ 850
Liabilities and Stockholders' Equity		
Current Liabilities		
Short-Term Bank Loans	¥ 185	¥ 200
Notes and Accounts Payable		
Trade Notes and Account	140	164
Affiliated Company	25	20
Other Current Liabilities	40	50
Total Current Liabilities	¥ 390	¥ 434
Long-Term Liabilities		
Bonds Payable (Note 7)	¥ 20	¥ 20
Convertible Debt	20	20
Retirement and Severance Allowance (Note 8*)	122	153
Total Long-Term Liabilities	¥ 162	¥ 193
Stockholders' Equity		
Common Stock, ¥10 par value	¥ 15	¥ 15
Capital Surplus	40	40
Legal Reserve (Note 9)	16	17
Retained Earnings (Note 9)	127	151
Total Stockholders' Equity	¥ 198	¥ 223
Total Liabilities and Stockholder' Equity	¥ 750	¥ 850

TANAGUCHI CORPORATION
Statement of Income and Retained Earnings for Fiscal Year 5
(in billions of yen)

Revenues

Sales (Note 10)	¥	1,200
Interest and Dividends (Note 11)		5
Total Revenues	¥	1,205

Expenses

Cost of Goods Sold	¥	878
Selling and Administrative		252
Interest		13
Total Expenses	¥	1,143
Income before Income Taxes	¥	62
Income Taxes (Note 12)		(34)
Net Income	¥	28

Retained Earnings

Balance, Beginning of fiscal Year 5	¥	127
Net Income		28
Deductions		
Cash Dividends		(3)
Transfer to Legal Reserve (Note 9)		(1)
Balance, End of Fiscal Year 5	¥	151

NOTE 1: Marketable Securities

Marketable securities appear on the balance sheet at acquisition cost.

NOTE 2: Accounts Receivable

Accounts and notes receivable are noninterest bearing. Within 15 days of sales on open account, customers typically sign noninterest-bearing, single-payment notes. Customers usually pay these notes within 60 to 180 days after signing. When Tanaguchi Corporation needs cash, it discounts these notes with Menji Bank. Tanaguchi Corporation remains contingently liable in the event customers do not pay these notes at maturity. Receivables from (and payable to) affiliated company are with Takahashi Corporation (see Note 4) and are noninterest bearing.

NOTE 3: Inventories

Inventories appear on the balance sheet at lower of cost or market. The measurement of acquisition cost uses a weighted average cost flow assumption.

NOTE 4: Investments and Loans to Affiliated Companies

Intercorporate investments appear on the balance sheet at acquisition cost. The balance in this account at the end of Year 4 and Year 5 comprise the following:

	Year 4	Year 5
Investments in Tanaka Corporation (25%)	¥ 15	¥ 15
Investment in Takahashi Corporation (80%)	70	70
Loans to Takahashi Corporation	25	55
	¥ 110	¥ 140

NOTE: 5 Investments in Other Companies

Other investments represent ownership shares of less than 20 percent and appear at acquisition cost.

NOTE 6: Property, Plant and Equipment

Fixed assets appear on the balance sheet at acquisition cost. The firm capitalizes expenditures that increase the service lives of fixed assets, while it expenses immediately expenditures that maintain the originally expected useful lives. It computes depreciation using the declining balance method. Depreciable lives for buildings are 30 to 40 years and for machinery and equipment are 6 to 10 years.

NOTE 7: Bonds Payable
Bonds payable comprises two bond issues as follows:

	Year 4	Year 5
12% semi-annual, ¥ 10 billion face value bonds, with interest payable on March 31 and September 30 and the principal payable at maturity on March 31, Year 20; the bonds were initially priced on the market to yield 10%, compounded semi-annually.	¥ 11.50	¥ 11.45
8% semi-annual, ¥ 10 billion face value bonds, with interest payable on March 31 and September 30 and the principal payable at maturity on March 31, Year 22; the bonds were initially priced on the market to yield 10%, compounded semi-annually	¥ 8.50	¥ 8.55
	¥ 20.00	¥ 20.00

NOTE: 8: Retirement and Severance Allowance
The firm provides amounts as a charge against income each year for estimated retirement and severance benefits but does not fund these amounts until it makes actual payments to former employees.

NOTE 9: Legal Reserve and Retained Earnings
The firm reduces retained earnings and increases the Legal Reserve account for a specified percentage of dividends paid during the year. The following plan for appropriation of retained earnings was approved by shareholders at the annual meeting held on June 29, Year 5:

Transfer to Legal Reserve	¥ (1)
Cash Dividend	(3)
Directors' and Statutory Auditors' Bonuses	(1)
Elimination of Special Tax Reserve Relating to Sale of Equipment	1

NOTE 10 Sales Revenue
The firm recognizes revenues from sales of machine tools at the time of delivery. Reported sales for Year 5 are net of a provision for doubtful accounts of ¥ 50 billion.

NOTE 11: Interest and Dividend Revenue
Interest and Dividend Revenue includes ¥ 1.5 billion from loans to Takahashi Corporation, an unconsolidated subsidiary.

NOTE 12: Income Tax Expenses
The firm computes income taxes based on a statutory tax rate of 55 percent for Year 5.

APPENDIX B
COMPARISON OF U.S. AND JAPANESE GAAP

1. STANDARD-SETTING PROCESS

U.S.   The U.S. Congress has the legal authority to prescribe acceptable accounting principles, but it has delegated that authority to the Securities and Exchange Commission (SEC). The SEC has stated that it will recognize pronouncements of the Financial Accounting Standards Board (FASB), a private-sector entity, as the primary vehicle for specifying generally accepted accounting standards.

Japan   The Japanese Diet has the legal authority to prescribe acceptable accounting principles. All Japanese corporations (both publicly and privately held) must periodically issue financial statements to their stockholders following provisions of the Japanese Commercial Code. This Code is promulgated by the Diet. The financial statements follow strict legal entity concepts.

Publicly listed corporations in Japan must also file financial statements with the Securities Division of the Ministry of Finance following accounting principles promulgated by the Diet in the Securities and Exchange Law. The Diet, through the Ministry of finance, obtains advice on account principles from the Business Advisory Deliberations Council (BADC), a body composed of representatives from business, the accounting profession and personnel from the Ministry of Finance. The BADC has no authority on its own to set acceptable accounting principles. The financial statements filed with the Securities Division of the Ministry of Finance tend to follow economic entity concepts, with intercorporate investments either accounted for using the equity method or consolidated.

All Japanese corporations file income tax returns with the Taxation Division of the Ministry of Finance. The accounting principles followed in preparing tax returns mirror closely those used in preparing financial statements for stockholders under the Japanese Commercial Code. The minister of Finance will sometimes need to reconcile conflicting preferences of the Securities Division (desiring financial information better reflecting economic reality) and the Taxation Division (desiring to raise adequate tax revenues to run the government).

2. PRINCIPAL FINANCIAL STATMENTS

U.S.   Balance sheet, income statement, statement of cash flows.

Japan   Balance sheet, income statement, proposal for appropriation of profit or disposition of loss. The financial statements filed with the Ministry of Finance contain some supplemental information on cash flows.

3, INCOME STATEMENT

U.S.   Accrual basis.

Japan   Accrual basis

4. REVENUE RECOGNITION

U.S. Generally at time of sale; percentage-of-completion method usually required on long-term contracts; installment and cost-recovery-first methods permitted when there is high uncertainty regarding cash collectibility.

Japan Generally at time of sale; percentage-of-completion method permitted on long-term contracts; installment method common when collection period exceeds two years regardless of degree of uncertainty of cash collectibility.

5. UNCOLLECTIBLE ACCOUNTS

U.S. Allowance method.

Japan Allowance method.

6. INVENTORIES AND COST OF GOODS SOLD

U.S. Inventories valued at lower of cost or market. Cost determined by FIFO, LIFO, weighted average, or standard cost. Most firms use FIFO, LIFO, or a combination of the two.

Japan Inventories valued at lower of cost or market. Cost determined by specific identification, FIFO, LIFO, weighted average, or standard cost. Most firms use weighted average or specific identification.

7. FIXED ASSETS AND DEPRECIATION EXPENSE

U.S. Fixed assets valued at acquisition cost. Depreciation computed using straight line, declining balance, and sum-of-the-years'-digits methods. Permanent declines in value are recognized. Most firms use straight line for financial reporting and an accelerated method for tax reporting.

Japan Fixed assets valued at acquisition cost. Depreciation computed using straight line, declining balance, and sum-of-the-years'-digits methods. Permanent declines in value are recognized. Most firms use a declining method for financial and tax reporting.

8. INTANGIBLE ASSETS AND AMORTIZATION EXPENSE

U.S. Internally developed intangibles expensed when expenditures are made. Externally purchased intangibles capitalized as assets and amortized over expected useful life (not to exceed 40 years). Goodwill cannot be amortized for tax purposes.

Japan The cost of intangibles (both internally developed and externally purchased) can be expensed when incurred or capitalized and amortized over the period allowed for tax purposes (generally 5 to 20 years). Goodwill is amortized over 5 years. Some intangibles (e.g., property rights) are not amortized.

9. LIABILITIES RELATED TO ESTIMATED EXPENSES (WARRANTIES, VACATION PAY, EMPLOYEE BONUSES)

U.S.	Estimated amount recognized as an expense and as a liability. Actual expenditures are charged against the liability.
Japan	Estimated amount recognized as an expense and as a liability. Actual expenditures are charged against the liability. Annual bonuses paid to members of the Board of Directors and to the Commercial Code auditors are not considered expenses, but a distribution of profits. Consequently, such bonuses are charged against retained earnings.

10. LIABILITIES RELATED TO EMPLOYEE RETIREMENT AND SEVERANCE BENEFITS

U.S.	Liability recognized for unfunded accumulated benefits.
Japan	Severance benefits more common than pension benefits. An estimated amount is recognized each period as an expense and as a liability for financial reporting. The maximum liability recognized equals 40 percent of the amount payable if all eligible employees were terminated currently. There is wide variability in the amount recognized. Benefits are deducted for tax purposes only when actual payments are made to severed employees. Such benefits are seldom funded beforehand.

11. LIABILITIES RELATED TO INCOME TAXES

U.S.	Income tax expense based on book income amounts. Deferred tax expense and deferred tax liability recognized for temporary (timing) differences between book and taxable income.
Japan	Income tax expense based on taxable income amounts. Deferred tax accounting not practiced. In consolidated statements submitted to the Ministry of Finance by listed companies (see No. 18), deferred tax accounting is permitted.

12. NONINTEREST-BEARING NOTES

U.S.	Notes stated at present value of future cash flows and interest recognized over term of the note.
Japan	Notes stated at face amount and no interest recognized over term of the note. Commonly used as a substitute for Accounts Payable.

13. BOND DISCOUNT OR PREMIUM

U.S.	Subtracted from or added to the face value of the bond and reported among liabilities on the balance sheet. Amortized over the life of the bond as an adjustment to interest expense.
Japan	Bond discount usually included among intangible assets and amortized over the life of the bonds. Bond discount and premium may also be subtracted from or added to face value of bonds on the balance sheet and amortized as an adjustment of interest expense over the life of the bonds.

14. LEASES

U.S.   Distinction made between operating leases (not capitalized) and capital leases (capitalized).

Japan   All leases treated as operating leases.

15. LEGAL RESERVE (PART OF SHAREHOLDERS' EQUITY)

U.S.   Not applicable.

Japan   When dividends are declared and paid, unappropriated retained earnings and cash are reduced by the amount of the dividend. In addition, unappropriated retained earnings are reduced and the legal reserve account is increased by a percentage of this dividend, usually 10 percent, until such time as the legal reserve equals 25 percent of stated capital. The effect of the latter entry is to capitalize a portion of retained earnings to make it part of permanent capital.

16. APPROPRIATIONS OF RETAINED EARNINGS

U.S.   Not a common practice in the U.S. Appropriations have no legal status when they do appear.

Japan   Stockholders must approve, each year, the "proposal for appropriation of profit or disposition of loss." Four items commonly appear: dividend declarations, annual bonuses for directors and Commercial Code auditors, transfers to legal reserves, and changes in reserves.

The income tax law permits certain costs to be deducted earlier for tax than for financial reporting and permits certain gains to be recognized later for tax than for financial reporting. To obtain these tax benefits, the tax law requires that these items "be reflected on the company's books." The pretax effect of these timing differences *do not appear* on the income statement. Instead, an entry is made decreasing unappropriated retained earnings and increasing special retained earnings reserves (a form of appropriated retained earnings). When the timing difference reverses, the above entry is reversed. The tax effects of these timing differences do appear on the income statement, however. In the year that the timing difference originates, income tax expense and income tax payable are reduced by the tax effect of the timing difference. When the timing difference reverses, income tax expense and income tax payable are increased by a corresponding amount.

17. TREASURY STOCK

U.S.   Shown at acquisition cost as a subtraction from total shareholders' equity. No income recognized from treasury stock transactions.

Japan   Reacquired shares are either canceled immediately or shown as a current asset on the balance sheet. Dividends "received" on treasury share are included in income.

18. INVESTMENTS IN SECURITIES

A. MARKETABLE SECURITIES (CURRENT ASSET)

U.S.   Lower of cost or market method.

Japan   Reported at acquisition cost, unless price declines are considered permanent, in which case lower of cost or market.

B. INVESTMENTS (NONCURRENT ASSET)

U.S.   Accounting depends on ownership: Less than 20%, lower of cost or market; 20% to 50%, equity method; greater than 50%, consolidated.

Japan   The principal financial statements are those of the parent company only (that is, unconsolidated statements). Intercorporate investments are carried at acquisition cost. Listed companies must provide consolidated financial statements as supplements to the principal statements in filings to the Ministry of Finance. The accounting for investments in securities in these supplementary statements is essentially the same as in the U.S.

19. CORPORATE ACQUISITIONS

U.S.   Purchase method or pooling of interests method.

Japan   Purchase method.

20. FOREIGN CURRENCY TRANSLATION

U.S.   The translation method depends on whether the foreign unit operates as a self-contained entity (all current method) or as an extension of the U.S. parent (monetary/nonmonetary method).

Japan   For branches, the monetary/nonmonetary translation method is used, with any translation adjustment flowing through income. For subsidiaries, current monetary items are translated using the current rate, other balance sheet items use the historical rate, and the translation adjustment is part of shareholders' equity.

21. SEGMENT REPORTING

U.S.   Segment information (sales, operating income, assets) disclosed by industry segment, geographical location, and type of customer.

Japan   Beginning in 1990, sales data by segment (industry, geographical location) are required. No disclosure by type of customer.

Sources: The Japanese Institute of Certified Public Accountants, *Corporate Disclosure in Japan* (July 1987); KPMG Peat Marwick, *Comparison of Japanese and U.S. Reporting and Financial Practices* (1989)

Wacoal Corp. is Japan's leading manufacturer and retailer of women's intimate apparel. The company's products are sold principally in Japan, Europe, the U.S., and certain Asian countries (i.e., China, Hong Kong, Indonesia, Korea, the Philippines, Singapore,Taiwan, and Thailand). In addition to being listed on the Tokyo, Osaka, and Kyoto stock exchanges, the company's common stock (¥50 par value) trades on the NASDAQ exchange in the U.S. as an American Depository Receipt (sponsored by Chase Manhattan Shareholder Services).

In compliance with its ADR listing on a major U.S. stock exchange, the company files financial statements in conformity with U.S. generally accepted accounting principles (hereafter GAAP).[1] According to the independent auditors' report issued by Deloitte Touche Tohmatsu International (see Exhibit 1), the company's financial statements conform to U.S. GAAP in all material respects except with regard to the accounting for certain investments in debt and equity securities.

Under generally accepted accounting practice in Japan, most debt and equity securities are accounted for on the historical cost basis (see Exhibit 3). However, under U.S. GAAP, effective 1995 such investments are accounted for under the provisions of Statement of Financial Accounting Standards ("SFAS") No. 115. Under SFAS No. 115, certain debt and equity investments must be classified according to their expected disposition: trading, available-for-sale, or held-to-maturity. While trading and available-for-sale securities are reported at their fair market value on an individual security basis, held-to-maturity securities are carried at their historical cost.

Required:

1. Using the data in Exhibits 2 and 3, recast Wacoal Corp.'s financial statements to reflect the use of SFAS No. 115. Calculate the following ratios for <u>both</u> the original financial statements (see Exhibit 2) and the restated financial statements:

    - Return on total assets
    - Return on owners' equity
    - Total debt-to-total assets
    - Long-term debt-to-shareholders' equity

Does the use of SFAS No. 115 create a material difference in the company's reported financial data?

2. Why do you think Wacoal Corp. chose <u>not</u> to restate its financial statements for SFAS No. 115?

3. Footnote 8 (see Exhibit 3) refers to a "legal reserve". What do you think is the purpose of this account? Has the company achieved the requirement that the reserve equal "25% of stated capital"?

---

[*] This case was prepared by Kenneth R. Ferris. Copyright © 1996 by The American Graduate School of International Management. All rights reserved.

[1] Foreign corporations listed on major U.S. exchanges must file with the Securities and Exchange Commission financial statements prepared according to U.S. GAAP, or if prepared under foreign GAAP, present a reconciliation of net income and shareholders' equity under U.S. GAAP, unless the foreign security is "unsponsored". An unsponsored foreign security (e.g., unsponsored ADR) is one in which listing is initiated by a U.S. financial institution without the request of the foreign issuer.

Exhibit 1
Wacoal Corporation
Independent Auditors' Report

Deloitte Touche Tohmatsu

Osaka Kokusai Building
3-13, Azuchimachi 2-chome
Chuo-ku, Osaka 541, Japan

To the Board of Directors and Shareholders of
Wacoal Corp.
Kyoto, Japan

We have audited the accompanying consolidated balance sheets of Wacoal Corp. and subsidiaries as of March 31, 1996 and 1995, and the related consolidated statements of income, shareholders' equity and cash flows for each of the three years in the period ended March 31, 1996, all expressed in Japanese yen. These financial statements are the responsibility of the Company's management. Our responsibility is to express an opinion on these financial statements based on our audits.

We conducted our audits in accordance with auditing standards generally accepted in the United States of America. Those standards require that we plan and perform the audit to obtain reasonable assurance about whether the financial statements are free of material misstatement. An audit includes examining, on a test basis, evidence supporting the amounts and disclosures in the financial statements. An audit also includes assessing the accounting principles used and significant estimates made by management, as well as evaluating the overall financial statement presentation. We believe that our audits provide a reasonable basis for our opinion.

Wacol Corp. and subsidiaries have not applied Statement of Financial Accounting Standards ("SFAS") No. 115 in accounting for certain investments in debt and equity securities but have provided the disclosures required by SFAS No. 115. The effects on the consolidated financial statements of not adopting SFAS No. 115 are summarized in Note 3 to the consolidated financial statements.

In our opinion, except for the effects of not adopting SFAS No. 115 in accounting for certain investments in debt and equity securities as discussed in the preceding paragraph, the consolidated financial statements referred to above present fairly, in all material respects, the financial position of Wacoal Corp. and subsidiaries as of March 31, 1996 and 1995, and the results of their operations and their cash flows for each of the three years in the period ended March 31, 1996 in conformity with accounting principles generally accepted in the United States of America.

As discussed in Note 1 to the consolidated financial statements, the Company changed its method of accounting for income taxes effective April 1, 1993 to conform with SFAS No. 109.

Our audits also comprehended the translation of the Japanese yen amounts into U.S. dollar amounts and, in our opinion, such translation has been made in conformity with the basis stated in Note 2. The translation of the financial statement amounts into U.S. dollars has been made solely for convenience.

Deloitte Touche Tohmatsu

June 7, 1996

Exhibit 2
Wacoal Corporation
Selected Financial Statements

Panel A.   Consolidated Balance Sheets (March 31, 1995 and 1996)

Assets	Millions of Yen		Thousands of U.S. Dollars (Note 2)
	1996	1995	1996
Current Assets:			
Cash and cash equivalents:			
Cash	¥ 4,102	¥ 5,390	$ 38,337
Time deposits and certificates of deposit	37,248	33,053	348,112
Total	41,350	38,443	386,449
Marketable securities (Note 3)	18,511	15,885	173,000
Notes and accounts receivable:			
Trade notes	5,274	4,858	49,290
Trade accounts	23,576	20,865	220,336
Allowance for returns and doubtful receivables	(2,346)	(2,304)	(21,925)
Inventories (Note 4)	24,290	22,322	227,009
Other current assets	6,050	5,084	56,542
Total current assets	116,705	105,153	1,090,701
Property, Plant and Equipment (Note 5):			
Land	25,948	25,912	242,505
Buildings	45,999	45,385	429,897
Machinery and equipment	9,647	9,974	90,159
Construction in progress	4	5	37
Total	81,598	81,276	762,598
Accumulated depreciation	(30,684)	(29,578)	(286,766)
Net property, plant and equipment	50,914	51,698	475,832
Other Assets:			
Investments (Notes 3 and 5)	23,370	20,890	218,411
Lease deposits and other	6,588	6,568	61,570
Total other assets	29,958	27,458	279,981
Total	¥197,577	¥184,309	$1,846,514

Exhibit 2
Wacoal Corporation
Selected Financial Statements
(continued)

Panel A. Consolidated Balance Sheets (March 31, 1995 and 1996)

Liabilities and Shareholders' Equity	Millions of Yen		Thousands of U.S. Dollars (Note 2)
	1996	1995	1996
Current Liabilities:			
Short-term bank loans (Note 5)	¥ 5,929	¥ 4,981	$ 55,411
Notes and accounts payable:			
Trade notes	6,272	5,462	58,617
Trade accounts	6,544	6,401	61,159
Accrued payroll and bonuses	8,879	7,765	82,981
Income taxes payable	7,134	2,956	66,673
Other current liabilities	6,752	6,155	63,103
Current portion of long-term debt (Note 5)	351	2,000	3,280
Total current liabilities	41,861	35,720	391,224
Long-Term Liabilities:			
Long-term debt (Note 5)	1,318	1,702	12,318
Liability for termination and retirement benefits (Note 6)	7,844	6,021	73,308
Deferred income taxes (Note 9)	603	460	5,636
Total long-term liabilities	9,765	8,183	91,262
Preferred Auction Rate Stock (Note 7)	4,983	4,832	46,570
Shareholders' Equity (Notes 3, 8 and 12):			
Common stock–authorized, 240,000,000 shares; issued and outstanding, 154,116,685 shares with par value of ¥50 per share	13,260	13,260	123,925
Additional paid-in capital	25,242	25,242	235,907
Legal reserve	3,747	3,704	35,019
Retained earnings	99,416	94,527	929,121
Cumulative translation adjustments	(697)	(1,159)	(6,514)
Total shareholders' equity	140,968	135,574	1,317,458
Total	¥197,577	¥184,309	$1,846,514

Exhibit 2
Wacoal Corporation
Selected Financial Statements
(continued)

Panel B. Consolidated Statements of Income (Years ended March 31, 1994, 1995, and 1996)

	Millions of Yen			Thousands of U.S. Dollars (Note 2)
	1996	1995	1994	1996
Revenues:				
Net sales	¥159,162	¥153,170	¥150,830	$1,487,495
Interest income	965	1,355	1,615	9,019
Other–net	2,039	1,217	1,427	19,056
Total revenues	162,166	155,742	153,872	1,515,570
Costs and Expenses:				
Cost of sales	85,470	83,162	83,421	798,785
Selling, general and administrative	61,942	59,353	57,677	578,897
Interest expense	346	420	477	3,234
Total costs and expenses	147,758	142,935	141,575	1,380,916
Income before Income Taxes and Cumulative Effect of Accounting Change	14,408	12,807	12,297	134,654
Income Taxes (Note 9):				
Current	8,098	5,600	7,155	75,682
Deferred	(917)	(519)	(170)	(8,570)
Total income taxes	7,181	6,119	6,985	67,112
Income before Cumulative Effect of Accounting Change	7,227	6,688	5,312	67,542
Cumulative Effect on Prior Years of Change in Accounting for Income Taxes (Note 9)			1,917	
Net Income	¥ 7,227	¥ 6,688	¥ 7,229	$ 67,542

	Yen			U.S. Dollars
Amounts per American Depositary Share (5 shares of common stock) (Note 10):				
Income before cumulative effect of accounting change	¥228	¥211	¥167	$ 2.13
Cumulative effect on prior years of change in accounting for income taxes			62	
Net income	¥228	¥211	¥229	$ 2.13
Cash dividends	¥ 68	¥ 68	¥ 68	$ 0.64

Exhibit 3
Wacoal Corporation
Selected Footnote Disclosures

1. Summary of Significant Accounting Policies

Basis of Financial Statements

Wacoal Corp. (the "Company") and its subsidiaries are predominantly engaged in one industry, the manufacture and sale of apparel, including foundation garments, lingerie, nightwear and outerwear in Japan, the United States of America, Europe and certain Asian countries.

The accompanying financial statements, stated in Japanese yen, differ from the financial statements issued by the Company for domestic purposes in Japan. In addition to the consolidation of subsidiaries, they reflect certain adjustments and reclassifications, not recorded on the books of account, to present them in accordance with accounting principles generally accepted in the United States of America, except that the provisions of Statement of Financial Accounting Standards ("SFAS") No. 115 have not been applied (see Note 3). The principal adjustments include the recognition of currency exchange gains or losses on noncurrent assets and liabilities, accounting for investments in affiliated companies (companies in which the Company's ownership is from 20% to 50%) on the equity method, the charge of stock issuance expenses to the additional paid-in capital account, accrual or deferral of certain expenses, recognition of warrant value and recognition of deferred income taxes relating to these adjustments, other temporary differences and loss carryforwards.

Certain reclassifications have been made to amounts previously reported to conform with the current year presentation.

Marketable Securities and Investments

The current and noncurrent portfolios of marketable debt and equity securities are each stated at the lower of aggregate cost or market value. The cost of marketable securities and investments sold is determined using the average cost method.

In May 1993, SFAS No. 115 regarding accounting for certain investments in debt and equity securities was issued. The Companies, however, have not applied SFAS No. 115 (see Note 3).

Exhibit 3
Wacoal Corporation
Selected Footnote Disclosures
(continued)

3. Marketable Securities and Investments

SFAS No. 115, "Accounting for Certain Debt and Equity Securities" has been effective since fiscal 1995. This Statement requires that certain debt and equity securities be classified as trading, available-for-sale or held-to-maturity. SFAS No. 115 requires that those investments classified as available-for-sale should be reported at fair value with unrealized gains and losses, net of applicable income taxes, excluded from earnings and reported in a separate component of shareholders' equity.

Most Japanese companies prepare financial statements under accounting principles generally accepted in Japan which report such debt and equity securities on the historical cost basis. In order to maintain comparability with such Japanese companies' financial statements, the Companies have not applied the provisions of SFAS No. 115. If the provisions of SFAS No. 115 had been applied, all of the Companies' marketable securities and investments would be classified as available-for-sale, and the consolidated balance sheets as of March 31, 1996 and 1995 would change as follows:

	Millions of Yen		Thousands of U.S. Dollars
	1996	1995	1996
Shareholders' equity as reported	¥ 140,968	¥ 135,574	$ 1,317,458
Net increase in the carrying amount of:			
Marketable securities	31		290
Investments	41,042	30,483	383,570
Net decrease in deferred income taxes in other current assets	(16)		(150)
Net increase in deferred income taxes in long-term liabilities	(21,089)	(15,682)	(197,093)
Minority interests included in other current liabilities	(10)	15	(94)
Total	19,958	14,816	186,523
Shareholders' equity in accordance with U.S. generally accepted accounting principles	¥ 160,926	¥ 150,390	$ 1,503,981

The fair value, gross unrealized gain and loss amounts reported below include the effect of related foreign currency and interest rate hedge transactions. The carrying amount, gross unrealized gains, gross unrealized losses and fair value for the available-for-sale securities by major security type at March 31, 1996 and 1995 were as follows:

1996	Millions of Yen			
	Carrying Amount	Gross Unrealized Gain	Gross Unrealized Loss	Fair Value
Current:				
Japanese and foreign governmental bond securities	¥ 134	¥ 2		¥ 136
Corporate debt securities	2,141	7	¥ 4	2,144
Bank debt securities	9,524	22	2	9,544
Fund trusts	6,712	6		6,718
Total	¥18,511	¥ 37	¥ 6	¥18,542
Noncurrent:				
Corporate debt securities	¥ 1,318	¥ 2		¥ 1,320
Bank debt securities	1,308	11		1,319
Fund trusts	120		¥ 4	116
Equity securities	13,378	41,250	217	54,411
Total	¥16,124	¥41,263	¥221	¥57,166

Exhibit 3
Wacoal Corporation
Selected Footnote Disclosures
(continued)

3. Marketable Securities and Investments (continued)

1995	Millions of Yen			
	Carrying Amount	Gross Unrealized Gain	Gross Unrealized Loss	Fair Value
Current:				
Japanese and foreign governmental bond securities	¥ 336	¥ 3	¥ 3	¥ 336
Corporate debt securities	2,909		18	2,891
Bank debt securities	9,979	12		9,991
Fund trusts	2,661	6		2,667
Total	¥15,885	¥ 21	¥ 21	¥15,885
Noncurrent:				
Corporate debt securities	¥ 1,083		¥ 6	¥ 1,077
Bank debt securities	1,279		7	1,272
Fund trusts	90		11	79
Equity securities	12,781	¥31,032	525	43,288
Total	¥15,233	¥31,032	¥ 549	¥45,716

1996	Thousands of U.S. Dollars			
	Carrying Amount	Gross Unrealized Gain	Gross Unrealized Loss	Fair Value
Current:				
Japanese and foreign governmental bond securities	$ 1,252	$ 19		$ 1,271
Corporate debt securities	20,010	65	$ 37	20,038
Bank debt securities	89,009	206	19	89,196
Fund trusts	62,729	56		62,785
Total	$173,000	$ 346	$ 56	$173,290
Noncurrent:				
Corporate debt securities	$ 12,318	$ 18		$ 12,336
Bank debt securities	12,224	103		12,327
Fund trusts	1,121		$ 37	1,084
Equity securities	125,028	385,514	2,028	508,514
Total	$150,691	$385,635	$2,065	$534,261

Net unrealized gain on available-for-sale securities, net of related income taxes and minority interests, for the year ended March 31, 1996 increased by ¥5,142 million ($48,056 thousand) and for the year ended March 31, 1995 decreased by ¥4,567 million. Maturities of marketable debt securities classified as available-for-sale at March 31, 1996 were as follows:

	Millions of Yen		Thousands of U.S. Dollars	
	Carrying Amount	Fair Value	Carrying Amount	Fair Value
Due within one year	¥11,838	¥11,850	$ 110,635	$110,748
Due after one year through five years	5,369	5,382	50,178	50,299
Due after five years	4,050	4,065	37,850	37,990
Total	¥21,257	¥21,297	$ 198,663	$199,037

Proceeds from sales of available-for-sale securities were ¥5,866 million ($54,822 thousand) and ¥8,149 million for the years ended March 31, 1996 and 1995, respectively. Gross realized gains and losses during the years ended March 31, 1996 and 1995 were insignificant except the gross realized gains of ¥294 million ($2,748 thousand) in 1996.

Exhibit 3
Wacoal Corporation
Selected Footnote Disclosures
(continued)

8. Shareholders' Equity

Under the Japanese Commercial Code (the "Code"), the amount available for dividends is based on retained earnings as recorded on the Company's books. Certain adjustments, not recorded on such books, are reflected in the financial statements as described in Note 1. At March 31, 1996, retained earnings recorded on the Company's books were ¥89,980 million ($840,935 thousand). Such retained earnings included ¥82,957 million ($775,299 thousand) which are designated as general reserves but are available for future dividends subject to the approval by shareholders and legal reserve requirements.

Under the Code, Japanese companies are required to appropriate as a legal reserve a portion of retained earnings in an amount equal to at least 10% of cash payments, including dividends and bonuses for directors and statutory auditors, in each financial period until the reserve equals 25% of stated capital. This reserve is not available for dividends, but may be used to reduce a deficit by resolution of shareholders or may be capitalized by resolution of the Board of Directors.

Under the Code, at least 50% of the issue price of new shares with a minimum of the par value thereof, is required to be designated as stated capital. The portion which is to be designated as stated capital is determined by resolution of the Board of Directors. Proceeds in excess of the amounts designated as stated capital, as reduced by stock issue cost less the applicable tax benefit, have been credited to additional paid-in capital. The Company may, by resolution of the Board of Directors, distribute additional paid-in capital or the portion of the stated capital in excess of the aggregate amounts of the par value by means of stock splits.

10. Amounts per American Depositary Share

The computation of net income per American Depositary Share, each share representing 5 shares of common stock, is based on the weighted average number of common shares outstanding. The average number of common shares outstanding used in the computations was 154,116,685 shares for 1996, 1995 and 1994. Cash dividends paid on Preferred Auction Rate Stock were deducted from net income for the computation of amounts per American Depositary Share.

Aussie Traders Ltd. is a large publicly-owned retail organization with headquarters in Melbourne, Australia. During the late 1980's, economic and competitive factors resulted in management looking outside of their traditional area of operations in pursuit of new growth opportunities. A decision was made to establish a retailing operation in South East Asia to capitalize on both local demand and the booming tourist market in that region. Singapore was chosen as the most suitable location because of its political stability, tourist industry, and well disposed attitude toward foreign investment.

These plans came to fruition with the establishment in June, 1992 of Aussie Retailers Ltd., a wholly-owned subsidiary of Aussie Traders Ltd. Aussie Retailers was established with an issued and paid-up capital of 500,000 shares, paid to their par value of S$25 (A$10).[1] A S$30 million (A$12 million) three year revolving credit facility (guaranteed by Aussie Traders) had also been arranged with a Singaporean bank and S$25 million of this facility was drawn down in late June, 1992 to provide for working capital requirements. The acquisition of suitable retail premises, office accommodation and all necessary equipment had been negotiated and these deals were finalized in mid-1992.

On July 1, 1992, after these transactions, Aussie Retailers Ltd. had the following balance sheet:

Aussie Retailers Ltd.
Balance Sheet
As of July 1, 1992
(S$000's)

Assets		Equities	
Cash	$ 6,000	Trade Creditors	$ 7,500
Stock	20,500	Loan	25,000
Fixed Assets (net)	18,500	Issued and Paid-up Capital	12,500
Total assets	$45,000	Total Equities	$45,000

(Exchange Rate: July 1, 1992   A$1 = S$2.50.)

The management of Aussie Traders Ltd. was aware of the fact that under Australian Accounting Standard (AAS) No. 20, two alternative methods were permitted to translate the financial statements of foreign subsidiaries for incorporation into the domestic consolidated accounts. The substance of AAS No. 20 (subsequently replaced by ASRB No. 1012) was that for *integrated foreign operations,* the temporal method was to be applied and any translation gain (loss) booked to the income statement; for *self-sustaining operations,* the current rate method was required and any resultant translation gain (loss) was to be taken directly to a foreign currency translation reserve.

AAS No. 20 provides a number of factors (e.g., see Exhibit 1) which might, either individually or collectively, suggest that a foreign operation is self-sustaining, but these are not definitive and in many cases a company may be able to justify the application of either method to account for its foreign operations. Given the potential for the choice of translation method to significantly impact upon reported

---

[*] This case was prepared by Kenneth R. Ferris and Barry R. Graham. Copyright © 1993 by Kenneth R. Ferris. All rights reserved.

[1] For convenience, the letter "S" denotes Singapore dollars and the letter "A" denotes Australian dollars.

profits and shareholders' equity, it was decided to ascertain the effects of an expected devaluation of the Australian dollar against the Singaporean dollar under both translation methods. The results of this analysis were to be a key component in reaching a final decision on the accounting method adopted.

Aussie Retailers Ltd. commenced trading in July, 1992. Its inventory was sold only in Singapore and its prices, which were denominated in Singapore dollars, were primarily determined by local competitive conditions. However, as inventory was sourced from around the world, including some from Aussie Traders in Australia, its pricing policy was not totally immune from the influence of exchange rate fluctuations. Other operating expenses (e.g., staff and overhead costs) were mostly local.

The performance of Aussie Retailers for the year ended June 30, 1993 met expectations (see Exhibits 2 and 3). However, due to a number of unforeseen economic circumstances, the expected devaluation of the A$ against the S$ did not occur. In fact, the trend was in the opposite direction such that at June 30, 1993 the exchange rate was A$1 = S$3. This change in the exchange rate had occurred gradually over the year such that the average exchange rate for the year was A$1 = S$2.75.

Required:

1. Assume that Aussie Retailers had no transactions for the year ending June 30, 1993 and that the A$ devalued by 20 percent against the S$ (i.e., A$1 = S$2.00). Using the July 1, 1992 balance sheet, compute the translation gain (loss) incurred for the year under the following translation methods:

    *   temporal
    *   current rate

2. If the bank loan had been from an Australian source and denominated in $A, what effect would this have had upon your computations in question one?

3. Translate the financial statements of Aussie Retailers (see Exhibits 2 and 3) using:

    *   the temporal method
    *   the current rate method.

4. Evaluate the relative merits of the current rate and temporal methods with respect to:

    (a) their usefulness for translating foreign currency statements for inclusion in domestic consolidated financial reports, and

    (b) their usefulness in evaluating the performance of managers of foreign subsidiaries.

5. Compare the foreign currency translation practices of Australia to those utilized in Canada, France, Germany, Italy, Japan, the U.K., the U.S., and as prescribed by the IASC. Are the practices similar or different?

Exhibit 1
Translation of Foreign Currency Financial Statements: A Summary of AAS No. 20

♦ The objective of translating the financial statements of foreign operations into domestic currency terms is to enable incorporation of the financial statements into the company or group accounts.

♦ The method used to translate foreign currency financial statements should reflect the financial and operational relationships which exist between the reporting entity and its foreign operations.

♦ Some foreign operations are inter-related with those of the domestic operations, (called "integrated foreign operations"), and expose the reporting entity to exchange gains or losses. For these foreign operations, the temporal method should be used.

♦ Some foreign operations are relatively unrelated to those of the domestic operations, and are "self-sustaining" in nature. These operations may expose the reporting entity to exchange gains or losses, but not through day-to-day operations. For these foreign operations, the current rate method should be used.

♦ Factors that might suggest that a foreign operation is self-sustaining include:

(a) the cash flows of the reporting entity are largely unaffected by the activities of the foreign operations;

(b) the sale prices of the foreign operation's products or services are not materially influenced by domestic conditions and such prices are primarily determined by factors other than changes in exchange rates;

(c) the foreign operation's major markets do not include the reporting entity's country;

(d) the foreign operation's costs are not materially affected by domestic prices;

(e) the foreign operation's day-to-day financing is not supplied by the reporting entity; and,

(f) there are no material inter-company transactions or other interchanges with the foreign operation in the course of normal activities.

Exhibit 2
Aussie Retailers Ltd.
Profit and Loss Statement
For the Year Ended June 30, 1993
(S$000's)

Sales		$ 90,000
Cost of Goods Sold		
Stock, July 1, 1992	20,500	
Purchases	48,000	
	68,500	
Less: Stock, 30 June 1993[2]	22,000	
		(46,500)
Gross Profit		43,500
Selling and Admin. Expenses	33,000	
Depreciation	1,500	
Interest	2,700	
		(37,200)
Net Income after Taxes[3]		$ 6,300

Exhibit 3
Aussie Retailers Ltd.
Balance Sheet
As of June 30, 1993
(S$000's)

Current Assets			**Current Liabilities**		
Cash	$ 2,100		Trade Creditors		$12,100
Trade Debtors	16,800				
Stock	22,000				
		40,900			
			Non Current Liabilities		
			Bank Loan		27,000
Fixed Assets (net)		17,000			
			Shareholders' Equity		
			Paid up Capital	12,500	
			Retained Earnings	6,300	
					18,800
Total Assets		$ 57,900	Total Equities		$57,900

---

[2] Stock at June 30, 1993 was acquired over a period when the average exchange rate was A$1 = S$2.85.
[3] The Singaporean government granted a tax "holiday" for the first year of operation.

Newcastle Ltd. is an integrated minerals and metals company headquartered in Woollongong, Australia. Since its inception in the 1930's, the company had been involved in the extraction, production, and marketing of a range of iron and steel products to both local and international markets. The company maintained operations in the states of New South Wales, Queensland, and South Australia.

In the early 1960s, the company went public with an initial offering of 2.5 million shares of ordinary stock ($.50 par value).[1] The public offering was oversubscribed, and within a decade, the price of the shares had increased ten-fold to more than $10 per share.

Other than the sale of stock, the company generated capital for its new exploration projects primarily through bank borrowing. By the late 1970s, however, interest rates had begun to climb sharply, and by 1980, the preferred client rate of interest (i.e., that rate charged by banks to their most preferred customers) had reached 20 percent.

To escape the high bank rates of interest, the management of Newcastle Ltd. decided to undertake a public offering of unsecured debentures. On July 1, 1982, the company successfully completed the sale of 10 year, 15.50 percent coupon rate, subordinated debentures having a maturity value of $50 million. The bonds required semiannual interest payments and were sold to yield 16 percent. They were callable at any time after July 1, 1987, at a price of $105 per bond,[2] and were convertible into Newcastle Ltd. ordinary shares at any time after July 1, 1985 at a rate of 60 shares of ordinary stock per $1,000 bond.

Over the next several years, interest rates fell by nearly 50 percent. By July of 1984, the preferred client rate of interest had fallen to 11 percent, and the equity market had, in turn, moved into a bullish trend. In response to these economic events, the share price of Newcastle Ltd. rose to $15 per share.

---

[*] This case was prepared by Kenneth R. Ferris. Copyright © 1996 by The American Graduate School of International Management. All rights reserved.
[1] All amounts are in Australian dollars unless otherwise noted.
[2] Although debentures are most commonly sold in units of $1,000, a widely accepted convention is to quote the value of such securities in hundreds of dollars; hence, a bond quoted for sale at $102 will actually cost $1,020.

Questions:

Use Exhibits 1 and 2 in calculating the following:

1. Determine the proceeds to be received by Newcastle Ltd. on July 1, 1982, from the sale of its unsecured debentures. (Ignore any anticipated transaction costs.)

2. Determine the interest expense for the year ended December 31, 1983. (Use the effective interest method.)

3. Assume that bonds having a maturity value of $5 million are converted into ordinary shares on July 1, 1985. Describe the balance sheet and income statement effects of the conversion. (Use specific dollar amounts.) Would your answer change if you knew that the ordinary shares were trading at $18.00 per share?

4. Assume that on July 1, 1987, the company decides to repurchase on the open market bonds having a maturity value of $20 million. At the time of the repurchase, the market yield on the outstanding bonds is 12 percent. Describe the balance sheet and income statement effects of this transaction. (Use specific dollar amounts.)

5. Assume that the company decides to call the remaining $25 million in outstanding bonds on July 1, 1989. At the time that the formal call notice is issued, the company's ordinary shares are trading at $25 per share. Show the journal entries needed to record the calling of the debt. If you were a bondholder, how would you respond?

Exhibit 1
Present Value of $1 Per Period

Periods	6%	8%	12%	15%	16%
1	0.943	0.926	0.893	0.870	0.862
2	1.833	1.783	1.690	1.626	1.605
3	2.673	2.577	2.402	2.283	2.246
4	3.465	3.312	3.037	2.855	2.798
5	4.212	3.993	3.605	3.352	3.274
6	4.917	4.623	4.111	3.784	3.685
7	5.582	5.206	4.564	4.160	4.039
8	6.210	5.747	4.968	4.487	4.344
9	6.802	6.247	5.328	4.772	4.607
10	7.360	6.710	5.650	5.019	4.833
11	7.887	7.139	5.937	5.234	5.029
12	8.384	7.536	6.194	5.421	5.197
13	8.853	7.904	6.424	5.583	5.342
14	9.295	8.244	6.628	5.724	5.468
15	9.712	8.559	6.811	5.847	5.575
16	10.106	8.851	6.974	5.954	5.669
17	10.477	9.122	7.120	6.047	5.749
18	10.828	9.372	7.250	6.128	5.818
19	11.158	9.604	7.366	6.198	5.877
20	11.470	9.818	7.469	6.259	5.929

Exhibit 2
Present Value of $1

Periods	6%	8%	12%	15%	16%
1	0.943	0.926	0.893	0.870	0.862
2	0.890	0.857	0.797	0.756	0.743
3	0.840	0.794	0.712	0.658	0.641
4	0.792	0.735	0.636	0.572	0.552
5	0.747	0.681	0.567	0.497	0.476
6	0.705	0.630	0.507	0.432	0.410
7	0.665	0.583	0.452	0.376	0.354
8	0.627	0.540	0.404	0.327	0.305
9	0.592	0.500	0.361	0.284	0.263
10	0.558	0.463	0.322	0.247	0.227
11	0.527	0.429	0.287	0.215	0.195
12	0.497	0.397	0.257	0.187	0.168
13	0.469	0.368	0.229	0.163	0.145
14	0.442	0.340	0.205	0.141	0.125
15	0.417	0.315	0.183	0.123	0.108
16	0.394	0.292	0.163	0.107	0.093
17	0.371	0.270	0.146	0.093	0.080
18	0.350	0.250	0.130	0.081	0.069
19	0.331	0.232	0.116	0.070	0.060
20	0.312	0.215	0.104	0.061	0.051

In his 1994 letter to shareholders, Mr. John Gough, Chairman of Pacific Dunlop Ltd. commented:

The past year's performance of Pacific Dunlop and our growth prospects are very positive. Profit increased by 17.8 percent to $307 million. This is the highest profit before abnormal items we have achieved...

There has been much public comment regarding accounting for goodwill. Let me say at the outset that we believe that we comply with the Accounting Standard on goodwill, our auditors believe we comply, and the Institute of Chartered Accountants in Australia has written to us saying that in their view the inverted sum of the years' digits method is a legitimate option under the standard...it is important that Australian companies which are growing internationally, are not disadvantaged by accounting standards exclusive to Australia.

The Company

Pacific Dunlop Ltd., headquartered in Melbourne, Australia, is an international marketing and distribution company with operations in over 80 countries. Among its achievements, the company is:

- The world's leading manufacturer and distributor of latex medical and industrial gloves.

- The world's leader in Cochlear bionic ear implants.

- The world's largest industrial battery manufacturer and second largest automotive battery manufacturer.

- Australia and New Zealand's largest tire manufacturer, marketer, and exporter.

- Australia and New Zealand's largest automotive parts and electrical goods distributor.

- Australia's largest manufacturer and supplier of branded footwear, clothing, and sporting goods.

- Australia's largest marketer of branded packaged food products.

- China's largest ice cream manufacturer and marketer.

- Asia's largest bedding supplier.

In 1994, Pacific Dunlop achieved sales of over $7 billion worldwide, an increase of over 10 percent as compared to the prior year. [1]

---

[*] This case was prepared by Kenneth R. Ferris and Bruce McDonald from publicly-available documents. Copyright © 1996 by The American Graduate School of International Management. All rights reserved.
[1] Unless otherwise noted, all values are stated in Australian dollars.

Accounting Controversy

In 1994, Pacific Dunlop found itself at the center of a controversy surrounding the accounting for goodwill. Under Australian generally accepted accounting principles (GAAP), purchased goodwill should be capitalized to the balance sheet at the time of acquisition, and then amortized to income over the period a company is expected to benefit from the goodwill, but under no circumstances should the expected period exceed 20 years. [2]

Executives for Pacific Dunlop, however, believed that under certain circumstances, the value of some intangible assets had an indefinite life, and therefore that no amortization, or at most minimal amortization, was appropriate. According to company representatives, the appropriate treatment was that:

> Acquired goodwill should be capitalized, regularly reviewed and valued, and only written down in circumstances where there is a diminution in the value of the business to which the acquired goodwill pertains. As an alternative, companies should be permitted to immediately write-off goodwill on acquisitions against their share premium reserve which had been established by the issue of shares at a premium.

The company's 1994 financial statement footnotes disclosed the following policy with regard to Pacific Dunlop's treatment of goodwill:

> Goodwill is capitalized and amortized to the Profit and Loss Account. In determining the period and method of amortization, each acquisition is separately assessed. The benefits from the goodwill acquired may exceed 20 years but the goodwill is written off over periods not exceeding 20 years to comply with Australian Accounting Standards.

> The unamortized balance of goodwill is reviewed semi-annually and any material diminution in value is charged to the Profit and Loss Account.

> The [company] uses both the inverted sum of the years' digits method and the straight-line method for goodwill amortization...The [company] has adopted the inverted sum of the years' digits method of amortization in respect of four of its major business groups...The benefits of acquiring these businesses are expected to exceed the mandated goodwill write-off period of 20 years from date of acquisition. Earnings are expected to grow over the period and not remain static, and therefore the inverted sum of the years' digits method had been adopted (which results in an annually growing amortization charge) rather than straight-line amortization (which results in a fixed annual charge).

---

[2] Australian Accounting Research Foundation, AASB No. 1013.

In response to the Pacific Dunlop amortization policy, the Urgent Issues Group of the Australian Accounting Research Foundation (AARF) issued a moratorium in 1995 on the use of the inverted sum of the years' digits (ISOYD) method until the appropriateness of the method could be studied.[3] According to representatives of the AARF;

> We had a number of companies using the ISOYD method in their financial accounts and it was having a very big impact on their reported profits. But several overseas countries have said that they simply found the use of this method in annual reports unacceptable.
>
> It would be irresponsible for us to allow this practice to continue, as eventually it would have undermined the strength of our capital markets here in Australia.

In opposition to the AARF position, companies employing the ISOYD method argued that if they were not permitted to use the approach, it would inhibit their ability to launch takeover bids for overseas companies and consequently place them at a competitive disadvantage to their international counterparts.

Required:

1. What method of goodwill amortization do you prefer? Why? If fixed assets, such as property and equipment, can be depreciated using a variety of depreciation methods (e.g. straight-line, units-of-production, sum of the years' digits, declining balance, etc.), should these same alternatives be available for the amortization of goodwill?

2. Compare Pacific Dunlop's "profit after goodwill and brandname amortization but before abnormal items and income taxes" under Australian, Canadian, German, U.K., and U.S. GAAP for the amortization of goodwill.[4] Are the differences in profit significant from that obtained using the ISOYD method?

3. Does the use of the ISOYD method impact the ability of companies (like Pacific Dunlop) to launch takeover bids for overseas companies? If so, explain how.

4. For an asset with a 20 year expected life, the ISOYD method assigns less than one percent of the asset's cost to year 1, and approximately 10 percent to year 20. What are the implications of this allocation scheme?

---

[3] In response to the controversy, the AARF issued an exposure draft proposing to permit only the straight-line method for purposes of goodwill amortization.

[4] Generally accepted practice with respect to the amortization of goodwill is as follows:

Country	Method	Period
Australia	Straight-line	20 years
Canada	Straight-line	40 years
Germany	Charge-to-equity	N.A.
U.K.	Charge-to-equity	N.A.
U.S.A.	Straight-line	40 years

Among the above countries, goodwill is tax deductible in Germany (over 5 years), the U.S. (over 15 years), and Canada (at a rate of 7 percent per annum to a maximum of 75 percent of capitalized cost).

5. Company executives frequently argue that two of a firm's most important assets are never disclosed on the balance sheet: the value of its work force and the value of internally-generated goodwill. Should GAAP be amended to permit the inclusion of these unreported assets? If so, what are the risks of doing so?

6. Review the accompanying financial data (see Exhibits 1-2) for Pacific Dunlop. Prepare a list of the differences that you observe between Australian and U.S. GAAP.

Exhibit 1
Pacific Dunlop Ltd.
Financial Statements

Profit and Loss Accounts of Pacific Dunlop Limited and Controlled Entities for the year ended 30th June 1994

The Company				Consolidated	
1994 ($'000)	1993 ($'000)		Notes	1994 ($'000)	1993 ($'000)
		Operating profit before abnormal items			
249,560	253,695	**and income tax**	1	436,734	384,740
9,738		Abnormal items before income tax	5	(4,881)	(9,533)
259,298	253,695	**Operating profit before income tax**		431,853	375,207
37,371	43,901	Income tax attributable to operating profit	6	123,321	108,952
221,927	209,794	**Operating profit after income tax**		308,532	266,255
		Outside equity interests in operating profit after income tax		5,038	5,845
		Operating profit after income tax attributable			
221,927	209,794	**to Pacific Dunlop Limited shareholders***		303,494	260,410
99,069	101,965	Retained profits at the beginning of the financial year		133,696	85,892
		Aggregate of amounts transferred (to)/from reserves	3	(35)	84
320,996	311,759	Total available for appropriation		437,155	346,386
		Dividends provided for or paid			
116,304	97,379	Interim dividend for year ended 30/6/94	7	116,304	97,379
123,465	113,982	Final dividend for year ended 30/6/94	7	123,465	113,982
367	1,329	Under provision for prior year interim and final dividends	7	367	1,329
80,860	99,069	Retained profits at the end of the financial year		197,019	133,696
		Summary of profit for the year			
		*Operating profit after income tax attributable to			
221,927	209,794	Pacific Dunlop Limited shareholders		303,494	260,410
		Abnormal items after tax attributable to			
9,738	(6,600)	Pacific Dunlop Limited shareholders	5	(3,296)	27
		Operating profit after tax before abnormal items			
212,189	216,394	**attributable to Pacific Dunlop Limited shareholders**		306,790	260,383

				1994 ¢	1993 ¢
		Earnings per share based on operating profit after income tax attributable to Pacific Dunlop Limited shareholders			
		Basic earnings per share before goodwill amortisation and abnormal items	34	31.5	27.0
		Basic earnings per share before abnormal items	34	29.2	25.7
		Basic earnings per share inclusive of abnormal items	34	28.9	25.7
		Diluted earnings per share before goodwill amortisation and abnormal items	34	30.6	26.2
		Diluted earnings per share before abnormal items	34	28.4	25.0
		Diluted earnings per share inclusive of abnormal items	34	28.1	25.0

Exhibit 1
Pacific Dunlop Ltd.
Financial Statements
(continued)

Balance Sheets of Pacific Dunlop Limited and Controlled Entities at 30th June 1994

	Notes	Consolidated 1994 ($'000)	Consolidated 1993 ($'000)	The Company 1994 ($'000)	The Company 1993 ($'000)
Current Assets					
Cash	9	1,012,104	1,206,621	35,545	44,059
Receivables	10	1,070,503	996,990	2,554,948	1,903,780
Inventories	12	1,252,492	1,155,818	263,061	261,414
Prepayments		76,901	62,987	22,855	20,141
Total Current Assets		3,412,000	3,422,416	2,876,409	2,229,394
Non-Current Assets					
Receivables	10	54,096	43,078	39,608	25,379
Investments	11	206,980	173,448	3,088,161	2,900,052
Property, plant and equipment	13	1,571,261	1,496,776	272,583	252,369
Intangibles	14	1,153,481	968,072	62,009	59,420
Other	15	346,987	346,462	39,857	36,168
Total Non-Current Assets		3,332,805	3,027,836	3,502,218	3,273,388
Total Assets		6,744,805	6,450,252	6,378,627	5,502,782
Current Liabilities					
Creditors and borrowings	16	2,717,869	2,588,554	3,038,346	2,234,147
Provisions	19	548,690	526,392	340,809	351,484
Other	20	12,020	38,290	8,285	7,239
Total Current Liabilities		3,278,579	3,153,236	3,387,440	2,592,870
Non-Current Liabilities					
Creditors and borrowings	16	975,204	978,965	677,434	725,594
Provision for deferred income tax		121,332	119,803		
Other	20	994	7,238		7,125
Total Non-Current Liabilities		1,097,530	1,106,006	677,434	732,719
Total Liabilities		4,376,109	4,259,242	4,064,874	3,325,589
Net Assets		2,368,696	2,191,010	2,313,753	2,177,193
Shareholders' Equity					
Share capital	2	529,676	464,561	529,676	464,561
Reserves	3	1,611,152	1,561,390	1,703,217	1,613,563
Retained profits		197,019	133,696	80,860	99,069
Shareholders' equity attributable to Pacific Dunlop Limited shareholders		2,337,847	2,159,647	2,313,753	2,177,193
Outside equity interest in controlled entities	8	30,849	31,363		
Total Shareholders' Equity		2,368,696	2,191,010	2,313,753	2,177,193

Exhibit 1
Pacific Dunlop Ltd.
Financial Statements
(continued)

Statement of Cash Flows of Pacific Dunlop Limited and Controlled Entities for the year ended 30th June 1994

	Notes	Consolidated 1994 ($'000) Inflows (Outflows)	Consolidated 1993 ($'000) Inflows (Outflows)	The Company 1994 ($'000) Inflows (Outflows)	The Company 1993 ($'000) Inflows (Outflows)
Cash flows from operating activities					
Receipts from customers		6,843,614	6,242,232	2,466,754	2,286,777
Payments to suppliers and employees		(6,138,363)	(5,622,839)	(2,189,595)	(2,111,795)
Interest received		48,149	65,644	104,992	102,553
Interest and other finance costs paid		(157,565)	(174,224)	(154,401)	(148,910)
Income taxes paid		(118,561)	(72,199)	(62,815)	(15,623)
Dividends received		6,292	7,037	122,650	196,527
Net cash provided by operating activities	29(e)	483,566	445,651	287,585	309,529
Cash flows from investing activities					
Purchase of businesses, net of cash acquired	29(b)	(293,724)	(40,210)	(13,194)	(8,231)
Purchase of property, plant and equipment	29(c)	(269,090)	(237,381)	(45,364)	(43,586)
Capitalised research and development expenditure		(52,561)	(60,433)		
Proceeds from sale of businesses	29(b)	1,975	152,101	968	
Proceeds from sale of plant and equipment –					
in the ordinary course of business		28,889	27,762	8,380	7,192
Loans (made)/repaid		(2,811)	(28,397)	3,721	(35,269)
Net loans from/(to) controlled entities	29(f)			46,896	(221,984)
Purchase of investments in controlled entities				(135,633)	(185,497)
Sale of other investments		95,433	147,552		
Purchase of other investments		(49,784)	(74,938)	(41,748)	
Net cash used in investing activities		(541,673)	(113,944)	(135,974)	(487,375)
Cash flows from financing activities					
Proceeds from issue of shares		7,574	5,933	5,230	4,382
Proceeds from borrowings		551,049	673,706	495,186	584,123
Repayment of borrowings		(550,697)	(607,738)	(540,190)	(432,760)
Lease payments		(43,929)	(97,670)	(20,232)	(18,003)
Dividends paid		(98,923)	(91,002)	(90,857)	(85,783)
Net cash (used in)/provided by financing activities		(134,926)	(116,771)	(150,863)	51,959
Net (decrease)/increase in cash held		(193,033)	214,936	748	(125,887)
Cash at the beginning of year		1,154,297	928,294	29,262	155,149
Effects of exchange rate changes on the balances of cash held in foreign currencies at the beginning of the financial year		(10,330)	11,067		
Cash at end of year	29(a)	950,934	1,154,297	30,010	29,262

Exhibit 2
Pacific Dunlop Ltd.
Selected Footnotes

Notes on the Accounts

These explanatory notes form part of both the consolidated accounts and the accounts of Pacific Dunlop Limited.

STATEMENT OF ACCOUNTING POLICIES

The significant accounting policies used in the preparation of these accounts are as follows:

Basis of Preparation of the Accounts

The accounts are drawn up in accordance with the conventions of historical cost accounting as practiced in Australia and using a going concern basis of accounting except to the extent that certain non-current assets are included at valuation.

The carrying amounts of non-current assets have been reviewed to ensure that such assets are not carried at a value in excess of their recoverable amount. In determining recoverable amounts the relevant cash flows have not been discounted to their present value.

The accounts have been prepared in accordance with the requirements of Australian Accounting bodies, applicable Accounting Standards and to comply with the requirements of the Corporations Law. Where appropriate, the accounts contain the terminology of the Corporations Law whereby Pacific Dunlop Limited is the chief entity and is referred to in the accounts as The Company and the economic entity (Group) comprises The Company and its controlled entities.

Consolidation Practices

The consolidated accounts comprise the accounts of Pacific Dunlop Limited (The Company), being the chief entity and all its controlled entities which are listed in Note 35.

Equity in Associated Companies

Equity accounting for associated companies was discontinued effective 1st July 1988, as the investments in such companies are not considered material. These investments are valued in the consolidated accounts at Directors' Valuation at 30th June 1994, and are disclosed in Note 11.

Depreciation and Amortisation of Property, Plant and Equipment

Depreciation on freehold buildings is provided by Pacific Dunlop Limited and all Australian controlled entities at the rate of 2.5% per annum on cost or valuation.

Overseas controlled entities depreciate freehold buildings at allowable taxation rates. Amortisation of leasehold properties is provided in equal monthly instalments over the period of the leases.

Depreciation on plant is provided so as to write off the asset over its useful life on a straight line basis.

Research and Development Expenditure

Expenditure is written off in the period in which it is incurred except in respect of the Medical Products Group (Nucleus Group).

Research and development expenditure is an integral feature of the Medical Products Group (Nucleus Group). Costs of projects for which total expenditure is expected to exceed $50,000 are capitalised to the extent that future benefits are expected, beyond reasonable doubt, to exceed these costs. The amount of the capitalised expenditure is reduced by any government grants received in relation to the expenditure. Grants received during the year in relation to costs previously charged to the operating profit, are brought to account as income.

Amortisation of capitalised costs commences in the half-year period immediately following their capitalisation and continues for either three or five years depending upon the nature of the expenditure and expected future benefits.

Research and development costs capitalised in previous periods are regularly reviewed and when the criteria for capitalisation is no longer met, the unamortised balance is charged to the operating profit for the period.

Income Tax

Income tax expense is calculated at current rates on the accounting profit adjusted for permanent differences and income tax over/under provided in the previous year. The estimated liability for income tax outstanding in respect of the period's operations is included in the Balance Sheet as a current liability.

Future income tax benefits and liabilities arising because some items are included in accounting profit in a period different from that in which the items are assessed for income tax, are included in the Balance Sheet as a non-current asset and a non-current liability respectively. As provided for in Accounting Standard AASB 1020, these deferred tax balances have been offset, where applicable, in the accounts of the individual entities.

The eventual recoverability of future income tax benefits and payment of the non-current tax liability is contingent upon taxable income being earned in future periods, continuation of the relevant taxation laws and each relevant company continuing to comply with the appropriate legislation.

Future income tax benefits attributable to tax losses (including capital losses) are only recorded where virtual certainty of recovery exists.

Provision is made for overseas taxes, which may arise in the event of retained profits of foreign controlled entities being remitted to Australia, when the dividend is declared.

Provision is made for capital gains tax, which may arise in the event of sale of revalued assets, only when such assets are sold.

Valuation of Inventories

Stock on hand and work in progress are consistently valued on the basis of the lower of cost and net realisable value. The methods generally adopted throughout the economic entity in determining costs are:
Raw materials and other stock –
Actual costs, determined on a first in, first out basis or standard costs approximating actual costs.
Finished goods and work in progress –
Standard costs approximating actual costs including an appropriate allocation of overheads. Merchant lines are valued at actual cost into store, determined on a first in, first out or average cost basis.

Obsolete and slow moving stocks are written down to net realisable value where such value is below cost.

Valuation of Property, Plant and Equipment

The bases of valuation of Freehold and Leasehold Land and Buildings are detailed in Note 13. Buildings and Plant under Construction and Plant and Equipment are recorded in the accounts at cost. The revaluation content of properties disposed of is transferred to Retained Profits.

Leases of Property, Plant and Equipment

Finance leases are capitalised at the present value of the minimum lease payments and amortised over the estimated useful life of the assets on a straight line basis. Operating lease payments are expensed as incurred.

**Exhibit 2
Pacific Dunlop Ltd.
Selected Footnotes**
(continued)

Accounting for Acquisitions

Acquired businesses are accounted for on the basis of the cost method. Fair values are assigned at date of acquisition to all the identifiable underlying assets acquired and to the liabilities assumed. Specific assessment is undertaken at the date of acquisition of any additional costs to be incurred.

Brandnames acquired are recorded in the accounts at cost.

Goodwill is capitalised and amortised to the Profit and Loss Account. In determining the period and method of amortisation, each acquisition is separately assessed. The benefits from the goodwill acquired may exceed 20 years but the goodwill is written off over periods not exceeding 20 years to comply with Australian Accounting Standards.

The unamortised balance of goodwill is reviewed semi-annually and any material diminution in value is charged to the Profit and Loss Account.

The bases of valuation of goodwill are detailed in Note 14.

The economic entity uses both the inverted sum of the years' digits method and the straight line method for goodwill amortisation:

Goodwill at Cost/Valuation – 30/6/94 ($million)	Amortisation Method	Amortisation Period
6	Straight Line	Up to 5 years
3	Straight Line	6 to 10 years
131	Straight Line	11 to 20 years
614	Inverted Sum of the Years' Digits	20 years
754		

The economic entity has developed both domestically and internationally by organic growth and acquisition. The general philosophy of the economic entity is that business acquisitions are fundamental to its growth strategy and thus it buys businesses for the long term. Upon acquisition, the economic entity sets about enhancing the value of these businesses.

The economic entity has adopted the inverted sum of the years' digits method of amortisation in respect of four of its major business groups:

* *Repco Australia/New Zealand (acquired 1988 and 1990):*
Australia's and New Zealand's leading auto parts retailer and wholesaler (established in Australia in 1928).

* *Edmont USA (acquired 1989):*
One of the world's leading manufacturers and distributors of industrial gloves (established 1934).

* *GNB USA (acquired 1987):*
Leading world manufacturer of auto and industrial batteries (established 1925).

* *Petersville/Plumrose Australia (acquired 1991 and 1993):*
Australia's leading food companies with significant Asia Pacific growth opportunities (long established businesses eg. Peters Ice Cream 1904, Herbert Adams 1909, Edgell 1926, Leggos 1888).

The benefits of acquiring these businesses are expected to exceed the mandated goodwill write off period of 20 years from date of acquisition. Earnings are expected to grow over that period and not remain static and therefore the inverted sum of the years' digits method has been adopted (which results in an annually growing amortisation charge) rather than straight line amortisation (which results in a fixed annual charge).

Brandnames

Brandnames acquired since 1st July 1987 are recorded in the accounts at cost. Brandnames are reviewed annually and any diminution in value is charged to the Profit and Loss Account.

An independent valuation was performed as at 30th June 1994 and supported the Directors' view that no diminution in value of brandnames had occurred since 30th June 1993, and accordingly no charge to the Profit and Loss Account has been made for the year. Details are included in Note 14.

Valuation of Investments

The bases of valuation of Investments are detailed in Note 11.

Deferred Expenditure

Deferred expenditure represents major industry restructuring costs which have future economic benefits over more than one accounting period and are amortised over the periods of their expected benefit on a straight line basis. The amortisation period will not exceed 5 years and the annual amortisation value is charged against trading profit.

Foreign Currency Translations

Transactions in foreign currencies are recorded at the rate of exchange ruling on the date of each transaction. At balance date, amounts payable and receivable in foreign currencies are converted at the rates of exchange ruling at the end of the financial period. Where forward currency contracts have been arranged, the contract settlement rate (approximating the spot rate) is used.

Exchange differences arising on foreign currency amounts payable and receivable are brought to account in the Profit and Loss Account. On consolidation, exchange differences on long term foreign currency amounts payable and receivable that hedge a net investment in an overseas controlled entity are transferred to the foreign currency translation reserve on a net of tax basis.

The accounts of overseas controlled entities are converted using the current rate method. Variations occurring from year to year arising from this translation method are transferred to the foreign currency translation reserve.

Employee Entitlements

Employee entitlements in respect of both annual and long service leave are provided by the economic entity in accordance with the vested legal entitlements of the country of employment. Provisions relating to these entitlements are classified as current liabilities.

Rounding Off to the Nearest Thousand Dollars

Pacific Dunlop Limited is a company of the kind referred to in the Corporations Law Regulation 3.6.05(6) and unless otherwise shown, the amounts in the accompanying accounts and in the Directors' Report have been rounded off to the nearest thousand dollars in accordance with section 311 of the Corporations Law.

Certain comparatives have been reclassified to ensure consistency with current classification requirements.

Exhibit 2
Pacific Dunlop Ltd.
Selected Footnotes
(continued)

	Consolidated		The Company	
	1994 ($'000)	1993 ($'000)	1994 ($'000)	1993 ($'000)

1 Operating Profit

Sales revenue	6,966,823	6,304,624	2,478,005	2,298,103
Dividend income	6,292	7,037	122,650	196,527
	6,973,115	6,311,661	2,600,655	2,494,630
Operating expenses	6,426,738	5,828,531	2,301,989	2,197,193
Loss/(gain) on sale of non-current assets	1,096	(8,771)	(163)	(422)
Net foreign exchange gain	(869)	(1,419)	(140)	(2,193)
Operating profit before net interest and income tax	546,150	493,320	298,969	300,052
Net interest expense on borrowings	62,771	54,673	26,441	20,540
Net interest expense on trade bills and finance leases	46,645	53,907	22,968	25,817
Operating profit before abnormal items and income tax	436,734	384,740	249,560	253,695
Income tax attributable to operating profit before abnormal items	124,906	118,380	37,371	37,301
Outside equity interests in operating profit before abnormal items	5,038	5,977		
Operating profit after tax and before abnormal items attributable to Pacific Dunlop Limited shareholders	306,790	260,383	212,189	216,394
Abnormal items after income tax attributable to Pacific Dunlop Limited shareholders	(3,296)	27	9,738	(6,600)
Operating profit inclusive of abnormal items attributable to Pacific Dunlop Limited shareholders	303,494	260,410	221,927	209,794

Operating profit before abnormal items and income tax is arrived at after charging:

Interest Paid or Due and Payable				
To wholly owned controlled entities			47,431	29,027
To others	110,920	120,317	74,744	80,022
Interest on Trade Bills	32,326	34,106	20,928	26,977
Finance Charges on Finance Leases	14,319	19,801	11,298	12,884
Depreciation and Amortisation				
Property, plant and equipment	156,682	134,507	25,324	22,048
Leased assets	34,199	36,807	23,205	24,085
Goodwill (refer also to Note 14)	23,695	13,270	4,002	1,032
Capitalised research and development expenditure	58,361	40,021		
Deferred expenditure	4,041	853		
Diminution in Brandnames		1,217		315
Bad Debts				
Trade debtors	3,755	6,824	3,369	4,683
Other amounts receivable	20	92		
Provision for Doubtful Debts				
Trade debtors	5,715	5,567	872	(115)
Other Provisions				
Provision for employee entitlements	34,323	25,708	14,824	9,261
Provision for deferred maintenance and contingencies	(3,075)	17,751	(2,880)	18,258
Provision for rationalisation and restructuring costs	1,486	3,976	(1,006)	3,502
Provision for rebates, allowances and warranty claims	3,445	6,635	843	1,636
Provision for insurance claims	(52)	751	(17)	102
Research and Development Costs Expensed as Incurred	13,935	14,395	3,272	2,240

Exhibit2
Pacific Dunlop Ltd.
Selected Footnotes
(continued)

	Consolidated		The Company	
	1994 ($'000)	1993 ($'000)	1994 ($'000)	1993 ($'000)

1 Operating Profit (continued)

Auditors' Remuneration

Amounts received and receivable for audit of accounts –

Auditors of Pacific Dunlop Limited	3,616	3,589	2,269	2,320
Other auditors	2,490	2,390		

For other services –

Auditors of Pacific Dunlop Limited	1,447	1,384	1,338	1,226
Other auditors	316	455		

No other benefits were received by auditors of
entities controlled by Pacific Dunlop Limited

Losses Arising from Sale of Non-Current Assets	4,515	1,770	1,241	384
Operating Lease Rentals	91,468	94,502	39,669	44,249

2 Share Capital

Authorised Capital

1,600,000,000 (last year 1,600,000,000) ordinary shares
of 50 cents each

	800,000	800,000	800,000	800,000

The 509,545,770 unissued ordinary shares are unclassified
shares.

Paid up capital

1,048,017,022 (last year 922,135,862) ordinary shares
of 50 cents each, fully paid

	524,009	461,068	524,009	461,068

10,699,958 (last year 6,546,119) ordinary plan shares
of 50 cents each, fully paid

	5,350	3,273	5,350	3,273

31,737,250 (last year 22,043,800) ordinary plan shares
of 50 cents each, paid to 1 cent

	317	220	317	220
	529,676	464,561	529,676	464,561

Shares issued during the year

107,556 ordinary shares of 50 cents each, fully paid, pursuant
to the conversion of subordinated convertible bonds.
95,643,010 ordinary shares of 50 cents each, fully paid, by way
of bonus issue.
25,743,476 ordinary shares of 50 cents each, fully paid, under
the dividend reinvestment plan.
13,325,500 ordinary plan shares of 50 cents each, paid to 1 cent.
4,281,000 ordinary plan shares of 50 cents each, fully paid.
627,907 ordinary plan shares of 50 cents each, fully paid, by way
of bonus issue.

The terms of these issues are explained in the Directors' Report
(pages 51 and 52).

Exhibit 2
Pacific Dunlop Ltd.
Selected Footnotes
(continued)

	Consolidated		The Company	
	1994 ($'000)	1993 ($'000)	1994 ($'000)	1993 ($'000)

3 Reserves and Retained Profits

Share premium reserve	1,655,879	1,573,601	1,655,879	1,573,601
Capital redemption reserve	28,000	28,000	28,000	28,000
Asset revaluation reserve	39,336	39,417	16,463	16,463
General reserve	4,724	4,724		
Foreign currency translation reserve	(114,375)	(81,940)	2,875	(4,501)
Equity reserve in associated companies	(2,412)	(2,412)		
Retained profits	197,019	133,696	80,860	99,069
	1,808,171	1,695,086	1,784,077	1,712,632

Movements during the year

Share premium reserve

Premium on plan shares converted	2,890	2,325	2,890	2,325
Premium on convertible notes converted	259		259	
Premium on shares issued	108,000	93,526	108,000	93,526
Premium on plan shares issued	19,264		19,264	
Issue of bonus shares	(48,135)		(48,135)	

Asset revaluation reserve

Transfer from/(to) retained profits	35	(84)		
Revaluation decrement for property revalued to recoverable amount*	(116)			
Tax benefit in respect of previous revaluation*		2,579		2,579

Foreign currency translation reserve
Exchange fluctuations on assets and liabilities held in foreign currencies

net (loss)/gain on translation	(79,680)	46,958		
net gain/(loss) on hedge transactions	47,245	(71,921)	7,376	(11,427)

Retained profits

Transfer (to)/from reserves	(35)	84		
Trading profits	306,790	260,383	212,189	216,394
Abnormal items	(3,296)	27	9,738	(6,600)
Dividends provided+	(240,136)	(212,690)	(240,136)	(212,690)
Net increase in reserves and retained profits	113,085	121,187	71,445	84,107

* This item has not been brought to account in determining the profit for the year.

+ The interim dividends and final dividends include amounts following from conversion of plan shares after balance date but prior to books closing date of $367,000 (30/6/93 $1,329,000)

Exhibit 2
Pacific Dunlop Ltd.
Selected Footnotes
(continued)

	Consolidated		The Company	
	1994 ($'000)	1993 ($'000)	1994 ($'000)	1993 ($'000)

4 Other Operating Revenue

Interest Received or Due and Receivable				
From wholly owned controlled entities			86,137	60,987
From partly owned controlled entities			358	1,444
From Directors of Pacific Dunlop Limited and controlled entities	138	126	138	126
From others	48,011	65,518	9,101	25,952
Interest on Trade Bills Received or Due and Receivable				
From wholly owned controlled entities			8,629	13,900
From partly owned controlled entities			629	144
Income from Investments				
On shares in associated companies	6,259	2,682		
On shares in other companies	33	4,355		
On shares in wholly owned controlled entities			119,243	193,667
On shares in partly owned controlled entities			3,407	2,860
Research and Development Grants Received		254		
Proceeds from the Sale of Investments	18,452	80,573	968	
Proceeds from the Sale of Other Non–Current Assets in the Normal Course of Business	28,889	27,762	8,380	7,192
Other Operating Revenue	101,782	181,270	236,990	306,272
Gains Arising from the Sale of Non–Current Assets in the Normal Course of Business	3,419	10,541	1,404	806
Bad Debts Recovered	837	759	392	503

5 Abnormal Items

Net (loss)/gain on sale of controlled entities and businesses	(4,881)		9,738	
Income tax benefit	1,585			
Net gain on sale of investments and properties		25,072		
Income tax expense				
Rationalisation		(33,641)		
Income tax benefit		14,226		
Litigation		(964)		
Income tax benefit		376		
Restatement of deferred tax balances resulting from change in income tax rates		(5,174)		(6,600)
Abnormal items after income tax	(3,296)	(105)	9,738	(6,600)
Less outside equity interest		132		
Abnormal items after income tax attributable to Pacific Dunlop Limited shareholders	(3,296)	27	9,738	(6,600)
Analysis of Abnormal Items				
Abnormal items before income tax	(4,881)	(9,533)	9,738	
Income tax benefit on abnormal items	1,585	14,602		
Abnormal tax charge due to change in tax rates		(5,174)		(6,600)
Outside equity interest in abnormal items		132		
Abnormal items after income tax attributable to Pacific Dunlop Limited shareholders	(3,296)	27	9,738	(6,600)

Exhibit 2
Pacific Dunlop Ltd.
Selected Footnotes
(continued)

	Consolidated		The Company	
	1994 ($'000)	1993 ($'000)	1994 ($'000)	1993 ($'000)

6 Income Tax

Tax at standard rate on operating profit	142,512	146,331	85,568	98,942
Add increased taxation arising from:				
Depreciation on buildings not allowable	2,258	2,245	259	231
Other non-allowable permanent differences	14,897	35,507	5,852	18,977
Income tax under/(over) provided in previous years	2,367	1,556	(1,340)	(264)
Deduct reduced taxation arising from:				
Tax rebate on dividends from investments	1,444	5,083	30,433	62,184
Tax exempt dividends from foreign companies	318	52	10,042	17,017
Investment and export incentive allowances	10,828	9,997	749	41
Capital receipts not assessable	2,122	11,064	4,384	(52)
Net lower overseas tax rates	7,307	21,033		
Other allowable permanent differences	16,694	34,632	7,360	1,395
Income tax as per Profit and Loss Accounts attributable to operating profit before effect of tax rate changes	123,321	103,778	37,371	37,301
Effect of tax rate changes (refer Note 5)		5,174		6,600
Income tax as per Profit and Loss Accounts attributable to operating profit	123,321	108,952	37,371	43,901
Income tax provided comprises:				
Provision attributable to current year	86,269	75,372	42,467	35,367
Adjustments to provision in respect of previous years	2,367	1,556	(1,340)	(264)
Provision attributable to future years				
Deferred tax liability	8,643	15,974		
Future income tax benefit	26,042	10,876	(3,756)	2,198
Effect of tax rate changes (refer Note 5)		5,174		6,600
	123,321	108,952	37,371	43,901

7 Dividends Paid and Proposed

Dividends paid or declared by The Company are:
(a) an interim dividend of 11 cents (1993 10½ cents) franked
    to 60% (1993 55%) has been declared by the Directors

Dividends taxed at 39%				97,497*
Dividends taxed at 33%			116,304	
			116,304	97,497

(b) a final dividend of 11½ cents (1993 11 cents) franked to
    60% (1993 55%) has been declared by the Directors

Dividends taxed at 39%				114,231*
Dividends taxed at 33%			123,465	
			123,465	114,231

*The interim and final dividends paid in respect of 1993 include amounts that were underprovided in the 1993 accounts of $118,000 and $249,000 respectively. These amounts have been charged to retained profits in 1994.

Dividend Franking Account
    After the payment of the final dividend which is proposed to be franked to 60% the balance of available franking credits in the franking account of Pacific Dunlop Limited will be Nil (1993 Nil).

Exhibit 2
Pacific Dunlop Ltd.
Selected Footnotes
(continued)

	Consolidated		The Company	
	1994 ($'000)	1993 ($'000)	1994 ($'000)	1993 ($'000)

8 Outside Equity Interest

Outside equity interest comprises:

Issued capital	29,798	27,515		
Reserves	(5,795)	(5,682)		
Retained profits at the beginning of the financial year	9,530	8,917		
Profits for the year	5,038	5,845		
Dividends provided for during the year	(8,066)	(5,219)		
Outside equity interest acquired/disposed of during the year	344	(13)		
Retained profits at the end of the financial year	6,846	9,530		
Total outside equity interest	**30,849**	**31,363**		

Details of share capital held by outside equity interests:

	Outside Equity Interest %	No. of Shares 1994	No. of Shares 1993	Consolidated 1994 ($'000)	Consolidated 1993 ($'000)
adidas (Australia) Pty. Ltd.	49	11,107,568		1,307	
adidas New Zealand Ltd.	49	1,090,584		332	
Ansell Malaysia Sdn. Bhd.	25	2,300,001	2,300,001	1,072	1,072
Ansell Medical Sdn. Bhd.	25	250,000	250,000	106	106
Ansell Steritech Ltd.			333,333		282
Beijing Pacific Dunlop Textiles Ltd.*	30	30%	30%	1,025	1,025
Dunlop Shelter Singapore Pte. Ltd.	40	4,001	4,001	3	3
Grosby (China) Ltd.	49	490	490		
Loscam Ltd.	19	24,266,195	24,266,195	4,853	4,853
Mates Vending Ltd.	25	497,250	596,700	1,063	1,278
Nicks Sports & Leisure Footwear Ltd.	1	20,000	20,000	46	46
Optix Australia Ltd.	49	1,960,900	1,960,000	1,960	1,960
Pacific Dunlop Garments Ltd.			1,402,000		234
Pasta House Mfg. Co. Pty. Ltd.	25	3,000,000	3,000,000	3,000	3,000
Restonic (M) Sdn. Bhd.	50	12,250,000	12,250,000	7,077	7,077
Serenity Asia Pte. Ltd. (Joint Venture interest)	50	50%		706	
Shanghai Holeproof Garments Ltd.*	30	30%	30%	1,027	358
Shenzhen Olex Cables Ltd.*	20	20%	20%	2,613	2,613
Tianjin Olex Cables Ltd.*	30	30%	30%	3,257	3,257
Union Knitting Mills Pty. Ltd.	12½	350,879	350,879	351	351
				29,798	27,515

*Ownership in the People's Republic of China is denominated in percentage terms.

Exhibit 2
Pacific Dunlop Ltd.
Selected Footnotes
(continued)

	Consolidated		The Company	
	1994 (S'000)	1993 (S'000)	1994 (S'000)	1993 (S'000)

9 Cash

Cash on hand	1,696	1,838	159	209
Cash at bank	119,199	90,595	33,069	20,850
Short-term deposits	891,209	1,114,188	2,317	23,000
	1,012,104	1,206,621	35,545	44,059

10 Receivables

Current				
Trade debtors	1,000,251	863,846	192,367	179,590
Less provision for doubtful debts	22,154	27,346	5,400	5,694
Less provision for rebates, allowances and warranty claims	25,440	22,424	7,121	6,278
	952,657	814,076	179,846	167,618
Amounts owing by wholly owned controlled entities			2,282,378	1,646,278
Amounts owing by partly owned controlled entities			25,273	25,551
Trade bills receivable	645	1,099		
Other amounts receivable	117,201	181,815	67,451	64,333
	1,070,503	996,990	2,554,948	1,903,780
Non-current				
Other amounts receivable	54,096	43,078	39,608	25,379
	1,124,599	1,040,068	2,594,556	1,929,159
Bad debts written off during the year against provision for doubtful debts				
Trade debtors	10,033	4,933	837	1,230

Included in other amounts receivable at 30/6/1994 are:
(i) Loans to employees in relation to the employee share plan

- current	2,406	1,407	2,406	1,407
- non-current	35,475	19,128	35,475	19,128

(ii) Loans to shareholders of controlled entity acquired during the year

- non-current		2,700		

(iii) Loans to Executive Directors of Pacific Dunlop Limited and certain controlled entities secured under the Pacific Dunlop Housing Scheme repayable at a future date at concessional interest rates

- non-current	3,139	3,139	3,139	3,139
- new loans made		1,591		1,591

(iv) Other loans to Directors of controlled entities

- current	103	270		
- non-current	23	122		
- new loans made	13	269		
- repayments received	261	95		

A new loan was made to J. Strafe. The loan is interest free
and repayable at the end of three years.
Repayment received from W. Chan.

Exhibit 2
Pacific Dunlop Ltd.
Selected Footnotes
(continued)

	Consolidated		The Company	
	1994 ($'000)	1993 ($'000)	1994 ($'000)	1993 ($'000)

11 Investments

Shares in Controlled Entities				
Not quoted on a prescribed stock exchange:				
Pre 1/7/1987 – Directors' Valuation 30/6/1987			440,949	439,439
Post 1/7/1987 – At cost			2,604,976	2,460,125
Total investment in controlled entities as per Note 35			3,045,925	2,899,564
Shares in Other Companies				
Quoted on a prescribed stock exchange:				
At cost	8	1,744	8	8
Market value 1994 $9,000				
1993 $3,474,000				
Not quoted on a prescribed stock exchange:				
At cost	3,184	16,627		
Shares in Unlisted Associated Companies				
Directors' Valuation 30/6/1994	76,611		42,228	
Directors' Valuation 30/6/1993		35,936		480
Interest in Partnerships				
South Pacific Tyres	123,701	116,360		
Tecbelt Pacific	3,476	2,781		
	206,980	173,448	3,088,161	2,900,052

Investments in associated companies were revalued by the Directors at 30th June 1994 based on their assessment of the underlying net worth of investments in associated companies at that time. No adjustments to book values resulted from this process. This revaluation is an annual process.

Investments in controlled entities in the books of The Company that were acquired prior to 1st July 1987 were valued by the Directors at 30th June 1987 based on their net tangible asset value at that date.

12 Inventories

At cost				
Raw materials	192,472	166,428	46,303	43,762
Work in progress	137,572	135,497	29,988	36,395
Finished goods	865,980	763,518	156,841	148,044
Other stock	18,790	9,957	553	310
	1,214,814	1,075,400	233,685	228,511
At net realisable value				
Raw materials	5,472	25,606	4,231	6,096
Work in progress	5,610	8,425	3,623	2,777
Finished goods	26,596	46,387	21,522	24,030
	37,678	80,418	29,376	32,903
	1,252,492	1,155,818	263,061	261,414

Exhibit 2
Pacific Dunlop Ltd.
Selected Footnotes
(continued)

	Consolidated		The Company	
	1994 ($'000)	1993 ($'000)	1994 ($'000)	1993 ($'000)

13 Property, Plant and Equipment

(a) Freehold land

Independent valuation 31/12/1991	61,298	64,652	15,421	15,421
Independent valuation 30/6/1994	230			
Directors' valuation 31/12/1991	21,262	21,669		
At cost	50,773	43,078	4,361	1,391
	133,563	129,399	19,782	16,812

(b) Freehold buildings

Independent valuation 31/12/1991	97,560	102,690	18,887	18,965
Independent valuation 30/6/1994	500			
Directors' valuation 31/12/1991	43,119	45,297		
	141,179	147,987	18,887	18,965
Less provision for depreciation	10,123	7,792	1,180	711
	131.056	140,195	17,707	18,254
At cost	155.305	122,702	11,557	6,803
Less provision for depreciation	18,596	10,712	459	134
	136,709	111,990	11,098	6,669
	267,765	252,185	28,805	24,923

(c) Leasehold land and buildings

Independent valuation 31/12/1991	36,058	38,284		
Directors' valuation 31/12/1991	13,899	15,022		
	49,957	53,306		
Less provision for amortisation	3,082	2,439		
	46.875	50,867		
At cost	29,738	26,434	2,787	2,697
Less provision for amortisation	9,506	6,995	1,366	1,008
	20,232	19,439	1,421	1,689
	67.107	70,306	1,421	1,689

(d) Plant and equipment

At cost	1,751,162	1,684,412	295,247	288,265
Less provision for depreciation	941,776	865,574	165,259	168,738
	809.386	818,838	129,988	119,527

(e) Leased plant and equipment

At cost	197,877	188,249	96,634	100,975
Less provision for amortisation	72.889	67,886	38,879	34,659
	124,988	120,363	57,755	66,316

(f) Buildings and plant under construction

At cost	168,452	105,685	34,832	23,102
	1,571,261	1,496,776	272,583	252,369

The independent valuations of freehold and leasehold land and buildings were carried out as at 31st December 1991 by Jones Lang Wootton, on various bases being market value, existing use value and market value subject to their continued occupation. The majority of sites were valued on these bases. However, certain other freehold and leasehold properties including both operative and idle sites were discounted below market value. A valuation of freehold and leasehold land and buildings is obtained every three years in accordance with the requirements of the Corporations Law.

Certain freehold land and buildings were revalued downwards as at 30th June 1994. This valuation was performed by Neil A. Harvey A.V.L.E. (Val.) of JLW Advisory – Corporate Property Services on the basis of existing use value. This downwards revaluation was not performed as part of a revaluation of the entire portfolio of land and buildings.

240

Exhibit 2
Pacific Dunlop Ltd.
Selected Footnotes
(continued)

	Consolidated		The Company	
	1994 ($'000)	1993 ($'000)	1994 ($'000)	1993 ($'000)
14 Intangibles				
Brandnames				
At cost	318,923	247,924	6,142	4,800
Capitalised research and development expenditure				
At cost	204,651	195,544		
Less provision for amortisation	76,585	79,005		
	128,066	116,539		
Goodwill				
Directors' valuation 30/6/1992	40,066	43,600		
Less provision for amortisation	884	321		
	39,182	43,279		
At cost	713,514	584,396	61,929	56,863
Less provision for amortisation	46,204	24,066	6,062	2,243
	667,310	560,330	55,867	54,620
Total goodwill	706,492	603,609	55,867	54,620
Total intangibles	1,153,481	968,072	62,009	59,420

Capitalised brandnames were subjected to an independent valuation by Interbrand UK Limited as at 30th June 1994. The bases of valuation used by the independent valuer were the earnings multiple basis and the discounted cash flow basis. Both bases valued the brandnames at a value in excess of the book value at 30th June 1994. The increment has not been booked and the brandnames remain at cost.

Research and development expenditure capitalised during the year amounted to $79,848,000 (1993 – $81,548,000). This is net of government grants of $318,000 (1993 – $275,000).

Certain goodwill values were revalued downwards by the Directors at 30th June 1992. This resulted from the annual review of carrying values of goodwill performed as at 30th June 1992. The basis of valuation used to determine recoverable amount was the earnings multiple basis.

Exhibit 2
Pacific Dunlop Ltd.
Selected Footnotes
(continued)

	Consolidated		The Company	
	1994 ($'000)	1993 ($'000)	1994 ($'000)	1993 ($'000)

15 Other Non-Current Assets

Deferred expenditure	24,684	17,397		
Less provision for amortisation	4,728	853		
	19,956	16,544		
Future income tax benefit arising from:				
Accumulated timing differences	119,885	152,022	39,857	36,168
Accumulated tax losses	207,146	177,896		
	327,031	329,918	39,857	36,168
	346,987	346,462	39,857	36,168

Future income tax benefits of $2,525,000 (1993 – $739,000) relating to trading tax losses of controlled entities and of $65,000,000 (1993 – $60,000,000) relating to capital tax losses of controlled entities have not been recognised in the accounts. The assets to which most of these capital losses relate were acquired with the purchase of Petersville Sleigh Ltd. in 1991. The benefit of these trading and capital tax losses will only be obtained if:

(a) the controlled entities derive future assessable income of a nature and an amount sufficient to enable the benefits from the deductions for the losses to be realised;
(b) the controlled entities continue to comply with the conditions for deductibility imposed by tax legislation; and
(c) no changes in tax legislation adversely affect the controlled entities in realising the benefits from the deductions for the losses.

16 Creditors and Borrowings

Current				
Creditors (refer Note 17)	1,737,184	1,504,131	2,428,993	1,581,407
Borrowings (refer Note 18)	980,685	1,084,423	609,353	652,740
	2,717,869	2,588,554	3,038,346	2,234,147
Non-current				
Creditors (refer Note 17)	84,072	115,575	24,664	54,256
Borrowings (refer Note 18)	891,132	863,390	652,770	671,338
	975,204	978,965	677,434	725,594

17 Creditors

Current				
Amounts owing to wholly owned controlled entities			1,668,289	928,051
Amounts owing to partly owned controlled entities			3,127	4,969
Trade creditors	698,217	610,568	122,441	122,886
Bills payable	827,378	717,271	542,262	457,334
Other creditors	155,544	139,650	59,661	52,209
Lease liabilities	56,045	36,642	33,213	15,958
	1,737,184	1,504,131	2,428,993	1,581,407
Non-current				
Other creditors	11,276	22,630	599	3,320
Lease liabilities	72,796	92,945	24,065	50,936
	84,072	115,575	24,664	54,256
	1,821,256	1,619,706	2,453,657	1,635,663

Exhibit 2
Pacific Dunlop Ltd.
Selected Footnotes
(continued)

	Consolidated		The Company	
	1994 ($'000)	1993 ($'000)	1994 ($'000)	1993 ($'000)
18 Borrowings				
Current				
Bank overdrafts	61,170	52,324	5,535	14,797
Bank loans repayable in:				
Australian dollars	26,500	45,770		20
Belgian francs		18,573		
French francs	5,427	13,242		
Malaysian ringgits	30,087	50,260	26,346	46,216
New Zealand dollars	16,371	4,041		
U.S. dollars	12,363	110,800		89,686
Other currencies	9,544	20,539		
Other loans repayable in:				
Australian dollars	229,531	23,517	189,437	23,425
Belgian francs	20,604		20,604	
French francs	12,098		12,098	
Malaysian ringgits	15,808		15,808	
New Zealand dollars	31,595	14,091	31,595	14,091
Thai baht	48,934		48,934	
U.S. dollars	444,288	712,007	242,675	445,328
Other currencies	16,365	19,259	16,321	19,177
	980.685	1,084,423	609,353	652,740
Non-current				
Subordinated convertible bonds – U.S. dollars	99.258	108,311	99,258	108,311
Bank loans repayable in:				
Malaysian ringgits		34,662		34,662
Other currencies	5			
Other loans repayable in:				
Australian dollars	74,461	74,483	73,438	73,438
Belgian francs		44,444		44,444
Canadian dollars	23,574	8,833	23,574	8,833
Malaysian ringgits	40,889	21,721	40,889	21,721
New Zealand dollars	65,319	69,824	65,319	69,824
Sterling pounds	14,831		14,831	
Thai baht	6,834	52,553	6,834	52,553
U.S. dollars	559,921	413,622	322,905	223,007
Other currencies	6,040	34,937	5,722	34,545
	891,132	863,390	652,770	671,338
	1,871,817	1,947,813	1,262,123	1,324,078

Exhibit 2
Pacific Dunlop Ltd.
Selected Footnotes
(continued)

	Consolidated		The Company	
	1994 (S'000)	1993 (S'000)	1994 (S'000)	1993 (S'000)

18 Borrowings (continued)

Subordinated convertible bonds

- The Company on 12th August 1986, completed its first US$ Convertible Bond Issue, comprising US$65,000,000 bonds of US$1,000 each, bearing interest of 7% per annum and having a maximum term of 10 years. In respect of bonds converted during the financial year, 107,556 ordinary shares at A$0.50 each of The Company were issued at A$2.91 per share. At 30th June 1994, bonds to the value of US$27,000 remained to be converted (30/6/1993 – US$227,000).

	37	339	37	339

- The Company on 3rd July 1987, completed its second US$ Convertible Bond Issue, comprising US$75,000,000 bonds of US$1,000 each, bearing interest of 6.75% per annum and having a maximum term of 10 years. No bonds were converted during the financial year. At 30th June 1994, bonds to the value of US$72,233,000 remained to be converted (30/6/1993 – US$72,233,000).

	99,221	107,972	99,221	107,972
	99,258	108,311	99,258	108,311

For additional details refer to the Directors' Report (page 52).
The long-term foreign currency monetary liabilities predominantly represent the acquisition cost of investments in overseas countries and are therefore matched by assets in matching currencies.
There are no material monetary assets or liabilities that are not effectively hedged for the next 12 months.

19 Provisions

Provision for employee entitlements	136,965	123,066	38,442	38,124
Provision for deferred maintenance and contingencies	15,944	19,836	12,156	16,344
Provision for rationalisation and restructuring costs	43,296	69,452	5,310	9,712
Provision for claims	9,043	7,413	656	87
Provision for dividend	239,769	211,361	239,769	211,361
Provision for income tax	103,673	95,264	44,476	75,856
	548,690	526,392	340,809	351,484

20 Other Liabilities

Current

Deferred income	10,175	11,384	6,440	7,239
Amounts due under contractual arrangements	1,845	26,906	1,845	
	12,020	38,290	8,285	7,239

Non-current

Deferred income	994	7,238		7,125
	13,014	45,528	8,285	14,364

Exhibit 2
Pacific Dunlop Ltd.
Selected Footnotes
(continued)

	Consolidated		The Company	
	1994 ($'000)	1993 ($'000)	1994 ($'000)	1993 ($'000)

21 Dissection of Liabilities

Secured

Bank Loans	2,222	1,084		
Other Loans	3,757	5,595		
	5,979	6,679		

Unsecured

Amounts owing to wholly owned controlled entities			1.668,289	928,051
Amounts owing to partly owned controlled entities			3,127	4,969
Bank overdrafts	61,170	52,324	5,535	14,797
Bank loans	98,075	296,803	26,346	170,584
Subordinated convertible bonds	99,258	108,311	99,258	108,311
Other loans	1,607,335	1,483,696	1.130,984	1,030,386
Lease liabilities	128,841	129,587	57,278	66,894
Trade creditors	698,217	610,568	122,441	122,886
Bills payable	827,378	717,271	542,262	457,334
Other creditors	166,820	162,280	60,260	55,529
Provisions (as per Note 19)	548.690	526,392	340,809	351,484
Provision for deferred income tax	121,332	119,803		
Other liabilities (as per Note 20)	13.014	45,528	8,285	14,364
	4.370,130	4,252,563	4.064,874	3,325,589
	4.376.109	4,259,242	4.064,874	3,325,589

For secured liabilities, security is predominantly over the assets of the relevant controlled entities.

22 Contingent Liabilities

Secured

Other amounts arising in the ordinary course of business	673			

Unsecured

Bills receivable discounted	10.785	36,282		
Other amounts arising in the ordinary course of business	38,114	22,842	8,449	9,274
	49,572	59,124	8.449	9,274

Pacific Dunlop Limited has guaranteed the performance of certain controlled entities that participate in commercial paper, medium term note and bond issues. The extent of the paper issued by these controlled entities as at 30th June 1994 was $632,155,000 (30/6/1993 $612,287,000).

Pacific Dunlop Limited has also guaranteed the performance of any wholly owned controlled entities that have negative shareholders' funds.

Tax authorities in Australia and the United States have, for some time, been reviewing the affairs of Pacific Dunlop Limited and certain controlled entities. A number of the issues raised by the authorities have been resolved during the period. Some of the issues raised which are still outstanding may eventually need to be tested in the Courts. These items have not been finalised, and there is no basis at this stage to estimate the likely outcome. However, it is considered that the probable outcome of these items will not have any material effect on The Company, or its controlled entities.

The potential after tax future liability of the economic entity for post retirement health benefits of employees of certain controlled entities in the United States amounts to approximately $19,704,000 (30/6/1993 $20,440,000).

Put and Call Options - Put and call options in relation to potential assets and liabilities of material significance to the economic entity as at 30th June 1994 relate to the acquisition of outside equity interests in the entities set out below. Due to the period of the options and the variability of the factors upon which future transaction prices will be set, it is not possible to accurately quantify the potential financial effect on the carrying amounts of assets and liabilities and the effect on the profit in the accounts for the year ended 30th June 1994 in the event that the outcome differs from that brought to account.

Entities in relation to which put and/or call options exist at 30th June 1994:

Pasta House Mfg. Co. Pty. Ltd.
The Meadow Gold Co. Ltd.

Exhibit 2
Pacific Dunlop Ltd.
Selected Footnotes
(continued)

	Consolidated		The Company	
	1994 ($'000)	1993 ($'000)	1994 ($'000)	1993 ($'000)

23 Expenditure Commitments

(a) Contracts for capital expenditure for which no amounts have been provided

Land and buildings	12,045	5,695		75
Plant	79,528	29,168	17,623	9,062
Investments	21,663		19,500	
	113,236	34,863	37,123	9,137
Payable within one year	100,026	34,097	23,913	8,371
Later than one but within two years	6,710	766	6,710	766
Later than two but within five years	6,500		6,500	
	113,236	34,863	37,123	9,137

(b) Lease commitments
Finance leases
Expenditure contracted and provided for

Payable within one year	65,190	48,890	37,256	22,831
Later than one but within two years	33,477	56,719	9,667	37,301
Later than two but within five years	45,390	41,376	15,415	15,367
Later than five years	6,318	10,254	4,701	7,088
Minimum lease payments	150,375	157,239	67,039	82,587
Less future finance charges	21,534	27,652	9,761	15,693
Lease Liability	128,841	129,587	57,278	66,894
Current portion (as per Note 17)	56,045	36,642	33,213	15,958
Non-current portion (as per Note 17)	72,796	92,945	24,065	50,936
	128,841	129,587	57,278	66,894

Operating leases
Expenditure contracted but not provided for

Payable within one year	83,399	75,002	19,976	19,323
Later than one but within two years	65,729	60,055	16,685	17,064
Later than two but within five years	99,030	101,332	28,836	34,109
Later than five years	53,298	62,760	22,868	25,287
	301,456	299,149	88,365	95,783

24 Superannuation Commitments

A total of 40 Superannuation Funds have been established worldwide.
The major funds are:

Country	Fund	Benefit Type	Basis of Contribution	Date of Last Actuarial Valuation	Actuary
Australia	Pacific Dunlop Superannuation Fund	Defined Benefit/ Accumulation	Balance of Cost/ Defined Contribution	1/7/1993	William M. Mercer Pty. Ltd.
Australia	Pacific Dunlop Executive Fund	Defined Benefit	Balance of Cost	1/7/1993	William M. Mercer Pty. Ltd.
Australia	Pacific Dunlop Group Staff Superannuation Fund	Defined Benefit	Balance of Cost	1/7/1993	William M. Mercer Pty. Ltd.
U.S.A.	GNB Incorporated Pension Plan	Defined Benefit	Balance of Cost	1/7/1993	Towers Perrin

The liabilities of all the Superannuation Funds are covered by the assets in the funds or by specific provisions within the economic entity. The economic entity is obliged to contribute to the Superannuation Funds as a consequence of Legislation or Trust Deeds; legal enforceability is dependent on the terms of the Legislation and the Trust Deeds.

Definitions:
Balance of Cost — The economic entity's contribution is assessed by the actuary after taking into account the members' contribution and the value of the assets.
Defined Contribution - The economic entity's contribution is set out in the appropriate fund rules, usually as a fixed percentage of salary.

Exhibit 2
Pacific Dunlop Ltd.
Selected Footnotes
(continued)

Statement by Directors

In the opinion of the Directors of Pacific Dunlop Limited ("The Company") –

(a) the accounts of The Company are drawn up so as to give a true and fair view of the profit of The Company for the year ended 30th June 1994 and the state of affairs of The Company as at 30th June 1994;

(b) at the date of this statement there are reasonable grounds to believe that The Company will be able to pay its debts as and when they fall due; and

(c) the consolidated accounts of the economic entity have been made out in accordance with Divisions 4A and 4B of Part 3.6 of the Corporations Law and so as to give a true and fair view of the profit of the economic entity for the year ended 30th June 1994 and the state of affairs of the economic entity as at 30th June 1994.

This statement is made in accordance with a resolution of the Board of Directors and is signed for and on behalf of the Directors.

J.B. Gough
Director

P. Brass
Director

Dated at Melbourne this 9th day of September 1994.

Auditors' Report to the members of Pacific Dunlop Limited

Scope

We have audited the financial statements of Pacific Dunlop Limited for the financial year ended 30th June 1994, consisting of the profit and loss accounts, balance sheets, statements of cash flows, accompanying notes, and the statement by Directors set out on pages 54 to 97. The financial statements comprise the accounts of The Company and the consolidated accounts of the economic entity, being The Company and its controlled entities. The Company's Directors are responsible for the preparation and presentation of the financial statements and the information they contain. We have conducted an independent audit of these financial statements in order to express an opinion on them to the members of The Company.

Our audit has been planned and performed in accordance with Australian Auditing Standards to provide reasonable assurance as to whether the financial statements are free of material misstatement. Our procedures included examination, on a test basis, of evidence supporting the amounts and other disclosures in the financial statements, and the evaluation of accounting policies and significant accounting estimates. These procedures have been undertaken to form

an opinion as to whether, in all material respects, the financial statements are presented fairly in accordance with Australian Accounting Standards and Statutory requirements so as to present a view which is consistent with our understanding of The Company's and the economic entity's financial position and the results of their operations.

The names of the subsidiaries audited by overseas KPMG member firms and other auditors are set out in Note 35. We have received sufficient information and explanations concerning these controlled entities to enable us to form an opinion on the consolidated accounts.

The audit opinion expressed in this report has been formed on the above basis.

Audit Opinion

In our opinion, the financial statements of Pacific Dunlop Limited are properly drawn up:

(a) so as to give a true and fair view of:
i) the state of affairs of The Company and the economic entity at 30th June, 1994 and the results and cash flows of The Company and the economic entity for the financial year ended on that date; and

ii) the other matters required by Divisions 4, 4A and 4B of Part 3.6 of the Corporations Law to be dealt with in the financial statements;

(b) in accordance with the provisions of the Corporations Law; and

(c) in accordance with applicable Accounting Standards.

KPMG Peat Marwick
Chartered Accountants

B. Jamieson
Partner

Dated at Melbourne this 9th day of September 1994.

247

Baycorp Holdings was publicly listed in New Zealand 1986, after acquiring the mercantile and debt collection companies of the McLaughlin family. After listing, the company expanded its interest to include credit reporting, computer-based business information services, and debt collection arrangements. The company suffered a serious loss in 1990, due to uncontrolled expansion in the Australia market, together with the depressed state of the New Zealand economy. In its 1990 annual report, company directors made the following comment:

> *Shareholders should be under no illusions as to the seriousness of the situation currently facing Baycorp Holdings Ltd. Its future is entirely dependent upon the company's ability to collect the funds owed to it through recoverable disbursements and factored ledgers and to trade within budgeted levels. While the directors believe that the company's goals are achievable, much hard work is required to reduce debt levels.*

With respect to the level of indebtness, the directors commented:

> *Some time ago the directors indicated a desire for a 50/50 gearing ratio within the medium term. With the write-downs in the company's balance sheet, this is an unrealistic expectation. However, recognising the type of business Baycorp is, that is a service activity, in the long term the directors do not believe Baycorp should have any term debt, apart from perhaps specific facilities for capital expenditure. Assuming therefore that your Board is successful in its endeavours to restore Baycorp's trading profits and balance sheet strength, our long term goal is for a debt-free company.*

> *Baycorp has debt totalling $20 million. With only a moderate surplus predicted from trading during the present financial year, the company has no realistic possibility of making any worthwhile reduction in principal as well as servicing interest rates at current market levels.*

In response to this setback the company made several management changes. It cut dividends. It sold investment property such that the company no longer had any investment in commercial real estate. It withdrew from the Australian market. To reassure customers and maintain customer confidence, it established trust accounts to handle client's funds. It centralized and appointed a manager to take specific control of its factored ledger (i.e. receivables) investment. The company also approached its financiers with a debt re-construction plan, which committed the funds collected from factored receivables and recoverable disbursements along with trading surpluses to reduce debt.

---

[*] This case was prepared by Michael E. Bradbury. Copyright © 1997 by Michael E. Bradbury. All rights reserved

The 1991 annual report made the following statements regarding the outlook of the company:

Despite the difficult market in which we operate, the company has budgeted to return to profitability during the year ending June 1992. In the period since the end of the 1991 financial year to the date of reporting, the company's performance indicates that acceptable profitability will be achieved.

Baycorp's prime objective however, remains the reduction of its debt levels and the improvement of its balance sheet position. A programme has been set in place to ensure that the balance sheet will be in a satisfactory position by June 1994, that is within the next three financial years. Given a continuation of the on-going support of the company's bankers and reasonable trading conditions, Baycorp's Directors are confident that this target will be achieved. However, the importance of the continued satisfactory collection of the company's financial assets through factored ledgers and recoverable disbursements cannot be over-stated. The desire expressed in the 1990 report for a debt-free company still exists but is clearly a long-term goal.

On June 4, 1992, an Extraordinary General Meeting of the Company resolved:

- To reduce capital (1) by cancelling capital to the extent of 15 cents per share on each of the 72,802,210 issued and fully paid shares (i.e., the nominal value was reduced from 25 cents to 10 cents); and (2) by cancelling the $834,648 of share premium.

- To authorize the directors to issue 3 million stock options to executive directors and senior managers.

- To authorize the directors to issue 6 million stock options to parties (non-directors) involved in the restructuring.

The 1992 directors' report to shareholders observed:

It is too early to say that Baycorp's recovery is complete. It is, however, now trading profitably and in a satisfactory financial position.

Gradual financial improvement continued in 1993, and on December 31, 1993 Baycorp acquired 92.7% of Creditcorp Holdings Limited, another listed company.

Required:

In late April 1994, the Directors of Baycorp approach you for advice. They wish to enter the final phase of the company's reconstruction. They propose a cash (rights) issue to existing shareholders to eliminate term liabilities, one of the major objectives of the Directors. Following the successful completion of a cash issue, the company's balance sheet (as at June 30, 1994) will be conservatively structured with no term debt. The company will have relatively low overheads. These factors, combined with upgraded technology and software, will place the company in a strong competitive position.

The Directors seek your advice in connection with the proposed cash issue. You are required to prepare a forecast for the year to December 31, 1994 for inclusion in the issue prospectus. To assist you with this forecast the following information is summarized in Exhibit 1:

- The current unaudited half-year financial statements to December 31, 1993.
- The unaudited half-year financial statement for the previous period to December 31, 1992.
- The audited financial statements for the full years from June 30, 1990 to June 30, 1993.

Exhibit 2 provides information about the recent share price of Baycorp. The Directors offer the following additional information:

- They expect annual operating revenue to increase by 19% over the full 1993 year.
- Operating expenditure is mostly variable.
- The tax effect of losses carried forward amounts to $526,000. The statutory tax rate is 33%. Currently there are no major timing differences between accounting and taxable income.
- Additional restructuring costs of $1,439,000 are expected. These charges are considered to be a nondeductable expenditure for tax purposes.
- Expenditures on fixed assets for the second half year are expected to be $1,541,000.
- Payables will remain at current levels. Receivables are expected to decrease by $585,000.
- The minority interest and share premium in the half-year accounts resulted from the consolidation of Creditcorp.
- There will be no material changes to existing political, fiscal and economic conditions in New Zealand which will materially affect the company or the competitive environment of the industry.

Prior to the cash issue, accumulated losses will need to be eliminated. The company proposes to reduce capital by cancelling the share premium account. The ordinary shares are to be consolidated into 30 cent shares.

The directors also wish to make the following accounting policy changes:

- In prior years, "work in progress" represented a proportion of commissions due on debts that were in process of collection. The value was frozen at 30 June 1989, subject to the lower of cost or market rule. The Directors have resolved to adopt a new accounting policy to only recognise commission income when debts are actually collected. Therefore, work in progress is to be written off as an abnormal expense for the year. For taxation purposes you may regard the work in progress adjustment as non-deductable (i.e., a permanent difference).

- In prior years, purchased goodwill arising on consolidation was recorded as a long term asset and was amortized. The Directors consider this goodwill to actually involve the purchase of a database. Due to the purchase of the Creditcorp database in the current year, the Directors have decided to adopt a policy of revaluing the database to its current value. The Directors have obtained an independent valuation of the database at $20 million. As the data bases will be regularly maintained, the Directors consider no depreciation will be necessary. The costs of all maintenance is expensed in the period incurred.

You estimate that the costs of a share issue, including share registry expenses, legal expenses, underwriting expenses, printing and postage, to be about $350,000. The directors wish these costs to be written off against the share premium reserve arising from the issue of shares above par.

You are required to prepare a forecast for the year to December 31, 1994 for inclusion in the issue prospectus. This will involve the following steps:

1. Forecast the income statement and balance sheet, assuming no change to the existing accounting policies and excluding any change to the financing activities.
2. Adjust the forecasted financial statements for the capital reduction and accounting policy changes required by the directors.
3. Decide on the equity issue. How many shares should be issued? At what price? The method (rights issue to shareholders or issue to the public)?
4. Include the effect of the proposed equity issue in the financial forecasts.

Exhibit 1
Baycorp Holdings Limited
Summarized Financial Statements

	Full Year June 30, 1990 $000	Full Year June 30, 1991 $000	Full Year June 30, 1992 $000	Full Year June 30, 1993 $000	Half Year December 31, 1992 $000	Half Year December 31, 1993 $000
Income Statement						
Operating revenue	22,799	14,213	16,672	21,288	10,631	10,540
Depreciation	1,866	1,179	1,186	1,015	604	581
Interest costs	3,658	1,186	943	103	54	34
Rent	51	1.093	1,169	1088	539	591
Goodwill amortisation	280	200	200	200	100	0
Other expenses	24,527	11,100	11,690	15,538	7,851	8,114
	30,382	14,736	15,181	17,944	9,148	9,320
Operating profit (loss)	(7,583)	(1,113)	838	3,344	1,483	1,220
Unusual gains (losses)	(18,249)	66	2095	0	0	0
Non-operating income	213	147	164	160	71	90
Net profit before tax	(25,619)	(900)	3,097	3,504	1,554	1,310
Income tax expense	(2,480)	0	0	0	0	382
Net profit after tax	(23,139)	(900)	3,097	3,504	1,554	928
Statement of Retained Earnings						
Opening retained earnings	6,241	(16,898)	(17,798)	(2,945)	(2,945)	559
Net profit after tax	(23,139)	(900)	3,097	3,504	1,554	928
Capital writedown			11,756			
Closing retained earnings	(16,898)	(17,798)	(2,945)	559	(1,391)	1,487

Exhibit 1
Baycorp Holdings Limited
Summarized Financial Statements
(continued)

	Full Year June 30, 1990 $000	Full Year June 30, 1991 $000	Full Year June 30, 1992 $000	Full Year June 30, 1993 $000	Half Year December 31, 1992 $000	Half Year December 31, 1993 $000
Unusual Items						
Write downs						
- development costs	(1,845)					
- work in progress	(1,190)					
- goodwill	(968)					
- receivables	(10,895)					
- inventory	(634)					
- fixed assets	(521)					
- cost of subsidiary	(479)					
Provision for future losses	(1,386)					
Claim under guarantee	(100)					
Loss on sale of property	(231)					
Profit on sale of subsidiary		66				
Recovery on receivables			2,095			
	(18,249)	66	2,095			

254

Exhibit 1
Baycorp Holdings Limited
Summarized Financial Statements
(continued)

	Full Year June 30, 1990 $000	Full Year June 30, 1991 $000	Full Year June 30, 1992 $000	Full Year June 30, 1993 $000	Half Year December 31, 1992 $000	Half Year December 31, 1993 $000
Statement of Financial Position						
Capital	18,201	18,201	7,280	7,280	7,280	9,168
Share premium	0	0	0	0	0	8,957
Retained earnings	(16,898)	(17,798)	(2,945)	559	(1,391)	1,487
Capital and reserves	2,138	1,238	4,335	7,839	5,889	19,612
Minority interest	0	0	0	0	0	854
Term liabilities	437	13,508	11,985	5,777	10,340	4,701
Current liabilities						
Provision for losses	1,386	0	0	0	0	0
Accounts payable	3,224	2,267	1,616	1,548	1,697	3,256
Current term liabilities	21,790	7,062	3,442	3,107	2,768	
Total current liabilities	26,400	9,329	5,058	4,655	4,465	7,115
Total funds employed	28,975	24,075	21,378	18,271	20,694	3,859

Exhibit 1
Baycorp Holdings Limited
Summarized Financial Statements
(continued)

	Full Year June 30, 1990 $000	Full Year June 30, 1991 $000	Full Year June 30, 1992 $000	Full Year June 30, 1993 $000	Half Year December 31, 1992 $000	Half Year December 31, 1993 $000
Long term assets						
Fixed assets	6,385	4,530	4,049	3,572	3,942	3,712
Database	3,947	3,747	3,547	3,347	3,447	16,347
Work in progress	7,874	7,874	7,874	7,874	7,874	7,874
Long term assets	18,206	16,151	15,470	14,793	15,263	27,933
Deferred tax benefit	0	0	0	0	0	60
Current assets						
Cash	32	0	649	78	491	188
Recoverable disbursements	3,249	1,663	1,265	736	992	480
Receivables - factored	2,054	2,497	1.513	1.434	1,656	2,404
Receivables - trade	3,520	2,065	1,604	372	1,416	294
Other receivables	1,914	1,699	877	858	876	923
Total current assets	10,769	7,924	5,908	3,478	5,431	4,289
Total assets	28,975	24,075	21,378	18,271	20,694	32,282

Exhibit 2
Baycorp Holding Ltd.
Recent Share Price History

Date	Price (cents)			Volume
	High	Low	Closing	
04/27/94	83	76	77	117.5
04/26/94	83	82	83	421
04/22/94	82	80	82	74.6
04/21/94	80	80	80	58.5
04/20/94	81	80	80	428.7
04/19/94	83	80	80	158.2
04/18/94	84	84	84	41.6

"Nokia needs to make sure that its gold mine doesn't cave in.

After selling its TV-manufacturing business and reducing its share in the tire and cable company, this Finnish powerhouse now derives nearly 100% of its revenues from the wireless-telecommunications industry. It was in this sector that Nokia built its name in the 1990s. Almost out of nowhere, Nokia grabbed a 22% share of the cellular-handset market, second only to Motorola. And the prospects for further growth in handset and infrastructure sales are tremendous.

The sky seems to be the limit for Nokia, but it will encounter some turbulence along the way. The lucrative business has not escaped the notice of some of the world's largest electronics companies. Handsets are fast becoming a commodity business, just as margins are getting off the ground; firms such as Sony and Toshiba have entered the ring.

It's the decision-making issue that has rattled investor confidence in Nokia lately. In the first quarter, Nokia posted a 70% drop in pretax profits, and a loss in its mobile phone division due to 'poor organization and logistics.'

They trade at 12 times earnings before one-time charges--well below the company's revenue growth rate." [+]

Karla Sibelius, Director of Research for a small Phoenix-based investment management firm specializing in U.S.-listed foreign securities, noted the positive review of Nokia written by Michael Porter in International Stocks (July 25, 1996). However, Karla became somewhat concerned as she looked at Nokia's recent stock price performance (see Exhibit 1). Nokia's shares began trading on the NYSE in July 1994 as American Depository Receipts (ADRs). One ADR represents one share of Nokia's common stock. Shares had traded as high as $US78 per share in September 1995, but by the end of July 1996, the stock price had dropped to around $US35 per share. Karla's confidence in Nokia was further eroded as she looked over the analyst's report highlighting the fact that Nokia's net profit had fallen by more than 43 percent from FIM3,939 million in 1994 to FIM2,232 million in 1995.[++] The analyst also noted that the decline would have been greater if Nokia had not benefited from a FIM485 million boost in net profit by changing its method of accounting for research and development.

The analyst's report had also included a discussion of academic research on companies initiating voluntary accounting changes[1] The study classified companies according to whether the accounting change had boosted (e.g., accelerated depreciation to straight-line depreciation) or reduced income (e.g., FIFO to

* This case was prepared by Graeme Rankine for the purpose of class discussion using publicly available data. Erik Solomon provided valuable assistance in the preparation of the case. Copyright © 1997 by American Graduate School of International Management. All rights reserved.

[+] Reproduced with permission from Morningstar, Inc

[++] FIM refers to the Finnish markka, the currency of Finland. At December 31, 1995, the exchange rate was FIM4.359 per $US1.

1 B. Dharan and B. Lev. 1993. "The Valuation Consequences of Accounting Changes: A Multi-Year Examination" *Journal of Accounting Auditing and Finance*, 8 (4): 475-494.

LIFO). According to the report, firms adopting income-increasing (income-decreasing) accounting changes would have otherwise experienced a decrease (increase) in earnings. In addition, the research showed that firms undertaking income-increasing (income-decreasing) accounting changes experienced negative (positive) stock returns relative to comparable size firms for up to seven years subsequent to the change. Karla wondered whether Nokia's change in research and development accounting was an ominous sign about the company's future. Yet, the analyst's report also included a discussion of other academic research in which the authors estimated the relationship between R&D expenditures and subsequent earnings to determine the unrecorded book value of a firm's R&D assets.[2] According to the report, the research suggested that in determining equity values, the capital market adjusts reported earnings and R&D book values to reflect the capitalization and amortization of R&D expenditures. That is, the capital market apparently viewed R&D as an investment which should be capitalized on the balance sheet and then amortized against earnings because it generated future benefits.

Karla realized that since the firm's investment committee was likely to have many questions, she would have to carefully and thoroughly review Nokia's financial statements.

The Company

Nokia Corporation is a leading international telecommunications group which is now Europe's largest and the world's second largest manufacturer of mobile phones with sales in 120 countries. It is also a world leading supplier of GSM (Global System for Mobile Communications) / DCS (Digital Cellular System) cellular networks as well as a significant supplier of access networks, multimedia equipment and of other telecom-related products. The company operates through three business groups -- Nokia Telecommunications (digital exchanges, transmission systems), Nokia Mobile Phones (digital and analog cellular phones, pagers), and Nokia General Communications Products (satellite and cable TV products, PC and workstation monitors, car audio products, and mobile handset components). Nokia moved closer to having 100 percent of its operations in the telecommunications industry by divesting its tire and cable machinery businesses, announcing its intention to reduce its share in the cable business to under 50 percent, and withdrawing from the color television business.

Nokia was formed out of an alliance between a pulp mill, a rubber factory, and a cable manufacturer. The pulp mill had been situated on the Nokia river in Finland and originally began operations in 1865. Just after the turn of the century, Finnish Rubber Works moved across the river and began operations. In the 1920s, Finnish Rubber Works took over a struggling metal manufacturer, Finnish Cable Works. Each of these companies functioned independently until 1967, when they merged to form the basis for the present telecommunications conglomerate. After the establishment of the new company, Nokia shifted its focus away from the domestic Finnish market as it pushed to become a regional power.

Many of Nokia's foreign dealings were with the Soviet Union in countertrade agreements. In 1973, the first international oil crisis adversely affected the entire Finnish economy, and consequently, had a substantial impact on Nokia's operations. Nokia began to reassess its operating strategy and heavy reliance on the Soviet Union. By this time, an electrical products business had grown up around the cable manufacturing operations. It was decided to extend the electrical goods product line and begin concentrating on manufacturing products with higher value added.

---

[2] B. Lev and T. Sougiannis. 1996. "The Capitalization, Amortization, and Value-Relevance of R&D" *Journal of Accounting and Economics*, 21 (1): 107-138.

In 1975, Kari Kairamo, previously the head of Nokia's Pulp, Paper & Power Division, was promoted to Chief Executive Officer. Kairamo's main priorities were to improve Nokia's product line, its reputation for quality and production techniques, and to move the company from its low value-added focus on paper, chemicals, electricity, and heavy machinery. Out of these relatively low-tech product lines, Kairamo began to create core competencies in high-tech fields such as robotics, fiber optics, telecommunications, and high-grade tissues. In 1979, Nokia increased its interest in telecommunications and mobile telephones with the establishment of Mobira Oy (Nokia Mobile Phones), a venture jointly-owned with Salora, a Swedish consumer electronics manufacturer.

During the 1980s, Nokia increased its interests in the telecommunications industry by acquiring a majority interest in Finland's state-owned telecommunications company, which was subsequently named Telenokia. At the same time, Karaimo sought to make Nokia a household name in consumer electronics through aggressive acquisitions. By early 1988, Nokia was Europe's third-largest television manufacturer and Scandinavia's largest telecommunications company. However, incorporating the newly-acquired businesses under one roof did not occur without difficulties. The problems were exacerbated by heavy price competition in the consumer electronics field which slashed the value of the company's investments. In the face of these problems, Kairamo committed suicide in December 1988.

Nokia's problems were to continue into the early 1990s. Finland fell into a deep recession causing a steep decline in Nokia's stock price. Nokia attempted to survive by selling off businesses and focusing on the telecommunications sector. In 1991, the company acquired the British company Technophone, which had been the second largest manufacturer of mobile phones in Europe. The acquisition cemented Nokia's position in the worldwide cellular phone market and made the company the second largest producer of cellular phones behind Motorola.

Mr. Jorma Ollila, the new Chief Executive Officer appointed in 1992, increased Nokia's focus on the mobile telecommunications industry. In 1993, Nokia acquired manufacturing facilities in South Korea and Texas, and entered a joint venture agreement with Mitsui of Japan to become the first foreign firm to enter the Japanese cellular phone market.

Competitive Environment

The mobile phone industry moved from its introductory stages in the 1970s and 1980s, to its consolidation stage in the 1990s. During this time, many small firms, which had caught the initial wave of cellular phone technology, were consolidated into a few surviving firms. At present, Motorola of the U.S. is the number one maker of mobile phones in the world, followed by Nokia, and Ericsson of Sweden. Together, these firms make up roughly three-quarters of the mobile telecommunications market. Of the three companies, Motorola and Ericsson have the most experience -- both of them have been involved in telecommunications for nearly a century. Ericsson was the first Swedish company to produce telephones after starting out as a telegraph company, whereas Motorola was one of America's first producers of wireless radios.

Within the past few years, both Nokia and Ericsson have made aggressive entries into the Far East. Ericsson is especially strong in China with a 40% market share. Nokia, likewise, is especially strong in Japan and in South Korea, where it recently acquired a manufacturing facility. Motorola's attempts to enter the Japanese market have also been aggressive, though with less success than Nokia. Motorola's strong position in the United States has been weakened by Nokia and Ericsson. In September 1996, Motorola announced its third quarter earnings would be significantly down due to weaknesses in international mobile phone sales during the preceding two months. Analysts attributed Motorola's weakness to a product line which relies on the older analog technology. Nokia and Ericsson have invested heavily in new GSM and PCS (Personal Communications Services) markets based on digital technologies. By early 1996, Ericsson announced that it had succeeded in capturing a third of the digital mobile phone market in the United States. Both Motorola and Nokia have recently begun marketing ultra-small mobile phones which have been well received. Ericsson has not yet developed a competing product and industry analysts believe Ericsson's product line to be one of the 'oldest' in the industry.

In Nokia's 1995 annual report, Chairman Jorma Ollila, indicated that the company's goal was to become one of the leading focused telecommunications companies. With operations in 120 countries, manufacturing facilities in four continents and with improved brand-recognition worldwide, Nokia's goal was becoming a reality. Ollila emphasized the importance of the company's strength in technology management and the challenge of achieving and maintaining world-class operational efficiencies through improved business processes.

Research and Development

Since the push by Kairamo to make Nokia known for high quality products, Nokia has made substantial investments in research and development. This has yielded many innovations, including the world's first portable NMT (Nordic Mobile Telephone) car phone in 1984 (see Exhibit 2).

R&D expenses totalled FIM2,531 million during 1995, an increase of 31% over the prior year. By year-end, more than 7,000 Nokia employees were dedicated to R&D. Nokia Research Center, the company's corporate R&D organization, grew rapidly in 1995 and increased its staff to 500, of which 15 percent hold post-graduate degrees. The unit, considered the "technological pathfinder" for the Nokia Group, covers the full range of activities from exploration of new technologies and product/systems concepts to exploitation in actual product development; it also interacts closely with the R&D units from all of Nokia's business groups.

Accounting for Research and Development

In the U.S., Financial Accounting Standard (FAS) No. 2 requires that companies expense R&D expenditures in the period in which they are incurred. The logic underlying this standard is captured by the following excerpts:

"Moreover, even if at some point in the process of an individual research and development project the expectation of future benefits becomes sufficiently high to indicate that an economic resource has been created, the question remains whether that resource should be recognized as an asset for financial accounting purposes. Although future benefits from a particular research and development project may be foreseen, they generally cannot be measured with a reasonable degree of certainty." [paragraph 45]

"Because there is generally no direct or even indirect basis for relating costs to revenues, the Board believes that the principles of 'associating cause and effect' and 'systematic and rational allocation' cannot be applied to recognize research and development costs as expenses." [paragraph 49]

Although Nokia is a Finnish company, its financial statements are prepared according to International Accounting Standards (IAS). Under IAS 9 (revised), research expenditures are expensed in the period they are incurred, whereas development expenditures meeting certain criteria are permitted to be capitalized and amortized. IAS 9 (revised) specifies that the development costs of a project may be deferred to future periods if all of the following criteria are met:

(a)   the product or process is clearly defined and the costs attributable to the product or process can be separately identified;

(b)   the technical feasibility of the product or process has been demonstrated;

(c)   the management of the enterprise has indicated its intention to produce and market, or use, the product or process;

(d)   there is a clear indication of a future market for the product or process or, if it is to be used internally rather than sold, its usefulness to the enterprise can be demonstrated; and

(e)   adequate resources exist, or are reasonably expected to be available, to complete the project and market the product or process. [Paragraph 17]

Under IAS 9 (revised), if development costs of a project are deferred, they should be amortized over a period not exceeding five years.[+++] The standard requires firms to conduct an impairment test at the end of each period so that: (a) when the criteria above used to justify the deferral of the costs, no longer apply, the unamortized balance should be charged as an expense immediately, and (b) when the criteria for deferral continue to be met but the amount of deferred development costs that can reasonably be expected to be recovered from related future revenues is exceeded by the unamortized balance of the costs, the excess should be charged as an expense immediately. The standard also requires that firms disclose (a) the total of research and development costs, including amortization of deferred development costs, charged as expense, (b) the movement in and the balance of unamortized deferred development costs, and (c) the basis, proposed or adopted, for the amortization of the unamortized balance.

The capitalization/amortization treatment permitted under IAS 9 (revised) with regard to development expenditures is similar to the treatment of software development expenditures in the U.S. Under FAS 86, software development expenditures which also generate uncertain future benefits, may be capitalized and amortized after the project becomes "technologically feasible". Under this standard, capitalized software development costs are amortized either on the basis of current and future revenues for each product or using the straight-line method, which ever generates the greater amount of amortization.

[+++]   The original version of IAS 9 specified that if development costs were deferred, "they should be allocated on a systematic basis to future accounting periods by reference either to the sale or use of a product or process or to the time period over which the product or process is expected to be sold or used." Thus, IAS 9 (revised) effectively changed the amortization period from an indefinite length of time to five years or less.

Required:

1. Consider the five-year summary data presented in Exhibit 3. Evaluate Nokia's growth in net sales, operating profit, net profit, total assets and stockholders' equity over the period 1991-1995. Consider the company's statement of cash flows. How has Nokia financed its growth?

2. Consider the balance sheet and income statement and the information in Note 3. Would you say that 1995 was a good year? Why or why not? Evaluate Nokia's profit performance through December 31, 1995. Evaluate Nokia using a Dupont analysis. [A Dupont analysis breaks return on equity into the product of three components as follows: return on equity (net income / stockholders' equity) = return on sales (net income / revenues) * asset turnover (revenues / total assets) * leverage (total assets / stockholders' equity)] What does the Dupont analysis tell you about the company's performance?

3. Describe Nokia's business strategy. What role does R&D play in achieving competitive advantage? What is your assessment of this strategy?

4. Consider the justification for expensing R& D expenditures provided by the Financial Accounting Standards Board and the criteria for capitalizing/amortizing R&D provided under IAS 9 (revised). What are the key assumptions underlying Nokia's accounting policy with regard to R&D expenditures? Do you agree with the company's decision to switch? Why or why not? Setting aside accounting-based justifications for the change in R&D accounting (i.e, asset recognition, matching etc.), what other reasons might motivate Nokia to make the change? What is your assessment of Nokia's earnings quality?

5. If analysts' criticism of Nokia's R&D accounting reduces the company's stock price, should the company change its accounting policy again? Why or why not? What should management do to restore confidence to the capital market?

6. Consider the information on capitalized R&D costs in Note 13 and the information about amortization of R&D costs in Note 7. What is the gross and net carrying amount of capitalized R&D cost at January 1, 1995. What transaction did Nokia record at January 1, 1995 to effect the change in R&D accounting? What was the impact on the balance sheet at January 1, 1995 of this transaction? If Nokia had continued to expense development costs, what would be the impact on the balance sheet at December 31, 1995 and the income statement and statement of cash flows for the year ending December 31, 1995?

7. Should Karla recommend that the investment committee buy Nokia's stock at its current price of $US35.25 per share on July 31, 1996? Why or why not?

DATE	HIGH PRICE	LOW PRICE	CLOSE PRICE	VOLUME	CUM.ADJ FACTOR
Jul96	$39.00	$32.25	$35.25	14,869,398	1.000000
Jun96	$42.88	$35.63	$37.00	15,847,000	1.000000
May96	$44.75	$33.50	$43.50	41,238,199	1.000000
Apr96	$36.63	$31.13	$36.50	47,195,898	1.000000
Mar96	$37.13	$33.88	$34.25	25,914,199	1.000000
Feb96	$39.63	$34.25	$34.88	25,168,598	1.000000
Jan96	$40.88	$33.13	$37.38	28,677,500	1.000000
Dec95	$54.13	$31.25	$39.00	73,286,563	1.000000
Nov95	$59.13	$50.75	$54.25	15,988,398	1.000000
Oct95	$69.75	$54.50	$55.75	38,355,797	1.000000
Sep95	$78.00	$62.25	$69.75	16,076,796	1.000000
Aug95	$70.13	$64.50	$69.25	12,211,796	1.000000
Jul95	$70.75	$59.38	$66.00	14,660,597	1.000000
Jun95	$61.25	$46.63	$59.88	20,718,000	1.000000
May95	$47.88	$41.00	$46.50	2,811,300	1.000000
Apr95	$41.63	$36.56	$41.00	462,800	2.000000
Mar95	$39.75	$35.38	$36.75	13,903,398	2.000000
Feb95	$40.13	$35.38	$37.63	19,577,594	2.000000
Jan95	$40.81	$36.38	$36.56	11,803,398	2.000000
Dec94	$37.88	$33.81	$37.50	9,672,796	2.000000
Nov94	$37.94	$33.63	$34.94	16,348,796	2.000000
Oct94	$39.00	$27.63	$37.56	18,764,195	2.000000
Sep94	$29.50	$27.31	$29.25	5,762,199	2.000000
Aug94	$26.88	$23.63	$26.50	5,535,000	2.000000
Jul94	$24.75	$20.63	$24.56	9,030,593	2.000000
Jun94	@NA	@NA	@NA	0	4.000000
May94	@NA	@NA	@NA	0	4.000000
Apr94	@NA	@NA	@NA	0	4.000000
Mar94	@NA	@NA	@NA	0	4.000000
Feb94	@NA	@NA	@NA	0	4.000000
Jan94	@NA	@NA	@NA	0	4.000000
Dec93	@NA	@NA	@NA	0	4.000000
Nov93	@NA	@NA	@NA	0	4.000000
Oct93	@NA	@NA	@NA	0	4.000000
Sep93	@NA	@NA	@NA	0	4.000000
Aug93	@NA	@NA	@NA	0	4.000000
Jul93	@NA	@NA	@NA	0	4.000000
Jun93	@NA	@NA	@NA	0	4.000000
May93	@NA	@NA	@NA	0	4.000000
Apr93	@NA	@NA	@NA	0	4.000000
Mar93	@NA	@NA	@NA	0	4.000000
Feb93	@NA	@NA	@NA	0	4.000000
Jan93	@NA	@NA	@NA	0	4.000000
Dec92	@NA	@NA	@NA	0	@NA
Nov92	@NA	@NA	@NA	0	@NA
Oct92	@NA	@NA	@NA	0	@NA
Sep92	@NA	@NA	@NA	0	@NA
Aug92	@NA	@NA	@NA	0	@NA
Jul92	@NA	@NA	@NA	0	@NA

NOKIA CORP -ADR
NOK.A
MONTHLY ADJUSTED PRICES

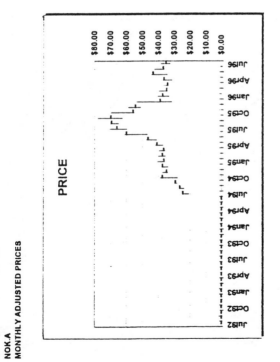

PRICE

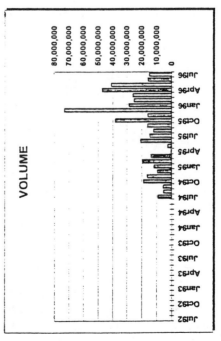

VOLUME

Exhibit 2:
**Nokia Corporation - Chronological List of Nokia's Recent Technological
and Product Developments**

Year	Technological and Product Developments
1986	Introduces an NMT (Nordic Mobile Telephone) cellular mobile exchange Introduces a low-radiation monitor
1987	Designs and manufactures nationwide pagers Introduces the world's first NMT pocket phone
1990	Introduces the world's first radio data system (RDS) pager
1991	Supplies equipment for world's first GSM (Global System for Mobile Communications)
1992	Introduces its first GSM handportable phone
1993	First manufacturer to launch handportable phones for all existing cellular digital systems
1995	Introduces the world's smallest base station for GSM / DCS (Digital Cellular System) cellular mobile networks (Nokia Primesite)
1996	Introduces the world's first all-in-one communicator (Nokia 9000 Communicator)

Exhibit 3:
Nokia Corporation - Abridged 1995 Annual Report

Prepared according to International Accounting Standards

Consolidated Profit and Loss Account

	1995	1994
Financial year ended December 31	**MFIM**	MFIM
Net sales	**36,810**	30,177
Costs of goods sold	**-25,518**	-20,808
Research and development expenses	**-2,531**	-1,937
Selling, general and administrative expenses	**3,749**	-3,836
Operating profit	**5,012**	3,596
Share of results of associated companies	**85**	22
Financial income and expenses	**-164**	384
Profit before tax and minority interests	**4,933**	4,002
Tax	**-769**	-932
Minority interests	**-77**	-75
Profit from continuing operations	**4,087**	2,995
Discontinued operations	**-2,340**	-
Profit from ordinary activities before cumulative effect of change in accounting policies	**1,747**	2,995
Cumulative prior year effect (after tax) of change in accounting policies	**485**	-
Profit from ordinary activities	**2,232**	2,995
Extraordinary items	**-**	944
Net profit	**2,232**	3,939

Key Ratios

	1995	1994
Earnings per share, FIM:		
Continuing operations[1]	**14.36**	10.97
Ordinary activities before cumulative effect of change in accounting principles[2]	**6.14**	10.97
Dividend per share,[3] FIM	**3.00**	2.50
Shareholders' equity per share,[4] FIM	**48.55**	43.65

[1] Profit from continuing operations divided by average of adjusted number of shares

[2] Profit from ordinary activities after discontinued operations out before cumulative effect of change in accounting policies divided by average of adjusted number of shares.

[3] The Board's proposed dividend for 1995.

[4] Adjusted number of shares at the end of the year.

Prepared according to International Accounting Standards

Consolidated Balance Sheet

December 31	1995 MFIM	1994 MFIM
ASSETS		
Fixed assets and other non-current assets		
Goodwill and other intangible assets	1,581	541
Property. plant and equipment	6,109	5,097
Investments	837	1,810
Long-term loan receivables	234	222
Other non-current assets	286	273
	9,047	7,943
Current assets		
Inventories	9,982	6,803
Accounts receivable, less allowances for doubtful accounts (31.12.1995 MFIM 155, 31.12.1994 MFIM 197)	9,518	7,835
Short-term investments	2,888	3,989
Bank and cash	1,326	1,279
	23,714	19,906
Total assets	32,761	27,849

December 31	1995 MFIM	1994 MFIM
SHAREHOLDERS' EQUITY AND LIABILITIES		
Shareholders' equity		
Share capital	1,498	1,498
Other restricted equity	5,455	5,494
Treasury shares	-470	-437
Untaxed reserves	1,873	1,727
Retained earnings	5,450	4,136
	13,806	12,418
Minority interests	422	555
Long-term liabilities		
Long-term debt	2,121	3,071
Other long-term liabilities	457	486
	2,578	3,557
Current liabilities		
Short-term borrowings	4,332	2,453
Current portion of long-term debt	187	278
Accounts payable and accrued liabilities	9,388	8,086
Advance payments	396	502
Provision for discontinued operations	1,652	-
	15,955	11,319
Total shareholders' equity and liabilities	32,761	27,849

Consolidated Cash Flow Statement

Financial year ended December 31	1995 MFIM	1994 MFIM
Cash flow from operating activities		
Profit before tax and minority interests	**4,933**	4,002
Adjustments, total	**1,533**	886
Operating profit before change in net working capital	**6,466**	4,888
Change in net working capital	**-5,351**	-1,450
Cash generated from operations	**1,115**	3,438
Interest received	**508**	349
Interest paid	**-667**	-568
Income taxes paid	**-1,102**	-326
Cash flow before extraordinary items	**-146**	2,893
Extraordinary expenses paid	**-496**	-350
Net cash used in/from operating activities	**-642**	2,543
Cash flow from investing activities		
Acquisition of Group companies, net of acquired cash	**-27**	-80
Treasury shares acquired	**-**	-78
Investments in other shares	**-69**	-351
Additions in capitalized R&D costs	**-742**	-
Capital expenditures	**3,299**	-1,967
Proceeds from disposal of shares in Group companies, net of disposed cash	**876**	45
Proceeds from sale of other shares	**1,850**	634
Proceeds from sale of fixed assets	**396**	24
Dividends received	**75**	142
Net cash used in investing activities	**-940**	**-1,631**
Cash flow from financing activities		
Proceeds from issuance of share capital	**-**	2,490
Capital investment by minority shareholders	**37**	23
Proceeds from (+), payments of (-) long-term liabilities	**-754**	-26,
Proceeds from (+), payments of (-) short-term borrowings	**1,976**	-571
Proceeds from (f), payments of (-) long-term receivables	**-41**	29
Proceeds from (+), payments of (-) short-term receivables	**186**	-145
Dividends paid	**-789**	-211
Net cash from financing activities	**615**	**1,348**
Net decrease/increase in cash and cash equivalents	**-967**	2,260
Cash and cash equivalents at beginning of period	**5,181**	3,008
Cash and cash equivalents at end of period	**4,214**	5,268

The above figures cannot be directly traced from the balance sheet without additional information as a result of acquisitions and disposals of subsidiaries and net foreign exchange differences arising on consolidation.

The schedule shown below reconciles cash and cash equivalents at the end of the previously reported period to cash and cash equivalents reported for the beginning of the current period.

Reconciliation:		
As previously reported for 1994 and 1993, respectively	**5,268**	3,297
Foreign exchange adjustment	**-87**	-289
	5,181	3,008
Net decrease/increase in cash and cash equivalents	**-967**	2,260
As reported for 1995 and 1994	**4,214**	5,268

Selected Notes to the Financial Statements

1. Accounting principles

The consolidated financial statements of Nokia Corporation (Nokia or the Group) prepared in accordance with International Accounting Standards (IAS) are presented on pages 23-25, while financial statements prepared in accordance with Finnish Accounting Standards (FAS) are on pages 27-30 and 50-53.

Apart from the exceptions indicated in italic type in the following, the accounting principles adopted by Nokia are in compliance with IAS. A reconciliation between the financial statements under FAS and IAS is presented on page 26.

Changes in accounting principles

Effective from the beginning of 1995, the Group has adopted the revised IAS 9, Research and development costs, and capitalized the development expenses meeting the criteria stated in the standard. See note 2.

In 1995 the Group has recognized the revenue of large long-term contracts in accordance with the percentage of completion method. See note 4.

Accounting convention

The financial statements are presented in Finnish markkas and are prepared under the historical cost convention.

Principles of consolidation

The consolidated financial statements include the accounts of the parent company, Nokia Corporation, and each of those companies in which it owns, directly or indirectly through subsidiaries, over 50% of the voting rights. The accounts of certain companies in which Nokia has management control are also consolidated. Certain real estate and housing companies. as well as small companies which had no operations during the financial year, have, however, been left out of the consolidated financial statements. The effect of these companies on the Group's result and distributable reserves is immaterial. The companies acquired during the financial period have been consolidated from the date the responsibility for their operations was transferred to the Group. Similarly, the result of a Group company divested during an accounting period is included in the Group accounts only to the date of disposal.

All inter-company transactions are eliminated as part of the consolidation process. Minority interests are presented separately in arriving at the results before extraordinary items cut after taxes. They are also shown separately from shareholders' equity and liabilities in the consolidated balance sheet.

Acquisitions of companies are accounted for using the purchase method. Goodwill represents the excess of the purchase cost over the fair value of assets less liabilities of acquired companies, after provision for direct reorganization costs. Goodwill is amortised over a period not exceeding five years, unless a longer period not exceeding 20 years from the date of acquisition can be justified.

The Group's share of profits and losses of associated companies (voting rights between 20% and 50%) is included in the consolidated profit and loss account in accordance with the equity method of accounting. The Group's share of post acquisition reserves (retained earnings. untaxed reserves and other restricted equity) is added to the cost of associated company investments in the consolidated balance sheet.

Profits incurred in connection with the sale of fixed assets between the Group and associated companies are eliminated in the IAS financial statements in proportion to share ownership. Such profits are deducted from the Group's equity and fixed assets and released in Group accounts over the same period as

270

depreciation is made. *Sales profits that arose before January 1, 1994, have not been eliminated in FAS financial statements.*

Investments in other companies (voting rights less than 20%) and also some joint ventures in start-up phase are stated at cost; provision is made where necessary to reduce the cost to estimated net realisable value.

Transactions in foreign currencies

Transactions in foreign currencies are recorded at the rates of exchange prevailing at the dates of the transactions. For practical reasons, a rate that approximates the actual rate at the date of the transaction is often used. At the end of the accounting period the unsettled balances on foreign currency receivables and liabilities are valued at the rates of exchange prevailing at the balance sheet date. Foreign exchange gains and losses related to normal business operations are treated as adjustments to cost of goods sold. Foreign exchange gains and losses associated with financing are entered as a net amount under financial income and expenses.

Foreign Group companies

In the consolidated accounts all items in the profit and loss accounts of foreign subsidiaries are translated into Finnish markka at the average exchange rates for the accounting period. The balance sheets of foreign Group companies are translated into Finnish markka at the rates of exchange ruling at the balance sheet date. Exchange differences arising from the application of the purchase method are treated as an adjustment affecting consolidated shareholders equity. Translation differences related to the restricted equity at the time of acquisition are treated as a part of restricted equity and exchange differences on the other reserves of foreign subsidiaries are credited or charged to retained earnings. Differences resulting from the translation of profit and loss account items at the average rate and the balance sheet items at the closing rate are taken to retained earnings. On the disposal of a foreign Group company, the cumulative amount of the translation difference is recognized as income or as expense in the same period in which the gain or loss on disposal is recognized.

The Group's policy is to hedge a portion of foreign subsidiaries' shareholders' equity and untaxed reserves to reduce the effects of exchange rate fluctuations on the Group's net investments in foreign Group companies. Exchange gains and losses resulting from the hedging transactions are offset against the translation differences arising from consolidation and recorded in the shareholders' equity.

Revenue recognition

Sales are recorded upon shipment of products and customer acceptance, if any, or performance of services, net of sales taxes and discounts. Revenues from large long-term contracts are recognized on the percentage of completion method. Provisions are made to cover anticipated losses on contracts.

Research and development

Research and development costs are expensed in the financial period during which they are incurred, except certain development costs which are capitalized when it is probable that a development project will be a success, and certain criteria, including commercial and technological feasibility, have been met. Capitalized development costs are amortized on a systematic basis over their expected useful lives. The amortisation period is between 3 and 5 years.

Maintenance, repairs and renewals

Maintenance, repairs and renewals are generally charged to expense during the financial period in which they are incurred. However, major renovations are capitalized and depreciated over their expected useful lives.

Property, plant and equipment

Property, plant and equipment are stated at cost less accumulated depreciation.

Depreciation is recorded on a straight-line basis over the expected useful lives of the assets, based on the following useful lives:

Buildings	20-40 years
Machinery and equipment	3-15 years

Land and water areas are not depreciated.

Gains and losses on the disposal of fixed assets are included in operating profit/loss.

Cash and cash equivalents

Cash and cash equivalents consist of cash on hand and balances with banks and liquid financial instruments.

Discontinued operations

A discontinued operation results from the sale or abandonment of an operation that represents a separate, major line of business of an enterprise and of which the assets, net profit or losses and activities can be distinguished physically, operationally and for financial reporting purposes. The profit effect of discontinued operations is separately disclosed.

Extraordinary items

In previous years certain income and expenses of abnormal nature, such as divestments of operations, were presented, net of tax, as extraordinary items in the consolidated profit and loss account. In accordance with the revised IAS 8 they would be classified as components of continuing or discontinued operations, as appropriate (see proforma result note 2.).

Appropriations

In Finland and certain other countries, companies are permitted to reduce or increase taxable income by net charges or by income representing adjustments to untaxed reserve accounts, provided that such amounts are reflected in the Group companies' financial statements.

In the consolidated IAS financial statements, accumulated appropriations are included in the balance sheet as part of shareholders' equity as "Untaxed reserves." Transfers to and from untaxed reserves are reflected through retained earnings.

2. Proforma profit in accordance with the revised IAS standards

	GROUP	
	1995	1994
Proforma profit from ordinary activities restated to reflect the new accounting policies (MFIM)		
Profit from continuing operations	**4,087**	2,982
Discontinued operations	**-2,340**	1,125
Profit from ordinary activities	**1,747**	4,107
Proforma earnings per share (FIM)		
From continuing operations	**14.36**	10.93
From ordinary activities	**6.14**	15.05

The Nokia Group has adopted the revised IAS accounting principles that came into effect at the beginning of 1995.

In accordance with the revised IAS 9, certain research and development costs are capitalized and amortized on a systematic basis over their expected useful lives. The amortization period is between 3 and 5 years. The cumulative prior year net effect (FIM 485 million) of R&D expenses has been included in the first four months' profit for 1995.

The revised IAS 8 requires that the profit effect of discontinued operations be presented separately. From the extraordinary items in Nokia's 1994 Financial Statements, the sale of Power division and the effect of the discontinued Picture Tubes unit would have been treated as discontinued operations. In 1995 the Financial Statements, discontinued operations include the financial impact of the decision to withdraw from the TV business.

The proforma result for year 1994 is presented above as if the revised IAS standards had already been adopted for 1994. The positive net profit effect of the capitalization of R&D expenses in 1994 would have been FIM 168 million.

3. Segment information

	Telecommu-nications	Mobile Phones	General Commu-nications Products	Other Operations	Eliminations	Group Total
Net sales						
1995, MFIM	**10,341**	**16,052**	**10,837**	**458**	**-878**	**36,810**
1994, MFIM	6,906	10,702	11,530	1,589	-550	30,177
Operating profit/loss, IAS						
1995, MFIM	**2,722**	**1,753**	**584**	**47**	**-**	**5,012**
1994, MFIM	1,700	1,745	210	-59	-	3,596
Capital expenditures						
1995, MFIM	**1,106**	**1,606**	**482**	**105**	**-**	**3,299**
1994, MFIM	506	971	381	109	-	1,967
Identifiable assets, IAS						
1995, MFIM	**8,208**	**12,781**	**7,047**	**6,251**	**-1,526**	**32,761**
1994, MFIM	4,448	6,772	7,765	9,584	-720	27,849

*Excluding acquisitions and R&D capitalization.

4. Percentage of completion method

Profit on large long-term contracts is recognized when sale is recorded on part-delivery of products or part performance of services, provided that the outcome of the contract can be assessed with reasonable certainty. This represents a change in accounting policy with effect from January 1,1995 in order to comply with the revised IAS.

Most of the Group's net sales arise from businesses other than those of a long-term project nature. Project deliveries occur in Cellular Systems, where part of its net sales (3.8 billion FIM) was of a long-term project nature. This change in accounting principle, which was due to the revised IAS 11, had a positive (76 MFIM) impact on operating profit in 1995. In 1994 the profit impact would have been immaterial.

7. Depreciation

	GROUP		PARENT COMPANY	
	1995 **MFIM**	1994 MFIM	**1995** **MFIM**	1994 MFIM
Depreciation according to plan				
Goodwill and other intangible assets				
Capitalized R&D costs	**435**	-		-
Intangible rights	**55**	38	**4**	4
Goodwill	**59**	69	-	-
Other intangible assets	**20**	20	**3**	2
Property, plant and equipment				
Buildings and constructions	**80**	77	**4**	4
Machinery and equipment	**1,046**	691	**12**	9
Other tangible assets	**130**	114	-	-
Total	**1,825**	1,009	**23**	19
Change in accumulated depreciation in excess of plan				
Goodwill and other intangible assets				
Intangible rights	**-15**	-3	-	-
Other intangible assets	**-3**	-21	-	-
Property, plant and equipment				
Buildings and constructions	**-187**	-106	**8**	3
Machinery and equipment	**-282**	-224	**1**	4
Other tangible assets	**6**	-2	-	2
Total	**481**	-356	**9**	9
Depreciation by function				
Costs of goods sold	**815**	574	-	-
R&D	**697**	171	**10**	6
Selling, marketing and administration	**177**	156	**13**	13
Other operating expenses	**77**	39	-	-
Goodwill	**59**	69	-	-
Total	**1,825**	1,009	**23**	19

8. Financial income and expenses

	GROUP		PARENT COMPANY	
	1995 **MFIM**	1994 MFIM	**1995** **MFIM**	1994 MFIM
Dividend income	**75**	142	**268**	83
Interest income from long-term investments	**29**	26	**108**	147
Interest income from short-term investments	**559**	379	**693**	395
Other financial income	**3**	22	**3**	3
Exchange gains and losses	**-10**	450	**-3**	243
Interest expenses	**-745**	-580	**-436**	-426
Other financial expenses	**-75**	-55	**-14**	-28
Total	**-164**	384	**619**	417

10. Discontinued operations

In February 1996, Nokia announced its intention to exit the TV business. The Group anticipates that the exit plan will be completed during 1996.

The financial impact of this decision is reported in the 1995 accounts as discontinued operations. The estimated exit costs include the write-down of property, plant and equipment and other assets to estimated net realisable value, severance payments and the estimated operating loss through the date of discontinuance.

The 1995 operating loss of the TV business has been included as a component of discontinued operations in the consolidated profit and loss account. The 1994 operating loss was 136 MFIM. The net sales of the TV business were 3,229 MFIM in 1995 (3,841 MFIM in 1994).

	GROUP	
	1995 **MFIM**	1994 MFIM
Operative loss 1995	-352	-
Discontinuation cost	-1,988	-
Total discontinuity cost	-2,340	-

11. Extraordinary items

	GROUP	
	1995 **MFIM**	1994 MFIM
Cumulative effect of change in accounting principles	485	-
Discontinued operations	-2,340	-
Valuation difference of shares	-	-134
Profits incurred in divesting operations	-	552
Gain on the sale of Tubes unit's fixed assets	-	318
Extraordinary items, FAS	-1,855	736
IAS adjustments and reclassifications	1,855	208
Extraordinary items. IAS	-	944

The parent company's extraordinary income is mainly profits on the sale of fixed assets. Extraordinary expenses principally include write-offs of Group company shares.

13. Goodwill and other intangible assets

	GROUP		PARENT COMPANY	
	1995 **MFIM**	1994 MFIM	**1995** **MFIM**	1994 MFIM
Capitalized ROD costs				
Acquisition cost Jan. 1	1,115	-		
Additions	742	-		
Accumulated depreciation Dec. 31	-902	-		
Net carrying amount Dec. 31	955	-		
Intangible rights				
Acquisition cost Jan. 1	362	324	**21**	19
Additions	149	66	**9**	3
Disposals	-21	-28	**-2**	-1
Accumulated depreciation Dec. 31	-254	-226	**-15**	-13
Net carrying amount Dec. 31	236	136	**13**	8
Goodwill				
Acquisition cost Jan. 1	1,3051	1,306	-	2
Additions	-	4	-	-
Disposals	-651	-5	-	-
Accumulated depreciation Dec. 31	-979	-972	-	-2
Net carrying amount Dec. 31	261	333	-	-
Other intangible assets				
Acquisition cost Jan. 1	255	239	**137**	137
Additions	80	26	**2**	2
Disposals	-136	-9	**-105**	-2
Translation differences	-	-1	-	-
Accumulated depreciation Dec. 31	-70	-183	**-12**	-114
Net carrying amount Dec. 31	129	72	**22**	23

Auditors' Report

To the shareholders of Nokia Corporation

We have audited the accounting records, the accounts and the administration of Nokia Corporation for the year ended December 31, 1995. The accounts prepared by the Board of Directors and the President and Chief Executive Officer include the report of the Board of Directors, consolidated financial statements prepared in accordance with International Accounting Standards (IAS), consolidated and Parent company profit and loss accounts, balance sheets, cash flow statements and notes to the financial statements. Based on our audit we express an opinion on these accounts and the Parent company's administration.

We conducted our audit in accordance with Finnish Generally Accepted Auditing Standards. Those standards require that we plan and perform the audit in order to obtain reasonable assurance about whether the financial statements are free of material misstatement. An audit includes examining, on a test basis, evidence supporting the amounts and disclosures in the financial statements, assessing the accounting principles used and significant estimates made by the management, as well as evaluating the overall financial statement presentation. The purpose of our audit of the administration has been to examine that the Board of Directors and the President and Chief Executive Officer have complied with the rules of the Finnish Companies' Act.

In our opinion, the financial statements prepared in accordance with International Accounting Standards (IAS) present fairly, in all material respects, the financial position of Nokia Corporation and subsidiary companies at the end of the financial period and the consolidated results of their operations, for the year then ended in accordance with International Accounting Standards.

The accounts showing a consolidated profit of FIM 1 971 260 000 have been prepared in accordance with the Accounting Act and other rules and regulations governing the preparation of financial statements in Finland. The financial statements give a true and fair view, as defined in the Accounting Act, of both the consolidated and Parent company result of operations, as well as of the financial position. The accounts can be adopted and the members of the Board of Directors and the President and Chief Officer of the Parent company can be discharged from liability for the period audited by us. The proposal made by the Board of Directors concerning the disposition of the profit for the year is in compliance with the Companies' Act.

We have acquainted ourselves with the interim reports published by the company during the year. In our opinion, they have been prepared in accordance with the rules and regulations governing the preparation of such reports in Finland.

Helsinki, February 28, 1996

Eric Haglund
Authorised Public Accountant
(KPMG)

Lars Blomquist
Authorised Public Accountant
(Coopers & Lybrand)

Prepared according to International Accounting Standards

NOKIA 1991-1995, IAS

	1995	1994	1993	1992	1991
Profit and Loss Account, MFIM					
Net sales	**36,810**	30,177	23,697	18,168	15,457
Costs and expenses	**-31,798**	-26,581	-22,232	-17,880	-15,553
Operating profit/loss	**5,012**	3,596	1,465	288	-96
Share of results of associated companies	**85**	22	28	-5	9
Financial income and expenses	**-164**	384	-347	-441	-237
Profit/loss before tax and minority interests	**4,933**	4,002	1,146	-158	-324
Tax	**-769**	-932	-299	-167	-231
Minority interests	**-77**	-75	-80	-88	-49
Profit/loss from continuing operations	**4,087**	2,995	767	-413	-604
Discontinued operations	**-2,340**	-	-	-	-
Profit/loss from ordinary activities before cumulative effect of change in accounting policies	**1,747**	2,995	767	-413	-604
Cumulative prior year effect (after tax) of change in accounting policies	485	-	-	-	-
Profit/loss before extraordinary items	**2,232**	2,995	767	-413	-604
Extraordinary items	**-**	944	-1,917	-310	393
Net profit/loss	**2,232**	3,939	-1,150	-723	-211
Balance Sheet Items, MFIM					
Fixed assets and other non-current assets	**9,047**	7,943	7,994	7,630	8,263
Current assets	**23,714**	19,906	14,653	13,605	11,890
Inventories	**9,982**	6.803	5,129	3,840	3,409
Accounts receivable and prepaid expenses	**9,518**	7,835	6,227	6,650	2,754
Cash and cash equivalents	**4,214**	5,268	3,297	3,118	3,727
Shareholders' equity	**13,806**	12,418	6,511	6,727	7,393
Minority shareholders' interests	**422**	555	536	695	600
Long-term liabilities	**2,578**	3,557	4,080	3,705	4,373
Long-term debts	2,121	3,071	3,397	3,124	3,896
Other long-term liabilities	457	486	683	581	477
Current liabilities	**15,955**	11,319	11,520	10,111	7,787
Short-term borrowings	**4,332**	2,453	3,435	3,835	2,797
Current portion of long-term loans	**187**	278	139	1,221	1,086
Accounts payable and accrued liabilities	**9,388**	8,086	5,976	4,314	3,389
Advance payments	**396**	502	534	399	202
Discontinuity/restructuring provision	**1,652**	-	1,436	342	313
Total assets	**32,761**	27,849	22,647	21,238	20,153
Key Ratios					
Earnings per share, FIM	**14.36**	10.97	3.07	neg.	neg.
Dividend per share, FIM	**3.00**	2.50	0.70	0.50	0.50
Profit/loss before tax and minority interests, % of net sales	**13.4**	13.3	4.8	-0.9	-2.1

LVMH: MOËT HENNESSY LOUIS-VUITTON[*]

The merger of Louis-Vuitton and Moët Hennessy in 1987 brought together under one roof some of the world's most prestigious products: Dom Perignon and Moët-Chandon champagnes, Hennessy cognacs, Louis Vuitton luggage, and Christain Dior and Givenchy fashions, among others. The conglomerate born of that merger, France's LVMH, was now the world's largest producer of luxury goods. It recorded sales of FF23.8 billion in 1993 (see Exhibit 1), or approximately $4.8 billion U.S.

An international company with American Depository Receipts actively traded on the NYSE (Symbol: LVMHY), LVMH nonetheless chose to prepare its financial statements according to the accounting standards of France, the country in which the company is headquartered. As part of its 20-F filing with the U.S. Securities and Exchange Commission, LVMH provides a reconciliation of its net income and shareholders' equity to U.S. generally accepted accounting principles (GAAP), as required.[1]

French vs. U.S. GAAP

French GAAP differs from U.S. GAAP in a number of areas. This case concerns some of those differences. For example, French companies often record treasury stock as an asset[2]. LVMH proves no exception: At December 31, 1993, LVMH's balance sheet shows 49,741 of its own shares reported as an asset valued at FF169 million (see Exhibits 2 and 3). French accounting standards also diverge from U.S. GAAP in that they do not require the amortization of such intangible assets as trademarks (or "brands") and patents. Accordingly, LVMH does not amortize the costs associated with the acquisition of its numerous brand names. As an explanation of this policy, LVMH's footnotes (see Exhibit 4) disclose the following:

> "Brands very often represent the most significant component of costs in excess of net assets acquired in connection with the Company's investments. Only brands which are very well known and established, individually identifiable and for which it is possible to verify their utility, are assigned values in the Company's financial statements. Brands are stated at cost, valued by reference to their contribution to the earnings of the related activity acquired. Provision for depreciation is recorded only in those instances where a permanent impairment of value, using the same criteria established at the date of acquisition, arises."

---

[*] This case was prepared by Kenneth R. Ferris and Renee A. Flinn. Copyright © 1995 by The American Graduate School of International Management. All rights reserved.

[1] Foreign companies desiring to sell or list debt or equity securities on a national exchange in the U.S. must file certain documents with the Securities and Exchange Commission. For example, Form 20-F is the required disclosure of a company's annual financial statements. As part of this filing, a non-U.S. company must either present its financial statements prepared according to U.S. generally accepted accounting principles or, as more commonly practiced, present a reconciliation of its net income and shareholders' equity under foreign accounting principles to U.S. GAAP.

[2] Under U.S. accounting standards, it was accepted practice to classify treasury shares as an asset until the issuance of S.E.C. Accounting Series Release No. 6 in 1938. Thereafter, treasury shares were principally classified as a contra-equity account, with all gains (losses) arising from reissue treated as additions (reductions) to capital surplus.

Under International Accounting Standards Commission (IASC) accounting standards (Exposure Draft E50, "Intangible Assets", May 1995), intangible assets with indeterminate lives should be written off over a maximum of 20 years from the date of initial recognition. The IASC exposure draft observes that "it is impossible to state with sufficient reliability that the useful life of most intangible assets exceeds twenty years."

Finally, French accounting for liabilities provides several alternative treatments. In 1991, for example, LVMH acquired the Pommery Champagne Group and partially financed the acquisition with a non-interest bearing note of FF1,600 million. In France, opinions differ as to whether or not loans and receivables (i.e. monetary assets and liabilities) should be discounted (using a constant periodic rate approximating the market rate).[3] In the absence of guidelines, companies choose themselves whether to state these financial assets and liabilities at "fair value" or at nominal value. In this case, LVMH recorded the note at its future settlement value of FF1,600 million.

Required:

1. Do you agree with LVMH's treatment of its treasury shares? If so, why? If not, why not? Calculate LVMH's long-term debt-to-equity ratio under U.S. and French accepted accounting practice; which calculation best reflects the company's solvency? How does LVMH's treatment of treasury stock affect its calculation of net income and earnings per share? Do you agree?

2. Do you agree with LVMH's amortization policy with respect to brand names? Explain your position. Restate LVMH's net income to reflect the amortization of brand names as required under U.S. accepted accounting practice, assuming an expected useful life of 10, 20, and 40 years. Calculate the company's return-on-sales under French and U.S. accounting for brand names; which calculation best reflects the company's profitability?

3. Restate LVMH's financial statements to reflect the discounting of the Pommery acquisition notes. (Assume that the notes have a 10 year life, and that in recent years, LVMH has paid on average 10 percent annually for similar borrowings.) Which accounting treatment do you prefer, and why?

4. Using your answers to questions 1, 2, and 3, prepare LVMH's reconciliation statement of French to U.S. GAAP as it might appear in the company's 20-F filing. Your reconciliation statement should have two parts: 1) a reconciliation of net income, and 2) a reconciliation of shareholders' equity.

---

[3] The National Accounting Board of France believes that monetary assets and liabilities should be stated at their nominal value, without discounting, whereas the Institute of Public Accountants and the Stock Exchange Commission believe that they should be stated at "fair value", and hence discounted. It is noteworthy that for tax purposes, imputed interest is not tax deductible, and hence discounting is discouraged.

Exhibit 1
LVMH: Moët Hennessy Louis Vuitton and Subsidiaries

CONSOLIDATED STATEMENT OF INCOME
(In millions of French francs, except per share amounts)

| | Years ended December 31, | | |
	1993	**1992**	**1991**
Net sales	**23,819**	**21,658**	**22,036**
Cost of products sold	(8,810)	(7,516)	(7,663)
Selling expenses	(6,900)	(6,278)	(5,624)
General and administrative expenses	(2,495)	(2,378)	(2,334)
Income from operations	**5,614**	**5,486**	**6,415**
Financial expense - net	(1,921)	(1,848)	(1,546)
Other income - net	57	39	2
Unusual items	778	-	-
Income before income taxes	**4,528**	**3,677**	**4,871**
Income taxes	(1,611)	(1,172)	(1,923)
Income before equity in associated companies	2,917	2,505	2,948
Equity in net income (losses) of associated companies	834	688	1,085
Income before minority interests	**3,751**	**3,193**	**4,033**
Minority interests	(177)	(186)	(296)
Net income	**3,574**	**3,007**	**3,737**
Earnings per share [4]	**43.77**	**36.89**	**46.55**
Average number of common shares outstanding during the year[5]	81,651,125	81,514,460	80,276,664
Fully diluted earnings per share	**43.64**	**36.75**	**45.82**
Number of common shares and share equivalents after dilution[2]	81,899,801	81,820,156	81,946,936

---

[4] Earnings per share, excluding unusual items **36.39** **36.89** **46.55**

[5] The number of shares has been adjusted to take into account the 5 for 1 stock split carried out in March 1994 and the 11 for 10 stock split announced by the shareholders in June 1994.

Exhibit 2
LVMH: Moët Hennessy Louis Vuitton and Subsidiaries

CONSOLIDATED BALANCE SHEETS
(In millions of French francs)

ASSETS	Dec. 31, 1993	Dec 31, 1992
Current assets		
Cash (of which time deposits 306; 1992: 460)	2,489	2,163
Short-term investments	1,500	1,263
Treasury shares	169	307
Accounts receivable-trade (less allowances of 197; 1992: 161)	4,966	4,916
Deferred income taxes	401	501
Inventories	13,992	14,404
Prepaid expenses and other current assets	2,210	1,926
Total current assets	25,727	25,480
Investments and other assets		
Investments in equity-accounted-for companies	11,336	10,196
Unconsolidated subsidiaries and other investments	1,015	1,087
Other non-current assets	386	319
Cost in excess of net assets of acquired businesses (less amortization of 883: 1992: 580)	5,273	5,507
Brands and other intangible assets (less amortization of 226; 1992: 183)	2,234	2,294
	20,244	19,403
Property, plant and equipment		
At cost less allowance for depreciation (of 3,713; 1992: 3,277)	7,614	7,947
Total	53,585	52,830

LIABILITIES AND STOCKHOLDERS' EQUITY		
Current liabilities		
Short-term borrowings	7,488	8,145
Accounts payable	2,535	2,683
Accrued expenses and other current liabilities	4,312	3,979
Income taxes	879	463
Total current liabilities	15,214	15,270
Deferred income taxes	860	881
Long-term debt	7,740	9,796
Other long-term liabilities	1,588	1,229
Minority interests in subsidiaries	238	367
Repackaged subordinated notes	4,548	4,729
Stockholders' equity		
Common stock:		
Par value 50.00 French francs, authorized 18,151,959 shares, issued 15,780,690 in 1993 and 15,765,438 in 1992	789	788
Additional paid-in capital and retained earnings	24,695	22,093
Cumulative translation adjustment	(2,087)	(2,323)
Total stockholders' equity	23,397	20,558
Total	FF 53,585	FF 52,830

284

Exhibit 3
LVMH: Moët Hennessy Louis Vuitton and Subsidiaries

CONSOLIDATED STATEMENTS OF CASH FLOWS
(In millions of French francs)

	1993	1992	1991
I. OPERATING ACTIVITIES			
Net income	3,574	3,007	3,737
Adjustments to reconcile net income to net cash provided by operating activities:			
Minority interests	177	185	296
Equity interest in undistributed earnings of associated companies	(423)	(265)	(724)
Depreciation and amortization	1,188	825	811
Change in provisions	368	333	150
(Gain) loss on sale of fixed assets and disposals of consolidated companies	(1,250)	(227)	(70)
NET CASH PROVIDED BY OPERATING ACTIVITIES BEFORE CHANGES IN OPERATING ASSETS AND LIABILITIES	**3,634**	**3,858**	**4,200**
Changes in operating assets and liabilities net of effects from acquisition of companies:			
Inventories	572	(1,114)	(1,446)
Accounts receivable-trade	220	234	(319)
Accounts payable	(161)	(277)	(301)
Other operating assets and liabilities	329	(535)	380
NET CHANGE IN OPERATING ASSETS AND LIABILITIES	**960**	**(1,722)**	**(1,686)**
NET CASH PROVIDED BY OPERATING ACTIVITIES	**4,594**	**2,136**	**2,514**
II. INVESTING ACTIVITIES			
Purchase of property, plant and equipment	(622)	(1,271)	(1,154)
Purchase of brands and other intangible assets	(29)	(46)	(37)
Acquisition of other investments	(225)	(182)	(461)
Proceeds from sale of fixed assets and other investments	488	169	289
Change in other non-current assets	(173)	15	(38)
Net effect of acquisition and disposals of consolidated companies (including in 1993, the disposal of Roc for 1,447, and the acquisition of Christian Lacroix, Kenzo and Desfossés International for respectively 90, 495 and 126; in 1992, purchase of Guinness PLC and Louis Vuitton shares for respectively 536 and 292; in 1991, purchase of Guinness PLC shares for 2,352 and acquisition of Pommery for 1,811)	723	(908)	(4,176)
NET CASH PROVIDED BY (USED IN) INVESTING ACTIVITIES	**162**	**(2,223)**	**(5,577)**
III. FINANCING ACTIVITIES			
Proceeds from issuances of common stock	27	56	67
Treasury shares	263	109	61
Dividends paid by the parent company	(1,065)	(1,066)	(962)
Proceeds from issuances of repackaged subordinated notes	-	1,129	-
Dividends paid to minority interests of consolidated subsidiaries	(229)	(198)	(223)
Proceeds from short-term borrowings and long-term debt	1,150	4,405	3,434
Principal payment on short-term borrowings and long-term debt	(4,503)	(4,353)	(2,024)
NET CASH PROVIDED BY (USED IN) FINANCING ACTIVITIES	**(4,357)**	**82**	**353**
IV. EFFECT OF EXCHANGE RATE CHANGES	**(49)**	**73**	**(99)**
NET INCREASE/(DECREASE) IN CASH AND CASH EQUIVALENTS	**350**	**68**	**(2,809)**
CASH AND CASH EQUIVALENTS AT BEGINNING OF YEAR (net of bank overdrafts)	**2,994**	**2,926**	**5,735**
CASH AND CASH EQUIVALENTS AT END OF YEAR (net of bank overdrafts)	**3,344**	**2,994**	**2,926**

Non-cash investing and financing activities:

	1993	1992	1991
-common stock issued upon conversion of bonds	1	511	415
-capital lease obligations	1	46	250

The change during the period in cash and cash equivalents includes the change in cash and time deposits, net of cash overdrafts, and short-term investments.

Exhibit 4
LVMH: Moët Hennessy Louis Vuitton and Subsidiaries

Selected Notes to the Financial Statements

1. Accounting Policies

Brands and Other Intangible Assets:

Brands very often represent the most significant component of costs in excess of net assets acquired in connection with the Company investments. Only brands which are very well known and established, individually identifiable and for which it is possible to verify their utility, are assigned values in the Company's financial statements. Brands are stated at cost, valued by reference to their contribution to the earnings of the related activity acquired. Provision for depreciation is recorded only in those instances where a permanent impairment of value, using the same criteria established at the date of acquisition, arises.

Earnings per share:

Earnings per share are calculated on the weighted average number of common shares outstanding during the year after deduction of shares effectively held by LVMH itself or its subsidiaries.

4. Treasury Shares

In accordance with authorizations given by the shareholders in general meetings, LVMH sold 39,265 of its own shares in 1993. These operations resulted in a gain before tax of FF16 million. The 49,741 remaining shares have been reserved for the stock option purchase plan approved during the year, as authorized by the law.

At December 31, 1993, the average purchase price per treasury share was FF3,405, unadjusted neither for the 5 for 1 stock split carried out in March 1994, nor for the 11 for 10 stock split announced in June 1994.

9. Brands And Other Intangible Assets

(in millions of French francs)	1993		1992	
	Gross	Accumulated amortization	Gross	Accumulated amortization
Brands	2,169	53	2,157	40
Patented and proprietary products	16	14	16	13
Leasehold rights	113	56	109	49
Other	162	103	195	81
		226	2,477	183

286

29.   Summary Of Differences Between Accounting Principles Adopted By LVMH And US GAAP

f.   Pommery Group Acquisition (Undiscounted Notes)

The Pommery Group was financed in part by a non-interest bearing note of FF1,600 million. Under US GAAP interest would be imputed to the note at a rate that approximates the rate that an independent borrower and lender would have negotiated in a similar transaction. As a result, interest expense would have increased and less cost would have been allocated to Pommery brands.

g.   Treasury Shares

At December 31, 1993, LVMH owned 49,741 of its own shares at a cost of FF169 million (1992: FF307 million; 1991: FF326 million). These shares have been shown as an asset carried at cost in the consolidated financial statements and accordingly have not been taken into account in the earnings per share calculations. Under US GAAP the cost of treasury shares would be shown as a deduction from stockholders equity and treated similarly in the calculations of earnings per share.

Gains realized in 1993, 1992, 1991 resulted from the sale of respectively 39,265, 58,494, and 7,680 shares of the company's common stock (1993: FF16 million; 1992: FF147 million; 1991: FF22 million). These gains have been included in the heading "other income - net" in the accompanying financial statements. Under US GAAP, these items would be recorded as an adjustment to stockholders' equity. The impact of these transactions, net of tax, was to increase 1993, 1992 and 1991 net income by respectively FF13 million, FF121 million and FF18 million.

k.   Amortization of Brands

Since the beginning of 1990, LVMH has decided to discontinue amortization of costs assigned to brands. Under US GAAP costs assigned to brands would be amortized on a straight-linebasis over their estimated useful lives, limited to forty years.

On October 25, 1991, TOTAL became the second French company to obtain a listing on the New York Stock Exchange (NYSE symbol: TOT). At the time of its listing, TOTAL was ranked third among European publicly traded oil and gas companies and eighth among publicly traded oil and gas companies worldwide. In 1990, the company, which engages in all aspects of the petroleum industry, generated seventy-two percent of its revenues outside France and operated in approximately eighty countries.

TOTAL prepares its financial statements in conformity with French generally accepted accounting principles (GAAP). Financial accounting and reporting in France is governed by the national accounting code, the *Plan comptable général*. The objectives of the code are to standardize the practice of accounting. Companies are obliged to use a prescribed chart of accounts for classifying transaction entries and they must use standardized terminology for describing the effects of financial transactions. To provide a true and fair view (*image fidèle*) of their operating performance and financial position, French companies must present their results in accordance with a model set of financial statements and schedules. In France, accounting records are meant to serve the legal purposes of proof and verification, rather than provide information for decision making.

French accounting principles are somewhat conservative and are likely to yield balance sheets that understate net assets and income statements that understate earnings. Replacement value or the LIFO method may be used to report inventory in consolidated financial statements and purchased goodwill is generally amortized over periods ranging from five to twenty years. Discretionary reserves may be used for reasonably estimated losses. Excess depreciation to reduce a company's tax liability is permitted, but accumulated excess depreciation must be classified as a liability. This treatment is required by the tax law which stipulates that tax-deductible expenses must also be reported in the financial statements. A statement of cash flows is recommended, but not required.

Like other non-U.S. companies which have registered their securities with the U.S. Securities and Exchange Commission (SEC), TOTAL must file a form 20-F annually. This form is quite similar to the form 10-K that U.S. registrants file with the SEC. The annual 20-F must include a reconciliation of the difference between the registrant's reported earnings and what they would have been if U.S. GAAP had been observed in their measurement. Reconciliations of shareholders' equity and earnings per share are also required. The purpose of these reconciliations is to provide analysts and investors with additional information which should be useful for decision making.

The following items, which are taken from TOTAL's 1994 form 20-F, appear in exhibits 1-8: the auditor's report, the accounting policies note, consolidated income statements, balance sheets, and cash flow statements, a summary of the differences between accounting principles followed by TOTAL and U.S. GAAP, reconciliations of net income and shareholders' equity to U.S. GAAP, and income statements and statements of changes in shareholders' equity restated to U.S. GAAP. All amounts are in millions of French francs, except for per-share items.

---

[*] This case was prepared by Stephen Tomczyk. Copyright ©1997 by Stephen Tomczyk. All rights reserved.

Required:

1. Compare the principles of consolidation observed by TOTAL for its investments in joint ventures (see exhibit 2) with the requirements under U.S. GAAP and discuss the impact of TOTAL's practice on its financial statements.

2. Using the information presented in exhibit 7, compare TOTAL's net income and shareholders' equity as measured under French GAAP with amounts determined according to U.S. GAAP. Does it appear that French GAAP are more conservative than U.S. GAAP? Are the differences in net income and shareholders' equity significant? Compute return on shareholders' equity under both sets of GAAP and compare the results. Are the differences significant?

3. TOTAL's accounting for treasury shares is described in exhibits 6 and 7. Compare the treatment of treasury shares under French GAAP with the treatment required by U.S. GAAP and discuss the effect of TOTAL's practice on its financial statements.

4. Compare TOTAL's income statements prepared according to French GAAP (see exhibit 3) with those presented according to U.S. GAAP (see exhibit 8). Which are more informative?

5. Examine the restated statements of income and changes in shareholders' equity presented in Exhibit 8. Why might TOTAL have elected to voluntarily make these financial disclosures?

Exhibit 1

Report of Independent Auditors

To the Shareholders and the Board of Directors of TOTAL

We have audited the accompanying consolidated balance sheets of TOTAL and its subsidiaries (together, the Company) as of December 31, 1994, and 1993, and the related consolidated statements of income, shareholders' equity and cash flows for each of the three years in the period ended December 31, 1994, all expressed in French francs. These financial statements are the responsibility of the Company's management. Our responsibility is to express an opinion on these financial statements based on our audits.

We conducted our audits in accordance with generally accepted auditing standards in the United States. Those standards require that we plan and perform the audit to obtain reasonable assurance about whether the financial statements are free of material misstatement. An audit includes examining, on a test basis, evidence supporting the amounts and disclosures in the financial statements. An audit also includes assessing the accounting principles used and significant estimates made by management, as well as evaluating the overall financial statement presentation. We believe that our audits provide a reasonable basis for our opinion.

In our opinion, the financial statements referred to above present fairly, in all material respects, the financial position of the Company as of December 31, 1994 and 1993 and the results of its operations and its cash flows for each of the three years in the period ended December 31, 1994 in conformity with generally accepted accounting principles in France.

Further, in our opinion, the reconciliation of net income for each of the three years in the period ended December 31, 1994 and shareholders' equity as of December 31, 1994 and 1993, presented in Note 3 to the financial statements referred to above, which reconciles net income and shareholders' equity, as reported in the financial statements, to net income and shareholders' equity as determined in conformity with generally accepted accounting principles in the United States, presents fairly the information shown therein on a consistent basis.

Arthur Andersen LLP
Paris, France
March 29, 1995

Exhibit 2

Accounting Policies

The consolidated financial statements of TOTAL and its subsidiaries (together, the "Company") have been prepared in accordance with French Generally Accepted Accounting Principles ("French GAAP"). They also include certain additional information required by the Securities and Exchange Commission of the United States.

Principles of consolidation

The consolidated financial statements include the accounts of all significant subsidiaries. The Company's interests in oil and gas-related joint ventures are proportionately consolidated. Investments in 20-50% owned significant companies are accounted for by the equity method. Companies in which ownership interest is less than 20%, but over which the Company has the ability to exercise significant influence, are also accounted for by the equity method. Under this method, the investment represents the Company's share of the underlying equity of the investee (including income or loss for the period) and is reflected in the consolidated balance sheets in "Equity affiliates". The Company's share of the income or loss of its equity investees is reflected in the consolidated statements of income as "Equity in income (loss) of affiliates".

Foreign currency translation

Transactions denominated in foreign currencies are translated at the exchange rate prevailing when the transaction is realized. Monetary assets and liabilities denominated in foreign currencies are translated at the exchange rates prevailing at the end of the period. The resulting gains or losses are recorded in "Other income (expense)" in the consolidated statements of income. Translation differences arising on foreign currency loans which are specifically contracted to hedge the value of a net investment in a consolidated subsidiary or equity investee from the effect of exchange rates fluctuations are reflected as an adjustment to shareholders' equity.

The balance sheets of consolidated subsidiaries or equity affiliates are translated into French francs on the basis of exchange rates at the end of the period. The consolidated statements of income and consolidated statements of cash flows are translated using the average exchange rates during the period. Foreign exchange differences resulting from such translation are recorded either in "Cumulative translation adjustment" (for the Company's share) or in "Minority interest".

Financial instruments

Financial instruments are used for hedging purposes. The Company enters into interest rate and foreign currency swap agreements to minimize its borrowing cost and reduce its exposure to interest rate and foreign currency changes. The differential between interest to be paid and interest to be received is recognized in income, over the life of the hedged item. Changes in the market value of interest rate futures options, caps and floors are recognized as gains or losses in the period of the change. However, when the contracts qualify as hedges, gains and losses on such contracts are recognized in income in the same period as the gains and losses on the item being hedged.

Exhibit 2

In connection with its trading activities, the Company uses hedging strategies to help moderate its exposure to fluctuations in the price of crude oil and related products. Gains and losses on these contracts are recognized or accrued as a component of the related transactions.
Changes in the market value of commodity hedges of petroleum products inventories are accounted for as additions to or reductions in inventory. The Company also enters into contracts that are not specific hedges. Gains and losses resulting from changes in the market value of these
types of contracts are recorded as follows: a) forward contracts: unrealized losses are recognized currently while unrealized gains are deferred until the contract is closed out; b) futures contracts: unrealized gains and losses are recognized in income or expensed currently.

Intangible assets

Acquisition goodwill is being amortized using the straight-line basis over periods not exceeding 30 years.

Property, plant and equipment

The Company applies the successful efforts method of accounting for its oil and gas exploration and producing properties. Costs of acquiring unproved properties are capitalized and impairment of those properties is provided by amortizing the cost thereof. Geological and geophysical costs are expensed as incurred. Drilling in progress and wells where proved reserves have been discovered are capitalized. Costs of exploratory drilling are expensed if the wells are determined to be unsuccessful. The costs of productive leasehold and other capitalized costs related to producing activities including tangible and intangible costs are amortized on a unit-of-production basis using the estimated proved reserves.

Other property, plant and equipment are carried at cost with the exception of assets that have been acquired before 1976 whose cost has been revalued under French regulations. The revaluation adjustment is included in shareholders' equity in "Revaluation reserve". This surplus is credited to income over the useful life of the related depreciable fixed assets using the corresponding rates of depreciation and depletion or upon disposal of the revalued assets.

Fixed assets of significant value which are held under hire purchase and similar agreements are capitalized and depreciated using the straight-line method. The corresponding commitment is recorded as a liability. Assets and capitalized leases are depreciated by the straight-line method over their estimated useful life.

Routine maintenance and repairs are charged to income as incurred. However, estimated costs of major refinery turnarounds are accrued over the period from the prior turnaround to the next planned turnaround.

Other investments

Investees over which the Company does not have the ability to exercise significant influence (generally less than 20% owned) or subsidiaries excluded from consolidation after consideration of their materiality to the Company's operations are valued at acquisition cost less allowance for impairment in value.

Exhibit 2

Accounting Policies
(continued)

Inventories

Inventories are stated at the lower of cost or market value. Cost is determined on a first-in, first-out basis (FIFO) for crude oil and refined product inventories. Other inventories are stated primarily on a weighted average basis.

Operating expenses - reserve for crude oil price changes

Net income is presented according to the replacement cost method. Under this method, monthly consumption of petroleum inventories (crude oil and refined products) is valued at the replacement cost of crude oil and refined products over the month instead of the historical cost value. When replacement cost exceeds historical cost value (positive inventory effect), a reserve for crude oil price changes is charged against operating income. This reserve is classified as a long-term liability. When the inventory effect is negative, the reserve for crude oil price changes is reversed up to the previously recorded amount.

Short-term investments

Short-term investments are valued at the lower of cost or market value. Non-publicly traded equity securities are stated at cost.

Dismantlement, removal and environmental costs

Environmental expenditures that relate to current operations are expensed or capitalized as appropriate. Expenditures that relate to an existing condition caused by past operations, and which do not contribute to current or future revenue generation, are expensed. Liabilities are recorded when environmental assessments and/or remedial efforts are probable, and the cost can be reasonably estimated.

The estimated costs of dismantlement and removal of major oil and gas exploration and production facilities including necessary site restoration are accrued on a unit-of-production basis.

Deferred taxes

In February 1992, the Financial Accounting Standards Board ("FASB") issued Statement of Financial Accounting Standards ("SFAS") No. 109. This standard requires, among other things, recognition of future tax benefits, measured by enacted tax rates, attributable to deductible temporary differences between financial reporting and income tax bases of assets and liabilities and to net operating loss ("NOLs") and tax credit carryforwards, to the extent that realization of such benefits is more likely than not.

Effective January 1, 1993, the Company adopted SFAS No. 109 and has reported the cumulative effect of the change as of the beginning of the 1993 fiscal year in the consolidated statement of income.

Exhibit 2

Accounting Policies
(continued)

Under its previous method, the Company applied the liability method but did not recognize the tax consequences of loss and tax credit carryforwards and did not record deferred taxes on certain temporary differences to the extent that their realization or reversal was not certain.

Sales, costs and expenses

Sales are recorded as products are shipped and services are rendered. Sales are presented net of excise taxes. Taxes paid to Middle East producing countries are included in operating expenses. Costs and expenses are charged to income in the period in which the related sales are recognized.

Research and development expenses

Research and development expenses are charged to income as incurred. The total of such costs expensed for the years ended December 31, 1994, 1993, and 1992 was MFF 1,053, MFF 1,108, and MFF 978, respectively.

Interest expense

Interest charges relating to the direct financing of major projects under construction, including development works on unproved oil and gas properties, are capitalized. All other interest is expensed currently.

Consolidated statements of cash flows

The Company applies the requirements of SFAS No. 95.

Employee benefits

In accordance with the laws and practices of each country, the Company participates in employee benefit pension plans offering death and disability, retirement and special termination benefits. About 54 % of active employees are covered through defined benefit pension plans. Most of continental European pension plans are not funded. United Kingdom, South African and United States plans are funded through pension funds, with investments made in various instruments such as insurance contracts and securities.

For defined contribution plans and multi-employer plans, expenses correspond to the contributions paid. For defined benefit pension plans, accruals and prepaid expenses are determined using the projected unit credit method. Accruals and prepaid expenses are recorded in accordance with the prevailing accounting practice in each country. Special termination benefits are recorded on an accrual basis at the time the offer is accepted and can be reasonably estimated to the employees or their representatives.

Exhibit 2

Accounting Policies
(continued)

Effective January 1, 1993, the Company adopted SFAS No. 106 "Employers' Accounting for Postretirement Benefits Other than Pensions" for eligible active and retired employees in the United States and elected to immediately recognize in income the cumulative effect of the change of MFF 170 (MFF 151 after taxes) which represents the unfunded accumulated postretirement benefit obligation (APBO) as of January 1, 1993. As a result of this change, the 1993 net income and minority interest have been reduced by MFF 132 (or FF 0.6 per share) and MFF 19, respectively.

In December 1992, the FASB issued SFAS No. 112 "Employers' Accounting for Postemployment Benefits". The effect of the new statement on 1994 net income is immaterial since the Company was already accounting for substantially all of this type of costs in accordance with SFAS No. 112.

Earnings per share

Earnings per common share is calculated by dividing net income by the weighted average number of common shares and common share equivalents outstanding during the period.

Exhibit 3

Consolidated Statements of Income

	Year ended December 31,		
	1994	1993	1992
Sales	136,743	135,478	136,608
Operating expenses	(125,214)	(124,377)	(125,063)
Depreciation, depletion and amortization	(5,135)	(4,858)	(4,674)
OPERATING INCOME:			
Corporate	(611)	(588)	(445)
Business Segments	7,005	6,831	7,316
Total operating income	6,394	6,243	6,871
Interest expense, net	(313)	(526)	(747)
Dividends on subsidiaries' redeemable preferred shares	(48)	(38)	(47)
Other income (expense)	(88)	(354)	(155)
Non-recurring items, net		177	(539)
Provision for income taxes	(1,730)	(1,645)	(1,734)
Equity in income (loss) of affiliates	69	(96)	(1)
INCOME BEFORE AMORTIZATION OF ACQUISITION GOODWILL	4,284	3,761	3,648
AMORTIZATION OF ACQUISITION GOODWILL	(556)	(566)	(585)
MINORITY INTEREST	(343)	(230)	(216)
NET INCOME	3,385	2,965	2,847
EARNINGS PER SHARE	14.6	13.5	13.8

Exhibit 4

Consolidated Balance Sheets

| | December 31, | |
	1994	1993
ASSETS		
NONCURRENT ASSETS:		
Intangible assets	12,737	12,601
Accumulated amortization	(4,146)	(3,477)
Intangible assets, net	8,591	9,124
Property, plant and equipment	94,870	89,333
Accumulated depreciation, depletion and amortization	(48,375)	(45,396)
Property, plant and equipment, net	46,495	43,937
Equity affiliates - Investments and loans	4,544	4,267
Other investments	6,535	7,047
Other noncurrent assets	5,435	8,479
Total noncurrent assets	71,600	72,854
CURRENT ASSETS:		
Inventories	11,867	11,732
Accounts receivable	19,668	17,707
Prepaid expenses and other current assets	7,167	6,590
Short-term investments	620	875
Cash and cash equivalents	23,893	23,966
Total current assets	63,215	60,870
TOTAL ASSETS	134,815	133,724

Exhibit 4

Consolidated Balance Sheets
(continued)

| | December 31, | |
	1994	1993
LIABILITIES AND SHAREHOLDER'S EQUITY		
SHAREHOLDERS' EQUITY:		
Common shares (FF50 par value; shares issued and		
outstanding: 1994 - 227,294,065; 1993 - 219,577,354)	11,365	10,979
Paid-in surplus	9,158	8,039
Retained earnings	32,452	30,785
Revaluation reserve	587	612
Cumulative translation adjustment	(2,214)	(976)
Perpetual subordinated securities repayable		
in shares (TSDIRAs)	648	1,955
Total shareholders' equity	51,996	51,394
SUBSIDIARIES REDEEMABLE		
PREFERRED SHARES	1,337	1,474
MINORITY INTEREST	2,421	2,218
COMMITMENTS AND CONTINGENCIES		
LONG-TERM LIABILITIES:		
Reserve for crude oil price changes	503	72
Deferred income taxes	4,797	6,093
Employee benefits	5,264	5,095
Other liabilities	4,332	4,336
Total long-term liabilities	14,896	15,596
LONG-TERM DEBT:		
Loans	22,141	23,540
Deposits	666	538
Total long-term debt	22,807	24,078
CURRENT LIABILITIES:		
Accounts payable	14,775	13,255
Other creditors and accrued liabilities	12,936	12,965
Current portion of long-term debt	2,605	2,514
Short-term borrowings	9,691	8,731
Bank overdrafts	1,351	1,499
Total current liabilities	41,358	38,964
TOTAL LIABILITIES AND SHAREHOLDERS' EQUITY	134,815	133,724

Exhibit 5

Consolidated Statements of Cash Flows

	Year ended December 31,		
	1994	1993	1992
CASH FLOWS FROM OPERATING ACTIVITIES			
Net income	3,385	2,965	2,847
Adjustments to reconcile net income to net cash flows from operating activities:			
Minority interest	343	230	216
Depreciation, depletion and amortization	6,639	5,803	5,449
Long-term liabilities, valuation allowances and deferred taxes	1,358	1,495	663
Unsuccessful exploration costs	547	862	777
Reserve for crude oil changes	435	(103)	101
Gains on sales of subsidiaries	(272)	(340)	
Gains on sales of assets	(840)	(539)	(14)
Gains from discontinued operations		(381)	
Equity in income of affiliates (in excess of)/less than dividends received	(28)	212	32
Changes in operating assets and liabilities	(755)	2,531	(648)
Other changes, net	228	115	(113)
NET CASH FLOWS FROM OPERATING ACTIVITIES	11,040	12,850	9,310
CASH FLOWS FROM INVESTING ACTIVITIES			
Intangible assets and property, plant and equipment additions	(9,874)	(10,436)	(10,468)
Exploration costs directly charged to expense	(473)	(599)	(627)
Investments in equity affiliates and equity securities	(633)	(3,481)	(1,176)
Increase in long-term loans granted	(2,277)	(3,775)	(2,219)
Acquisitions of subsidiaries, net of cash acquired	(380)	(139)	(346)
Proceeds from sale of assets, equity affiliates and equity securities	2,111	1,618	1,185
Proceeds from sale of subsidiaries, net of cash sold	932	1,288	
Proceeds from sale of discontinued operations		1,034	
Repayment of long-term loans (including cost-oil reimbursed) granted	886	1,120	888
(Increase) decrease in short-term investments	230	(343)	1,316
NET CASH FLOWS PROVIDED BY (USED IN) INVESTING ACTIVITIES	(9,478)	(13,713)	(11,447)

Exhibit 5

Consolidated Statements of Cash Flows
(continued)

	Year ended December 31,		
	1994	1993	1992
CASH FLOWS FROM FINANCING ACTIVITIES			
Proceeds from issuance of shares:			
Parent company's shareholders	496	4,071	679
Minority shareholders	16	18	86
Cash repayment of TSDIRAs	(1,264)		
Cash dividend paid:			
Parent company's shareholders and holders of TSDIRAs	(752)	(523)	(1,440)
Minority shareholders	(192)	(170)	(191)
Net issuance (repayment) of long-term debt	1,963	5,038	5,591
Increase (decrease) in short-term borrowings and bank overdrafts	(1,489)	971	(3,227)
Other changes, net	(40)	(49)	(244)
NET CASH FLOWS PROVIDED BY (USED IN) FINANCING ACTIVITIES	(1,262)	9,356	1,254
NET INCREASE (DECREASE) IN CASH AND CASH EQUIVALENTS	300	8,493	(883)
Effect of exchange rates and changes in reporting entity on cash and cash equivalents	(373)	212	(72)
Cash and cash equivalents at the beginning of the year	23,966	15,261	16,216
CASH AND CASH EQUIVALENTS AT THE END OF THE YEAR	23,893	23,966	15,261
SUPPLEMENTAL DISCLOSURES OF CASH FLOW INFORMATION			
Cash paid during the year for:			
Interest (net of amount capitalized)	2,474	2,585	2,055
Income taxes	1,007	1,374	843

301

Exhibit 6

Summary of Differences between Accounting Principles Followed by the Company and United States Generally Accepted Accounting Principles

Reserve for crude oil price changes

The replacement cost method adopted by the Company to reflect the impact of price changes on crude oil and refined products sold and the related reserve for crude oil price changes would not be acceptable under US GAAP.

Income taxes

As described in Note 1, Accounting Policies, the Company changed its method of accounting for income taxes, effective January 1, 1993.

Prior to the adoption of SFAS No. 109, the reconciliation between French GAAP and US GAAP (Accounting Principles Board's Opinion No. 11 "APB No. 11") was determined by measuring the difference between the liability method followed by the Company and the deferral method prescribed by APB No. 11. Consequently, the cumulative effect of the change in accounting principle reported for French GAAP purposes for the year ended December 31, 1993 differs from the cumulative catch-up amount calculated for the reconciliation to US GAAP as the latter represents the change from APB No. 11 to SFAS No. 109.

Further, the Company reported the effect of applying SFAS No. 109 on the difference between the reported amount and the tax basis of oil and gas properties acquired before January 1, 1993 as an adjustment to intangible assets. Under US GAAP, the gross-up resulting from the deferred tax liability on nondeductible fixed assets would have been recorded as an addition to the corresponding oil and gas properties with the related depreciation expense included in operating income.

Pension plans

a) The Company has applied the provisions of SFAS No. 87 as follows:

b) The transition obligation or fund excess has been determined as of January 1, 1987 as being the difference between the liabilities accounted for under prior years' accounting policies and the funded status of the plans resulting from SFAS No. 87 calculations.

c) The net transition obligation has been charged against shareholders' equity as of January 1, 1987.

d) For US GAAP reporting purposes, the transition obligation or fund excess has been amortized using the greater of 15 years and the average residual active life of the employees covered by each plan.

Revaluation

As described in Note 1, Accounting Policies, certain noncurrent assets have been revalued on the basis of their appraised value. US GAAP does not permit such revaluation. However, this revaluation has no impact on net income.

Exhibit 6

Summary of Differences between Accounting Principles Followed by the Company and United States Generally Accepted Accounting Principles
(continued)

Treasury shares

The Company has acquired some of its own shares mainly to be delivered to employees in connection with the implementation of share purchase plans. The cost of these shares is included in short-term investments. Under US GAAP, such treasury shares should be reflected as a reduction of shareholders' equity. Also, proceeds from common shares issued invested in shares of other companies carried at cost that may be exchanged for treasury shares should be classified outside of shareholders' equity.

In addition, under US GAAP, gains on disposals of treasury shares held in treasury should be excluded from the determination of net income and credited to paid-in surplus.

Equity securities

Under French GAAP, unrealized gains are not recognized and valuation allowances of marketable equity securities are generally determined based on year-end quotations.

Adoption of SFAS No. 115 by the Company as of January 1, 1994 (for US GAAP reconciliation purposes only) resulted in unrealized gains relating to available-for-sale securities of MFF 612 added to shareholders' equity. This new statement had no impact on the 1994 net income determined under US GAAP as the aggregate market value of securities classified as "trading" was lower than their aggregate cost as of January 1, 1994.

Intangible assets

The Company does not amortize all intangible assets. Under US GAAP, intangible assets should be amortized over the future periods estimated to be benefited, up to a maximum of 40 years. Under US GAAP, previously recorded write-downs may not be reversed in subsequent periods.

Interest on receivables

Non-interest bearing loans and low-interest housing loans are made to the Company's employees. Such loans are not discounted whereas under US GAAP they should be recorded at their present value.

LIFO inventory

Total Petroleum North America (TOP(NA)) follows the last-in, first-out method (LIFO) for financial reporting purposes. The inventories are adjusted to the first-in, first-out method (FIFO) in the consolidated financial statements. Under US GAAP, the inventories would not be restated to FIFO.

Exhibit 6

Summary of Differences between Accounting Principles Followed by the Company and United States Generally Accepted Accounting Principles
(continued)

Deferred compensation

The Company generally grants to its employees a discount from the market price for shares purchased pursuant to share subscription plans, share purchase plans and reserved capital increases. Accounting for this discount is not addressed by French GAAP and these transactions have no effect on the statement of income. Under US GAAP, the discount, measured at the date of grant, is considered as compensation to employees.

Accrual of loss contingencies

The Company has recorded loss contingencies in relation to future insurance premium increases based on retrospective rating provisions in multiple-year insurance contracts. Under US GAAP (SFAS No. 5 and Emerging Issues Task Force Issue No. 93-6) such losses should only be accrued to the extent that they were probable or known at year-end. Accordingly, the corresponding reserves classified as "Long-term liabilities" in the accompanying balance sheets must be reversed and retrospective premium payable must be recognized in the period in which they are incurred.

Consolidated statements of income presentation

Under US GAAP, depreciation and amortization of intangible assets (including goodwill) would have been deducted from operating income. In addition, miscellaneous valuation allowances or reversals included in "Other income (expense)" would have been deducted from or added to operating income.

Also, the cumulative effect of 1993 accounting changes would have been separately disclosed.

Exhibit 7

Reconciliation of Net Income and Shareholders' Equity to US GAAP

The following is a summary of the estimated adjustments to net income and shareholders' equity for the years ended December 31, 1994, 1993, and 1992 which would be required if US GAAP had been applied instead of French GAAP.

	Net income Year ended December 31,		
	1994	1993	1992
Amounts per accompanying consolidated financial statements	3,385	2,965	2,847
US GAAP adjustments (a)			
Increase (decrease) due to:			
Reserve for crude oil price changes	421	(74)	74
Income taxes		138	(79)
Pension plans	(10)	78	81
Treasury shares	1	(6)	(52)
Equity securities	(5)	(8)	(44)
Intangible assets	(50)	(21)	(111)
Interest on receivables	(37)	20	(38)
Deferred compensation	(144)		
LIFO inventory		52	(21)
Accrual of loss contingencies	39		
Other		4	6
Tax effect of US GAAP adjustments	(48)	(116)	
Approximate amounts under US GAAP	3,552	3,032	2,663

Exhibit 7

Reconciliation of Net Income and Shareholders' Equity to US GAAP
(continued)

| | Shareholders' equity Year ended December 31, | |
	1994	1993
Amounts per accompanying consolidated financial statements	51,996	51,394
US GAAP adjustments (a)		
Increase (decrease) due to:		
Reserve for crude oil price changes	511	90
Pension plans	661	671
Revaluation	(587)	(612)
Treasury shares	(1,611)	(1,595)
Equity securities	(18)	(172)
Intangible assets	(308)	(258)
Interest on receivables	(109)	(72)
LIFO inventory	6	6
Deferred compensation	(144)	
Accrual of loss contingencies	39	
Tax effect of US GAAP adjustments	(202)	(154)
Cumulative translation adjustment of US GAAP adjustments	(41)	(43)
Approximate amounts under US GAAP	50,193	49,255

(a) US GAAP adjustments are presented net of the portion applicable to minority interest.

Exhibit 8

Consolidated Statements of Income and Changes in Shareholders' Equity
Restated to US GAAP

The consolidated statements of income for the years ended December 31, 1994, 1993, and 1992 and statements of changes in shareholders' equity for the years ended December 31, 1994 and 1993 presented below have been restated to reflect the principal differences between US GAAP and French GAAP.

| | Year ended December 31, | | |
	1994	1993	1992
Sales	136,743	135,478	136,101
Cost of sales	(120,859)	(120,376)	(121,461)
Other operating expenses	(11,203)	(11,501)	(9,072)
OPERATING INCOME	4,681	3,601	5,568
Interest expense	(792)	(853)	(1,015)
Dividend income	479	327	281
Dividends on subsidiaries redeemable preferred shares	(48)	(38)	(47)
Other income (expense)	1,307	1,030	(110)
Provision for income taxes	(1,788)	(1,769)	(1,822)
Equity in income (loss) of affiliates	69	(96)	(1)
Minority interest	(356)	(261)	(222)
NET INCOME FROM CONTINUING OPERATIONS BEFORE EXTRAORDINARY ITEM AND CUMULATIVE EFFECT OF ACCOUNTING CHANGES	3,552	1,941	2,632
Extraordinary item:			
Income (loss) from discontinued operations (after income taxes)			31
Gain on sale of discontinued operations (after income taxes)		381	
Cumulative effect of accounting changes:			
Income taxes		842	
Health-care and life insurance benefits (US plans)		(132)	
NET INCOME	3,552	3,032	2,663

Exhibit 8

Consolidated Statements of Income and Changes in Shareholders' Equity
Restated to US GAAP
(continued)

| | Year ended December 31, | | |
	1994	1993	1992
PRIMARY EARNINGS PER SHARE (a)			
Average common shares and common			
share equivalents outstanding	231,675,234	219,235,628	206,834,701
Net income from continuing			
operations before extraordinary item and			
cumulative effect of accounting changes	15.3	8.9	12.7
Extraordinary item - Discontinued operations		1.7	0.2
Cumulative effect of accounting changes:			
Income taxes		3.8	
Health-care and life insurance			
benefits (US plans)		(0.6)	
NET INCOME PER SHARE	15.3	13.8	12.9

(a) The Company reports earnings per share using the method described in Note 1, Accounting Policies. Under US GAAP, treasury shares would not have been considered as outstanding. Also, earnings per share calculations assuming full dilution are not given as its effect is immaterial.

Shareholders' equity as of December 31, 1992	43,821
Net income for 1993	3,032
Cash dividend	(523)
Issuance of common shares	4,071
Treasury shares	(1,453)
Translation adjustment	307
Shareholders' equity as of December 31, 1993	49,255
Unrealized gains on marketable equity securities,	
net of tax - As of January 1, 1994	612
Unrealized gains (losses) on marketable equity	
securities, net of tax - 1994	(453)
Net income for 1994	3,552
Cash dividend	(752)
Issuance of common shares	496
Cancellation of TSDIRAs repaid in cash	(1,264)
Treasury shares	(17)
Translation adjustment	(1,236)
Shareholders' equity as of December 31, 1994	50,193

The BASF Group, headquartered in Germany, is one of the world's leading chemical companies. The company's 1995 sales of over DM 46 million were distributed worldwide as follows: Asia, Pacific area, and Africa -- 11 percent; Europe (excluding Germany) - 37 percent; Germany - 27 percent; North America - 19 percent; and South America - 6 percent. With the exception of its audio and video tapes and computer diskettes, few of the company's products are "end-user", and consequently BASF markets itself with the following theme:

> We don't make a lot of the products you buy.
> We make a lot of the products you buy **better**.

Like most manufacturing companies, BASF is both capital and inventory-intensive. As of year-end 1995, over 52 percent of the company's assets were composed of either inventory (16 percent) or tangible assets (36.7 percent) This case focuses on the accounting for BASF's inventory.

Accounting for Inventory

There are few accounting issues that generate more controversy than the accounting for inventories. Almost all nations permit the use of First-in, First-out (FIFO) and various permutations of the average cost method (e.g. the weighted-average cost approach), but a far smaller number of countries allow the use of Last-in, First-out (LIFO), or its close variant (when prices are rising), Highest-in, First-out (HIFO).[1] Nations permitting the use of LIFO include Argentina, Brazil, Canada, Denmark, Germany, India, Italy, Japan, Mexico, Spain, and the United States, among others. Opponents of LIFO point out that the approach bears no resemblance to the actual flow of inventory through the vast majority of companies, and that the method often produces a questionable valuation of ending inventory on the balance sheet. Proponents, on the other hand, point to the improved matching of revenues and expenses that results on the income statement -- a particularly desirable feature for those nations experiencing modest to high levels of inflation -- and to LIFO's income tax advantages as compared to FIFO and average cost, a fact which largely accounts for its popularity in such countries as Germany, Italy, Japan, and the U.S.

Concerns regarding the quality of the valuation of ending inventory under LIFO have led the regulatory agencies of some countries to require the disclosure of a "LIFO reserve", an approximation of the difference between the LIFO cost basis of ending inventory and its current cost. Disclosure of the LIFO reserve in the footnotes to the financial statements is intended to permit financial statement users to assess the relative impact of LIFO on a company's inventory values; and, if the impact is deemed to be material, to enable the user to restate the relevant balance sheet accounts.[2] Thus, disclosure of the LIFO reserve is designed to enable companies to retain the superior income statement matching and income tax advantages provided by LIFO, while overcoming its balance sheet limitations.

---

[*] This case was prepared by Kenneth R. Ferris. Copyright © 1996 by The American Graduate School of International Management. All rights reserved.
[1] As of 1996, no country permits the use of such replacement cost methods as Next-in, First-out (NIFO) for financial reporting purposes, although such methods are sometimes available for income tax purposes.
[2] Restatement of LIFO ending inventory using the LIFO reserve yields an approximation of the equivalent ending inventory under FIFO (i.e., on a current cost basis).

Financial Analysts have also found the LIFO reserve to be useful for purposes of comparing the reported performance of a LIFO-based company with that of a FIFO-based company. The change in the LIFO reserve, a cumulative measure, from one period to the next approximates the difference in the cost of goods sold attributable to the inventory price changes reflected in using LIFO versus FIFO. In essence, subtracting the change in the LIFO reserve from the LIFO cost of goods sold provides an estimate of a company's cost of goods sold under FIFO. With this in mind, analysts are able to restate the income statements of LIFO-based companies to a common data benchmark (i.e., FIFO).[3]

Questions:

1. Using the financial data for BASF presented in Exhibits 1 and 2:

    (a) calculate the current value of the company's inventory at year-end 1993, 1994, and 1995;

    (b) calculate the company's cost of goods sold and pre-tax net income under FIFO for 1994 and 1995;

    (c) calculate the company's inventory turnover ratio and the days-inventory-on-hand ratio under LIFO and FIFO for 1994 and 1995.

2. Estimate the income tax savings experienced by BASF for 1994, 1995, and for all years in total, that resulted from using LIFO instead of FIFO.[4]

3. It has been suggested by some accounting standard-setters that companies should be permitted to use LIFO for income statement preparation purposes and FIFO for balance sheet preparation purposes; do you agree with this proposal? Why or why not?

---

[3] There is no such thing as a "FIFO reserve", and hence no equivalent way to restate the results of a FIFO-based company to approximate the results under the LIFO method.

[4] Effective 1995, the statutory tax rate for German corporations subject to unlimited tax liability is 45 percent (30 percent for distributed profits). Also, corporations are subject to a "solidarity surcharge" of 7.5 percent.

Exhibit 1
1993 Financial Statements and Selected Footnote Information
BASF

A. Balance Sheet

as of December 31, 1993
million DM

Assets	Notes	Dec. 31, 1993	Dec. 31, 1992
Intangible assets	(7)	638.0	683.7
Tangible assets	(7)	17,721.6	15,213.7
Financial assets	(8)	1,929.0	2,954.8
Fixed assets	(3)	20,288.6	18,852.2
Goods on lease		277.3	306.8
Inventories	(9)	6,039.4	6,441.7
Accounts receivable-trade		5,748.0	5,445.8
Receivables from affiliated companies		624.4	1,089.8
Miscellaneous receivables and other assets		1,654.7	1,841.6
Receivables and other assets	(10)	8,027.1	8,377.2
Securities	(3)	2,921.1	2,904.6
Checks, cash on hand, central bank and postal giro balances, bank balances		2,318.2	1,652.3
Current assets	(3)	19,583.1	19,682.6
Prepaid expenses	(11)	486.3	438.4
		40,358.0	38,973.2

Equity and Liabilities			
Subscribed capital	(12)	2,922.5	2,852.0
Capital surplus	(13)	4,463.9	4,329.8
Revenue reserves and profit retained	(14)	7,629.4	7,315.0
Translation adjustment	(6)	−231.5	−
Minority interests	(3)	159.8	85.8
Equity		14,944.1	14,582.6
Special reserves	(3/15)	50.2	74.2
Pension provisions and similar obligations		6,725.4	6,681.9
Provisions for taxes	(16)	809.4	803.1
Other provisions	(16)	6,420.8	6,216.6
Provisions	(3/16)	13,955.6	13,701.6
Bonds and other liabilities to the capital market		3,462.5	3,206.2
Liabilities to credit institutions		1,901.9	1,755.4
Accounts payable-trade		2,801.5	2,891.9
Liabilities to affiliated companies		1,215.0	545.5
Miscellaneous liabilities		1,878.0	2,072.8
Liabilities	(17)	11,258.9	10,471.8
Deferred income		149.2	143.0
		40,358.0	38,973.2

B. Profit and Loss Account

January 1 – December 31, 1993
million DM

	Notes	**1993**	1992
Sales	(20)	**43,122.7**	44,522.4
– Petroleum and natural gas taxes		**2,554.3**	2,589.6
Sales (without petroleum and natural gas taxes)		**40,568.4**	41,932.8
Cost of sales		**27,646.8**	28,236.8
Gross profit on sales		**12,921.6**	13,696.0
Selling expense		**7,591.1**	7,868.6
General administration expense		**1,052.4**	1,076.7
Research and development expense		**1,934.4**	2,048.4
Other operating income	(21)	**2,111.2**	1,548.6
Other operating expense	(21)	**3,423.3**	2,939.5
Income from operations		**1,031.6**	1,311.4
Net income from financial assets	(22)	**0.4**	−151.6
Amortization of financial assets and securities held as current assets		**9.5**	20.2
Interest result	(23)	**35.1**	129.7
Results from ordinary activities		**1,057.6**	1,269.3
Extraordinary results		**–**	− 29.9
Profit before taxes		**1,057.6**	1,239.4
Income taxes	(24)	**296.2**	626.3
Net income		**761.4**	613.1
Minority interests in profit/loss	(27)	**− 96.3**	−1.5
Net income after minority interests		**857.7**	614.6

C. Selected Footnote Information

(9) Inventories

Inventories are broken downs as follows:

million DM	BASF Group		BASF AG	
	1993	1992	**1993**	1992
Raw materials and supplies			**305.9**	395.6
Work in process, finished goods and merchandise	**5,886.8**	6,293.8	**1,445.1**	1,627.0
Uncompleted contracts	**147.3**	136.7	**136.1**	190.5
Payment on account	**5.3**	11.2	**2.0**	0.3
	6,039.4	6,441.7	**1,889.1**	2,213.4

For inventories valued on the LIFO basis, LIFO reserves approximated DM 132 million for the BASF Group, and DM 8 million for raw materials and DM 72 million for work in process, finished goods and merchandise for BASF Aktiengesellschaft.

Exhibit 2
1995 Financial Statements and Selected Footnote Information
BASF

A. Balance Sheet

million DM

Assets	Notes	Dec. 31, 1995	Dec. 31, 1994
Intangible assets	(7)	1,730.0	511.7
Tangible assets	(7)	15,399.3	15,993.1
Financial assets	(8)	2,615.5	2,068.5
Fixed assets	(3/4)	**19,744.8**	**18,573.3**
Goods on lease		183.3	223.7
Inventories	(9)	6,541.6	6,037.9
Accounts receivable – trade		6,563.9	6,483.3
Receivables from affiliated companies		703.7	574.6
Miscellaneous receivables and other assets		1,638.7	1,552.6
Receivables and other assets	(10)	**8,906.3**	**8,610.5**
Securities		3,865.4	3,614.2
Checks, cash on hand, central bank and postal bank balances, bank balances		2,328.0	2,334.6
Current assets	(3)	**21,824.6**	**20,820.9**
Prepaid expenses	(11)	**465.9**	**464.6**
		42,035.3	39,858.8

Equity and Liabilities			
Subscribed capital	(12)	3,048.8	3,048.8
Capital surplus	(13)	4,703.9	4,703.9
Revenue reserves and profit retained	(14)	10,317.0	8,440.8
Translation adjustment	(6)	−495.4	−453.1
Minority interests	(3)	353.2	179.4
Equity		**17,927.5**	**15,919.8**
Special reserves	(4/15)	**77.9**	**49.7**
Pension provisions and similar obligations		6,657.5	6,602.0
Provisions for taxes		1,234.7	1,092.8
Other provisions	(16)	6,485.9	6,259.3
Provisions	(3/16)	**14,378.1**	**13,954.1**
Bonds and other liabilities to the capital market		1,387.9	1,831.0
Liabilities to credit institutions		1,444.9	1,801.3
Accounts payable – trade		2,770.7	2,995.1
Liabilities to affiliated companies		459.1	1,119.6
Miscellaneous liabilities		3,444.2	2,021.7
Liabilities	(17)	**9,506.8**	**9,768.7**
Deferred income		**145.0**	**166.5**
		42,035.3	39,858.8

*For 1994 inventories valued on the LIFO basis, LIFO reserves were approximately DM 140 million for the BASF Group.

B. Profit and Loss Account

January 1 – December 31, 1995
million DM

	Notes	1995	1994
Sales	(20)	**49,402.6**	46,564.6
– Petroleum and natural gas taxes		**3,173.5**	2,890.6
Sales (without petroleum and natural gas taxes)		**46,229.1**	43,674.0
Cost of sales		**29,766.5**	29,162.2
Gross profit on sales		**16,462.6**	14,511.8
Selling expense		**7,747.9**	7,647.0
General administration expense		**1,087.4**	1,002.5
Research and development expense		**2,087.9**	1,916.2
Other operating income	(21)	**2,013.8**	1,850.3
Other operating expense	(21)	**3,530.4**	3,647.5
Income from operations		**4,022.8**	2,148.9
Net income from financial assets	(22)	**128.3**	114.4
Amortization of financial assets and securities held as current assets		**44.2**	109.2
Interest result	(23)	**21.3**	– 42.8
Profit before taxes*		**4,128.2**	2,111.3
Income taxes	(24)	**1,704.9**	941.1
Net income		**2,423.3**	1,170.2
Minority interests in profit/loss	(27)	**–47.2**	–113.8
Net income after minority interests		**2,470.5**	1,284.0

* Results from ordinary activities

*For 1994 inventories valued on the LIFO basis, LIFO reserves were approximately DM 140 million for the BASF Group.

C. Selected Footnote Information*

Inventories

Work in progress and finished goods, as well as merchandise, are combined into one item for BASF Aktiengesellschaft due to the production conditions of the chemical industry. Uncompleted contracts are mainly plants under construction for third parties at home and abroad.

Inventories are carried at acquisition or production cost or at the lower quoted or market values, or at such lower values as appropriate.

Production cost includes direct costs and an appropriate portion of the production overhead allocated using normal utilization rates of the production plants, but excludes financing costs for the production period.

The acquisition or production cost of raw materials, work in progress, finished goods and merchandise is mainly determined by the LIFO method (annual-period LIFO), factory supplies generally by the average cost method. The inventories of certain foreign companies for which a similar LIFO method is not allowed under local valuation rules are carried at average cost in the Group financial statements. The lower market value represents in the case of raw materials and factory supplies the replacement costs thereof, and in the case of work in progress and finished products the reproduction cost or the expected sales proceeds less costs to be incurred prior to sale and an average profit margin.

million DM	BASF Group 1995	1994	BASF AG 1995	1994
Raw materials and supplies			**425.4**	380.6
Work in progress, finished goods and merchandise	**6,399.9**	5,894.8	**1,787.3**	1,479.2
Uncompleted contracts	**126.5**	130.2	**146.1**	130.5
Payment on account	**15.2**	12.9	**4.6**	1.1
	6,541.6	6,037.9	**2,363.4**	1,991.4

For inventories valued on the LIFO basis, LIFO reserves were approximately DM 192 million for the BASF Group and approximately DM 13 million for raw materials and approximately DM 95 million for work in progress, finished goods and merchandise for BASF Aktiengesellschaft.

*For 1994 inventories valued on the LIFO basis, LIFO reserves were approximately DM 140 million for the BASF Group.

On March 25, 1993, *The Wall Street Journal* carried an article with the following title:

> Daimler-Benz Discloses Hidden
> Reserves of $2.45 Billion,
> Seeks Big Board Listing

According to the article, Daimler-Benz AG, Germany's largest industrial company, would report $2.45 billion U.S. (or 4 billion marks) as an unexpected addition to its 1992 balance sheet. The disclosure apparently came as part of Daimler's efforts to become the first German company to list its shares on the New York Stock Exchange (NYSE).

According to U.S. Securities and Exchange Commission representatives, many foreign companies would like to gain access to the huge U.S. equity and debt markets; however, a major stumbling block for those companies is complying with U.S. reporting and disclosure practices designed to protect investors. In a statement to financial analysts, Gerhard Liener, Daimler's chief financial officer, reported that the company had already adopted some U.S. accounting practices: It had been reporting quarterly data to shareholders for the past two years, and its method of reporting cash flows had conformed to U.S. practice since 1992.

With respect to the previously undisclosed reserve of $2.45 billion, financial analysts observed that German companies "were notorious for squirreling away cash that never appears on their balance sheet." According to a Daimler spokesperson, "This is money that we've had in the back room, but it will be visible now. The company will continue to retain the cash as an internal cash reserve."

Analysts familiar with German accounting practice note that there are a variety of ways that companies can create hidden or "silent" reserves -- understating revenues, overstating expenses, and overstating charges for "provisions for contingencies," amongst others.[1] With respect to Daimler's reserve, the $2.45 billion resulted from an inconsistent application of pension valuation methods throughout the company. Daimler's operating companies apparently discounted their pension fund commitments at 6 percent, whereas the holding company discounted those same commitments at 3.5 percent.

Daimler-Benz officials stated that they hope that the recent disclosures will help the company attain NYSE listing by year-end 1993. A remaining problem, however, may be the company's accounting for goodwill. Under U.S. practice, goodwill arising from a merger or acquisition must be capitalized to the balance sheet and then amortized off against earnings over the asset's expected useful life (but not to exceed 40 years). In recent years, Daimler acquisitions have produced over $2.0 billion in goodwill, which under German accounting practice has been charged off in total against retained earnings.

---

[1] Provision for contingencies is analogous to the creation of a loss (or expense) reserve in the U.S. The principal difference, however, is that in Germany, provisions for normally occurring expenses (e.g., maintenance) may be created often with the explicit purpose of smoothing reported earnings. Under U.S. practice, the creation of reserves is usually limited to unusual or nonrecurring events.

QUESTIONS

Presented in the following exhibits are the Daimler-Benz consolidated balance sheet and consolidated statement of income as of December 31, 1991. Recast the company's 1991 financial statements to reflect the previously hidden reserves and the goodwill charged to equity. Consider the ways that companies reporting their financial results under U.S. GAAP can "smooth" their reported earnings (e.g., create hidden reserves). Make a list of these methods and the reasons why a company might want to smooth its reported results.

Exhibit 1
DAIMLER-BENZ AG

Consolidated Statement of Income

	1991 In Millions of DM	1990 In Millions of DM
Sales	**95,010**	**85,500**
Increase in Inventories and Other Capitalized In-House Output	3,556	2,840
Total Output	**98,566**	**88,340**
Other Operating Income	3,545	3,598
Cost of Materials	(49,456)	(44,477)
Personnel Expenses of which for Old-Age Pensions DM 1,511 million (1990: DM 1,347 million)	(29,372)	(26,890)
Amortization of Intangible Assets, Depreciation of Fixed Assets and Leased Equipment	(5,977)	(5,169)
Other Operating Expenses	(13,824)	(12,016)
Income from Affiliated, Associated and Related Companies	56	4
Net Interest Income	623	989
Write-Downs of Financial Assets and of Securities	(134)	(158)
Results from Ordinary Business Activities	**4,027**	**4,221**
Extraordinary Result	(544)	-
Income Taxes	(1,039)	(1,814)
Other Taxes	(502)	(612)
Net Income	**1,942**	**1,795**
Profit Carried Forward from Previous Year	8	5
Transfer to Retained Earnings	(1,275)	(1,124)
Income Applicable to Minority Shareholders	(99)	(145)
Loss Applicable to Minority Shareholders	29	34
Unappropriated Profit of Daimler-Benz AG	**605**	**565**

Exhibit 2
DAIMLER-BENZ AG

Consolidated Balance Sheet

Assets	December 31, 1991 In Millions of DM	December 31, 1990 In Millions of DM
Non-Current Assets		
Intangible Assets	774	304
Fixed Assets	16,574	15,057
Financial Assets	3,758	1,569
Leased Equipment	8,092	6,518
	29,198	23,448
Current Assets		
Inventories	20,732	18,855
Advance Payments Received	(5,827)	(5,727)
	14,905	13,128
Receivables	12,370	11,321
Other Assets	9,783	9,019
Securities	5,725	5,154
Cash	2,010	3,786
	44,793	42,408
Prepaid Expenses and Deferred Taxes	1,723	1,483
	75,714	67,339
Stockholders' Equity and Liabilities		
Stockholders' Equity		
Capital Stock	2,330	2,330
Paid-in-Capital	2,117	2,117
Retained Earnings	13,182	11,934
Minority Interests	1,214	881
Unappropriated Profit of Daimler-Benz AG	605	565
	19,448	17,827
Provisions		
Provisions for Old-Age Pensions and Similar Obligations	10,790	10,831
Other Provisions	17,239	16,536
	28,029	27,367
Liabilities	7,015	6,469
Accounts Payable Trade		
Other Liabilities	20,713	15,312
	27,728	21,781
	509	364
Deferred Income	75,714	67,339

319

In June of 1993, Holzmann AG, one of Germany's largest construction companies, was employed by the municipal government of Bonn, Germany, to assist in the construction of a convention/trade center complex. The company was to construct the superstructure of a multistory building as part of that city's downtown redevelopment. The construction agreement called for work to begin not later than August of 1993, and required Holzmann to construct the concrete frame for the building.

Under the terms of the three-year contract agreed to, the company was to receive a total of DM 16 million [1] in cash payments from the City of Bonn to be paid as follows: 25 percent when the work was 30 percent complete, 25 percent when the work was 60 percent complete, and the remaining 50 percent when the contracted work had been fully completed. The contract, which was of a fixed-price variety and hence did not provide for cost overrun recoupment, required that completion percentage estimates be certified by an independent engineering consultant before any cash progress payments would be made.

In preparing its bid, Holzmann had estimated that the total cost to complete the project would be DM 14.4 million, assuming no cost overruns. Hence, under optimal conditions, the company anticipated a profit of approximately DM 1.6 million.

During the first year of the contract, Holzmann AG incurred actual costs of DM 4.32 million, and on June 30, 1994, the engineering consulting firm of Deutsche Babcock AG of Köln, Germany, determined that the project had attained a 30 percent completion level. In the following year, the company incurred actual costs of DM 4.68 million. As of June 30, 1995, the firm of Deutsche Babcock determined that the project had attained at least a 60 percent completion level. In their report to the Bonn city council, however, the consulting engineers noted that the company might be facing a potential cost overrun situation. In response to this observation, the directors of the company noted that they had anticipated that a number of economies of scale would arise during the final phases of construction and thereby offset any prior cost overruns.

By May of 1996, the company had completed the remainder of the project. Actual costs incurred during the year to June 30, 1996, amounted to DM 5.6 million. The firm received a certification for the fully completed work.

---

[1] Unless otherwise noted, all amounts are in German deutsche marks (DM).

Accounting Decision -- Revenue Recognition under Long-term Contracts

Prior to the issuance of the 1994 annual report, the controller's office of Holzmann AG determined that the proceeds from the convention/trade center contract would be accounted for using the completed contract method, as required under German accounting practice. Under this approach, the recognition of income is postponed until essentially all work on the contract has been completed. In essence, revenues (and thus expenses) are recognized upon completion or substantial completion of a contract. In general, a contract is regarded as substantially complete if the remaining costs to complete a project are insignificant in amount. Funds expended under the contract are accounted for in an asset account, "construction in progress," while progress payments received during the construction phase are accounted for in a deferred or unearned revenue account. Although income is not recognized until completion of the contract, any expected losses should be recognized immediately when identified.

The primary advantage of the completed contract method is that reported operating results are based on actual results, rather than on estimates. The principal disadvantage is that the method may produce results inconsistent with the actual performance of a firm if the contract extends over more than one reporting period.

In the process of reaching the decision to use the completed contract method, the controller's office of Holzmann AG had discussed the matter with the company's independent chartered accountant, KPMG Deutsche Treuhand-Gesellschaft. The accounting firm had provided the company with several position papers authored by the firm, which essentially identified the percentage of completion method as the preferred method of accounting for long-term construction contract income, at least when the estimated costs to complete a contract and the extent of construction progress can be reasonably estimated. Under this method, revenues are recognized in proportion to the amount of construction actually completed in a given period. The principal advantage of this method is that performance is reported as the work is actually undertaken, rather than at some later date; thus, accounting information users are provided with up-to-date information as to the relative effectiveness and performance of the company. The primary disadvantage is that the method requires the use of estimation procedures, thereby potentially allowing estimation error to enter into the performance reporting process.

Holzmann's auditors noted that despite the fact that the completed contract method was considered the preferred accounting treatment in Germany, in most other countries, the percentage of completion method was the preferred treatment. (Under IASC and EU accounting standards, either method is permitted.) Joseph Westphal, Holzmann's chief financial officer, indicated that despite the percentage of completion's overwhelming acceptability in other countries, Holzmann would continue to use the completed contract method because of tax considerations. Under German income tax regulations, if the completed contract method is utilized for income tax purposes, its use is required for financial reporting purposes.

Questions

1. Assuming that the company had no other sources of revenues or expenses, determine the level of profits to be reported for the years ended June 30, 1994, 1995, and 1996, utilizing the following revenue recognition methods:

   a. Percentage of completion
   b. Completed contract
   c. Cash basis. (Note: Assume that the City of Bonn remits cash payments on the same day as work completion certification.)

2. Which set of results (from Question 1) best reflects the economic performance of the company over the period 1994-1996? What criteria did you apply in the foregoing assessment?

3. a. Assuming that the company decided to change its method of accounting from the completed contract to the percentage of completion method on July 1, 1995, what journal entries would be required?

   b. How should the percentage of completion be determined? Explain why.

4. Assume that the company utilizes the completed contract method for tax purposes and the percentage of completion method for financial reporting purposes; calculate the company's deferred income taxes for 1994, 1995, and 1996. (Assume a tax rate of 45 percent.[2])

---

[2] At the beginning of 1994, several amendments to German tax law came into effect. As a consequence, the normal tax rate for corporations subject to unlimited tax liability became 45 percent on retained profits and 30 percent for distributed profits. Effective 1995, a "solidarity surcharge" of 7.5 was also introduced. After deducting the imputed tax credit attached to dividends received from German companies, the tax rates for retained earnings and distributed profits become 48.375 and 32.25 percent, respectively.

Zoltek Companies, Inc., a United States corporation, was founded in 1975 by Zsolt Rumy, a native of Hungary. Zoltek's initial operations involved the manufacture and sale of industrial equipment and related services; however, in 1987, Zoltek began its current line of business -- the manufacture of carbon fiber products. Carbon fiber composites are an attractive material for a diverse range of applications based on their distinctive characteristics that include high strength, low weight, stiffness, toughness, resistance to corrosion, resistance to fatigue, capacity to dissipate heat and electrical conductivity. Until the 1980's, the high price of carbon fibers limited their use primarily to the aerospace industry.

During the past decade, the distinctive characteristics of carbon fibers and the techniques for fabricating carbon fiber composites became more broadly understood and a number of diverse applications developed. One of the earlier non-aerospace applications was in sporting goods for such products as golf club shafts, tennis racquets and bicycle frames. Today, approximately 50 percent of Zoltek's carbon fibers revenue is still derived from two customers, B.F. Goodrich and TRW, for use in aircraft brakes and automobile airbags, respectively.

Zoltek's strategy as a recognized leader in carbon fiber technology strategy is to manufacture and market carbon fibers at price points substantially lower than those generally prevailing in the industry, by becoming the low cost producer of carbon fibers used in current specialty markets and by working with customers to develop new, broad market applications. New commercial applications identified by Zoltek include cargo shipping containers, vehicle drive shafts, compressed natural gas tanks, civil engineering uses including wrappings for bridge abutments and structural supports, wood laminates, high strength piping, marine uses and alternative energy systems. Zoltek already serves specialty niche markets such as fire-retardant coatings and specialty friction products.

Currently, Zoltek has over three million pounds of carbon fiber capacity, slightly over 10 percent of worldwide capacity. Because of the potential for new applications and indications of much greater needs in the coming years for their existing client base, Zoltek has made aggressive plans to expand capacity to 50 million pounds and reduce costs through acquisition of a reliable, low-cost, source of acrylic fiber, which constitutes approximately 50 percent of the manufactured cost of carbon fiber. A key part of those plans involves the acquisition of Magyar Viscosa Rt. ("Viscosa"), a Hungarian manufacturer of acrylic and nylon fibers. Through Viscosa, Zoltek also expects to attain a strategic advantage over its competition by providing access to the technology underlying important raw materials, and an advantageous location to expand carbon fiber manufacturing capacity.

To acquire Viscosa, Zoltek plans to affect a secondary public offering of stock for $26.3 million (U.S.). $17.8 million will be used to acquire 95 percent of the assets of Viscosa along with certain liabilities, the remaining $8.5 million will be used for Viscosa's working capital needs and corporate capital expenditures. The 5 percent of Viscosa not purchased will be owned by Viscosa's employees.

Zoltek shares trade on the over-the-counter Nasdaq National Market. Share prices have fluctuated significantly in the weeks leading up to the planned secondary public offering. Exhibit 1 contains a history of these price movements. Exhibit 2 contains recent financial statements for Zoltek.

Background of the Viscosa Acquisition

Viscosa's predecessor was founded in April of 1941 in Budapest, Hungary, as a private company to produce rayon fiber, cellophane and rayon sponge. It was nationalized in 1948 and established as the Hungarian National Synthetic Fibers Company.

As a consequence of the discontinuance of financial support for most of Hungary's industrial companies associated with the country's move to privatize many of its previously state-controlled businesses, Viscosa's predecessor declared bankruptcy in November of 1992. Effective June 30, 1993, the former state-run company was transformed into a joint-stock company whose sole owner was the Hungarian State Property Agency (SPA). The SPA was charged with the task of restructuring Viscosa and preparing it for privatization.

Since June of 1993, Viscosa has issued additional shares from time to time to raise capital, principally by the conversion of debt obligations. As a final step to prepare Viscosa for privatization, in December 1994, the SPA caused state-owned bank lenders to consolidate their debt, and approximately $14 million of debt was forgiven. At present, the SPA owns approximately 54% of Viscosa's outstanding equity. Of the remaining equity, approximately 26% is owned by a consortium of three banks, 11 % by another state institute, 7% by two banks and a brokerage firm and the remaining 2% by three trade creditors.

In December 1994, the initial privatization tender invitation was advertised. Zoltek responded and was awarded the opportunity to negotiate the proposed acquisition. Over several months, Zoltek negotiated agreements with the SPA and Viscosa's other shareholders and lenders to effect the acquisition.

Required:

1. Assuming that the following events took place on July 1, 1995 (they actually took place around the end of November), prepare a pro forma consolidated balance sheet for Zoltek as of this date:

    •   Zoltek consummated its secondary public offering of common stock.

    •   Zoltek used a portion of the proceeds of its stock issuance to acquire 95 percent of the outstanding shares of Viscosa (the remaining 5 percent is owned by employees) for $17.8 million. The selling shareholders retained and/or forgave the liabilities for capital lease obligations and long-term debt. Except for inventories, the book values of Viscosa's assets approximate their fair value. The historical cost of inventory overstates its replacement cost by 96 million Hungarian forints (HUF). Zoltek believes that accrued expenses of Viscosa are understated by HUF500 million for the correction of deferred maintenance conditions, employee severance, enhancements of environmental compliance systems and termination of a third-party management consulting contract.

    •   On July 1, 1995, the exchange rate was approximately $1 U.S. : 123 HUF.

2. Describe the future accounting and economic foreign exchange exposure that Zoltek is likely to face as a result of the Viscosa acquisition and recommend strategies for dealing with this exposure.

3. To the maximum extent permitted by the data in the case, recommend an offering price for Zoltek's shares. Identify the qualitative and quantitative factors that you considered in making this recommendation.

Exhibit 1
Zoltek Daily Closing Share Prices

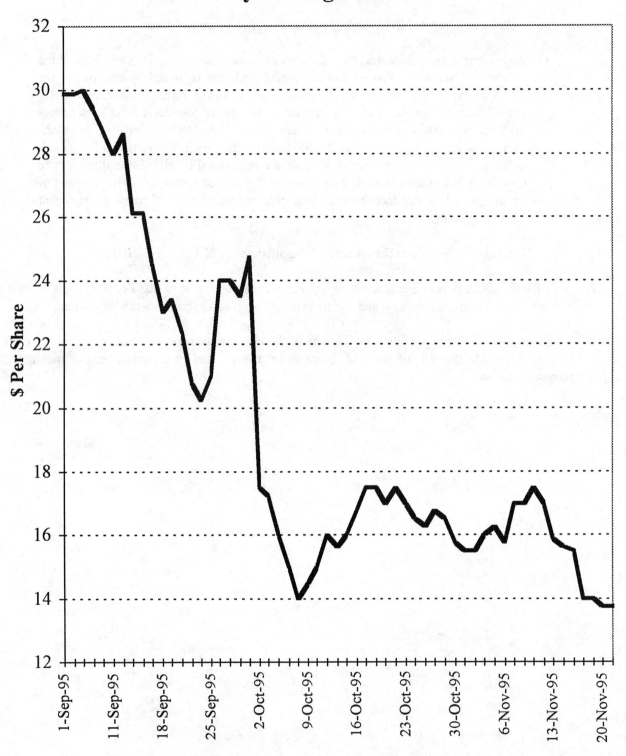

Exhibit 2
ZOLTEK COMPANIES
CONSOLIDATED BALANCE SHEET

ASSETS		Sept. 30, 1994		June 30, 1995
Current Assets:				
Cash	$	156,496	$	201,650
Accounts receivable, net		2,934,882		2,510,361
Inventories		3,657,924		3,425,489
Prepaid expenses		45,810		113,207
Refundable income taxes		200,820		1,818
Assets held for sale				2,089,693
Total current assets	$	6,995,932	$	6,995,932
Property and equipment, net		10,312,366		9,224,969
Loan origination and deferred costs		63,927		98,848
Other assets		500		500
Total assets	$	17,372,725	$	17,666,535

LIABILITIES AND SHAREHOLDERS' EQUITY				
Current liabilities:				
Revolving credit agreement	$	1,027,969		
Current maturities of long-term debt		633,702		728,240
Trade accounts payable		1,105,659		913,108
Accrued expenses		289,027		246,453
Income taxes payable		73,461		175,489
Total current liabilities	$	3,129,818	$	2,063,290
Deferred income taxes		580,000		580,000
Long-term debt, less current maturities		6,562,446		6,384,069
Shareholders' equity:				
Common stock, $.01 par value, 8,000,000 shares authorized, 3,100,000; 3,128,570; and 4,813,203 shares issued and outstanding respectively		31,285		48,132
Additional paid-in capital		3,823,342		4,102,336
Retained earnings		3,245,834		4,488,708
	$	7,100,461	$	8,639,176
Total liabilities and shareholders' equity	$	17,372,725	$	17,666,535

Exhibit 2 — Continued

ZOLTEK COMPANIES, INC.
CONSOLIDATED STATEMENT OF OPERATIONS

	Year Ended September 30, 1994	Nine Months Ended June 30, 1994	Nine Months Ended June 30, 1995
Net sales	$ 7,920,651	$ 5,826,027	$ 8,674,542
Cost of sales	4,502,263	3,371,844	5,117,932
Gross profit	3,418,388	2,454,183	3,556,610
Selling, general and administrative expenses	1,624,327	1,218,233	1,332,425
Income (loss) from continuing operations	1,794,061	1,235,950	2,224,185
Other income (expense):			
Interest expense	(616,608)	(445,936)	(561,784)
Interest income			11,644
Other, net	2,988	2,470	2,108
Income (loss) from continuing operations before income taxes	1,180,441	792,484	1,676,153
Provision (benefit) for income taxes	381,839	293,744	626,948
Net income (loss) from continuing operations	798,602	498,740	1,049,205
Income from discontinued operations, net of income taxes	208,006	151,617	209,713
Net income (loss)	$ 1,006,608	$ 650,357	$ 1,258,918
Net income (loss) per share:			
Income (loss) from continuing operations	$ 0.17	$ 0.11	$ 0.22
Discontinued operations	0.05	0.03	0.04
Net income (loss) per share	$ 0.22	$ 0.14	$ 0.26
Weighted average common shares outstanding	4,656,795	4,654,076	4,784,144

Exhibit 2 — Concluded

ZOLTEK COMPANIES, INC.
CONSOLIDATED STATEMENT OF CASH FLOWS

	Year Ended September 30, 1994	Nine Months Ended June 30, 1994	Nine Months Ended June 30, 1995
Cash flows from operating activities:			
Net income(loss)	$ 1,006,608	$ 650,357	$ 1,258,918
Adjustments to reconcile net income (loss) to net cash provided by operating activities:			
Depreciation	949,978	685,751	790,361
Changes in assets and liabilities:			
(Increase) decrease in accounts receivable	(815,423)	20,934	424,521
(Increase) decrease in inventories	(701,393)	(480,857)	(1,554,816)
(Increase) decrease in prepaid expenses	22,770	(55,728)	(67,397)
(Increase) decrease in refundable income taxes	(145,509)	55,311	199,002
Increase (decrease) in trade accounts payable	(335,805)	214,428	(192,551)
Increase (decrease) in accrued expenses	(6,013)	(23,562)	(42,574)
Increase in income taxes payable	73,461	70,640	102,028
Increase (decrease) in deferred income taxes	315,038	5,000	
Total adjustments	$ (642,896)	$ 491,917	$ (341,426)
Net cash provided by operating activities	$ 363,712	$ 1,142,274	$ 917,492
Cash flows from investing activities:			
Payments for purchase of property and equipment	(1,135,155)	(1,071,070)	(590,977)
Usage of proceeds from industrial revenue bonds			
Net cash used in investing activities	$ (1,135,155)	$ (1,071,070)	$ (590,977)
Cash flows from financing activities			
Net increase (decrease) in line of credit borrowings	(1,359,567)	(697,122)	(1,027,969)
Net proceeds from sale of common stock			
Proceeds from exercise of stock options and warrants	158,279	16,947	279,797
Proceeds from issuance of notes payable	5,297,500	1,210,500	5,650,000
Repayment of notes payable	(3,147,614)	(505,087)	(5,148,268)
Increase in loan origination costs and deferred costs	(63,927)	(62,685)	(34,921)
(Increase) decrease in deferred offering costs			
Net cash provided by(used in)financing activities	$ 884,671	$ (37,447)	$ (281,361)
Net increase(decrease)in cash	113,228	33,757	45,154

Exhibit 3

MAGYAR VISCOSA, RT.
CONSOLIDATED BALANCE SHEET

	December 31,1994 (HUF 000)		June 30,1995 (HUF 000)	
ASSETS				
Current assets:				
Cash	HUF	94,113	HUF	95,636
Securities		10,373		50
Accounts receivable, net		629,913		832,575
Other receivables		226,908		180,996
Inventory		930,653		912,678
Prepaid expenses		12,980		21,086
Total current assets		1,904,940		2,043,021
Property and equipment, net		5,317,500		5,098,793
Other assets:				
Investments		74,825		74,825
Intangibles, net		43,664		40,981
Loan receivables		25,818		20,890
Total assets	HUF	7,366,747	HUF	7,278,510
LIABILITIES AND SHAREHOLDERS' EQUITY				
Current liabilities:				
Accounts payable	HUF	849,288	HUF	1,299,734
Current maturities of long-term debt		235,213		680,736
Income taxes payable		38,206		38,206
Current portion of obligation under capital lease		337,709		741,529
Other short-term liabilities		319,630		299,564
Total current liabilities		1,780,046		3,059,769
Long-term capital lease obligation		1,581,064		1,596,968
Long-term debt, less current maturities		618,700		124,462
Other long-term liabilities		189,641		185,569
Shareholders' equity:				
Preferred stock, stated par, 110,000 shares authorized, issued and outstanding		1,100,000		1,100,000
Common stock, stated par, 117,618 shares authorized, issued and outstanding		1,176,180		1,176,180
Additional paid-in capital		974,802		974,792
Accumulated deficit		(53,686)		(939,230)
Total shareholders' equity	HUF	3,197,296	HUF	2,311,742
Total liabilities and shareholders' equity	HUF	7,366,747	HUF	7,278,510

Exhibit 3 — Continued

MAGYAR VISCOSA, RT.

CONSOLIDATED STATEMENT OF OPERATIONS

	Six Months Ended Dec. 31, 1993 (HUF 000)	Year Ended Dec. 31, 1994 (HUF 000)	Six Months Ended June 30, 1995 (HUF 000)
Net sales	HUF 2,486,731	HUF 5,282,460	HUF 3,147,553
Cost of sales	2,092,838	4,609,527	2,867,121
Gross profit	393,893	672,933	280,432
Selling, general and administrative expenses	551,303	1,210,638	529,718
Operating loss	(157,410)	(537,705)	(249,286)
Other income (expense):			
Interest income	18,831	27,872	7,908
Other income	454,624	75,195	3,327
Interest expense	(182,557)	(306,405)	(106,882)
Foreign currency loss	(311,119)	(402,220)	(538,749)
Other expense	(20,221)	(605,558)	(634,396)
Loss before income taxes	(177,631)	(1,143,263)	(883,682)
Income tax provision		(38,206)	(1,862)
Loss before extraordinary items	(177,631)	(1,181,469)	(885,544)
Extraordinary expense, loss on sale of flats		(232,753)	
Extraordinary income, debt restructuring		1,519,565	
Net income (loss)	HUF (177,631)	HUF 105,343	HUF (885,544)

333

Exhibit 3 — Concluded

MAGYAR VISCOSA, RT.
CONSOLIDATED STATEMENT OF CASH FLOWS

	Six Months Ended Dec. 31, 1993		Year Ended Dec. 31, 1994		Six Months Ended June 30, 1995	
	(HUF 000)		(HUF 000)		(HUF 000)	
Cash flows from operating activities:						
Net income (loss)	HUF	(177,631)	HUF	105,343	HUF	(885,544)
Adjustments to reconcile net income (loss) to net cash provided by operating activities:						
Extraordinary gain, debt restructuring				(1,519,565)		
Extraordinary loss, sale of flats				232,753		
Unrealized exchange loss		335,845		323,332		558,376
Unrealized exchange gain		(51,741)		(38,812)		(44,384)
Depreciation and amortization		248,839		509,791		253,817
Write off investments				5,000		
(Gain) loss on fixed asset sales		(3,397)		(3,181)		1,362
Other		2,553		(2,229)		737
Provision for doubtful accounts		7,508		81,007		6,395
Provision for inventories		17,732		55,361		10,310
Provision for early retirements		42,801				
Changes in assets and liabilities:						
(Increase) decrease in receivables		61,995		4,268		(113,833)
(Increase) decrease in inventories		(235,082)		18,188		7,665
(Increase) decrease in prepaid expenses		12,707		5,931		(8,105)
Increase in payables		31,444		259,223		327,512
Decrease in other liabilities		(31,923)		(36,187)		(7,903)
Total adjustments	HUF	439,281	HUF	(105,120)	HUF	991,949
Net cash provided by operating activities		261,650		223		106,405
Cash flows from investing activities:						
Payments for purchase of property and equipment		(68,582)		(114,154)		(35,032)
Proceeds from fixed asset sales		7,086		14,125		444
Proceeds (purchase) of investments				(11,373)		10,373
Net cash used by investing activities		(61,496)		(111,402)		(24,215)
Cash flows from financing activities:						
Proceeds from issuance of notes payable				191,048		176,221
Repayment of notes payable		(91,660)		(129,080)		(256,888)
Payment of finance lease		(88,521)		(200,909)		
Net cash used by financing activities		(180,181)		(138,941)		(80,667)
Net increase (decrease) in cash	HUF	19,973	HUF	(250,120)	HUF	1,523

Exhibit 4
Hungarian Forint Exchange Rates

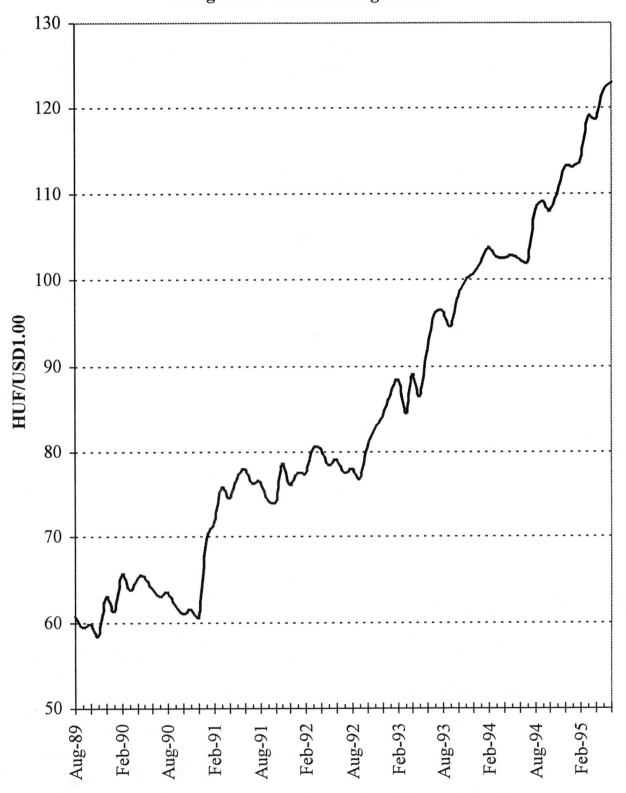

BENETTON GROUP S.P.A. [*]

Benetton Group S.p.A. is a well-known manufacturer of casual apparel which it markets under the brand name The United Colors of Benetton. The company was founded in 1965 by the Benetton family in Ponzano Veneto, Italy, and became a public company in 1978. In 1989, the company made its first public offering of American depository receipts, each representing two ordinary shares (par value L 500), which trade on the NYSE; consequently, the company files a form 20-F (annual report) with the S.E.C. Presented below are excerpts from Benetton's 1993 20-F filing. Exhibit 1 contains a "summary of significant accounting policies" used in the preparation of Benetton's 1993 financial statements, whereas Exhibit 2 excerpts the company's report relating to its reconciliation of net income and stockholders' equity under Italian GAAP versus U.S. GAAP. Exhibit 3 provides information regarding Benetton's changes in shareholders' equity.

Required:

1. Review the accounting policies utilized by the Benetton Group (see Exhibit 1) and indicate where (and how) they differ from policies under U.S. GAAP.

2. (a) Using the information in Exhibit 2, recreate the journal entries necessary to (1) revalue Benetton's fixed assets and trademarks and (2) write off purchased goodwill to stockholders' equity.

   (b) Compare and contrast Benetton's return on equity under Italian GAAP with its return on equity under U.S. GAAP. What generalizations can you draw about the profitability of Italian companies under Italian GAAP versus U.S. companies under U.S. GAAP.

3. Using the information in Exhibit 3, explain (using journal entries) the changes in Benetton's stockholders' equity accounts from year-end 1992 to year-end 1993.

Exhibit 1
Benetton Group S.p.A.
Summary of Significant Accounting Policies

- **Form and content of consolidated financial statements**

  The financial statements conform to the accounting policies established by the Italian accounting profession, and are reclassified in accordance with the standards generally followed in international practice. In addition, the financial statements of minor subsidiaries located in highly inflationary countries are restated to reflect changes in the purchasing power of the local currencies in accordance with inflation accounting policies.

- **Consolidation policy**

  The difference between the cost and appropriate fair market value of stockholders' equity of subsidiary companies at the time they were acquired (goodwill) was recorded directly to consolidated equity.

- **Foreign Currency Translation policies**

  The financial statements of foreign subsidiaries, including those operating in countries with hyper-inflationary economies are translated into Italian lire using end-of-period exchange rates for balance sheet items and the average exchange rate for the period for income statement items. Any translation differences are reflected directly in consolidated stockholders' equity (i.e., the Exchange Fluctuation Reserve).

- **Marketable securities**

  Marketable securities are stated at lower-of-cost-or-market value at the balance sheet date. Securities subject to resale commitments are recorded at cost.

- **Inventories**

  Inventories are stated at the lowest of cost, on a weighted average basis, or net realizable value.

- **Investments**

  Investments of between 20% and 50% in associated companies are accounted for on an equity basis. Less significant investments are valued at cost.

- **Fixed assets**

  Fixed assets are recorded at either purchase or construction cost. Revaluation of the majority of those assets in accordance with Italian Law No. 72 of 19 March 1983 occurred as of 31 December 1983. Real estate holdings were revalued under Law No. 413 as of 31 December 1991. Depreciation is computed on a straight-line basis using rates that reflect the estimated useful lives of the assets.

- **Trademarks**

  Trademarks are stated at registration or purchase cost, revalued at 31 December 1983. The related revaluation surplus was credited to a specific stockholders' equity reserve.

- **Income taxes**

  Current income taxes are provided for on the basis of a reasonable estimate of the liability for the year. Deferred taxes, principally arising from the reversal of excess depreciation and from lease accounting adjustments, are also provided for.

- **Reserve for termination indemnities**

  The majority of the company's employees are covered by a plan required under Italian law and labor contracts which grant a termination indemnity based on compensation and years of service. As is normal in Italy, the Group has accrued the amount due to each employee as of year-end, but does not fund this liability.

- **Revenue recognition**

  Revenue from product sales are recognized at the time of shipment, which represents the moment when ownership passes.

- **Expense recognition**

  Expenses are recorded in accordance with the matching principle. Advertising costs are charged to income in the year in which they are incurred.

Exhibit 2
Benetton Group S.p.A.
Reconciliation of Net Income and Stockholders' Equity:
Italian vs. U.S. GAAP

Differences which have an effect on net income and stockholders' equity:

- Revaluation of Fixed Assets and Trademarks
  In 1991 and prior years, certain categories of property, plant and equipment and trademarks were revalued to amounts in excess of historical cost. This procedure, which was authorized by Italian law, was allowed under Italian accounting practice to give consideration to the effects of local inflation. Revaluations (totaling L46,222 million) were credited to stockholders' equity and revalued assets are depreciated over their remaining useful lives on a straight-line basis.

- Accounting for Goodwill
  In prior years, goodwill on investments acquired were charged or credited to stockholders' equity at the date of purchase. The adjustment in the accompanying reconciliation has been made to recognize the goodwill on acquisitions, originally amounting to L11,519 million. Goodwill is amortized over a 10 year period, corresponding to the estimated useful lives of the underlying assets acquired. The relevant decrease in 1992 is due to the sale of the company's interest in Prince Holdings, Inc., and the consequent reversal of the related goodwill.

	Year Ended December 31 (lire, millions)		
	1991	*1992*	*1993*
Net income, per Italian GAAP	164,783	184,709	208,038
Reduction in depreciation and amortization on revalued fixed assets and trademarks	2,067	2,575	3,134
Amortization of goodwill	(6,724)	(338)	(1,252)
Net income per U.S. GAAP	160,126	186,946	209,920
Stockholders' equity per Italian GAAP	716,532	922,761	1,063,278
Elimination of revaluations of fixed assets and trademarks	(19,494)	(16,919)	(13,785)
Reinstatement of goodwill previously written off	57,101	7,295	6,043
Stockholders' equity per U.S. GAAP	754,139	913,137	1,055,536

Exhibit 3
Benetton Group S.p.A.

. Statement of Changes in Consolidated Stockholders' Equity
For the Years ended December 31, 1991, 1992, and 1993
(in millions of lire)

	Capital Stock	Additional Paid-in Capital	Surplus from Monetary Revaluation of Assets	Other Reserves and Prior Years' Retained Earnings	New Income for the Year	Total
BALANCES AS OF DECEMBER 31, 1990	81,777	186,661	19,118	165,776	133,271	586,603
Allocation of 1990 net income to reserves	—	—	—	133,271	(133,271)	—
Dividends distributed, as approved at the stockholders' meeting of April 30, 1991	—	—	—	(40,888)	—	(40,888)
Effect of monetary revaluation	—	—	27,104	(23,074)	—	4,030
Differences arising from the translation of foreign currency financial statements	—	—	—	2,004	—	2,004
Net income for the year	—	—	—	—	164,783	164,783
BALANCES AS OF DECEMBER 31, 1991	81,777	186,661	46,222	237,089	164,783	716,532
Allocation of 1991 net income to reserves	—	—	—	164,783	(164,783)	—
Dividends distributed, as approved at the stockholders' meeting of April 29, 1992	—	—	—	(49,066)	—	(49,066)
Disposal of Prince Holdings Inc.: recovery of goodwill on acquisition previously charged against consolidation reserves	—	—	—	56,534	—	56,534
Differences arising from the translation of foreign currency financial statements	—	—	—	14,052	—	14,052
Net income for the year	—	—	—	—	184,709	184,709
BALANCES AS OF DECEMBER 31,1992	81,777	186,661	46,222	423,392	184,709	922,761
Allocation of 1992 net income to reserves	—	—	—	184,709	(184,709)	—
Dividends distributed, as approved at the stockholders' meeting held on April 29, 1993	—	—	—	(57,244)	—	(57,244)
Differences arising from the translation of foreign currency financial statements	—	—	—	(10,277)	—	(10,277)
Net income for the year	—	—	—	—	208,038	208,038
BALANCES OF DEC. 31, 1993	81,777	186,661	46,222	540,580	208,038	1,063,278

The company's footnotes to the 20-F report also contained the following information about "Other Reserves," which are aggregated with retained earnings:

Other Reserves are as follows (lire, in millions):

	31 December	
	1992	*1993*
Exchange fluctuation reserve	20,055	55,561
Risk reserve	14,210	7,099
Taxation reserve	—	7,580
Reserve for agents' termination indemnities	8,992	9,219
	43,257	79,459

The exchange fluctuation reserve reflects the net effect of adjusting foreign currency balances of payables and receivables of the Italian companies in the Group using year-end exchange rates.

The risk reserve prudently covers various business contingencies, including outstanding legal cases.

The taxation reserve prudently covers liabilities which may arise on the final settlement of outstanding tax disputes with the authorities.

Luxottica Group S.p.A. is an Italian-based corporation involved in the design, manufacture, distribution, and marketing of traditional and designer lines of frames for eyeglasses and sunglasses. The company's products which include more than 700 traditional eyeglass frame styles and over 500 designer frame styles, are principally manufactured in Italy and are distributed worldwide by a variety of wholly-owned foreign subsidiaries.

The company's shares trade on the New York Stock Exchange via American Depository receipts (one ADR is equivalent to one ordinary Luxottica share, par value of L 1,000) under the symbol LUX. Consequently, Luxottica files form 20-F with the Securities and Exchange Commission to report its annual financial results and form 6-K to report its quarterly financial results.

Exhibit 1 presents the company's balance sheet for the years ended 31 December, 1992 and 1993 as they appeared in its 20-F filing with the S.E.C. The following information was also revealed in that filing:

- 1993 net income of L 91,914 million.

- At the company's annual shareholders' meeting in April 1993, cash dividends of L 27,030 million were approved and were subsequently paid in July. Italian civil code requires that 5 percent of net income be retained as a legal reserve until this reserve is equal to one-fifth of the issued share capital.

- Part of Luxottica's property, plant, and equipment was revalued in accordance with the provisions of Italian Laws No. 576 as of December 2, 1975, No. 72 as of March 19, 1985, and No. 413 as of December 30, 1991.[1] The revaluation was undertaken to partially account for the change in the purchasing power of money (i.e., monetary revaluation). 1993 Depreciation and amortization amounted to L 24,695 million.

- Currency translation effects of L 21,748 million (relating to the translation of foreign subsidiary financial statements into the Italian lire, the functional currency), was recorded directly in retained earnings.

- Goodwill, the excess purchase price paid in the acquisition of another company over the fair market value of identifiable assets acquired less liabilities assumed, is amortized over a 10 year period. (Under Italian GAAP, purchased goodwill is usually recorded as an asset and amortized over a 5 to 10 year period, although it is permissible to immediately write-off goodwill against retained earnings.)

---

[*] This case was prepared by Kenneth R. Ferris. Copyright © 1995 by Kenneth R. Ferris. All rights reserved.

[1] On December 31, 1991 (effective January 1, 1992), the Italian government passed a law requiring the compulsory revaluation of industrial buildings. This revaluation resulted in a net write-up of the carrying value of assets and, accordingly, an increased charge for depreciation over a building's remaining useful life, such lives approximating 15 years. For financial reporting purposes, building costs and accumulated depreciation were increased by a like amount, resulting in no net write-up to either fixed assets or shareholders' equity.

The company's intangible asset balances of L 32,721 million and L 28,207 million at year-end 1992 and 1993, respectively, were composed as follows:

	December 31	
	1992	*1993*
Goodwill which arose in connection with the acquisition of the remaining 50% interest in Luxottica United Kingdom—net of amortization of L 300 million and L 450 million at December 31, 1992 and 1993, respectively.	1,197	1,047
Goodwill which arose in connection with the acquisition of Florence Line S.r.l.—net of accumulated amortization of L 3,237 million and L 4,316 million at December 31, 1992 and 1993, respectively.	7,554	6,475
Goodwill which arose in connection with the acquisition of Fidia S.p.A.—net of accumulated amortization of L 4,253 million and L 5,672 million at December 31, 1992 and 1993, respectively.	9,925	8,506
Goodwill which arose from the acquisition of the remaining 50% interest in Avant Garde Optics Inc. net of accumulated amortization of L 22,736 million and L 25,984 million at December 31, 1992 and 1993, respectively.	9,744	6,496
Other, principally trademarks net of accumulated amortization	4,301	5,683
Total	32,721	28,207

The company's footnotes also revealed the following in regard to its "commitments and contingencies":

The company is obligated under noncancelable distribution agreements with designers which expire at various dates through 2002. In accordance with the provisions of such agreements, the Company is required to pay royalty and advertising fees based on a percentage of sales with, in certain agreements, minimum guarantees of such payments in each year of the agreements. Minimum payments required in each of the years subsequent to December 31, 1993 aggregated Lire 17,207 million, Lire 17,907 million, Lire 12,863 million and Lire 10,360 million in each of 1994, 1995, 1996, and 1997 respectively.

A subsidiary of the Company leases factory and office space under an agreement which expires in 2005 and provides for minimum annual rentals of approximately Lire 603 million.

Years ending December 31,	
1994	603
1995–1998	2,411
1999–2005	4,149
TOTAL	7,163

Required:

1. Using the available information, prepare a statement of cash flows for 1993 for Luxottica and comment on the company's financial health vis-à-vis its cash flows.

2. (a) Calculate the required value of Luxottica's legal reserve. Where would you expect this reserve to be disclosed? Do you think that the legal reserve constrained Luxottica's ability to declare dividends?

(b) Use journal entries to explain how the account Surplus from Monetary Revaluations of Assets was created and why it declined from 1992 to 1993.

3.   Restate Luxottica's 1993 net income and balance sheet assuming the following:

(a)   A 40-year amortization period for goodwill (as per U.S. GAAP).

(b) The direct write-off of goodwill against retained earnings (as per Italian GAAP).

4.   (a) Based on the available information, calculate the present value of Luxottica's commitments under its (1) distribution agreements and (2) lease agreements.

(b) Assume that the noncancelable distribution and lease agreements should be capitalized to the company's balance sheet. Calculate Luxottica's long-term debt to equity both with and without capitalization of the commitments. Does capitalization materially affect the company's solvency?

Exhibit 1

LUXOTTICA GROUP S.p.A. AND SUBSIDIARIES
Consolidated Balance Sheets
December 31, 1992 and 1993

Assets	(millions of lire)	
	1992	1993
Current assets		
Cash	48,390	30,568
Marketable securities	16,741	77,373
Accounts receivable		
Less: Allowance for doubtful accounts, L 3,776 and L 4,565, respectively)	135,732	168,928
Sales and income taxes receivable	12,507	5,150
Inventories	88,345	88,870
Prepaid expenses and other	7,167	19,895
Deferred income tax benefits	10,488	8,142
Total current assets	319,370	398,926
Property, plant and equipment—net	122,335	139,449
Other assets		
Intangible assets-net	32,721	28,207
Investments	803	705
Security deposits and other	1,308	1,365
Sales and income taxes receivables	2,081	2,915
Total other assets	36,913	33,192
Total	478,618	571,567

Liabilities and Shareholders' Equity	(millions of lire)	
	1992	1993
Current liabilities		
Bank overdrafts	54,138	39,341
Current portion of long-term debt	2,400	10,890
Accounts payable	35,381	59,669
Accrued expenses and other	36,557	40,847
Accrual for customers' right of return	5,148	6,791
Income taxes payable	24,008	5,881
Total current liabilities	157,632	163,419
Long-term debt	20,450	14,181 *
Liability for termination indemnities	17,553	21,100
Deferred income taxes	20,698	22,970
Minority interests in consolidated subsidiaries	3,078	5,695
Shareholders' equity		
Capital stock; par value L 1,000 − 45,050,000 ordinary shares authorized and issued, 44,584,500 shares outstanding	45,050	45,050
Surplus from monetary revaluations of assets	7,828	6,191
Retained earnings	223,788	310,420
Total	276,666	361,661
Less: Treasury shares at cost	17,459	17,459
Shareholders' equity	259,207	344,202
Total	478,618	571,567

* The long-term debt reflects notes payable to banks, with interest payable at 9 to 13 percent, depending on maturity, and payable in installments through 2000.

Strategic alliances refer to those formal relationships between business entities, entered into with the explicit goal of protecting or enhancing marketshare. These contractual relations may be as simple as a written agreement not to compete in a particular marketplace, or as complex as a full integration of operations and product-lines. Strategic alliances can be particularly effective in those industries wherein the barriers to entry are significant because such agreements provide a relatively low cost approach to market penetration and/or protection. This case concerns the accounting for such alliances in one such industry -- the airline industry.

Air transportation remains one of the most regulated, yet privatized industries worldwide. Not only are the permitted flying hours of a commercial pilot often set by governmental regulation, but so are the allowable flying hours of an aircraft engine between required maintenance. Some of the most critical regulations from a business perspective, however, involve access to passenger markets. Governments control not only which airlines fly to and from a given passenger-market place, but also how frequently, often by merely controlling the allocation and distribution of airport docking-gates. International airlines face the added constraint of governmental politics -- access to foreign passengers may be obtained or denied solely on the basis of the existing political climate. Thus, international air carriers in particular find the use of strategic alliances beneficial as a means to overcome barriers to entry to foreign-passenger marketplaces.

Accounting Issues

The accounting for strategic alliances is as diverse as the agreements themselves. Noncompete agreements, for example, wherein one entity agrees not to seek access to a particular market in return for a similar commitment from another entity, are rarely if ever disclosed on the face of the financial statements. The value of these commitments cannot be measured with reasonable certainty, and in most cases, no existing assets or consideration are exchanged. Where a noncomplete agreement is perceived to have material value to an entity, it may be disclosed in the footnotes to the financial statements; and, where consideration is given or received as part of the alliance, some accounting recognition of the receipt or disbursement will be required.

More frequently, strategic alliances are entered into as a means to increase revenue flows and/or reduce costs. In the airline industry, this may involve linking route networks through codesharing, joint sales efforts, and joint frequent-flyer programs.[1] This type of alliance is usually accompanied by a significant equity investment. When one entity makes an investment in another, the accounting for that investment is often dictated by the size and intent of the investment. For example, for relatively small equity investments (e.g. 0-20% of the voting shares), the investor may use either the **cost method** (i.e. in China), the **lower of cost or market method** (i.e. in Canada, France, Germany, and Korea), or the **mark-to-market method** (i.e. in Argentina, Israel, and the U.S.), to account for its investment. When an entity makes a sufficiently large investment in another, such that the investor company can influence the operating decisions of the investee (e.g. 20-50% of the voting shares), most countries require that the investment be

---

* This case was prepared by Kenneth R. Ferris. Copyright © 1996 by the American Graduate School of International Management. All rights reserved.
[1] For example, as a direct result of this type of agreement, British Airways increased its USAir passenger traffic by 104 percent in one year alone (1994).

accounted for using the **equity method**.[2] Under the equity method, an investor's initial investment is subsequently increased (decreased) by the investor's proportionate share of the investee's earnings (losses), and is decreased by any dividend distributions made by the investee.

A strategic alliance, however, may also be evidenced by the creation of an entirely new entity, such as a joint venture. Joint ventures are most frequently accounted for using either the equity method or **proportionate consolidation** (e.g., see IAS No. 31). Under proportionate (or partial) consolidation, the investor consolidates its percentage ownership interest in the joint venture's assets, liabilities, and net earnings (or losses) with its own financial results.[3]

British Airways

British Airways, headquartered at London's Heathrow Airport, is the world's largest scheduled international passenger airline. In 1994, the airline ranked first both in terms of the number of international scheduled passengers carried and in terms of international scheduled revenue passenger kilometers. British Airways (BA) operates one the world's most extensive international scheduled airline route networks, comprising approximately 169 destinations in 80 countries.

As part of the airline's global strategy, BA has entered into a number of strategic alliances in the major markets of continental Europe, the Pacific region, and the United States. In 1993, for example, BA invested £263.7 million in convertible preferred stock in USAir and £304 million in Qantas, Australia's principal international air carrier. Additional investments in Deutsche BA Luftfahrtgesellschaft mbH (Deutsche BA) and TAT European Airlines S.A. (TAT), France's leading independent airline, were made in 1992 and 1993, respectively. The nature and status of these strategic investments is described further in Exhibit 1.

Questions:

1. How did BA account for its investments in Deutsche BA, Qantas, TAT, and USAir at year-end 1994? 1995? What changes in accounting occurred, and why?

2. Comment on the effect of FRS No. 5, "Reporting the Substance of Transactions" on BA's accounting for aircraft leases (see footnote no. 1). How did FRS No. 5 affect BA's debt position?

---

[2] Countries not requiring the use of the equity method for such investments include China, Indonesia, Sweden, and Switzerland.
[3] Proportionate consolidation, which is premised on the notion of "ownership", differs from **full consolidation,** which is premised on the notion of "control". Under full consolidation, even though an investor may own only, say, 75 percent of an investee's voting shares, the investor will consolidate 100 percent of the investee's net assets, using a "minority interest" account to reflect the value of those consolidated-but-unowned net assets. Under proportionate consolidation, however, only the value of the net assets actually owned are consolidated, eliminating the need for a minority interest account.

Strategic Investments

Investment in USAir

In January 1993, British Airways agreed terms for a new alliance between BA and USAir. The first stage was completed with the investment by the Group of $300 million (£198 million) in new convertible preferred stock of USAir and the signing of a flight codesharing agreement. Sir Colin Marshall (Chairman), Derek Stevens (Chief Financial Officer) and Roger Maynard (Director of Corporate Strategy) joined the 15-member USAir Board. The Group also agreed in early 1993 to invest an additional $100.7 million in convertible preferred stock of USAir pursuant to the exercise of pre-emption rights following the exercise of employee options and the public offering by USAir of $231 million (net) of common stock in the US market.

In recent years, USAir has been, and continues to be, affected by competition from low-cost, low-fare airlines in its principal geographic market area in the northeast United States. USAir has incurred operating losses in every year since 1990 and had a net capital deficiency at December 31, 1994. The payment of dividends on USAir's convertible preferred stocks was suspended in September 1994.

In the year ended December 31, 1994, USAir reported a loss before tax of $684.9 million on operating revenues of $6,997 million. For the six months ended June 30, 1995, USAir announced an unaudited operating income of $121 million (compared with a loss of $66 million for the comparable period in the prior year) on operating revenues of $3.7 billion and net income of $16 million (compared with a loss of $183 million for the comparable period in the prior year).

In 1994, USAir's management drew up a major restructuring program which included negotiations with unionized employees to obtain employee concessions. In the Company's Annual Report Form 20-F for fiscal 1994, it was noted that if negotiations with the leadership of the USAir's unionized employees regarding wage reductions, improved productivity and other cost savings were not successfully concluded within the timescale which the financial position of USAir required, the Directors believed that a provision for permanent diminution in value was likely to be required. The Directors have written down the carrying value of the Company's investment in USAir by 50% as at March 31, 1995. See "Item 9 — Management's Discussion and Analysis of Financial Condition and Results of Operations — Results of Operations" and Note 22 of Notes to Financial Statements. In late July 1995, negotiations with the unions reached an impasse and USAir announced its intention to concentrate its efforts to reduce labor costs through traditional collective bargaining.

Revenue benefits are generated by linking the British Airways and USAir route networks through codesharing, joint sales efforts and joint frequent flyer programs. Cost and revenue benefits from the USAir Alliance increased in line with our expectations in fiscal 1995. Combined codeshare and USAir interline connection traffic grew 104% over fiscal 1994, and USAir feed to/from BA now accounts for 42% of BA's total US carrier feed.

BA and USAir have entered into a codesharing agreement under which USAir flights from cities across the United States link with BA's trans-Atlantic services. On June 5, 1995, HM Government reached agreement with the US Government on a new "mini-deal" annex to the Bermuda 2 air service agreement which now permits codeshare services to any point in the US. See "Competition". Under the new agreement, the US Department of Transportation (the "DOT") has approved applications to add another 57 points to the 65 previously approved.

Codesharing services commenced on May 1, 1993. USAir codesharing services operate with both BA and USAir flight codes. Schedules are coordinated and through check-in has been introduced to facilitate smoother transfers for passengers and their baggage. USAir divested its routes from the United States to the United Kingdom upon implementation of the codesharing agreement, with these routes now operated under BA's route authority under a "wet lease" using USAir aircraft and crews. In June 1995, BA and USAir announced that services linking Gatwick with Charlotte, Pittsburgh and Baltimore will be flown by British Airways crews and aircraft from early next year, ending the "wet lease" agreement between the two carriers.

Investment in Qantas

On March 10, 1993, BA acquired a 25% interest in Qantas from the Australian Government for A$666 million (£304 million). Under the Australian Government's privatization plan, the remaining 75% of the shares in Qantas was offered to the public in Australia and to Australian and international institutional investors in July 1995 in an offering expected to close in early August 1995. A maximum of 49% of Qantas shares may be owned by foreign interests.

Qantas is a major carrier on the routes from Australia to Asia, the United Kingdom and Continental Europe, the United States, Southern Africa and New Zealand. At June 30, 1995, the group employed a work force of approximately 23,000 and operated a combined fleet of 136 aircraft. The average age of the core airline fleet was 6.3 years. In the financial year ended June 30, 1994, Qantas reported an operating profit before tax and abnormal losses of A$302 million on operating revenue of A$6.6 billion. Abnormal losses accounted for A$65 million relating to one-off non-operational costs. These abnormal losses and an income tax expense of A$81 million produced an after-tax profit of A$156 million compared with a loss of A$377 million, after abnormal losses of A$446 million in the previous year. As at June 30, 1994, Qantas had net assets of A$2.2 billion.

Qantas made an operating profit before tax of A$203 million on operating revenue of A$3.7 billion for the half year ended December 31, 1994. This compared with A$138 million profit for the comparable period in the prior year. The improvement was largely due to increased passenger volumes in international and domestic markets. Growth in the domestic market was particularly strong with an increase in capacity of 24% over the previous half year. This was achieved with constant seat factors, improved yields and Qantas regaining market leadership domestically. No abnormal losses were recorded in the half year and an income tax expense of A$74 million was incurred. This resulted in a group profit after tax of A$129 million compared with a profit of A$72 million for the comparable period in the prior year.

The strategic partnership between British Airways and Qantas continues to provide opportunities to enhance the range of products available to both companies' customers such as the "Global Explorer" round-the-world fares and reciprocal frequent flyer benefits between British Airways, Qantas and other members of the global alliance. Both companies are continuing to work on reducing costs by cooperating on purchasing, technical and support activities and by sharing assets and ground facilities, including shared offices in Japan and lounge facilities in Hong Kong. In particular, Qantas is currently installing the BABS computer reservation and COBRA yield management systems developed by British Airways.

TAT

In January 1993, BA invested £15 million to acquire 49.9% of TAT with an option to purchase the remaining shares, or a put option, exercisable on or after April 1997. TAT is France's leading independent airline operating, as of March 1995, to 23 destinations within France and on four international routes with a fleet principally of Fokker jet and ATR turboprop aircraft.

In the year ended March 31, 1995, TAT encountered extremely strong price competition from national airlines and, as a result, has withdrawn from almost all of its cross-border services except between France and the United Kingdom. See "Competition — Europe." The remaining international routes, Paris Orly to Heathrow, Marseille to Gatwick and Rome to Gatwick via Lyon, all provide connecting traffic to BA mainline services.

TAT has not substantially changed its domestic network but launched six daily services from Orly to Marseille in May 1995 and plans to operate from Orly to Toulouse later in 1995.

Deutsche BA

In June 1992, BA acquired 49% of Deutsche BA in a joint venture with three German banks. At the end of March 1995, Deutsche BA operated 18 domestic routes and 23 international routes with a fleet of twelve jet and nine turboprop aircraft. During the year, Deutsche BA further expanded its route network and incurred related development losses. However, the airline has secured a significant share of the German domestic air travel market.

Deutsche BA has closed its routes from Frankfurt to Paris and Munich to Ankara and commenced new routes from Munich to Gatwick and from Berlin to Vilnius and Riga. These new routes are expected to provide connecting traffic to BA mainline services.

Since March 1995, Deutsche BA has taken delivery of three SAAB 2000 50-seater turboprop aircraft. Two further aircraft are on order with delivery dates up to November 1995. These aircraft will replace the smaller SAAB 340 aircraft on a one-for-one basis.

Exhibit 2
British Airways Plc
Financial Statements: 1994-95

A. Profit and Loss Account (for the year ended 31 March 1995)

£ million	Note	1995	Group 1994*
Turnover	3	7,177	6,602
Cost of sales	4	(6,436)	(6,018)
Gross profit		741	584
Administrative expenses	4	(123)	(116)
Operating profit		618	468
Income from interests in associated undertakings	7	58	22
Other income and charges	8	1	9
Provision against investment in USAir Group, Inc.	18	(125)	
Loss on sale of fixed assets	9	(20)	(7)
Profit on sale of subsidiary undertaking	10	10	
Net interest payable	11	(215)	(212)
Profit before taxation		327	280
Before provision against investment in USAir Group, Inc.		452	
Provision against investment in USAir Group, Inc.		(125)	
Taxation	12	(77)	(6)
Profit for the year		250	274
Dividends	13	(119)	(106)
Retained profit for the year	29	131	168

	Note	1995	1994*
Earnings per share	14		
Basic earnings per share		26.2p	30.0p
Adjustment to exclude exceptional provision against investment in USAir Group, Inc.		13.1p	
Adjusted earnings per share		39.3p	30.0p
Fully diluted earnings per share		24.5p	27.6p
Adjustment to exclude exceptional provision against investment in USAir Group, Inc.		11.1p	
Fully diluted adjusted earnings per share		35.6p	27.6p
Dividends per share	13	12.40p	11.10p

* Restated in accordance with Financial Reporting Standard 5, see Note 1.

Exhibit 2
British Airways Plc
Financial Statements: 1994-95
(continued)

B.   Balance Sheets (at 31 March 1995)

£ million	Note	Group 1995	1994*	Company 1995	1994*
Fixed assets					
Tangible assets	15				
Fleet		**5,155**	*5,127*	**5,001**	*4,948*
Property		**801**	*484*	**716**	*415*
Equipment		**207**	*200*	**185**	*178*
		6,163	*5,811*	**5,902**	*5,541*
Investments	16				
Subsidiary undertakings and quasi-subsidiaries				**678**	*766*
Associated undertakings		**442**	*567*		
Trade investments		**29**	*28*	**27**	*26*
		471	*595*	**705**	*792*
		6,634	*6,406*	**6,607**	*6,333*
Current assets					
Stocks	20	**70**	*69*	**46**	*43*
Debtors	21	**1,182**	*1,130*	**1,062**	*1,083*
Short-term loans and deposits		**1,099**	*1,194*	**1,033**	*1,116*
Cash at bank and in hand		**64**	*40*	**48**	*25*
		2,415	*2,433*	**2,189**	*2,267*
Creditors: amounts falling due within one year	23	**(2,320)**	*(2,114)*	**(2,261)**	*(1,998)*
Net current assets/(liabilities)		**95**	*319*	**(72)**	*269*
Total assets less current liabilities		**6,729**	*6,725*	**6,535**	*6,602*
Creditors: amounts falling due after more than one year					
Borrowings and other creditors	24	**(4,267)**	*(4,610)*	**(4,429)**	*(4,740)*
Convertible Capital Bonds 2005	25	**(315)**	*(316)*		
		(4,582)	*(4,926)*	**(4,429)**	*(4,740)*
Provisions for liabilities and charges	27	**(57)**	*(69)*	**(54)**	*(66)*
		2,090	*1,730*	**2,052**	*1,796*
Capital and reserves					
Called up share capital	28	**239**	*239*	**239**	*239*
Reserves	29				
Share premium account		**460**	*457*	**460**	*457*
Revaluation reserve		**308**	*27*	**306**	*23*
Profit and loss account		**1,083**	*1,007*	**1,047**	*1,077*
		1,851	*1,491*	**1,813**	*1,557*
		2,090	*1,730*	**2,052**	*1,796*

*Restated in accordance with Financial Reporting Standard 5, see Note 1.

Exhibit 3
British Airways Plc
Footnotes: Selected Excerpts

1   CHANGES IN ACCOUNTING POLICIES

Adoption of new accounting standard

The Group has adopted the provisions of Financial Reporting Standard 5 'Reporting the Substance of Transactions' with effect from 1 April 1994 and corresponding amounts have been adjusted accordingly. As a consequence, the leases on twenty-four aircraft previously accounted for as operating leases are now accounted for as if they were finance leases and are aggregated with finance leases in the various disclosures in these accounts. The effect of this change on the balance sheet at 31 March 1995 has been to increase tangible fixed assets by £870 million (1994: £1,006 million) and borrowings by £905 million (1994: £1,041 million) and to reduce opening reserves by £52 million (1994: £45 million). The effect on the results for the year ended 31 March 1995 has been to increase operating profit by £53 million (1994: £43 million) and to increase interest payable by £54 million (1994: £52 million), thereby reducing profit before taxation for the year by £1 million (1994: £9 million).

In addition, the standard also introduced the concept of "quasi-subsidiaries" and requires companies to consolidate such entities in their group financial statements as if they are subsidiary undertakings. British Airways 49 per cent associated undertakings, Deutsche BA Luftfahrtgesellschaft mbH and TAT European Airlines S.A., are classified as "quasi-subsidiaries" under this standard. This new basis for presenting accounts has no effect on the legal status of the companies concerned. The Group previously accounted for these companies as associated undertakings with provisions being made against cost of advances. The effect on the balance sheet at 31 March 1995 has been to reduce net assets by £39 million (1994: £39 million). The effect on the results for the year ended 31 March 1995 has been to increase profit before taxation for the year by £12 million (1994: reduction of £3 million).

Accounting for the investment in Qantas Airways Limited

Qantas Airways Limited makes up its annual accounts to 30 June each year and also publishes a half-yearly statement of results covering the six months to 31 December each year. In the light of Qantas' impending privatisation, the Group has changed its policy of accounting for its share of post-acquisition results by only recognising its share of profits less losses on the basis of publicly reported information (as adjusted to conform with British Airways accounting policies); previously, results were included up to 31 March each year based on unaudited management accounts. Accordingly, the Group accounts have been amended to reflect British Airways share of Qantas' profits less losses for the twelve months to 31 December. The effect on reserves at 1 April 1994 is a reduction of £6 million.

2   ACCOUNTING POLICIES

Accounting convention

The accounts have been prepared under the historical cost convention modified by the inclusion of certain assets at valuation, as stated below, and in accordance with all applicable United Kingdom accounting standards and the Companies Act 1985.

Basis of consolidation

The Group accounts include the accounts of the Company, its subsidiary undertakings and quasi-subsidiaries, each made up to 31 March, together with the attributable share of results and reserves of associated undertakings, adjusted where appropriate to conform with British Airways accounting policies. Certain associated undertakings make up their annual audited accounts to dates other than 31 March. In the case of Qantas, published results up to the year ended 31 December are included; in other cases, results disclosed by subsequent unaudited management accounts are included. The attributable results of those companies acquired or disposed of during the year are included for the periods of ownership.

On the acquisition of a business, including an equity interest in an associated undertaking, fair values are attributed to the Group's share of net tangible assets. Where the cost of acquisition exceeds the values attributable to such net assets, the resulting goodwill is set off against reserves in the year of acquisition.

In accordance with section 230 of the Companies Act 1985, a separate profit and loss account dealing with the results of the Company only is not presented.

Quasi-subsidiaries

Where an entity, though not fulfilling the legal definition of a subsidiary or subsidiary undertaking, gives rise to benefits for the Group that are, in substance, no different than those that would arise were that entity a subsidiary or subsidiary undertaking, that entity is classified as a quasi-subsidiary. In determining whether the Group has the ability to enjoy the benefits arising from such entities' net assets, regard has to be given as to which party is exposed to the risks inherent in the benefits and which party, in practice, carries substantially all the risks and rewards of ownership.

Exhibit 3
British Airways Plc
Footnotes: Selected Excerpts
(continued)

Associated undertakings

Where the Group participates in the results of partnerships or companies in which it has an equity interest of 20 per cent or more, but not exceeding 50 per cent, and is in a position to exercise significant influence, those interests are classified as associated undertakings, except for those companies that are accounted for as quasi-subsidiaries. The Group's share of the profits less losses of associated undertakings is included in the Group profit and loss account and its share of the post-acquisition results of these companies is included in interests in associated undertakings in the Group balance sheet. The Group's interest in the results of USAir Group. Inc. is currently limited to its fixed preferred dividends and only such dividends as are declared are included in the accounts.

7 INCOME FROM INTERESTS IN ASSOCIATED UNDERTAKINGS

Attributable profits less losses	**51**	*6*
USAir preferred stock dividend received up to August 1994		
(1994: full year) (Note 18)	**7**	*16*
	58	*22*

16 INVESTMENTS
a Group
i) Associated Undertakings

£ million	Equity	Loans at cost	Provisions Shares	Loans	Group total 1995	1994
Balance at 1 April	518	98	(2)	(67)	547	448
Changes in accounting policies (Note 1)	51	(98)		67	20	4
Balance at 1 April as restated	569		(2)		567	452
Exchange movements	(40)				(40)	6
Additions		7	(125)		(118)	69
Repayments						(8)
Share of attributable results	33				33	1
Goodwill						(25)
Reclassification						72
Balance at 31 March	562	7	(127)		442	567

Equity comprises:		
Cost of shares	627	669
Goodwill set off	(94)	(94)
Share of post-acquisition profits/(losses)	29	(6)
	562	569

ii) Trade Investments

	Cost Shares	Loans	Group total 1995	1994
Balance at 1 April	26	2	28	98
Exchange movements				1
Additions	1		1	6
Reclassification				(77)
Balance at 31 March	27	2	29	28

Total Investments

	Associated undertakings	Trade investments
Listed		23
Unlisted	442	6

The listed investment is listed on the London Stock Exchange and its market value at 31 March 1995 was £13 million (1994: £22 million).

Exhibit 3
British Airways Plc
Footnotes: Selected Excerpts
(continued)

16 INVESTMENTS (continued)

b Company

i) Subsidiary Undertakings and Quasi-Subsidiaries

£ million	Cost		Provisions		Company total	
	Shares	Loans	Shares	Loans	**1995**	*1994*
Balance at 1 April	1,080	68	(317)	(65)	**766**	*668*
Changes in accounting policies (Note 1)	40		(40)			
Balance at 1 April as restated	1,120	68	(357)	(65)	**766**	*668*
Exchange movements	(25)				**(25)**	*7*
Additions/(reductions)	178		(238)	3	**(57)**	*89*
Transfer from subsidiary undertaking	1				**1**	
Repayments		(6)			**(6)**	
Disposal	(1)	(58)		58	**(1)**	
Reclassification						*2*
Balance at 31 March	1,273	4	(595)	(4)	**678**	*766*

ii) Associated Undertakings

			Shares		Company total	
			Cost	Provisions	**1995**	*1994*
Balance at 1 April			18	(18)		*11*
Changes in accounting policies (Note 1)			(18)	18		
Balance at 1 April as restated						*11*
Additions						*2*
Repayments						*(13)*
Balance at 31 March						

iii) Trade Investments

			Cost		Company total	
			Shares	Loans	**1995**	*1994*
Balance at 1 April			24	2	**26**	*22*
Additions			1		**1**	*6*
Reclassification						*(2)*
Balance at 31 March			25	2	**27**	*26*

Total Investments	Subsidiary undertakings and quasi-subsidiaries	Trade investments
Listed		23
Unlisted	678	4

The listed investment is listed on the London Stock Exchange and its market value at 31 March 1995 was £13 million (1994: £22 million).

Exhibit 3
British Airways Plc
Footnotes: Selected Excerpts
(continued)

17 INVESTMENT IN QANTAS AIRWAYS LIMITED

Summarised Financial Information

The published statements of operations for the Qantas group for the year ended 30 June 1994 and the six months ended 31 December 1994, and its balance sheets at these dates, as adjusted to accord with British Airways accounting policies are summarised below:

Year ended and at 30 June 1994

	As published by Qantas (audited) A$m	Adjustments A$m	Total A$m	Total £m
Operating revenue	6,602		6,602	3,017
Operating profit	480	189	669	306
Abnormal charges	(65)		(65)	(30)
Net interest	(178)	(195)	(373)	(170)
Profit/(loss) before taxation	237	(6)	231	106
Profit after taxation	156	45	201	92
Non current assets	6,799	2,125	8,924	4,229
Net current liabilities	(586)	(335)	(921)	(436)
Long term liabilities	(4,047)	(2,285)	(6,332)	(3,001)
Share capital	1,000		1,000	474
Reserves	1,166	(495)	671	318

Six months ended and at 31 December 1994

	As published by Qantas (audited) A$m	Adjustments A$m	Total A$m	Total £m
Operating revenue	3,672		3,672	1,736
Operating profit	285	103	388	183
Net interest	(82)	(94)	(176)	(83)
Profit before taxation	203	9	212	100
Profit after taxation	129	47	176	83
Non current assets	6,773	2,067	8,840	4,394
Net current liabilities	(494)	(525)	(1,019)	(506)
Long term liabilities	(3,998)	(1,990)	(5,988)	(2,976)
Share capital	1,000		1,000	497
Reserves	1,281	(448)	833	415

The Sterling equivalents for the statements of operations have been translated at the average exchange rates for the year ended 30 June 1994 and six months ended 31 December 1994; those for the balance sheets have been translated at the closing rate on those dates.

18 INVESTMENT IN USAir GROUP, INC.

Under an agreement made between British Airways and USAir in January 1993, British Airways undertook to invest US$750 million in USAir convertible preferred stock over a five year period. The investment was to occur in three stages and was subject to a number of conditions, including regulatory approval by the US Government. Approval of the first stage, involving the investment of US$300 million to give British Airways a holding equivalent to 24.6 per cent of USAir's equity share capital on an undiluted basis and an initial code sharing agreement, was given by the US Secretary for Transportation in March 1993. The preferred stock so acquired by the Group is convertible at the Group's option at any time on or after 21 January 1997 into USAir common stock. Until converted, the preferred stock is entitled to cumulative quarterly cash dividends of seven per cent per annum.

In order to maintain its holding equivalent to 24.6 per cent of USAir's equity capital, the Group invested a further US$100.7 million in convertible preferred stock in May 1993 pursuant to the exercise of pre-emptive rights relating to the issue of new common stock by USAir. This new series of convertible preferred stock is entitled to cumulative quarterly cash dividends of 0.5 per cent over LIBOR.

The present holdings of convertible preferred stock entitle the Group to 22 per cent of the current voting rights in USAir. If not converted, the preferred stock is finally redeemable in 2008. In certain extremely unlikely circumstances, the Group can be required to invest a further US$450 million over the next three years through two additional purchases of preferred stock in USAir.

Exhibit 3
British Airways Plc
Footnotes: Selected Excerpts
(continued)

18 INVESTMENT IN USAir GROUP, INC. (continued)

Under the above arrangements, the Group's current interest in the results of USAir is limited to its fixed preferred dividends, which are payable on a quarterly basis when declared. No such dividend has been paid by USAir to the Group since August 1994. In respect of the Group's present holdings, the last payment of dividends received from USAir was for the quarter ended 31 August 1994 (see Note 7). The book value of the Group's investment at 31 March 1995 was £125.4 million.

Summarised Financial Information

The audited statement of operations of USAir for the year ended 31 December 1994 and its balance sheet at that date, prepared in accordance with United States generally accepted accounting principles, are summarised below:

	USAir US$m	£m
Operating revenues	6,997	4,581
Operating loss	(491)	(321)
Net interest payable and other expenses	(194)	(128)
Net loss	(685)	(449)
Preferred dividend requirements	(78)	(51)
Net loss applicable to common stockholders	(763)	(500)
Total assets less current liabilities	4,548	2,911
Long-term debts and redeemable preferred stock	(3,654)	(2,339)
Deferred credits and other liabilities	(1,791)	(1,146)
Total stockholders' equity (deficit)	(897)	(574)

For the three months ended 31 March 1995, USAir announced an unaudited operating loss of US$42 million on operating revenues of US$1,763 million and a net loss of US$97 million.

The Sterling equivalents for the statements of operations have been translated at the average exchange rate for the year ended 31 December 1994 and the three months ended 31 March 1995; those for the balance sheet at 31 December 1994 have been translated at the closing rate on that date.

In its audit report on USAir's Annual Report on Form 10-K for the year ended 31 December 1994, filed with the US Securities and Exchange Commission, the auditors of USAir made the following statement:

"The accompanying financial statements have been prepared assuming that Group [USAir Group, Inc. and subsidiaries] will continue as a going concern. As discussed in Note 4(a) to the consolidated financial statements, Group [USAir Group, Inc. and subsidiaries] has suffered recurring losses from operations and has a net capital deficiency that raise substantial doubt about its ability to continue as a going concern. Management's plans in regard to these matters are also described in Note 4(a). The consolidated financial statements do not include any adjustments that might result from the outcome of this uncertainty.".

In Note 4(a) of its Annual Report on Form 10-K referred to above, USAir states that "…The Company [USAir Group, Inc.] has incurred annual operating losses for every year since 1990 and has a net capital deficiency at December 31, 1994. The Company [USAir Group, Inc.] is currently in negotiations with employee labor groups in an effort to obtain employee concessions that will substantially reduce operating costs. On March 29, 1995, USAir and the negotiating committee of the Air Line Pilots Association ('ALPA') Master Executive Council, which represents USAir's pilots, signed an agreement in principle on wage and other concessions in exchange for financial returns and governance participation for USAir pilots. The agreement in principle is subject to many significant conditions, including approval of the boards of directors of the Company [USAir Group, Inc.] and USAir and of the shareholders of the Company [USAir Group, Inc.] and the execution of definitive documentation. USAir continues to negotiate with representatives of its other unions but it is uncertain whether any final agreements will be reached. No assurance can be given whether or when any transactions with any of the unions will be consummated or what the terms of any such transactions might be. In addition, the Company [USAir Group, Inc.] is evaluating other strategic decisions that could be implemented to improve the operating results of the airline. The Company [USAir Group, Inc.] believes that it must reduce its operating costs substantially if it is to survive in this low cost, low fare competitive environment.".

On 3 May 1995, agreement in principle in similar terms to those described above was reached by USAir with the International Association of Machinists (the 'IAM').

In the corresponding note to last year's British Airways accounts, there was a warning that if negotiations with the leadership of USAir's unionised employees regarding wage reductions, improved productivity and other cost savings were not successfully concluded within the timescale which the financial position of USAir required, the Directors believed that a provision for permanent diminution in value was likely to be required.

Exhibit 3
British Airways Plc
Footnotes: Selected Excerpts
(continued)

18 INVESTMENT IN USAir GROUP, INC. (continued)

While acknowledging continuing uncertainties about the prospects for an early agreement with the unions and about the effect on USAir of possible new competition, and therefore the timing of a significant improvement in its financial position, the Directors presently believe that USAir's liquidity position will continue to be adequate during the period that is likely to be required to conclude agreements with the unions.

Because, under accounting rules, the investment is treated as a debt security, certain technical consequences follow the suspension of preferred dividends on the security. US accounting rules, set out in Financial Accounting Standards Board Statement No. 115, 'Accounting for Certain Investments in Debt and Equity Securities', effective for this year, require a provision to be made where a diminution of value is 'other than temporary'. The uncertainties referred to above, and the lack of clarity as to whether dividend payments on the security will be resumed in the near term, have led the Directors to conclude that a provision of US$200 million (50 per cent of original cost) should be made. Although the UK accounting rules differ in detail from those in the US, the Directors believe that, notwithstanding the synergy benefits flowing from the investment and their belief in the long term future of USAir, it would be prudent and consistent to make a similar provision in the UK accounts. The Directors consider the investment in USAir of strategic importance; the Company presently derives trading benefits which constitute significant contributions to profit as a result of additional traffic generated through USAir connections, as well as joint marketing arrangements and cost savings, and expects these to continue and grow.

19 QUASI-SUBSIDIARIES

Summarised financial information of Deutsche BA Luftfahrtgesellschaft mbH and TAT European Airlines S.A., prepared in accordance with British Airways accounting policies, is set out below. Transactions and balances between the two companies have been eliminated.

£ million	1995	Total 1994
Profit and Loss Account		
Turnover	368	319
Operating loss	(81)	(70)
Loss before taxation	(90)	(85)
Taxation (charge)/credit	(3)	7
Loss for the year	(93)	(78)
Balance Sheet		
Fixed assets	159	162
Current assets	82	83
Creditors: Amounts falling due within one year	(380)	(237)
Net current liabilities	(298)	(154)
Total assets less current liabilities	(139)	8
Creditors: Amounts falling due after more than one year	(122)	(151)
Provisions for liabilities and charges	(3)	(3)
Capital and reserves (deficits)	(264)	(146)
Cash Flow Statement		
Net cash inflow from operating activities	25	26
Net cash outflow from returns on investments and servicing of finance	(11)	(13)
Net cash (outflow)/inflow from investing activities	(4)	10
Net cash inflow before financing	10	23
Net cash outflow from financing	(22)	(24)
Decrease in cash and cash equivalents	(12)	(1)
Statement of Total Recognised Gains and Losses		
Loss for the year	(93)	(78)
Exchange movements	(25)	
Total gains and losses recognised for the year	(118)	(78)

Guinness PLC, founded in 1792, is one of the world's leading alcoholic beverage companies, producing such well-known brands as Johnnie Walker, Bell's and Dewar's Scotch whiskies, Gordon's and Tanqueray gins, and Guinness stout, the distinctive dark beer bearing the company's name. The company is headquartered in London, England, and consequently prepares its financial statements in accordance with the U.K. Companies Act of 1985 -- legislation on corporate organization that contains, among other things, accounting requirements for limited liability companies domiciled in the U.K. Guinness's financial data also conforms to the guidelines provided by the U.K.'s Accounting Standards Board, as specified in the Board's Statements of Standard Accounting Practice (SSAP). While the SSAPs are in many respects similar to the accounting standards (i.e. FASs) promulgated by the Financial Accounting Standards Board (FASB) in the U.S., some significant distinctions exist.

Accounting Policies

Goodwill. While Guinness initially began operations exclusively as a producer of ales and beer, it has since expanded into the manufacture of a variety of alcoholic beverages. In most instances, the expansion of the company's product lines was achieved by the acquisition of existing beverage producers with well established brandnames. For example, in the 1980's, Guinness acquired both Dewar PLC and Gordon PLC. A significant by-product of this growth-by-acquisition strategy was the creation of purchased "goodwill", or the excess purchase price paid for an existing company above and beyond the company's fair market value.

Under U.S. generally accepted accounting practice (or GAAP), goodwill must be capitalized to the acquiror's balance sheet and then amortized against earnings over a period not to exceed 40 years. Under U.K. GAAP, however, alternative accounting options exist. In addition to capitalization/amortization, U.K. companies may elect to write off all (or virtually all) of the purchased goodwill at the time of acquisition. This approach, commonly called the "charge-to-equity" method, is usually executed by a charge against the Profit and Loss Reserve (i.e. retained earnings) or against a specific reserve account created for this purpose[1]. In some instances companies have petitioned the U.K. courts for permission to write goodwill off against the "share premium" reserve (i.e. additional paid-in-capital). Guinness' balance sheet (see Exhibit 1) and footnotes thereto (see Exhibit 2) reveal that the company has charged all purchased goodwill against a specific equity reserve account called "Goodwill".

Brands. Brands, or brandnames, refer to well recognized product names or corporate logos. These intangible assets are usually difficult to accurately value. Where a brand has been internally-generated, for example, it is difficult to separate the revenue generated by advertising from benefits due to the brand's positive consumer image. In the case of purchased brands, it can be difficult to separate the value of a well recognized brandname from goodwill. As a result, unless the cost of a brandname is explicitly identified in an acquisition agreement, it is most often subsumed within the value assigned to

---

[1] Effective January 1, 1995, the International Accounting Standards Committee issued IAS No. 22 (revised), which prohibits the use of the immediate write-off method for goodwill: "positive goodwill should be recognized as an asset and amortized to income on a systematic basis over...[a] period not to exceed 5 years unless a longer life (not to exceed 20 years) can be justified and is explained in the financial statements."

goodwill. As a consequence, the capitalization of brands is rare.[2] A notable exception is the U.K., where purchased brands are often capitalized to the balance sheet following the acquisition of a company or product line.

A review of Guinness' balance sheet reveals, for example, that over 33 percent of the company's 1994 fixed assets of £ 4.3 billion are reflected in the account "Acquired brands at cost". Guinness' summary of significant accounting policies discloses the following:

> Brands represent the Group's most valuable asset.

> Acquired brands are only recognized on the balance sheet where they have a substantial and long-term value, title is clear, brand earnings are separately identifiable, the brand could be sold separately from the rest of the business, and where the brand achieves earnings in excess of unbranded products.

> Since only major acquired brands are included on the balance sheet, internally-generated brands including Guinness stout, are excluded, despite their immense value to the Group. The cost of acquired brands included in the balance sheet amounts to £1,824 million, which includes £429 million in respect of Moët-Hennessey brands. The economic lives and the value of brands are reassessed on an annual basis. The 1994 valuation indicated that the capitalized brands are worth significantly more than the value included in the balance sheet.

> Amortization is not provided except where the end of the useful economic life of the acquired brand can be foreseen.

Thus, not only does Guinness capitalize these intangible assets to the balance sheet, but amortization is **only** taken when the end of an asset's economic life can be predicted.

Asset Valuation. A fundamental tenet of U.S. GAAP is that assets are valued at their historical cost, unless an impairment of value has occurred, in which case a lower value may be used.[3] In the U.K., however, a variety of valuation options exist. Assets may, for example, be valued using the historical cost principle, alternative valuation rules, or a combination of such methods. Under the alternative valuation rules, assets may be revalued above historical cost as follows:[4]

- Tangible and intangible assets (except goodwill) may be written up to current costs, as estimated by an independent appraiser or by a company's directors; and,

- Long-term investments may be written up to current market value.

---

[2] Under International Accounting Standards Committee (IASC) Exposure Draft E50, Intangible Assets, the IASC has proposed to restrict the balance sheet recognition of brands to those assets that (a) can be identified, (b) their benefits can be measured separately from goodwill, (c) be revalued only by reference to an active secondary market, and (d) if capitalized, be amortized over a period not to exceed 20 years.

[3] The one exception to this tenet involves marketable securities, which may be revalued above historical cost in some circumstances. See Financial Accounting Standards Board, FAS No. 115, "Accounting for Certain Investments in Debt and Equity Securities," (May, 1993).

[4] The revaluation of assets above historical cost is permitted under IASC International Accounting Standard No. 16.

Thus, it is not uncommon for a U.K.-based company to periodically revalue those assets, such as land and buildings, that are subject to significant price appreciation. When such revaluations are undertaken, the amount of the write-up is debited to the asset account and a parallel amount is credited to an asset revaluation reserve account in the equity section of the balance sheet. These reserves are normally not legally available for distribution to shareholders as dividends, at least until such time as the revalued amounts are written off against earnings as depreciation, at which point a proportionate amount (representing the extra depreciation) is transferred from the revaluation reserve to retained earnings.

Guinness' footnotes (see Exhibit 2) disclose that, with the exception of land and buildings, its assets are valued using the historical cost convention. Land and buildings, however, are valued at "historical cost or valuation" less depreciation taken to date. Valuation is defined as "replacement cost" or "open market valuation" depending upon the class of asset involved (see Exhibit 2).

Required:

1. Consider the various U.K. alternatives to the accounting for goodwill; which method do you prefer, and why? Restate Guinness' financial statements for 1994 using U.S. accounting practice for goodwill; prepare a list of any assumptions that you make. Calculate Guinness' (a) return on sales, (b) return on equity, and (c) return on assets for 1994 under both the U.K. and U.S. treatment of goodwill; what generalizations can be drawn?

2. Evaluate Guinness' accounting for its acquired brands; do you agree? How would Guinness' financial statements be affected if U.S. standards were used when accounting for its brands?

3. Compare the U.K. and U.S. approaches to the valuation of tangible fixed assets; which approach do you prefer, and why? Restate Guinness' financial statements for 1994 assuming that tangible fixed assets are valued at historical cost; prepare a list of any assumptions that you make. Calculate Guinness' (a) return on sales, (b) return on equity, and (c) return on assets for 1994 using both the original and restated values; what generalizations are suggested by this data?

Exhibit 1
Guinness PLC
Financial Statements

Group profit and loss account

For the year ended 31 December 1994	Notes	1994 £m	1994 £m	1993 £m	Growth %
Turnover (continuing operations)	1		4,690	4,663	1
Net trading costs	2		(3,734)	(3,725)	
Profit before interest and taxation					
(excluding Moët Hennessy (MH) and LVMH) (continuing operations)	1		956	938	2
Share of profit before taxation of MH	3		89	–	
Share of profit before taxation of LVMH	4		–	125	
Disposal of investment in LVMH	5	(173)			
Provision against investment in LVMH made in 1993		173			
			–	(173)	
Profit before interest and taxation			1,045	890	17
Net interest charge	8		(130)	(188)	
Profit on ordinary activities before taxation			915	702	30
Taxation on profit on ordinary activities	9		(243)	(247)	
Profit on ordinary activities after taxation			672	455	48
Minority interests (equity)			(31)	(22)	
Profit for the financial year			641	433	48
Dividends	10		(279)	(258)	
Retained earnings			362	175	
EARNINGS PER SHARE	11				
Basic earnings per share			31.8p	22.9p	39
Diluted – before exceptional items			31.6p	31.7p	–
Disposal of investment in LVMH			–	(8.8)p	
Diluted earnings per share			31.6p	22.9p	38
DIVIDENDS PER SHARE	10				
Paid or payable			13.80p	12.80p	8
Gross equivalent			17.25p	16.00p	
Interest cover (times, before exceptional items)			8.0	5.7	
Dividend cover (times, before exceptional items)			2.3	2.5	

Exhibit 1
Guinness PLC
Financial Statements
(continued)

Group balance sheet

At 31 December 1994	Notes	1994 £m	1994 £m	1993 £m	1993 £m
NET ASSETS					
Fixed assets					
Acquired brands at cost	13		1,395		1,395
Tangible assets	14		1,784		1,725
Investment in MH	15	900		–	
Investment in LVMH	16	–		1,282	
Other long term investments	17	149		157	
			1,049		1,439
			4,228		4,559
Current assets					
Stocks	18	1,858		1,822	
Debtors	19	1,272		1,239	
Cash at bank and in hand		476		399	
		3,606		3,460	
Creditors (amounts falling due within one year)					
Short term borrowings	20	(778)		(907)	
Other creditors	21	(1,441)		(1,455)	
		(2,219)		(2,362)	
Net current assets			1,387		1,098
Total assets less current liabilities			5,615		5,657
Creditors (amounts falling due after more than one year)					
Long term borrowings	20	(1,113)		(1,366)	
Other creditors	22	(187)		(171)	
			(1,300)		(1,537)
Provisions for liabilities and charges	23		(256)		(282)
Total net assets	12		4,059		3,838
EQUITY					
Capital and reserves					
Called up share capital	24 (B)		505		503
Share premium account	24 (B)		544		522
			1,049		1,025
Other reserves	25 (A)		2,037		2,346
Profit and loss account	25 (A)		2,182		1,587
Goodwill	25 (B)		(1,321)		(1,229)
Shareholders' funds			3,947		3,729
Minority interests (equity)			112		109
Total equity			4,059		3,838

Exhibit 1
Guinness PLC
Financial Statements
(continued)

Statement of total recognised gains and losses

For the year ended 31 December 1994	1994 £m	1993 £m
Profit for the financial year attributable to shareholders	641	433
Share of LVMH profit after taxation relating to the Group not recognised in the profit and loss account	–	26
Exchange adjustments	(49)	(145)
Total recognised gains and losses	**592**	**314**

Note of historical cost profits and losses

There is no material difference between the reported profit for 1994 and 1993 shown on page 38 and the profit for those years restated on an historical cost basis.

Reconciliation of movements in shareholders' funds

For the year ended 31 December 1994	1994 £m	1993 £m
Profit for the financial year attributable to shareholders	641	433
Dividends	(279)	(258)
Retained earnings	362	175
Other recognised gains and losses relating to the year (net)	(49)	(119)
New share capital issued	24	27
Provision against value of LVMH goodwill made in 1993	(146)	146
Goodwill transferred to the profit and loss account on disposal of investment in LVMH	187	–
Goodwill deducted from shareholders' funds on acquisition of investment in MH	(104)	–
Goodwill deducted from shareholders' funds on other acquisitions and disposals	(29)	(48)
Attributable share of associates' reserve movements	(27)	(23)
Net increase in shareholders' funds	218	158
Shareholders' funds at start of year	3,729	3,571
Shareholders' funds at end of year	**3,947**	**3,729**

Exhibit 2
Guinness PLC
Selected Footnotes

Accounting policies

Basis of accounting
The accounts are prepared under the historical cost convention, modified to include the revaluation of land and buildings, and in accordance with applicable accounting and financial reporting standards.

Basis of consolidation
The Group accounts include the accounts of the Company and its subsidiary undertakings together with the Group's share of the profits and retained post-acquisition reserves of associated undertakings. Associated undertakings are those in which the Group holds a long-term equity interest and over which it is in a position to exercise a significant influence.

Where the Group's interest in unincorporated joint venture partnerships is determined on the basis of the contribution to the results of the partnership from the sale of the Group's products, the attributable results and the related underlying net assets and borrowings are consolidated.

Brands
The fair value of businesses acquired and of interests taken in associated undertakings includes brands, which are recognised where the brand has a value which is substantial and long-term. Acquired brands are only recognised where title is clear, brand earnings are separately identifiable, the brand could be sold separately from the rest of the business and where the brand achieves earnings in excess of those achieved by unbranded products.

Amortisation is not provided except where the end of the useful economic life of the acquired brand can be foreseen. The useful economic lives of brands and their carrying value are subject to annual review and any amortisation or provision for permanent impairment would be charged against the profit for the period in which they arose.

Tangible fixed assets and depreciation
Land and buildings are stated at cost or valuation less depreciation. In the case of distilleries, breweries and related specialised properties, valuations are principally on a depreciated replacement cost basis. Hotel and leisure business properties are valued on the basis of an open market valuation for existing use.

Freehold land is not depreciated. Other tangible fixed assets are depreciated on a straight line basis at annual rates estimated to write off their book values over their expected useful lives. Details of depreciation rates are given in Note 14(B).

Stocks
Stocks are stated at the lower of cost and net realisable value. Cost includes raw materials, duties where applicable, direct labour and expenses and the appropriate proportion of production and other overheads, including financing costs in respect of whisky and other spirit stocks during their normal maturation period.

Accounting for acquisitions and disposals
(A) Results
The results of businesses acquired or disposed of are consolidated from or to the effective dates of acquisition or disposal.

(B) Fair value adjustments and acquisition provisions
On the acquisition of a business or of an interest in an associated undertaking, the acquisition cost is allocated to the fair value of net tangible assets and the fair value of significant brands acquired, after adjustments to bring accounting policies into line with those of the Group.

(C) Goodwill
The goodwill arising on the acquisition of businesses and interests in associated undertakings is calculated by reference to the fair value of net assets acquired and is deducted in arriving at shareholders' funds. Where merger relief is taken under Section 131 of the Companies Act 1985, the difference between the fair value and the nominal value of shares issued as purchase consideration is treated as a merger reserve. Goodwill realised on disposals is included in the calculation of the gain or loss on disposal.

Exhibit 2
Guinness PLC
Selected Footnotes
(continued)

13. ACQUIRED BRANDS AT COST

The amount stated for brands represents the cost of acquired brands. Brands are only recognised where title is clear, brand earnings are separately identifiable, the brand could be sold separately from the rest of the business and where the brand achieves earnings in excess of those achieved by unbranded products.

The cost of brands is calculated at acquisition, as part of the fair value accounting for businesses acquired, on the basis of after tax multiples of pre-acquisition earnings after deducting attributable capital employed.

The acquired brands which have been recognised include Bell's, Dewar's, Johnnie Walker, Old Parr and White Horse Scotch whisky, Gordon's and Tanqueray gin and Asbach brandy.

The acquired brands of MH which have been recognised as part of the investment in MH are set out in Note 15(A).

The Directors have reviewed the amounts at which brands are stated and are of the opinion that there has been no impairment in the value of the brands recognised, that all brands recognised could be sold for amounts substantially greater than those recognised in the balance sheet and that the end of the useful economic lives of the brands cannot be foreseen.

14. TANGIBLE FIXED ASSETS

	Land and buildings (Note (A)) £m	Plant and machinery £m	Casks, containers and road vehicles £m	Total £m
Cost or valuation				
At 1 January 1994	845	1,142	246	2,233
Additions	44	125	52	221
Subsidiaries acquired	4	3	–	7
Disposals	(1)	(35)	(26)	(62)
Exchange adjustments	(1)	(17)	(3)	(21)
At 31 December 1994	891	1,218	269	2,378
Depreciation				
At 1 January 1994	28	409	71	508
Charge for the year	18	90	33	141
Disposals	–	(22)	(24)	(46)
Exchange adjustments	–	(7)	(2)	(9)
At 31 December 1994	46	470	78	594
Net book amount				
At 31 December 1994	845	748	191	1,784
At 31 December 1993	817	733	175	1,725

Exhibit 2
Guinness PLC
Selected Footnotes
(continued)

14. TANGIBLE FIXED ASSETS continued

(A) Land and buildings

	1994 £m	1993 £m
(i) The amount shown at cost or valuation includes the following:		
At cost	348	301
At valuation in 1992	543	544
	891	**845**
(ii) If shown on an historical cost basis, land and buildings would be stated at:		
Cost	762	715
Depreciation	(89)	(75)
Net book amount	**673**	**640**
(iii) The net book amount of land and buildings comprises:		
Freeholds	768	740
Long leaseholds (over 50 years)	75	75
Short leaseholds (under 50 years)	2	2
	845	**817**

(B) Depreciation rates
The following table shows the principal annual rates of depreciation:

Freehold buildings and long leaseholds	Straight line over 50 years
Short leaseholds	Straight line over the life of the lease
Distilling and bottling plant	2% – 10%
Brewing plant	5% – 12½%
Casks and containers	5% – 6⅔%
Distribution vehicles	12½% – 16⅔%
Motor cars	20% – 30%

18. STOCKS

	1994 £m	1993 £m
Raw materials and consumables	144	164
Work in progress	25	18
Stocks of maturing whisky and other spirits	1,505	1,470
Finished goods and goods for resale	184	170
	1,858	**1,822**

Stocks of maturing whisky and other spirits include financing costs amounting to £563m (1993 – £546m). A net adjustment to stocks of £17m (1993 – £17m) has been credited to the profit and loss account within net trading costs comprising £122m (1993 – £121m) of interest incurred during the year less £105m (1993 – £104m) in respect of sales during the year.

Exhibit 2
Guinness PLC
Selected Footnotes
(continued)

25. OTHER RESERVES AND GOODWILL

(A) Other reserves and profit and loss account

	Revaluation reserve £m	Capital redemption reserve £m	Merger reserve £m	Associated undertakings £m	Total other reserves £m	Profit and loss account £m
At 1 January 1994	177	49	1,781	339	2,346	1,587
Retained earnings	–	–	–	63	63	299
Other	(4)	–	–	(27)	(31)	4
Disposal of investment in LVMH	–	–	–	(381)	(381)	381
Exchange adjustments	(1)	–	–	41	40	(89)
At 31 December 1994	172	49	1,781	35	2,037	2,182

Exchange adjustments include a charge of £39m arising on the translation of foreign currency borrowings which is matched against the gain arising on the translation of the related net investment in overseas subsidiary and associated undertakings.

(B) Goodwill

	Year of acquisition	1 January 1994 £m	Additions £m	Disposals £m	31 December 1994 £m
Distillers	1986	284	–	–	284
Schenley	1987	92	–	–	92
LVMH	1988-90	187	–	(187)	–
Provision against LVMH goodwill made in 1993		(146)	–	146	–
Asbach	1991-92	112	–	–	112
Cruzcampo Group	1991	325	–	–	325
Glenmore	1991	47	–	–	47
MH	1994	–	104	–	104
Other		328	29	–	357
		1,229	133	(41)	1,321

There was already considerable pessimism amongst the traders of the London Stock Exchange (LSE) when the markets opened on September 20, 1990. The headlines of the morning edition of The Independent carried confirmation of what even the last few "bulls" had by now reluctantly accepted: a recession had arrived, not just in Britain, but worldwide. Within minutes of the opening bell, however, the attention of virtually every trader on the floor of the LSE became focused on a single issue -- Polly Peck International.

Polly Peck had traded as high as 462 pence earlier in the year, but opened on September 20 at 245 pence. Within minutes, the issue had dropped 25 pence, or more than 10 percent. The selling seemed driven by several rumors that quickly passed among the traders: Asil Nadir, then chairman of the company, was said to have shot himself; shortly thereafter, the rumor became that he had actually been assassinated by a Middle East gunman. By 11 a.m., the share price had dropped to 180 pence; and by 2:20 p.m., when trading in the shares was finally suspended at the request of the company, over 36 million shares had changed hands and the price was down to 108 pence. Polly Peck's market value had declined by £560 million in a single day. Many of the sellers that day had been banks that had taken Polly Peck shares as collateral against the borrowings of the company.

Company Background

Polly Peck International (PPI) was, until 1980, a marginally profitable U.K. textile company. The company began a dramatic revival in 1980, however, when Asil Nadir, a Cypriot, obtained a controlling stake in the company. Nadir was less interested in the company's prospects as a textile producer than in the fact that its shares were publicly listed. Nadir intended to use Polly Peck, then worth about £ 300,000, as a stock market vehicle to expand his personal wealth.

Nadir intended to turn PPI into a conglomerate, and he began by building upon the company's basic operations. In 1983, he significantly expanded PPI's textile business by purchasing a 76 percent stake in Santana Inc. in the U.S. and a majority stake in InterCity PLC in the U.K. Nadir then extended PPI's textile operations into the Far East by acquiring a majority stake in Impact Textile Group in 1986, and by increasing PPI's existing stake in Shuihing Ltd to 90 percent. Peck continued expanding in textiles and in July 1987, acquired a majority interest in Palmon (UAE) Ltd., a manufacturer of casual shirts.

In the early 1980s, PPI also diversified into the electronics business by acquiring a 82 percent ownership in Vestel Electronics, one of the largest publicly-traded companies in Turkey. Vestel manufactured color televisions, video recorders, audio equipment, microwave ovens, and washing machines. PPI's success in the electronics business was substantially enhanced in early 1986 ,when Akai of Japan decided to join Ferguson, Salora and Goldstar as licensors to Vestel. Subsequently, PPI also acquired Russell Hobbs PLC, a U.K. manufacturer of kitchen appliances, Tower Housewares PLC, a manufacturer of kitchen ware, and the Capitronic Group. In 1989, PPI became a major player in the international electronics industry with the purchase of a controlling stake in Sansui, a Japanese electronics manufacturer, thereby providing PPI with an internationally-recognized brand name (see Exhibit 1).

Beyond textiles and electronics, Nadir also invested in the leisure and food industries. PPI's hotel division included such five star facilities as the Crystal Cove in Cyprus and the Sheraton Voyager in Antalya, Turkey. The company's food division operated the Pizza Hut franchise for Turkey, as well as citrus and apple packing and juice bottling plants. PPI became an international force in the food industry in 1989 with the acquisition of Del Monte, one of the world's largest suppliers of fresh fruit and vegetables.

In less than 10 years, Nadir's growth-by-acquisition strategy had increased PPI's market capitalization from only £ 300,000 to over £ 731 million.

Problems at Polly Peck

The situation at Polly Peck deteriorated rapidly when trading in the company's shares was suspended on September 20, 1990. Although the main operating companies -- Sansui, Vestel, and Del Monte -- were reported to have financially sound operations, the group's lenders were wary of renewing the lines of credit to any of PPI's operating companies. Many of the lenders recalled PPI's earlier cash crisis in 1987 when PPI had failed to make timely payments to its creditors.

Regrettably, the company's fate appeared dependent on the willingness of its lenders to extend further, or renew existing, credit lines. According to one banker, PPI's problems were largely attributable to the structure of the group's debts. PPI had historically relied extensively on borrowings, a large proportion of which (i.e. in excess of £ 100 million) were short-term revolving lines of credit, which lenders could renew (or choose not to) at their discretion. The remaining portion of PPI's debt consisted of longer-term loans for which Asil had offered Polly Peck's shares as collateral. As the stock market declined, the value of these shares fell to less than one fourth of the related outstanding debt.[1] In response to the uncertainty regarding PPI's ability to renew its existing lines of credit, Moody's Investor Service, a U.S. debt-rating agency which rated about one third of PPI's borrowings, downgraded PPI's short and medium-term debt from Ba1 and Ba3 to Ba3 and B2. Even prior to the downgrading, however, the PPI debt had been classified as "speculative" because of the company's high debt levels.

Required:

1. Using the financial data in Exhibits 2-4, prepare a statement of cash flows for PPI for 1986-1989. (Hint: A statement of cash flows may be prepared using only Exhibit 4, or by using Exhibits 2, 3, and 4.)

2. Using the financial data in Exhibits 2-4, calculate the following ratios for 1987-1989:

   a. Total debt-to-equity ratio
   b. Cashflow from operations ÷ current liabilities ratio
   c. Times-interest-earned ratio
   d. Average days inventory-on-hand ratio

   e. Average receivable collection period
   f. Average payment period of accounts payable
   g. Current ratio
   h. Asset turnover ratio

---

[1] Lenders normally maintain collateral of 125 percent or more of a loan's outstanding balance for safety purposes.

3. Using the following formula, calculate the value of Altman's Z-score for bankruptcy prediction for PPI for the period 1987-1989:

$$Z = .063X_1 + .092X_2 + .057X_3 + .0014X_4,$$

where

X_1 = working capital ÷ total assets;
X_2 = earnings before interest and taxes ÷ total assets;
X_3 = retained earnings ÷ total assets; and,
X_4 = net worth ÷ total assets.

Assume a cut-off value of .037 for Z., how well does the Z-score predict PPI's financial problems?[2]

4. Using your analysis from questions 1-3, determine what Polly Peck's problems are and <u>when</u> they are first apparent.

---

[2] The interested reader is referred to R. Taffler, "Empirical Models for Monitoring U.K. Corporations," The Journal of Banking and Finance (June 1984).

Exhibit 1
Polly Peck International PLC
Summary Financial Results
(£ million)

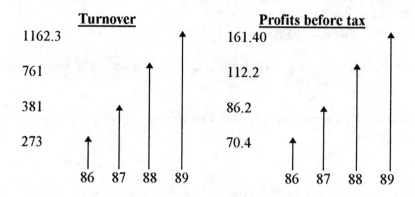

Turnover

1162.3			
761			
381			
273			
86	87	88	89

Profits before tax

161.40			
112.2			
86.2			
70.4			
86	87	88	89

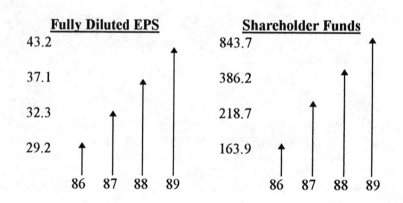

Fully Diluted EPS

43.2			
37.1			
32.3			
29.2			
86	87	88	89

Shareholder Funds

843.7			
386.2			
218.7			
163.9			
86	87	88	89

Exhibit 2
Polly Peck International PLC and its subsidiaries
CONSOLIDATED PROFIT AND LOSS ACCOUNT
(in millions of pounds)

	12 Months ended 31st Dec. 1989	16 Months ended 31st Dec. 1988	12 Months ended 29th Aug. 1987	12 Months ended 29th Aug. 1986
TURNOVER	1,162.3	967.1	380.8	273.7
Cost of sales	866.1	707.5	244.9	175.3
Gross Profit	296.2	259.6	135.9	98.4
Distribution costs	47.1	27.9	13.5	6.9
Administrative expenses	110.1	85.0	28.9	15.4
TRADING PROFIT	139.0	146.7	93.4	76.0
other income	77.4	38.0	0.8	0.5
	216.4	184.7	94.2	76.5
Interest payable	55.6	40.6	9.5	6.5
	160.8	144.1	84.7	70.0
Share of results of related companies	0.6	-	1.5	0.4
PROFIT ON ORDINARY ACTIVITIES BEFORE TAXATION	161.4	144.1	86.2	70.4
taxation on ordinary activities	22.8	24.5	16.6	9.1
Profit on ordinary activities after taxation	138.6	119.6	69.6	61.3
Minority interest	0.9	1.7	0.6	0.1
Profit before extraordinary items	137.7	117.9	69.0	61.2
Extraordinary items	-	0.9	0.4	-
Profit for the financial period:				
Parent	60.3	27.2	11.7	7.4
Subsidiaries	76.8	91.6	56.5	53.5
Related companies	0.6	-	1.3	0.3
	137.7	118.8	69.4	61.2
Dividends	49.3	26.1	11.9	7.4
RETAINED PROFITS FOR THE FINANCIAL PERIOD	88.4	92.7	57.5	53.8
EARNINGS PER ORDINARY SHARE				
Basic	44.6	53.0	51.0	46.9
Fully diluted	43.2	48.4	45.6	42.2

Exhibit 3
Polly Peck International PLC and its subsidiaries
CONSOLIDATED BALANCE SHEET
(in millions of pounds)

	As of			
	31 Dec. 1989	31 Dec. 1988	29 Aug. 1987	29 Aug. 1986
FIXED ASSETS	284.5	-	-	-
Acquired brands at cost	1,015.8	514.8	221.2	157.9
Tangible assets	51.1	-	-	-
Bank deposits	18.3	4.8	1.3	3.9
Investments	1,369.7	519.6	222.5	161.8
CURRENT ASSETS				
Stocks and work in progress	246.5	128.1	68.4	35.8
Debtors	459.6	203.1	158.8	113.0
Cash and bank balances	249.3	124.2	20.6	18.1
	955.4	455.4	247.8	166.9
CREDITORS				
Amounts falling due within one year*	723.7	276.4	136.5	100.1
NET CURRENT ASSETS	231.7	179.0	111.3	66.8
TOTAL ASSETS LESS CURRENT LIABILITIES	1,601.4	698.6	333.8	228.6
CREDITORS				
Amounts falling due after more than one year	753.5	295.7	127.6	63.8
PROVISION FOR LIABILITIES AND CHARGES				
Deferred tax	2.6	1.4	0.9	0.7
	845.3	401.5	205.2	164.0
CAPITAL AND RESERVES				
Called up share capital	38.5	25.1	15.6	12.2
Share premium account	478.3	186.5	47.0	24.5
Revaluation reserve	254.8	148.1	89.5	53.1
Other reserves	0.4	0.4	0.8	0.8
Retained profit	71.7	26.1	44.3	73.3
	843.7	386.2	197.2	163.9
Minority interest	1.6	15.3	7.9	0.1
	845.3	401.5	205.1	164.0
* Trade payables/creditors	108.0	75.0	35.0	13.0

Exhibit 4
Polly Peck International PLC and its subsidiaries
FUND FLOW STATEMENT
(in millions of pounds)

	12 months ended 31st Dec. 1989	16 months ended 31st Dec. 1988	12 months ended 29th Aug. 1987	12 months ended 29th Aug. 1986
SOURCE OF FUNDS				
Profit on Ordinary activities before taxation	161.4	144.1	86.2	70.4
Adjustment for items not involving the movement of funds:				
Depreciation	28.9	19.2	6.3	4.0
Provision against other investments	0.8	-	-	-
Minority interest	0.9	-	-	-
Exchange variances				
on results of overseas companies	(1.7)	(11.6)	(14.3)	(7.1)
on inter group funding	(19.3)	(98.9)	(14.4)	(4.5)
Related companies share of results less exchange variances	(0.6)	-	(1.3)	(0.3)
Loss on disposal of tangible fixed assets	1.6	0.2	(0.1)	-
	10.6	(91.1)	(23.8)	(7.9)
TOTAL GENERATED FROM OPERATIONS	172.0	53.0	62.4	62.5
FUNDS FROM OTHER SOURCES				
Bank loans (net)	686.9	76.2	39.8	28.5
Proceeds on sale of fixed assets	22.5	14.9	1.2	0.7
Divestments	51.8	-	-	-
Ordinary shares and guaranteed bonds issued net of loan stock conversion and expenses	323.6	297.1	75.0	-
	1,084.8	388.2	116.0	29.2
	1,256.8	441.2	178.4	91.7
APPLICATION OF FUNDS				
Acquisitions	582.6	74.6	4.5	-
Purchase of tangible assets	209.0	156.4	49.9	41.3
Purchase of other investments	17.8	9.9	1.0	2.6
Taxation paid	12.3	19.5	11.5	8.2
Dividends paid	18.7	14.4	7.4	5.6
Bank and mortgage loans paid	-	-	16.4	3.2
	840.4	274.8	90.7	60.9
	416.4	166.4	87.7	30.8
INCREASE (DECREASE) IN WORKING CAPITAL				
Stock and work in progress	77.4	60.6	37.1	11.6
Debtors	182.2	85.6	62.9	37.6
Creditors	28.8	(49.7)	(22.5)	(22.6)
	288.4	96.5	77.5	26.6
INCREASE IN LIQUID FUNDS	128.0	69.9	10.2	4.2

Jyoti Structures Ltd. (hereafter JSL) is the third largest manufacturer of steel power transmission towers in India. Power transmission towers are used to transmit electrical power from power generation plants to consumer sites. The towers are usually constructed of fabricated steel and range in height from 50 to 150 feet above ground. Since the introduction of liberalized economic policies in India in 1991, the power transmission industry has been the fastest growing industry in India. JSL was incorporated as a private company in 1974, and became a listed company on the Bombay Stock Exchange in 1989.

JSL's first manufacturing facility was established at Nasik (in the state of Maharashtra) in 1979 and had a production capacity of 5,000 million tonnes (MT) per annum. As a consequence of JSL's association with Tata Exports Ltd., India's premier export company, JSL received orders in excess of 10,000 MT. Faced with the decision of either expanding the Nasik facility or building an entirely new manufacturing plant to meet the excess demand, the directors of JSL chose the latter option, purchasing a nearby location where a second fabrication operation was established as a separate private company named Prakash Fabricators, Inc. (hereafter Prakash).

Prakash continued to work as an independent subcontractor for JSL from 1979 to 1989. During this period, JSL built a second facility at Raipur, near Calcutta, in Central India. During the financial year 1994-95, JSL floated a 100% owned subsidiary with a paid-up capital of Rs. 25,000.[1] The objective of floating JSL Finance (JSF) was to channel all diversification projects of JSL through JSL Finance.

Pursuant to this objective, JSF purchased 100% of the outstanding shares of Prakash from the original promoters at a price of Rs. 47,93,850, or Rs.45,225 per share. The amount represented the fair market value of Prakash's net assets.[2] As a result of this, Prakash became a wholly-owned subsidiary of JSF.[3] During 1995-96, a portion of Prakash was sold (at cost) to an outside investor, effectively reducing JSF's ownership interest from 100 to 80 percent.

Accounting for Investments

Under generally accepted accounting practices in India, there is no requirement to consolidate the financial statements of subsidiaries with those of the parent company.[4] In most cases, subsidiaries are accounted for as long-term investments by the parent company. Such investments are normally accounted for at their cost, unless a permanent decline in value occurs, in which case the investment is written down to its net realizable value. Accordingly, JSL accounted for JSF (and, by extension, Prakash) using the cost method.

---

* This case was prepared by Kenneth R. Ferris and Motilal Gyamlami. Copyright © 1997 by the American Graduate School of International Management. All rights reserved

[1] All values are in Indian rupees (Rs) unless otherwise noted.

[2] The total purchase price of Rs 47,93,850, is equivalent to 4,793,850 rupees (or 106 shares at 45,225 rupees per share).

[3] Other than its inital capitalization of 25,000 rupees, the only assets and liabilities held by JSF were those acquired from Prakash Fabricators, Inc. in 1995. JSF's acquisition of Prakash was funded by an advance from JSL, its parent company.

[4] In India, accounting standards are established by the Institute of Chartered Accountants of India (ICAI).

Under International Accounting Standards Commission recommended practice, a parent company **should** consolidate all majority-owned subsidiaries, except those held for disposal in the near future or those over whose assets and operations parental control is impaired by legal restrictions (e.g. control resides with a bankruptcy judge or other court-appointed entity). In the event that a majority-owned subsidiary is not consolidated, the reasons for that accounting treatment should be disclosed.

Exhibits 1 - 5, presented below, contain respectively:

1. JSL's independent auditors' report;
2. JSL's balance sheet as of 31 March 1996 and profit and loss account for the year ended 31 March 1996;
3. JSL's schedules A-M, which relate to the balance sheet;
4. JSL's schedules 1-8, which relate to the profit and loss account; and,
5. The footnotes to the JSL's 1996 statement of accounts.

According to the Director's report accompanying JSL's statement of accounts, JSF earned 1,986,000 rupees in 1996, and paid dividends totaling 190,000 rupees through 31 March 1996.

Required:

1. Assume that JSF's acquisition of Prakash was consummated on April 1, 1995, and that the sale of the 20 percent shareholding occurred on April 1, 1995. Recast JSL's balance sheet and income statement as of 31 March 1996 using the equity method of accounting for investments.

2. Assume that JSF's acquisition of Prakash was consummated on April 1, 1995. Recast JSL's balance sheet and income statement as of 31 March 1996 using the full consolidation approach. Would your answer change if you were using the partial consolidation approach instead? If so, explain how.

   For this analysis, assume that Prakash's abbreviated financial statements at 31 March 1996 were as follows:

Balance Sheet
(in rupees)

Current Assets	500,000	Long-term debt	1,000,000
Noncurrent assets	4,500,000	Shareholders' equity	4,000,000
Total	5,000,000	Total	5,000,000

Profit & Loss Account
(in rupees)

Sales	12,482,500
Expenditure	10,000,000
Profit-after-taxes	2,482,500

3. Review JSL's financial disclosures in Exhibits 1 - 5 and prepare a list of any differences between Indian and U.S. GAAP that you observe.

Exhibit 1
Jyoti Structures Ltd.
Independent Auditors Report

AUDITORS' REPORT

TO THE MEMBERS OF JYOTI STRUCTURES LIMITED

We have audited the attached Balance Sheet of JYOTI STRUCTURES LIMITED as at 31st March, 1996 and also the Profit and Loss Account of the Company for the year ended on that date, annexed thereto and report that :

1. As required by the Manufacturing and Other Companies (Auditors' Report) Order, 1988, issued by the Company Law Board in terms of Section 227 (4A) of the Companies Act, 1956, we annex hereto, a statement of the matters specified in paragraphs 4 and 5 of the said Order. We also draw the attention of the members to Note No. 13 of the Notes forming Part of the Accounts of the Company.

2. Further to our comments in the Annexure referred to in paragraph 1 above, we state that :

   a) we have obtained all the information and explanations which to the best of our knowledge and belief were necessary for the purposes of our audit;

   b) in our opinion, proper books of account as required by law have been kept by the Company so far as appears from our examination of the books;

   c) the Balance Sheet and Profit and Loss Account dealt with by this Report are in agreement with the books of account;

   d) in our opinion and to the best of our information and according to the explanations given to us, the said accounts give the information required by the Companies Act, 1956, in the manner so required and give a true and fair view :

      i) in the case of the Balance Sheet, of the state of affairs of the Company as at 31st March, 1996; and

      ii) in the case of the Profit and Loss Account, of the PROFIT for the year ended on that date.

For R.M. AJGAONKAR & CO.,
Chartered Accountants

Mumbai,
27th May, 1996

R.M. AJGAONKAR
Proprietor

ANNEXURE TO THE AUDITORS' REPORT
(Referred to in Paragraph 1 of our report of even date)

1. The Company has maintained proper records showing full particulars including quantitative details and situation of the fixed assets. As per the information and explanations given to us, the management has physically verified the fixed assets. In our opinion, the frequency of verification is reasonable, having regard to the size of the Company, nature of its business and value of the fixed assets. No material discrepancies were noticed on such verification.

2. None of the fixed assets have been revalued during the year.

3. The stocks have been physically verified during the year by the management. In our opinion, the frequency of verification is reasonable.

4. In our opinion and according to the information and explanations given to us, the procedures for physical verification of stocks followed by the management were reasonable and adequate in relation to the size of the Company and the nature of its business.

5. The discrepancies noticed on verification between the physical stocks and book records were not material in relation to the operations of the Company and the same have been properly dealt with, in the books of account.

6. In our opinion and according to the information and explanations given to us, the valuation of stocks is fair and proper, and is in accordance with the normally accepted accounting principles and is on the same basis as in the previous year.

7. In our opinion and according to the information and explanations given to us, the rates of interest and other terms and conditions of loans, secured or unsecured, taken by the Company from companies, firms and other parties listed in the register maintained under Section 301 of the Companies Act, 1956, and/or from companies under the same management as defined under Section 370(1B) of the Companies Act, 1956 are not prima facie prejudicial to the interest of the Company.

8. In our opinion and according to the information and explanations given to us, the rates of interest and other terms and conditions of loans, secured or unsecured, granted by the Company to companies, firms or other parties listed in the register maintained under Section

Exhibit 1
Jyoti Structures Ltd.
Independent Auditors Report
(continued)

301 of the Companies Act, 1956 and/or to the companies under the same management as defined under sub-section (1B) of Section 370 of the Companies Act, 1956 are prima facie not prejudicial to the interest of the Company.

9. In respect of loans and advances in the nature of loans given by the Company, where stipulations have been made, the parties are generally repaying the principal amounts as stipulated or as rescheduled and have also been regular in the payment of interest, wherever applicable.

10. In our opinion and according to the information and explanations given to us, there are adequate internal control procedures commensurate with the size of the Company and the nature of its business with regard to purchase of stores, raw materials including components, plant and machinery, equipments and other assets and for sale of goods.

11. In our opinion, the transactions of purchase of goods and materials and sale of goods and services, made in pursuance of contracts or arrangements entered in the register maintained under Section 301 of the Companies Act, 1956, and aggregating during the year to Rs 50,000 or more in respect of each party, were made at prices which are reasonable having regard to the prevailing market prices for such goods or materials or the prices at which transactions for similar goods or materials were made with other parties, wherever applicable.

12. As explained to us, the Company has a regular procedure for the determination of unserviceable or damaged stores, raw materials and finished goods. Adequate provision has been made in the accounts for the loss arising on the items so determined.

13. In our opinion and according to the information and explanations given to us, the Company has complied with the provisions of Section 58A of the Companies Act, 1956 and the Rules framed thereunder with regard to the deposits accepted from the public.

14. In our opinion, the Company has maintained reasonable records for sale and disposal of realisable by-products and scrap.

15. In our opinion, the Company has an adequate internal audit system commensurate with its size and nature of its business.

16. The Central Government has not prescribed maintenance of cost records under Section 209(1)(d) of the Companies Act, 1956 for the products of the Company.

17. The Company has generally been regular during the year in depositing Provident Fund and Employees' State Insurance dues with the appropriate authorities, wherever applicable.

18. According to the books and records examined by us and the information and explanations given to us, there were no undisputed amounts payable in respect of Income-tax, Wealth-tax, Sales tax, Customs Duty and Excise Duty which have remained outstanding as at 31st March, 1996 for a period exceeding six months from the date they became payable.

19. According to the information and explanations given to us and the records of the Company examined by us, prima facie, no personal expenses have been charged to revenue account other than those payable under contractual obligations or in accordance with the generally accepted business practices.

20. The Company is not a Sick Industrial Company within the meaning of clause (0) of Section 3(1) of the Sick Industrial Companies (Special Provisions) Act, 1985.

21. In respect of service activities, the Company has a reasonable system of recording receipts, issues and consumption of materials and stores and allocation of the materials consumed to the relevant jobs commensurate with its size and nature of its business.

22. In respect of service activities, the system of the Company provides for a reasonable allocation of manhours utilised to the relative jobs, commensurate with its size and nature of its business, wherever applicable.

23. In our opinion and according to the information and explanations given to us, there is a reasonable system of authorisation at proper levels and necessary controls on the issue of stores and where applicable, on allocation of stores and labour to jobs and there is a system of internal control generally commensurate with the size of the Company and the nature of its business.

For R.M. AJGAONKAR & CO.,
Chartered Accountants

Mumbai,
27th May, 1996

R.M. AJGAONKAR
Proprietor

Exhibit 2

Jyoti Structures Ltd.

Financial Statements as of 31 March 1996

BALANCE SHEET AS AT 31ST MARCH, 1996

	Schedule	Rupees	As at 31.3.1996 Rupees	As at 31.3.1995 Rupees
SOURCES OF FUNDS				
1. Shareholders' Funds				
a) Share Capital	A	4,91,13,150		4,90,73,890
b) Reserves & Surplus	B	20,11,10,421		11,49,28,892
			25,02,23,571	16,40,02,782
2. Loan Funds				
a) Secured Loans	C	16,46,88,390		10,28,37,440
b) Unsecured Loans	D	2,51,52,779		1,01,71,392
			18,98,41,169	11,30,08,832
			44,00,64,740	27,70,11,614
APPLICATION OF FUNDS				
1. Fixed Assets	E			
Gross Block		23,81,48,606		18,70,55,750
Less :Depreciation		4,14,68,187		2,17,59,343
Net Block		19,66,80,419		16,52,96,407
Add : Capital Work-in-Progress		36,87,982		—
			20,03,68,401	16,52,96,407
2. Investments	F		10,50,400	10,50,400
3. Current Assets, Loans and Advances				
a) Inventories	G	28,37,57,057		16,24,04,442
b) Sundry Debtors	H	22,12,46,290		8,53,48,252
c) Other Current Assets	I	5,39,88,428		2,55,52,791
d) Cash & Bank Balances	J	11,46,76,373		5,93,17,465
e) Loans & Advances	K	18,56,90,187		15,73,94,695
		85,93,58,335		49,00,17,645
Less :				
Current Liabilities & Provisions				
a) Current Liabilities	L	54,34,49,441		31,68,32,797
b) Provisions	M	7,80,79,975		6,35,34,128
		62,15,29,416		38,03,66,925
Net Current Assets			23,78,28,919	10,96,50,720
4. Miscellaneous Expenditure				
(to the extent not written off or adjusted)				
Share Issue Expenses			8,17,020	10,14,087
			44,00,64,740	27,70,11,614

As per our report attached
For R.M. AJGAONKAR & CO.,
Chartered Accountants
R.M. AJGAONKAR
Proprietor
Mumbai, 27th May, 1996

For and on behalf of the Board

K.R. BHAT
Company Secretary

V.P. VALECHA
Chairman

K.R. THAKUR
Managing Director

PROFIT & LOSS ACCOUNT FOR THE YEAR ENDED 31ST MARCH, 1996

	Schedule	Rupees	As at 31.3.1996 Rupees	As at 31.3.1995 Rupees
INCOME				
1. Sales	1		1,17,66,57,174	76,18,81,655
2. Other Income	2		2,01,43,298	77,98,347
			1,19,68,00,472	76,96,80,002
EXPENDITURE				
1. Cost of Materials Consumed	3		54,37,26,445	38,96,87,696
2. Erection & Sub-contracting Expenses	4		18,60,26,044	8,63,36,648
3. (Increase)/Decrease in stocks of Finished/ Semi-Finished goods	5		(3,04,85,100)	(2,73,28,150)
4. Personnel Expenses	6		3,89,36,627	2,44,57,162
5. Operating & Other Expenses	7		27,37,81,432	17,46,90,959
6. Interest	8		3,62,14,259	2,25,29,404
7. Depreciation		1,99,96,840		81,13,802
Less : Deferred Govt. Grant		1,43,130		—
			1,98,53,710	81,13,802
			1,06,80,53,417	67,84,87,521
8. Profit before taxes			12,87,47,055	9,11,92,481
9. Taxes			3,15,00,000	2,60,00,000
10. Profit after taxes			9,72,47,055	6,51,92,481
11. Balance brought forward from previous year			8,58,598	4,28,742
12 Prior year adjustment (Net)			4,85,058	43,753
13. Excess/(Short) Provision of Taxes for earlier years			(7,25,629)	—
14. Profit available for appropriations			9,78,65,082	6,56,64,976
APPROPRIATIONS				
a. Proposed Dividend			1,22,79,975	1,08,06,378
b. Transfer to Debenture Redemption Reserve			15,00,000	15,00,000
c. Transfer to General Reserve			8,25,00,000	5,25,00,000
d. Balance carried to Balance Sheet			15,85,107	8,58,598
			9,78,65,082	6,56,64,976

As per our report attached
For R.M. AJGAONKAR & CO.,
Chartered Accountants
R.M. AJGAONKAR
Proprietor
Mumbai, 27th May, 1996

For and on behalf of the Board

K.R. BHAT
Company Secretary

V.P. VALECHA
Chairman

K.R. THAKUR
Managing Director

Exhibit 3
Jyoti Structures Ltd.
Balance Sheet Schedules A-M

SCHEDULES FORMING PART OF BALANCE SHEET

			As at 31.3.1996	As at 31.3.1995
		Rupees	Rupees	Rupees

SCHEDULE - A

SHARE CAPITAL

Authorised :

60,00,000	Equity Shares of Rs. 10/- each (P.Y. 60,00,000 Equity Shares of Rs. 10/- each)		6,00,00,000	6,00,00,000

Issued :

49,11,990	Equity Shares of Rs. 10/- each (P.Y. 49,11,990 Equity Shares of Rs. 10/- each)		4,91,19,900	4,91,19,900

Subscribed & Paid-up :

49,11,990	Equity Shares of Rs. 10/- each fully called up			
---	(P.Y. 49,11,990 Equity Shares of Rs. 10/- each)		4,91,19,900	4,91,19,900
	Less : Allotment money in arrears - by others		6,750	46,010
			4,91,13,150	4,90,73,890

Notes :

Of the above Shares :

a) 67,530 Equity Shares were issued as fully paid-up Bonus Shares by capitalisation of General Reserve in the year 1985-86.

b) 16,51,330 Equity Shares of Rs. 10/- each were issued for cash on Rights basis, (including 28,000 Equity Shares issued to the employees of the Company) at a Premium of Rs. 25/- per share in the year 1992-93.

c) 16,37,330 Equity Shares were allotted as fully paid-up Bonus Shares by way of capitalisation out of Share Premium, in the year 1994-95.

SCHEDULE - B

RESERVES AND SURPLUS

			As at 31.3.1996	As at 31.3.1995
a)	M.P. State Govt. Grant	15,00,000		—
	Less : Deferred M.P. Govt. Grant	1,43,130		—
			13,56,870	—
b)	Share Premium	2,95,09,950		4,58,83,250
	Less : Transfer for Allotment of Bonus Shares	—		1,63,73,300
	Less : Allotment money in arrears	16,875		1,15,025
			2,94,93,075	2,93,94,925
c)	Debenture Redemption Reserve	75,00,000		60,00,000
	Add : Addition during the Year	15,00,000		15,00,000
			90,00,000	75,00,000
d)	Investment Allowance (Utilised) Reserve	6,75,369		6,75,369
	Less : Transfer to General Reserve	6,75,369		—
			—	6,75,369
e)	General Reserve as per Last Year	7,65,00,000		2,40,00,000
	Add : Transfer from Investment Allowance (Utilised) Reserve	6,75,369		—
	Add : Addition during the Year	8,25,00,000		5,25,00,000
			15,96,75,369	7,65,00,000
f)	Balance as per Profit and Loss Account		15,85,107	8,58,598
			20,11,10,421	11,49,28,892

Exhibit 3
Jyoti Structures Ltd.
Balance Sheet Schedules A-M
(continued)

SCHEDULES FORMING PART OF BALANCE SHEET

	As at 31.3.1996 Rupees	As at 31.3.1995 Rupees

SCHEDULE - C

SECURED LOANS

		As at 31.3.1996 Rupees	As at 31.3.1995 Rupees
a)	Banks (for Working Capital)	13,88,80,396	6,98,47,041

Secured by hypothecation of raw materials, work-in-progress, finished goods, stores/spares and consumables,book debts (to the extent of finance availed against the same, if any) and secured by a charge which is second & subservient to the charge created in favour of the Trustees to the Debentureholders of 14% secured Non-Convertible Debentures, by way of deposit of title deeds in respect of the Company's immovable property in M.I.D.C., Satpur Industrial Area, Nasik (Maharashtra)

b)	14% secured Non-Convertible Redeemable Debentures of Rs. 100/- each wholly subscribed by Canbank Financial Services Ltd.	1,00,00,000	1,00,00,000

    i) Secured by unattested Deed of Hypothecation dated 23rd January, 1991 charging the tangible movable property and assets (save and except book debts) subject to the prior charges, present or future, if any, in favour of bankers to the Company for the working capital facilities; and

    ii) Secured by mortgage by deposit of title deeds with effect from 23rd January, 1991 in respect of the Company's immovable property in M.I.D.C., Satpur Industrial Area, Nasik (Maharashtra)

    iii) These Debentures shall be repayable at a premium of 5% on the expiry of 6th, 7th and 8th year from the date of allotment in the ratio of 30:30:40 respectively

c)	IDBI - Equipment Finance Scheme Term Loan	31,02,166	51,70,278
	IDBI - Assets Credit Scheme - Term Loan	93,25,828	1,19,40,121

Secured by an exclusive first charge by way of hypothecation of specific machinery

d)	Madhya Pradesh Finance Corporation	33,80,000	58,80,000

    i) Secured by a charge created by way of deposit of title deeds in respect of Company's land & buildings in Urla Industrial Area, Raipur (Madhya Pradesh)

    ii) Secured by hypothecation of certain machinery & equipments situated in Company's factory in Urla Industrial Area , Raipur (Madhya Pradesh)

	As at 31.3.1996 Rupees	As at 31.3.1995 Rupees
	16,46,88,390	10,28,37,440

Exhibit 3
Jyoti Structures Ltd.
Balance Sheet Schedules A-M
(continued)

SCHEDULES FORMING PART OF BALANCE SHEET

		As at 31.3.1996 Rupees	As at 31.3.1995 Rupees
SCHEDULE - D			
UNSECURED LOANS			
a)	Term loan from Western Maharashtra Development Corporation Limited	**7,98,359**	7,98,359
b)	Sales Tax - Deferral Scheme 1988 - Western Maharashtra Development Corporation Limited	**64,67,708**	33,75,215
c)	Sales Tax - Deferral - Madhya Pradesh	**1,78,86,712**	59,47,818
d)	From Others	**—**	50,000
		2,51,52,779	1,01,71,392

SCHEDULE -E

FIXED ASSETS AND DEPRECIATION

	GROSS BLOCK					DEPRECIATION				(Rupees) NET BLOCK	
	As at 1.4.1995	Additions	Deletions	As at 31.3.1996	As at 1.4.1995	For the year	Deletions	As at 31.3.1996	As at 31.3.1996	As at 31.3.1995	
Land	13,12,866	30,11,351	—	43,24,217	64,238	13,455	—	77,693	42,46,524	12,48,628	
Buildings	1,59,08,605	25,87,981	—	1,84,96,586	14,89,254	4,84,545	—	19,73,799	1,65,22,787	1,44,19,351	
Plant & Machinery	8,35,45,014	2,97,35,326	4,79,596	11,28,00,744	1,45,71,065	71,65,855	2,13,007	2,15,23,913	9,12,76,831	6,89,73,949	
Leased Assets	6,84,41,523	50,51,314	—	7,34,92,837	14,50,902	1,00,46,624	—	1,14,97,526	6,19,95,311	6,69,90,621	
Furniture & Fixtures	38,60,305	14,63,895	—	53,24,200	6,26,496	2,80,022	—	9,06,518	44,17,682	32,33,809	
Office Equipments	62,23,692	17,16,341	—	79,40,033	14,70,911	8,96,068	—	23,66,979	55,73,054	47,52,781	
Air Conditioners & Water Coolers	12,55,173	1,72,365	—	14,27,538	2,53,675	63,269	—	3,16,944	11,10,594	10,01,498	
Vehicles	65,08,572	79,24,236	90,357	1,43,42,451	18,32,802	10,47,002	74,989	28,04,815	1,15,37,636	46,75,770	
TOTAL	18,70,55,750	5,16,62,809	5,69,953	23,81,48,606	2,17,59,343	1,99,96,840	2,87,996	4,14,68,187	19,66,80,419	16,52,96,407	
Capital Work-in-Progress	—	36,87,982	—	36,87,982	—	—	—	—	36,87,982	—	
TOTAL	18,70,55,750	5,53,50,791	5,69,953	24,18,36,588	2,17,59,343	1,99,96,840	2,87,996	4,14,68,187	20,03,68,401	16,52,96,407	
Previous Year	8,66,78,368	10,09,65,412	5,88,030	18,70,55,750	1,37,70,424	81,13,802	1,24,883	2,17,59,343	16,52,96,407	7,29,07,944	

Exhibit 3
Jyoti Structures Ltd.
Balance Sheet Schedules A-M
(continued)

SCHEDULES FORMING PART OF BALANCE SHEET

	As at 31.3.1996 Rupees	As at 31.3.1995 Rupees
SCHEDULE - F		
INVESTMENTS		
Unquoted (at cost)		
a) Janakalyan Sahakari Bank Ltd. (2,540 Shares of Rs. 10/- each fully paid-up)	25,400	25,400
b) IDBI Term Discount Bond (Series II) (100 Bonds of Rs. 5,000/- each fully paid-up)	5,00,000	5,00,000
c) SBI Bonds (500 Bonds of Rs. 1,000/- each fully paid-up)	5,00,000	5,00,000
d) JSL Finance Ltd. (a subsidiary company) (2,500 Shares of Rs. 10/- each fully paid-up)	25,000	25,000
	10,50,400	10,50,400
SCHEDULE - G		
INVENTORIES		
a) Raw Materials	17,76,66,000	9,71,29,000
b) Tools and Tackles	10,83,652	3,92,295
c) Stores and Spares	27,21,000	19,48,000
d) Work-in-Progress	2,79,19,000	1,83,83,000
e) Finished Goods	3,42,97,100	4,34,22,000
f) Stock-in-Transit (Finished Goods)	3,00,74,000	—
g) Construction Materials at site	99,96,305	5,32,827
h) Bought-out Components	—	5,97,320
	28,37,57,057	16,24,04,442
SCHEDULE - H		
SUNDRY DEBTORS		
(Unsecured and considered good)		
a) Outstanding for more than six months	1,99,08,357	1,28,16,595
b) Others	20,13,37,933	7,25,31,657
	22,12,46,290	8,53,48,252

Exhibit 3
Jyoti Structures Ltd.
Balance Sheet Schedules A-M
(continued)

SCHEDULES FORMING PART OF BALANCE SHEET

	As at 31.3.1996 Rupees	As at 31.3.1995 Rupees
SCHEDULE - I		
OTHER CURRENT ASSETS		
(Unsecured and considered good)		
Retentions and charges recoverable from clients	5,39,88,428	2,55,52,791
SCHEDULE - J		
CASH AND BANK BALANCES		
a) Cash on Hand	74,20,350	17,46,343
b) Current Accounts with Scheduled Banks	3,23,38,878	50,15,633
c) Fixed Deposits with Scheduled Banks	7,49,17,145	5,25,55,489
	11,46,76,373	5,93,17,465
SCHEDULE - K		
LOANS AND ADVANCES		
a) Advances to Suppliers	2,34,52,115	2,32,45,477
b) Advances to Subsidiary Companies	1,47,82,204	1,44,06,771
c) Advances recoverable in cash or in kind or for value to be received	5,13,07,534	4,47,51,648
d) Advances with public bodies and others	2,17,16,038	1,12,36,750
e) Pre-paid Expenses	1,76,01,419	1,35,26,641
f) Advance payment of Taxes	5,68,30,877	5,02,27,408
	18,56,90,187	15,73,94,695
SCHEDULE - L		
CURRENT LIABILITIES		
a) Sundry Creditors		
i) For goods/services	29,70,92,795	7,88,63,456
ii) Other Liabilities	7,07,50,110	6,46,50,123
iii) Unclaimed Dividend	1,51,998	1,26,071
b) Advances received from Customers	17,54,54,538	17,31,93,147
	54,34,49,441	31,68,32,797
SCHEDULE - M		
PROVISIONS		
a) Provision for Taxation	6,58,00,000	5,27,27,750
b) Proposed Dividend	1,22,79,975	1,08,06,378
	7,80,79,975	6,35,34,128

387

Exhibit 4
Jyoti Structures Ltd.
Profit and Loss Statement Schedules 1-8

SCHEDULES FORMING PART OF THE PROFIT AND LOSS ACCOUNT

		As at 31.3.1996 Rupees	As at 31.3.1995 Rupees
SCHEDULE - 1			
SALES			
a)	Sales/Erection of Towers, Structures & Components	1,14,05,45,819	73,77,51,635
b)	Conversion Charges	61,67,751	40,60,539
c)	Residuals & Scrap	2,99,43,604	2,00,69,481
		1,17,66,57,174	76,18,81,655
SCHEDULE - 2			
OTHER INCOME			
a)	Interest	81,55,306	32,36,818
b)	Dividend	1,53,810	—
c)	Lease Rental / Management Fees	98,43,864	14,97,594
d)	Miscellaneous Receipts	19,90,318	30,63,935
		2,01,43,298	77,98,347
SCHEDULE - 3			
COST OF MATERIALS CONSUMED			
a)	Opening Stock	9,77,26,320	7,22,87,000
b)	Add : Purchases	62,36,66,125	41,51,27,016
		72,13,92,445	48,74,14,016
c)	Less : Closing Stock	(17,76,66,000)	(9,77,26,320)
		54,37,26,445	38,96,87,696
SCHEDULE - 4			
ERECTION AND SUB-CONTRACTING EXPENSES			
a)	Construction Materials and Stores	4,77,16,707	1,35,91,964
b)	Tools & Tackles consumed	43,87,553	14,82,432
c)	Wages	1,58,33,264	1,59,02,254
d)	Sub-contracting Expenses	10,23,24,115	3,84,75,681
e)	Repairs to Equipment/Machinery	3,31,796	7,54,976
f)	Construction Transport	1,31,40,587	1,24,30,452
g)	Others	22,92,022	36,98,889
		18,60,26,044	8,63,36,648
SCHEDULE - 5			
(INCREASE)/DECREASE IN STOCK OF FINISHED AND SEMI-FINISHED GOODS			
a)	Opening Stock	6,18,05,000	3,44,76,850
b)	Less : Closing Stock	(9,22,90,100)	(6,18,05,000)
		(3,04,85,100)	(2,73,28,150)

SCHEDULES FORMING PART OF THE PROFIT AND LOSS ACCOUNT

		As at 31.3.1996 Rupees	As at 31.3.1995 Rupees
SCHEDULE - 6			
PERSONNEL EXPENSES			
a)	Salaries and Wages including Bonus	**3,20,88,519**	1,98,31,770
b)	Contribution to Provident Fund & Other Funds	**27,77,695**	17,49,455
c)	Welfare Expenses	**40,70,413**	28,75,937
		3,89,36,627	2,44,57,162
SCHEDULE - 7			
OPERATING AND OTHER EXPENSES			
a)	Excise Duty	**7,97,96,431**	7,27,39,086
b)	Stores & Consumables	**84,77,015**	78,60,644
c)	Power & Fuel	**92,66,453**	71,95,155
d)	Conversion Expenses	**3,19,66,020**	2,25,86,171
e)	Repairs to Buildings	**9,07,407**	5,55,278
f)	Repairs to Plant & Machinery and Others	**43,09,221**	35,43,518
g)	Testing & Designing Expenses	**52,58,381**	29,07,454
h)	Freight & Octroi	**4,29,51,363**	1,37,66,442
i)	Rent	**70,12,423**	13,69,115
j)	Rates & Taxes	**4,09,671**	1,88,041
k)	Insurance	**46,90,486**	28,15,289
l)	Travelling & Conveyance	**1,55,94,640**	72,94,612
m)	Postage, Telephone & Telex	**87,47,817**	53,77,098
n)	Printing & Stationery	**32,07,473**	22,48,888
o)	Professional & Legal Fees	**29,14,462**	9,00,117
p)	Service Charges	**1,00,08,061**	54,82,346
q)	Sales Tax	**52,27,813**	37,52,530
r)	Directors' Fees	**15,750**	9,500
s)	Auditors' Remuneration	**1,75,000**	1,30,000
t)	Bank Charges & Guarantee Commission	**2,36,67,400**	1,10,19,727
u)	Brokerage & Commission	**47,90,499**	5,16,446
v)	Miscellaneous Expenses	**38,37,077**	21,53,384
w)	Donations	**3,53,501**	83,050
x)	Amortisation of Share Issue Expenses	**1,97,068**	1,97,068
		27,37,81,432	17,46,90,959
SCHEDULE - 8			
INTEREST			
a)	On Term Loans	**50,44,165**	61,64,669
b)	On Bank Loans	**3,04,66,233**	1,58,93,587
c)	On Others	**7,03,861**	4,71,148
		3,62,14,259	2,25,29,404

NOTES FORMING PART OF ACCOUNTS 1995-96

1. **Significant Accounting Policies :**

   a) Generally Mercantile system of Accounting is followed unless otherwise stated.

   b) Valuation of inventories is made as under :-

       i) Raw materials and stores & spares are valued at cost and the scrap is valued at net realisable value.

       ii) Work-in-progress is valued at estimated cost.

       iii) Finished goods are valued at estimated cost or net realisable value whichever is lower.

       iv) Tools and Tackles are valued at estimated value.

   c) Investments are stated at cost.

   d) All fixed assets are capitalised at cost, inclusive of incidental expenses.

   e) Depreciation on Leased Assets has been provided on the basis of primary lease period of the assets. On all other fixed assets, depreciation is provided on Straight Line Method at the rate and in the manner prescribed in Schedule XIV of the Companies Act, 1956.

   f) Expenses for issue of equity shares made by the Company are written off over a period of 10 years and proportionate expenditure has been written off during the year.

   g) · Sales/income in case of Construction Contracts and orders to be executed over a period of more than one year are booked on the basis of running bills based on completed work.

   h) Leasing income is accounted on accrual basis.

   i) The amount of government grant received is credited to Deferred Government Grant Account and income therefrom is recognised over the life of assets for which it is received.

   j) All the assets and liabilities in foreign currency as on 31st March, 1996 are accounted for at the rate of exchange prevailing as on that date.

2. Contingent Liabilities not provided for :

   a) Outstanding Performance Guarantees given by banks **Rs. 33,22,79,383/-** (P.Y. Rs. 23,26,22,000/-).

   b) Bills discounted with banks and outstanding are **Rs. 2,67,98,829/-** (P.Y. Rs. 2,26,778/-).

3. During the year, M.P. State Government Subsidy of Rs. 15,00,000/- was received on account of new factory established in Raipur (M.P.). The amount received is credited to Deferred Government Grant Account and income of Rs. 1,43,130/- is accounted therefrom in the current year.

4. Dividend includes Rs. 1,50,000/- received from subsidiary company, viz : JSL Finance Ltd.

NOTES FORMING PART OF ACCOUNTS 1995-96

5. a) The amount of exchange difference (Net) between the values booked as on 31st March, 1996 and the values as on the date of shipments works out to a surplus of Rs. 3,15,103/- on deferred terms of contracts in respect of Imports and Exports.

    b) The amount of exchange difference (Net) adjusted in the carrying cost of fixed assets during the year works out to a deficit of Rs. 14,59,513/-.

6. The Company's contribution to the Gratuity Fund is towards premium on LIC's policy taken by the Trustees of the Fund to cover the gratuity liability. The Company is liable to make further contribution in case funds in the hands of the Trustees are not sufficient to meet the claims of the employees.

7. The total amount of Managerial Remuneration paid to Managing Director and Whole-Time Director is **Rs. 13,22,446/-** (P.Y. Rs. 5,85,266/-) which is inclusive of perquisites of **Rs. 2,30,446/-** (P.Y. Rs. 1,23,266/-).

8. Auditors' Remuneration :

		1995-96 Rupees	1994-95 Rupees
a)	For Audit Fees	125,000	75,000
b)	For Taxation Matters	25,000	20,000
c)	For Tax Audit	25,000	20,000
d)	For Other Services	—	15,000
		1,75,000	1,30,000

9. a) Capacity and Production of Transmission Lines, Towers & Structures :

		1995-96	1994-95
i)	Installed Capacity (MT p.a.)	34,000	34,000
ii)	Production (MT)	27,219	20,278

    b) Turnover, Opening and Closing Stock of Transmission Lines, Towers & Structures/Components & parts :

		1995-96		1994-95	
		MT	Rupees	MT	Rupees
i)	Turnover	26,520	1,14,67,13,570 #	19,386	74,18,12,174 #
ii)	Residuals & Scrap	—	2,99,43,604	—	2,00,69,481
iii)	Opening Stock (Finished Goods)	1,884	4,34,22,000	991	2,46,26,850
iv)	Closing Stock (Finished Goods)	2,583	6,43,71,100	1,884	4,34,22,000

#Value includes the turnover of Turnkey Projects

NOTES FORMING PART OF ACCOUNTS 1995-96

c) Consumption - Raw Materials / Bought-out Components etc. :

		1995-96		1994-95	
		MT	**Rupees**	MT	Rupees
i)	Steel	**30,011**	**42,30,94,239**	21,447	30,19,78,029
ii)	Zinc	**1,374**	**6,78,00,326**	963	4,87,64,990
iii)	Fasteners, ASCR Conductors, Accessories/Bought-out Towers & Structures/Components etc.	**—**	**5,28,31,880**	—	3,89,44,677

10. CIF Value of Imports (Direct) :

	1995-96	1994-95
	Rupees	Rupees
a) Capital Goods	**1,28,00,567**	1,37,71,880
b) Bought-out Components	**1,21,46,218**	—
c) Raw Materials	**23,56,28,164**	6,41,91,259
d) Spare parts	**6,67,127**	7,86,815

11. Value of Imported and Indigenous
    Raw Materials and Stores & components consumed :

		1995-96		1994-95	
		%	**Rupees**	%	Rupees
a)	Raw Materials :				
	i) Imported	**37.30**	**19,37,81,433**	23.78	8,88,60,626
	ii) Indigenous	**62.70**	**32,56,77,675**	76.22	28,47,97,681
b)	Stores & Spare parts :				
	i) Imported	**7.30**	**6,67,127**	1.92	1,54,200
	ii) Indigenous	**92.70**	**84,77,015**	98.08	78,60,644
c)	Components				
	i) Imported	**50.05**	**1,21,46,218**	—	—
	ii) Indigenous	**49.95**	**1,21,21,119**	100.00	1,60,29,389

Exhibit 5
Jyoti Structures Ltd.
Footnotes to Accompany Financial Statements
(continued)

12. Earnings and Expenditure in Foreign Currency :

		1995-96 **Rupees**	1994-95 Rupees
a)	Earnings (Including Deemed Exports and Sales through Export House)	27,81,34,099	7,47,41,454
b)	Expenditure - Travelling & Others	54,30,539	14,71,035

13. a) Interest received on allotment money, interest on Fixed Deposits with bankers and interest on Investments in SBI/IDBI Bonds is accounted for as and when received.

b) Excise Duty, Customs Duty & Octroi are accounted for as and when paid. Similarly bonus to employees is accounted at the time of payment.

14. Previous Year's figures have been regrouped wherever necessary.

As per our report attached
For R.M. AJGAONKAR & CO.,
Chartered Accountants
R.M. AJGAONKAR
Proprietor
Mumbai, 27th May, 1996

For and on behalf of the Board

K.R. BHAT
Company Secretary

V.P. VALECHA
Chairman

K.R. THAKUR
Managing Director

Lever Brothers West Indies Ltd. was incorporated in the Republic of Trinidad and Tobago in 1929.[1] The company was formed after Unilever PLC (a company incorporated in the United Kingdom) acquired two local firms, Trinidad Manufacturing and Refining Ltd. and West Indian Industries Ltd., involved in the manufacture of crude soap and cooking fat from coconut oil. The acquisitions provided Unilever entry to the growing Caribbean consumer marketplace. In 1964, the corporate name of Lever Brothers West Indies was adopted, and the company came public after Unilever distributed 10 percent of the firm's equity to its principal Caribbean distributors. Beginning in 1973, additional shares were sold into the local equity market following a wave of civil unrest related to a growing nationalistic movement in the island republic. Today, Unilever PLC, through its wholly-owned subsidiary Unilon AG, holds 50.01 percent of the firm's voting shares.

Lever Brothers' principal business activities include the manufacture and sale of detergents ("Sqezy" dish washing liquid and "Breeze" laundry detergent), food-related products ("Blue Band" margarine and "Golden Ray" cooking margarine), and personal products ("Close up" toothpaste and "Rexona" deodorant). The company's markets are, by agreement with its parent company, limited to the CARICOM countries[2]. Within the CARICOM market, Lever Brothers' products held the following market share at year-end 1996:

Detergents	29%
Food-related products	40%
Personal products	20%

In keeping with its policy of "least-cost sourcing," Lever Brothers also markets a variety of personal-care products (e.g., "Brut" after-shave lotion, "Dove" beauty bar, and "Vaseline Intensive Care" lotion, among others), that can be imported more cheaply than locally-manufactured.

The ordinary shares of Lever Brothers trade only on the Trinidad and Tobago stock exchange. During 1996, the company's shares traded in a range of $4.80 to $6.25 per share[3].

---

[*] This case was prepared by Kenneth R. Ferris and Laurens Albada-Jelgersma. Copyright © 1997 by the American Graduate School of International Management. All rights reserved.

[1] Trinidad and Tobago, the Southernmost Caribbean islands located seven miles off the Venezuelan coast, were first settled by the peaceful Arawak Indians, who were subsequently wiped out by the warmongering Carib Indians. The first reported European to visit the islands was Christopher Columbus in 1498, who claimed the land for Spain, naming Trinidad after the Trinity to show his gratitude for reaching land after a long Atlantic voyage. The islands remained under Spanish control until 1797, at which time Trinidad was invaded and captured by British forces. Great Britain gained possession of Tobago in 1814. In 1962, Trinidad and Tobago were granted their independence, and in 1976, the two islands became a republic within the United Kingdom Commonwealth. The Republic's national capital is Port of Spain, located on Trinidad, and elections for its democratic government are held every five years.

[2] CARICOM, or Caribbean Community, was formed in 1973 as an economic trading bloc amongst the 13 English-speaking countries of Barbados, Belize, Guyana, Jamaica, the eight Windward and Leeward Islands, and Trinidad and Tobago. Subsequently, Suriname also joined this Caribbean equivalent of the Common Market. (The eight Windward and Leeward Islands include: Dominica, Grenada, St. Lucia and St. Vincent, and Antigua, Montserrat, St. Kitts - Nevis - Anguilla and the Virgin Islands, respectively.)

[3] All values are in Trinidad/Tobago dollars (TT$), with an exchange rate of approximately $1 U.S. = $6 TT at year end 1996.

Accounting Policies: The Revaluation of Fixed Assets

According to the company's annual report, Lever Brothers prepares its financial statements (see Exhibits 1 and 2) according to International Accounting Standards as "approved in Trinidad and Tobago". The footnotes to the financial statements disclose that the company prepares these statements using the historical cost convention, except for certain fixed assets:

> These financial statements have been prepared under the historical cost convention except for certain fixed assets which were professionally valued on 30 September 1976 and 30 December 1995, and with reference to International Accounting Standards approved in Trinidad and Tobago. The existence of any material items covered by these Standards is disclosed.

It is the company's policy to revalue its properties at least every five years, the results of which are taken into account in the preparation of the financial statements. The directors review the value of the plant on an ongoing basis and adjustments, based on professional valuations, are made where considered appropriate. All other assets are stated at cost.

This case concerns the accounting for those revalued assets, which in recent years had been professionally revalued in 1983, 1988, 1993, and 1995.

1993 Asset Revaluation

In the Spring of 1993, the Board of Directors of Lever Brothers met to approve the appointment of Raymond & Pierre, Chartered Valuation Surveyors, to review and appraise the company's freehold properties. Raymond & Pierre, a respected West Indies' firm of appraisers, had been selected by Mr. Garry Voss, chairman and managing director of Lever Brothers, on the basis of discussions with the company's auditors and bankers. According to the revaluation policy of Lever Brothers, land and buildings were to be revalued every five years; and, if the value had significantly changed, the revalued amount would be booked. The last revaluation had taken place in 1988, and had also been undertaken by the firm of Raymond and Pierre. Plant and machinery, on the other hand, were generally not revalued on an on-going basis. The last revaluation of Lever Brothers' plant and machinery had been undertaken in 1976.

Under the approved accounting standards of Trinidad and Tobago, fixed assets are initially recorded at their purchase price or production cost. Thereafter, such assets (but excluding goodwill) may be stated either at their market value on the date at which they were last valued or at their current cost, with any resulting surplus (or reduction) credited (debited) to a revaluation reserve (a component of shareholders' equity). When fixed assets are revalued, any increment or decrement in value on individual assets must be determined and accounted for separately (i.e. on an individual asset basis). When a revalued asset is subsequently sold, any profit (loss) on the sale is computed by reference to the carrying value (i.e., revalued amount) of the asset; and, any revaluation gain (loss) realized on such a sale is transferred to the profit-and-loss account.

At the conclusion of their 1993 appraisal, Raymond & Pierre submitted a report to the directors of Lever Brothers (see Exhibit 3). This report indicated that the current value of the company's freehold land and buildings was now $31.359 million, an increase of over $9 million as compared to the 1988 valuation of $22.095 million. In a report prepared for the Lever Brothers' Board of Directors, Ms. Karlene Ammon, the firm's financial accountant responsible for financial disclosures, provided the following details regarding the revaluation appraisal results in 1993 and recent prior years:

	Freehold Land	Freehold Building	Adjustment to Capital Reserve
Historical cost	$ 246,000	$ 8,165,000	
1983 revaluation adjustment	10,791,000	19,686,000	$30,477,000
1983 Replacement cost	11,037,000	27,851,000	
1988 revaluation adjustment	(5,986,000)	(10,807,000)	(16,793,000)
1988 Replacement cost	5,051,000	17,044,000	
1993 revaluation adjustment	5,664,000	3,600,000	9,264,000
1993 Replacement cost	$ 10,715,000	$ 20,644,000	$22,948,000

1995 Asset Revaluation

In 1995, the Board of Directors of Lever Brothers concluded that it was necessary to change the basis upon which its fixed assets were revalued. Previously, the fixed assets had been revalued on a replacement cost basis. In the early 1990s, however, the directors had voted to implement a policy of "least-cost sourcing" under which the company would continue to manufacture only those products whose import cost exceeded local manufactured cost. This decision had been reached in anticipation of pending CARICOM import tariff reductions. The import tariffs on foreign goods had been implemented following the formation of CARICOM in an attempt to nurture the formation of local industry.

The impact of the Lever Brothers directors' decision was significant: By 1995, local production of all personal products except toothpaste had been discontinued. As a consequence, the directors became concerned that the revenue-producing potential of the company's fixed assets had become impaired, and in December of 1995, retained the appraisal firm of Linden Scott & Associates Ltd. to review the value of these assets. The directive given to the appraisal firm was to "appraise the Lever Brothers' fixed assets on an open market," or liquidation value, basis. This analysis revealed that the carrying value of the freehold assets exceeded their liquidation value by $10.669 million.

Ms. Ammon summarized the appraisal data for the directors as follows:

	Freehold Land	Freehold Building	Adjustment to Capital Reserve
1993 Replacement cost	10,715,000	20,664,000	
1995 revaluation adjustment	(1,915,000)	(8,754,000)	(10,669,000)
1995 Liquidation value	8,800,000	11,910,000	
Net additions and accumulated depreciation	--	(910,000)	
1995 Carrying value	$8,800,000	$11,000,000	

Questions:

1.   Using the information provided in the case, reconstruct the journal entries used by Lever Brothers in the valuation of freehold land and buildings, and for the Capital Reserve.

2.   Calculate the following ratios at year-end 1995 for the company **both** with and without the revaluation of freehold land and buildings:

   • Long-term debt-to-shareholders' equity
   • Return on total assets
   • Return on shareholders' equity

3.   Comment on the practice of revaluing noncurrent assets. Do you agree with the practice? If so, why? If not, why not?

4.   Do you agree with the Board of Directors decision in 1995 to change the basis for revaluing its fixed assets from replacement cost to liquidation value? If so, why? If not, why not?

A.   Auditors' Report

TO THE MEMBERS OF LEVER BROTHERS WEST INDIES LIMITED

We have examined the balance sheet of Lever Brothers West Indies Limited as at 31 December 1995 and the profit and loss account and cash flow statement for the year then ended, as set out on pages 12 to 21, and have obtained all the information and explanations we have required. Our examination was made in accordance with approved auditing standards.

In our opinion, according to the best of our information and the explanations given to us, and as shown by the books of the company, the balance sheet is properly drawn up so as to exhibit a true and correct view of the state of the company's affairs as at 31 December 1995 and the related financial statements present fairly the results of its operations and cash flow for the year then ended in accordance with approved accounting standards.

Price Waterhouse

9 February 1996
Port of Spain
Trinidad and Tobago.

Exhibit 1
Lever Brothers West Indies Ltd.
Financial Statements
(continued)

B.   **Profit and Loss Account**

	Notes	Year Ended 31 December 1995 $'000	1994 $'000
Turnover		$273,345	$255,192
Cost Of Sales		202,163	191,293
Gross Profit		71,182	63,899
Operating Expenses		(49,841)	(43,220)
Profit Before Taxation	3	21,341 -	20,679
Taxation	4	6,946	9,324
Profit After Taxation		14,395	11,355
Dividends			
– Interim		(4,199)	(2,886)
– Final proposed		(11,810)	(7,873)
		(16,009)	(10,759)
Retained (Loss)/Profit for the Year	11	$ (1,614)	$ 596

Exhibit 1
Lever Brothers West Indies Ltd.
Financial Statements
(continued)

C.   **Balance Sheet**

	Notes	Year Ended 31 December 1995 $'000	1994 $'000
Fixed Assets	5	$ 42,952	$ 56,330
Current Assets			
Cash at bank and in hand		15,388	6,055
Trade debtors		37,478	39,614
Other debtors		3,283	7,642
Inventories	6	39,730	42,516
		95,879	95,827
Current Liabilities			
Bank borrowings - unsecured	7	--	18,751
Trade creditors		26,755	11,418
Other creditors and accruals		6,383	5,634
Amounts due to parent and related companies	8	7,030	8,447
Proposed dividend		11,810	7,873
		51,978	52,123
Net Current Assets		43,901	43,704
		$ 86,853	$100,034
Share Capital	9	$ 26,244	$ 26,244
Capital Reserve	10	6,965	17,987
Retained Profits	11	34,131	35,745
Stockholders' Funds		67,340	79,976
Deferred Taxation	12	4,848	5,476
Retirement and Termination Benefits		14,665	14,582
		$ 86,853	$100,034

The attached statement and notes set out on pages
15 to 21 form an integral part of these financial statements.

Director   Director

Exhibit 1
Lever Brothers West Indies Ltd.
Financial Statements
(continued)

D. Cash Flow Statement

	Year Ended 31 December	
	1995 $'000	1994 $'000
Operating Activites		
Profit before taxation	$ 21,341	$ 20,679
Adjustment for:		
Depreciation	4,350	3,748
(Profit)/loss on disposal of fixed assets	(540)	22
Increase in retirement and termination benefits	83	2,289
Operating profit before working capital changes	25,234	26,738
Decrease/(increase) in trade debtors and other debtors	6,495	(14,076)
Decrease in inventories	2,786	10,898
Increase/(decrease) in trade creditors and other creditors	14,516	(7,972)
Cash Flows from Operating Activities	49,031	15,588
Taxation Paid	(7,421)	(8,547)
Net Cash Flows from Operating Activities	41,610	7,041
Investing Activities		
Purchase of fixed assets	(2,135)	(8,137)
Proceeds from sale of fixed assets	681	437
Cash Used in Investing Activities	(1,454)	(7,700)
Financing Activity		
Dividends paid	(12,072)	(9,973)
Net Increase/(Decrease) in Cash and Cash Equivalents	28,084	(10,632)
Cash and Cash Equivalents at Beginning of Year	(12,696)	(2,064)
Cash and Cash Equivalents at End of Year	$ 15,388	$ (12,696)
Cash at Bank and In Hand	$ 15,388	$ 6,055
Bank Borrowings	--	(18,751)
	$ 15,388	$ (12,696)

Exhibit 2
Lever Brothers West Indies Ltd.
Selected Footnotes

1   INCORPORATION AND NATURE OF ACTIVITIES

Lever Brothers West Indies Limited was incorporated in the Republic of Trinidad and Tobago in 1929. The principal business activities are the manufacture and sale of detergents, margarine, edible fats and oils and personal care products. The company is a subsidiary of Unilon AG which is itself a wholly owned subsidary of Unilever PLC, a company incorporated in the United Kingdom.

2   SIGNIFICANT ACCOUNTING POLICIES

Basis of preparation

These financial statements have been prepared under the historical cost convention except for certain fixed assets which were professionally valued on 30 September 1976 and 30 December 1995, and with reference to International Accounting Standards approved in Trinidad and Tobago. The existence of any material items covered by these Standards is disclosed.

Turnover

Turnover comprises sales of goods after deduction of discounts.

Fixed assets

Cost or revaluation

Land, building and plant are stated at valuation or, for additions subsequent to the date of revaluation, at cost. All other assets are stated at cost.

The directors review the value of land, buildings and plant on an ongoing basis and professional valuations, are conducted when these reviews indicate a pontentially significant variation from recorded values.

Depreciation

Freehold land and capital work in progress are not depreciated.

Depreciation is calculated on the straight line basis using the following rates:

Freehold buildings	-	2.5% per annum
Leasehold buildings	-	over the period of lease (7% - 20%)
Plant	-	7% and 20% per annum
Motor vehicles	-	20% per annum

Exhibit 2
Lever Brothers West Indies Ltd.
Selected Footnotes
(continued)

2   SIGNIFICANT ACCOUNTING POLICIES (Continued)

Inventories

Inventories are valued at the lower of cost and net realisable value, calculated on the following bases which have been consistently applied:

- Raw materials - oils, chemicals and packaging materials are valued at purchase cost on a FIFO basis.
- Raw materials - others are valued at purchase cost on an average cost basis.
- Finished goods and work in progress are valued at cost which includes a proportion of attributable production overheads.
- Engineering and general stores are valued at weighted average cost.

Foreign currencies

Transactions originating in foreign currencies are translated into Trinidad and Tobago dollars at the rates of exchange prevailing when recorded. Foreign currency monetary assets and liabilities are expressed in the balance sheet at rates prevailing at the balance sheet date. Gains and losses on exchange are dealt with in the current year's operating results.

Deferred taxation

The company follows the liability method of accounting for deferred taxation. Under this method, the future tax liability on timing differences, which results mainly from the excess of depreciation allowed for tax purposes over book depreciation, is provided for at the expected future corporation tax rate.

Retirement benefit plan

The company operates a defined benefit pension plan covering certain regular full time employees. The funds of the plan are administered by trustees and are separate from the company's assets. Contributions to the pension plan, which are based upon triennial actuarial valuations, are charged against profits on the accruals basis.

The industrial agreement covering the majority of employees provides for a termination benefit which functions as a retirement benefit for those employees who are not in the pension plan. The annual cost of providing for these benefits which is augmented at the discretion of management is charged against current earnings. Total charge in 1995 amounted to $17,602 (1994 - $2,549,963).

Exhibit 2
Lever Brothers West Indies Ltd.
Selected Footnotes
(continued)

3	PROFIT BEFORE TAXATION	1995 $'000	1994 $'000
	This is stated after charging/(crediting):		
	Depreciation (Note 5)	$ 4,350	$ 3,748
	Interest - net	(52)	522
	Audit fees	120	115
	Directors' fees	13	13
	Foreign exchange gain	(2,373)	(1,791)
	Pension contribution	1,565	1,479

4	TAXATION	1995	1994
	Corporation tax for the year	$ 7,574	$ 7,874
	Deferred taxation (see Note 12)	(628)	1,450
		$ 6,946	$ 9,324

5   FIXED ASSETS

	Freehold Land	Freehold Buildings	Leasehold Building	Plant	Work in Progress	Motor Vehicles	Total
31 December 1995							
Net book value at 31.12.94	$10,715	$20,068	$ 1,100	$22,310	$ 446	$ 1,691	$56,330
Additions	--	296	--	2,236	49	--	2,581
Revaluation deficit	(1,915)	(8,754)	--	--	--	--	(10,669)
Disposal and other adjustments	--	(91)	91	(413)	(446)	(81)	(940)
Depreciation charge	--	(519)	(129)	(3,210)	--	(492)	(4,350)
Net book value at 31.12.95	$ 8,800	$11,000	$ 1,062	$20,923	$ 49	$ 1,118	$42,952

Exhibit 2
Lever Brothers West Indies Ltd.
Selected Footnotes
(continued)

5 · FIXED ASSETS (Continued)

	Freehold Land	Freehold Buildings	Leasehold Building	Plant	Work in Progress	Motor Vehicles	Total
31 December 1995							
Cost or valuation	$ 8,800	$11,000	$ 1,958	$48,473	$ 49	$ 2,416	$72,696
Accumulated depreciation	--	--	896	27,550	--	1,298	29,744
Net book value -31.12.95	$ 8,800	$11,000	$ 1,062	$20,923	$ 49	$ 1,118	$42,952
31 December 1994							
Net book value at 31.12.93	$10,715	$19,821	$ 1,224	$17,959	$ 805	$ 1,691	$52,529
Additions	--	763	--	7,474	446	259	8,942
Disposals and other adjustments	--	(13)	--	(564)	(805)	(11)	(1,393)
Depreciation charge	--	(503)	(124)	(2,559)	--	(562)	(3,748)
Net book value at 31.12.94	$10,715	$20,068	$ 1,100	$22,310	$ 446	$ 1,377	$56,330
Cost or valuation	$10,715	$20,822	$ 1,867	$48,186	$ 446	$ 3,686	$85,722
Accumulated depreciation	--	754	767	25,876	--	1,995	29,392
Net book value -31.12.94	$10,715	$20,068	$ 1,100	$22,310	$ 446	$ 1,691	$56,330

The freehold properties were revalued on an open market basis by Linden Scott & Associates Limited, Professional Valuers in December 1995. The deficit arising on revaluation amounted to $10,669,000 (see Note 10).

The plant was revalued by George Chin & Partners, Professional Valuers in September 1976.

Exhibit 2
Lever Brothers West Indies Ltd.
Selected Footnotes
(continued)

6 INVENTORIES	1995 $'000	1994 $'000
Raw materials and supplies	$ 15,645	$ 20,051
Work in progress	3,393	4,413
Engineering and general stores	2,405	3,642
Goods in transit	5,167	3,689
Finished goods	13,120	10,721
	$ 39,730	$ 42,516

7 BANK BORROWINGS - UNSECURED		
Banker's acceptances	$ --	$ 9,918
Bank overdraft	--	8,833
	$ --	$ 18,751

8 AMOUNTS DUE TO PARENT AND RELATED COMPANIES		
Amounts due to parent company	$ 1,510	$ 1,903
Amounts due to related companies	5,520	6,544
	$ 7,030	$ 8,447

9   SHARE CAPITAL

	1995	1994
Authorised 100,000,000 ordinary shares of $1 each	$100,000	$100,000
Issued and fully paid 26,243,832 ordinary shares of $1 each	$ 26,244	$ 26,244

10 CAPITAL RESERVE		
Balance at beginning of year	$ 17,987	$ 18,158
Revaluation deficit (see Note 5)	(10,669)	--
Surplus on disposal of fixed assets	(353)	(171)
Balance at end of year	$ 6,965	$ 17,987

Exhibit 2
Lever Brothers West Indies Ltd.
Selected Footnotes
(continued)

		1995 $'000	1994 $'000
11	**RETAINED PROFITS**		
	Balance at beginning of year	$ 35,745	$ 35,149
	Retained profit for the year	(1,614)	596
	Balance at end of year	$ 34,131	$ 35,745
12	**DEFERRED TAXATION**		
	Balance at beginning of year	$ 5,476	$ 4,026
	Transfer to profit and loss account	(628)	1,450
	Balance at end of year	$ 4,848	$ 5,476

13 PENSION PLAN

The last actuarial valuation of the plan was carried out on 1 January 1995 by independent actuaries using the projected unit credit method. It revealed that the plan was adequately funded.

		1995	1994
14	**CONTINGENT LIABILITIES**		
	Custom bonds and other guarantees	$ 7,605	$ 7,674
15	**CAPITAL COMMITMENTS**		
	Authorised and contracted for but not provided for in the financial statements	$ 588	$ 31
16	**RELATED PARTY TRANSACTIONS**		
	Purchases from related companies	$ 28,844	$ 26,820
	Royalties and service fees charged to the company	$ 6,068	$ 5,837

All related party transactions during the year were made on an arms length basis.

17 LEASE COMMITMENTS

The company's total commitment as at 31 December 1995 under the terms of the leases for building and plant is $6,041,907 (1994 - $7,240,260) of which $974,454 is payable during the 1996 financial year. As at 31 December 1995 the remaining period of the leases was 7 years.

Exhibit 3
Lever Brothers West Indies Ltd.
Raymond and Pierre "Valuation Report[*]"

Terms of Reference

We received instructions to provide a Valuation Report as at 30th June 1993 on the Lands, Buildings and Site Improvements owned by the company for the purposes of incorporation in the Books of Accounts.

General Comment

We last reported on the Assets of the Company on the 30th June 1988. Full details of Information Sources, Bases of Valuation, Methods of Valuations, Structures and Accommodation with respect to both properties, including the land and site improvements, were given in the substantive report. Notwithstanding the fact that there has been no change in the physical characteristics of the properties since out 1988 report, our own research and our consultation with Cost Consultants have revealed that there was a substantial increase in building costs over the period June 1988 to June 1993.

The increases reflected in the 1993 costs were primarily due to the introduction of VAT with effect from 1st January 1990 and to the flotation of the dollar with effect from 8th April 1993. In arriving at the replacement cost of the buildings due regard was had to the increase in costs of components while appropriate adjustments were made to arrive at the overall depreciated replacement costs of building per se.

Basis of Valuation

During the past 5 years evidence of sales of comparable properties became scarce, and with the involvement of cost factors mentioned above, the integrated nature of the complex suggested as the best approach the adoption of the Depreciated Replacement Cost Basis of ascertaining the value in use of the lands and buildings. This basis requires estimates of the value of the land in its existing use and of the net replacement costs of the buildings and other site works.

Method of Valuation

Land

This was valued in its existing use assuming vacant possession. In this connection we had considerable evidence which led us to use the most appropriate method commonly known as the Direct Capital Comparison Method.

In this method evidence of arm's length open market transactions of similar lands was investigated and analyzed and the results applied to the subject land after making appropriate adjustments to take into account locational and other relevant factors.

---

[*] Report dated 13 September, 1993

Method of
Valuation
(continued)

Buildings

The adopted approach to the valuation of the buildings was the Depreciated Replacement Cost Method. This method requires the estimation of the cost of construction new with appropriate deductions made to allow for age, condition, depreciation, economic or functional obsolescence and environmental factors.

Condition

On the date of inspection, 30th July 1993, the buildings were found to be structurally sound and maintained to a high standard.

Valuation
Opinion

Having regard to the characteristics of the properties and to all relevant factors we have reached the following conclusion as regards to the Depreciated Replacement Costs of the Lands and Buildings as at 30th June 1993 as shown on the attached Schedules of the Valuation Summary:

Eastern Main Road Complex	-	$ 30,069,000
Macoya Industrial Site	-	$ 1,290,000
TOTAL		$ 31,359,000

ALPHABETICAL LISTING OF CASES AND THEIR AUTHORS

Accounting for Strategic Alliances	Kenneth R. Ferris
Aussie Traders Ltd.	Kenneth R. Ferris and Barry R. Graham
BASF	Kenneth R. Ferris
Baycorp Holdings	Michael E. Bradbury
Benetton Group S.p.A.	Kenneth R. Ferris
Buenos Aires Embotelladora S.A.	Kenneth R. Ferris and Shankar Venkataraman
Coca-Cola Femsa S.A. de C.V.	Graeme Rankine
CompX International, Inc.	Kenneth R. Ferris
Daimler-Benz AG	Kenneth R. Ferris
E.I. DuPont de Nemours	David Shields
Financial Analysis of International Energy Firms	Graeme Rankine
Grupo Embotellador de Mexico	Michael Moffett and Tomas Soto
Guinness PLC	Kenneth R. Ferris and Renee A. Flinn
Holzmann AG	Kenneth R. Ferris
Hong Kong Land Development Co. Ltd.	Kenneth R. Ferris
International Acquisitions, Inc.	Kenneth R. Ferris
Japan Airlines Company Ltd.	Kenneth R. Ferris
Jilin Chemical Industrial Company Ltd.	Kenneth R. Ferris and Teh-han Chow
Jyoti Structures Ltd.	Kenneth R. Ferris and Motilal Gyamlami
Lever Brothers West Indies Ltd.	Kenneth R. Ferris and Laurens Albada-Jelgersma
Luxottica Group S.p.A.	Kenneth R. Ferris
LVMH: Moët Hennessy Louis-Vuitton	Kenneth R. Ferris and Renee A. Flinn
Mitsui Oil Exploration Company	Kenneth R. Ferris
Newcastle Ltd.	Kenneth R. Ferris
Nokia Corporation	Graeme Rankine
Pacific Dunlop Ltd.	Kenneth R. Ferris and Bruce McDonald
Polly Peck International PLC	Kenneth R. Ferris and Motilal Gyamlami
Tanaguchi Corporation	Paul R. Brown and Clyde Stickney
The Constructive Capitalization of Leases	Kenneth R. Ferris
TOTAL	Stephen Tomczyk
Wacoal Corporation	Kenneth R. Ferris
Waterloo Enterprises	Kenneth R. Ferris and Michael F. van Breda
Zoltek Companies, Inc.	Thomas I. Selling

Accounting for Strategic Alliances

Country(s):   United Kingdom
Industry(s):   Airline
Company(s):   **British Airways**
Issue(s):   This case concerns the accounting for strategic alliances (i.e. investments) in the airline industry. As a means to expand its international passenger network, British Airways entered into alliances in continental Europe (with Deutsche BA in Germany and TAT European Airlines in France), the Pacific region (with Qantas), and the U.S. (with USAir). The case focuses on how BA accounted for each of these investments, particularly after the introduction of Financial Reporting Standard No. 5, "Reporting the Substance of Transactions," in April, 1994 in the U.K.

Aussie Traders Ltd.

Country(s):   Australia; Singapore
Industry(s):   Retail
Company(s):   **Aussie Traders Ltd.; Aussie Retailers Ltd.**
Issue(s):   This case provides a forum to evaluate the financial statement impact of translation exposure under alternative approaches to translating foreign financial statements. The setting involves an Australian parent company, with retail operations in Singapore.

BASF

Country(s):   Germany
Industry(s):   Chemical
Company(s):   **BASF Group**
Issue(s):   This case concerns the accounting for inventories, with specific attention to FIFO and LIFO. The case illustrates the LIFO reserve concept, and how it can be used to restate financial statements. It also gives students exposure to German accounting practices and financial statements.

Baycorp Holdings Ltd.

Country(s):   New Zealand
Industry(s):   Financial services
Company(s):   **Baycorp Holdings Ltd.**
Issue(s):   This case focuses on the preparation of pro forma financial statements in anticipation of a share or rights offering. Students are also requested to propose the method, number of shares, and price for the proposed offering.

Benetton Group S.p.A.

Country(s):   Italy
Industry(s):   Apparel manufacturing
Company(s):   **Benetton Group**
Issue(s):   This case focuses on the principal differences between Italian and U.S. accounting practices, with specific attention to the revaluation of assets, accounting for goodwill, and stockholders' equity. Students are asked to assess the impact of these differences on selected financial measures.

413

Buenos Aires Embotelladora S.A.

Country(s):	Argentina, Brazil, United States
Industry(s):	Beverage (soft-drink)
Company(s):	**Buenos Aires Embotelladora, PepsiCo**
Issue(s):	This case involves a financial analysis of the Argentine affiliate of PepsiCo. The company, in an effort to grow rapidly, expanded into Brazil, principally via debt financing. The competitive environment was such that the affiliate was unable to support the rapidly growing debt level, leading to near bankruptcy. A review of financial indicators enables students to pinpoint when the company's problems first began.

Coca-Cola Femsa S.A. de C.V.

Country(s):	Mexico
Industry(s):	Beverage (soft-drink)
Company(s):	**Coca-Cola Femsa, Gemex, Panamco**
Issue(s):	The purpose of this case is three-fold. First, to provide a forum to compare and contrast Mexican versus U.S. accounting practices. Second, to prepare a financial analysis of a Mexican beverage company. And third, to provide a forum to explore alternative methods of accounting for inflation.

CompX International, Inc.

Country(s):	Canada
Industry(s):	Manufacturing
Company(s):	**CompX International, Inc.**
Issue(s):	This relatively numerical case focuses on the accounting for and valuation of debt instruments. Students are requested to calculate the expected proceeds from five alternative debt offerrings: 1) interest-bearing debentures, 2) zero-coupon debentures, 3) payment-in-kind debentures (a hybrid security), 4) century bonds, and 5) perpetuity debentures. Students also consider the advantages and disadvantages of each type of security.

Daimler-Benz AG

Country(s):	Germany
Industry(s):	Industrial and consumer machine manufacturing
Company(s):	**Daimler-Benz AG**
Issue(s):	This case principally focuses on the creation of hidden reserves, in this instance via a company's pension fund. Students are asked to focus on the ways in which reserves can be created, and the motivation for their creation. The case also provides an opportunity for students to develop their financial restatement skills.

E.I. DuPont de Nemours

Country(s):	United States
Industry(s):	Chemical
Company(s):	**E.I.DuPont de Nemours**
Issue(s):	This case focuses on environmental liability disclosure by a large U.S.-based multinational firm. Students are asked to evaluate the company's footnote disclosures from 1992 to 1995, and then restate the financial statements for the off-balance sheet obligation.

Financial Analysis of International Energy Firms

Country(s):	France; Netherlands; United Kingdom
Industry(s):	Petroleum refining
Company(s):	**British Petroleum; Royal-Dutch Petroleum; Shell Transport and Trading; TOTAL**
Issue(s):	This case concerns the financial analysis of four international companies operating in the oil and gas industry. Students are requested to prepare selected financial ratios for one year, and then to develop an analysis of common-size data, financial ratios, and cash flow data for a three year period. Students are also requested to consider the effects of translation exposure and differences in generally accepted accounting practices on their analysis.

Grupo Embotellador de Mexico

Country(s):	Mexico
Industry(s):	Beverage (soft-drink)
Company(s):	**Grupo Embotellador de Mexico**
Issue(s):	This case focuses on the strategies employed by PepsiCo to expand its market share in Mexico, and the implications for these strategies associated with the peso devaluation in December 1994. Students are requested to evaluate the fit between PepsiCo's marketing plans and its financial position following the devaluation.

Guinness PLC

Country(s):	United Kingdom
Industry(s):	Beverage
Company(s):	**Guinness PLC**
Issue(s):	This case focuses on three key differences between U.K. and U.S. accounting standards: 1) accounting for goodwill, 2) the capitalization of brandnames, and 3) the revaluation of noncurrent assets. Students are asked to restate the company's financial statements to reflect U.S. GAAP, and to assess the impact of the accounting differences on various financial ratios.

Holzmann AG

Country(s):	Germany
Industry(s):	Construction
Company(s):	**Holzmann AG**
Issue(s):	This case concerns the accounting for revenues under long-term contracts, specifically in the construction industry. Students are requested to prepare income statements under both the completed contract and the percentage of completion methods. The concept of deferred income taxes is also introduced.

Hong Kong Land Development Company Ltd.

Country(s):	Hong Kong
Industry(s):	Real estate/property development
Company(s):	**Hong Kong Land Development Company**
Issue(s):	This case focuses on the basic issues of revenue recognition: What are "revenues"? When should revenues be recognized? What constitutes a "sale"? The case also explores the issues associated with related-party transactions and recurring versus nonrecurring transactions.

International Acquisitions, Inc.

Country(s):	Germany; Japan; United Kingdom; United States
Industry(s):	Hotel and resort
Company(s):	**International Acquisitions, Inc.**
Issue(s):	This case explores whether country differences in the accounting for goodwill affect merger and acquisition decisions. Students are asked to calculate the maximum price that a company should offer in an asset acquisition bid using German, Japanese, U.K., and U.S. goodwill accounting practices.

Japan Airlines Company Ltd.

Country(s):	Japan
Industry(s):	Airline
Company(s):	**Japan Airlines**
Issue(s):	During the period 1993-1996, Japan Airlines implemented a number of accounting policy changes involving (a) bond issuance costs, (b) deferred income taxes, (c) the estimated lives of its aircraft, and (d) the method of depreciating its aircraft. In each case, JAL's net income was enhanced (or net loss reduced). This case looks at the motivation for these accounting policy changes and asks students to recast JAL's operating results assuming the changes were not undertaken. The case also provides a forum to evaluate Japanese vs. U.S. GAAP.

Jilin Chemical Industrial Company Ltd.

Country(s):	China
Industry(s):	Diversified chemical manufacturing
Company(s):	**Jilin Chemical Industrial Company**
Issue(s):	This case compares and contrasts generally accepted accounting principles in China with those under IASC standards. Students are requested to restate Jilin Chemical's IAS-based financial statements to those that would be presented under Chinese GAAP. Various ratios are then computed to enable the magnitude of the accounting differences to be assessed. A sub-theme of the case involves a comparison of P.R.C. and U.S. accounting standards.

Jyoti Structures Ltd.

Country(s):	India
Industry(s):	Steel fabrication, power transmission
Company(s):	**Jyoti Structures Ltd., JSL Finance Ltd., Prakash Fabricators, Inc.**
Issue(s):	The principal focus of this case is a comparison of Indian and U.S. generally accepted accounting practice; however, a significant sub-theme involves the restatement of financial statements. Students are requested to recast the company's basic financial statements using (a) the equity method and (b) consolidated reporting practices for a wholly-owned subsidiary accounted for under the cost method.

LVMH: Moët Hennessy Louis-Vuitton

Country(s):	France
Industry(s):	Consumer luxury goods
Company(s):	**LVMH**
Issue(s):	This case contrasts French and U.S. accepted accounting practice in three areas: 1)classification of treasury shares, 2) amortization of intangible assets and 3) undiscounted notes. Students are asked to restate LVMH's financial statements as if they were prepared under U.S. GAAP, and to assess the impact of these national accounting differences on net income and shareholders' equity.

Lever Brothers West Indies Ltd.

Country(s):	Trinidad and Tobago, W.I.
Industry(s):	Consumer products manufacturer
Company(s):	**Lever Brothers West Indies Ltd.**
Issue(s):	This case focuses on the revaluation of noncurrent assets. Students are provided data regarding the company's actual revaluation of noncurrent assets and are asked to reconstruct the entries utilized, and then assess the impact of revaluation on selective financial ratios for the company. Students are also asked to evaluate the practice of asset revaluation, as well as management's decision to change the basis of valuation used in the revaluation process.

Luxottica S.p.A.

Country(s):	Italy
Industry(s):	Consumer products
Company(s):	**Luxottica S.p.A.**
Issue(s):	This case focuses on several issues. First, it contrasts the accounting practices of Italy and those of the U.S. with respect to goodwill, commitments and contingencies, and shareholders' equity in general. Second, it provides an opportunity for students to prepare and analyze cash flow data from Italian financial statements.

Mitsui Oil Exploration Company

Country(s):   Japan; Vietnam
Industry(s):   Oil and gas exploration
Company(s):   **Mitsui Oil Exploration Company**
Issue(s):   This numerical case illustrates the preparation and use of the statement of cash flows as a management tool, as well as the related concept of "discretionary" cash flows.

Newcastle Ltd.

Country(s):   Australia
Industry(s):   Integrated minerals and metals
Company(s):   **Newcastle Ltd.**
Issue(s):   This case is a straightforward illustration of the accounting for liabilities, specifically long-term unsecured debentures. Students are asked to determine the proceeds of an initial debt offering, as well as the financial statement effects of periodic interest charges, a debt-for-stock conversion, an open market repurchase, and a forced conversion.

Nokia Corporation

Country(s):   Finland
Industry(s):   Wireless communications
Company(s):   **Nokia Corporation**
Issue(s):   This case has two objectives. First, students are requested to prepare a financial analysis of a foreign firm. Second, students are asked to evaluate the company's recent decision to change its policy in regard to the accounting for R & D expenditures. The case also provides an opportunity to develop financial statement restatement skills.

Pacific Dunlop Ltd.

Country(s):   Australia
Industry(s):   Conglomerate
Company(s):   **Pacific Dunlop Ltd.**
Issue(s):   This case concerns the accounting for goodwill. It explores the use of the inverted sum of years' digits method to amortize goodwill, and students are asked to compare the reported profits of a company under the accepted goodwill treatment of Australia, Canada, Germany, the U.K., and the U.S. The case also involves a comparison of Australian and U.S. accounting practices.

Polly Peck International PLC

Country(s):   United Kingdom
Industry(s):   Conglomerate
Company(s):   **Polly Peck International**
Issue(s):   This relatively numerical case focuses on the preparation and use of the statement of cash flows. Students are also asked to calculate selected financial ratios and Altman's Z-score in an effort to predict the financial viability of Polly Peck International.

Tanaguchi Corporation

Country(s):	Japan
Industry(s):	Machine tool manufacturing
Company(s):	**Tanaguchi Corporation**
Issue(s):	This case concerns the differences between Japanese and U.S. generally accepted accounting practices, and the impact of those differences on reported net income, total assets, and various financial ratios. The case illustrates the impact of different economic, strategic, institutional and cultural factors on interpretations of profitability and risk.

The Constructive Capitalization of Leases

Country(s):	Chile; United States
Industry(s):	Retail Food
Company(s):	**Santa Isabel S.A.; Food Lion, Inc**
Issue(s):	This case focuses on the use of operating leases as a financing vehicle and its effect on the capital structure of companies. The case illustrates the constructive capitalization of leases as a means to achieve data comparably within and between countries. A sub-theme involves the issue of off-balance sheet financing and how to restate financial statements for off-balance sheet debt.

TOTAL

Country(s):	France
Industry(s):	Oil and gas
Company(s):	**TOTAL**
Issue(s):	This case focuses on the key differences in generally accepted accounting practice between France and the U.S. Students are requested to evaluate these differences and to assess their impact on selected financial ratios.

Wacoal Corporation

Country(s):	Japan, United States
Industry(s):	Apparel
Company(s):	**Wacoal Corp.**
Issue(s):	This case investigates the impact of SFAS No. 115 on the financial statements of a Japanese apparel manufacturer. The company reported its results under U.S. GAAP except in one material respect -- the accounting for debt and equity investments. Data is provided to enable students to restate the company's financial data for SFAS No. 115, and then to examine its impact. The secondary issue of Japan's requirement of a "legal reserve" is also explored.

Waterloo Enterprises

Country(s):	Canada
Industry(s):	Office equipment manufacturing
Company(s):	**Waterloo Enterprises**
Issue(s):	This case is a straightforward introduction to the accounting for inventories. Sufficient data is provided to compare and contrast the costs of goods sold and ending inventory under FIFO or LIFO (or any other inventory valuation method), as well as to illustrate the concepts of LIFO inventory layers, LIFO reserve, and LIFO liquidation. The case involves an inventory accounting method change, and thus the issue of how to account for accounting policy changes can also be covered.

Zoltek Companies, Inc

Country(s):	Hungary; United States
Industry(s):	Manufacturing
Company(s):	**Magyar Viscosa Rt.; Zoltek Companies, Inc.**
Issue(s):	This case concerns the acquisition of a Hungarian state-owned company by a U.S. public company. Students are asked to (1) prepare a proforma consolidated balance sheet for the pending acquisition, (2) evaluate the consolidated entity's foreign exchange exposure and recommend strategies for dealing with that exposure, and (3) recommend a proposed share price for the U.S. company's secondary public offering that will fund the acquisition.